STAN GETZ

OTHER BOOKS BY
DONALD L. MAGGIN

Bankers, Builders, Knaves, and Thieves

STAN GETZ

A LIFE IN JAZZ

DONALD L. MAGGIN

WILLIAM MORROW
AND COMPANY, INC. NEW YORK

Library of Congress Cataloging-in-Publication Data

Maggin, Donald L.
    Stan Getz : a life in jazz / by Donald L. Maggin. — 1st ed.
        p.   cm.
    Includes bibliographical references and index.
    ISBN 0-688-12315-5
    1. Getz, Stan, 1927–1991. 2. Jazz musicians — United States — Biography. I. Title.
ML419.C48M34   1996
788.7'165'092 — dc20
[B]   95-47748
                                                                                           CIP
                                                                                            MN

Printed in the United States of America

First Edition

1   2   3   4   5   6   7   8   9   10

BOOK DESIGN BY IRIS WEINSTEIN

FOREWORD

NATURE PROVIDED Stan Getz with abundant talents for music: perfect pitch, an uncanny feel for rhythmic nuance, great sight-reading skills, and a photographic memory. These attributes, however, were not what made him a great artist. The essence of his art was the ability to create fresh and beautiful melodies, to improvise; he was a giant of instantaneous composition. He spoke of improvisation as a way of conversing:

> It's like a language. You learn the alphabet, which are the scales. You learn sentences, which are the chords. And then you talk extemporaneously with the horn. It's a wonderful thing to *speak* extemporaneously, which is something I've never gotten the hang

of. But musically I love to talk just off the top of my head. And that's what jazz music is all about.

He made his conversations with his listeners particularly moving, because he added to his gift for melody a mastery of a wide range of sound—whispers, cries, shouts, purrs, wails. And he always projected his notes with a personal timbre, a poignant ache that penetrated to the listener's marrow.

Of the jazz greats who came to prominence in the decade following World War II, Stan's career most closely resembles, in shape and longevity, that of Sonny Rollins. These two were not innovators like Ornette Coleman, John Coltrane, or Miles Davis—men who changed the very grammar of jazz—but creators who achieved greatness while expanding the boundaries of the music they inherited.

In a profession noted for creative burnout, Stan maintained the highest aesthetic standards for more than forty-six years, from his first recorded solo on December 19, 1944, with the Stan Kenton Orchestra, to his final one in duet with Kenny Barron in Copenhagen on March 6, 1991. Over this span, he was recorded roughly three hundred times; despite decades of personal torment and turmoil, his playing on all but a handful of these occasions shines at the highest level.

His career had many peaks—his great big band work, from "Early Autumn" in 1949 to *Apasianado* in 1990; his 1961 masterpiece, *Focus*, the most successful marriage ever of jazz and classical music; his artistry in working with Antonio Carlos Jobim, Astrud and João Gilberto, and Charlie Byrd to take bossa nova from obscurity as a local Brazilian genre and to make it a force that stirred millions worldwide; his marvelous collaborations with Jimmy Raney, Bob Brookmeyer, Gary Burton, Chick Corea, Jimmy Rowles, and Albert Dailey; the magnificent quartet and duet recordings with Kenny Barron during his last decade, made while he conquered his addictions and other torments and fought a courageous four-year battle against cancer. He thrilled us, he healed us, and he always swung.

Stan wrote in 1978:

> My life is music. And in some vague, mysterious and subconscious way, I have always been driven by a taut inner spring which has propelled me to almost compulsively reach for perfection in music, often—in fact, mostly—at the expense of everything else in my life.

All of us who love music can be thankful that from 1940, when his father bought him his first saxophone, until his death in 1991, Stan was driven by that "taut inner spring."

ACKNOWLEDGMENTS

I MUST FIRST THANK Tom Bruce, my indispensable aide. He curtailed his career as an actor and playwright to contribute thousands of hours and an extraordinary array of skills to the making of this book; he is a formidable organizer, meticulous researcher and grammarian, probing interviewer, discerning editor, and computer wizard.

During her one and a half years on this project, Amy Ward Brimmer undertook many of the same tasks that Tom did—and handled them with energy and skill.

Arne Astrup's exhaustive *Stan Getz Discography*, covering more than three hundred recordings, was an essential tool, an illuminating road map that eased my task immeasurably. I cannot thank him enough.

I deeply appreciate the help given by Dan Morgenstern and his staff at the Institute of Jazz Studies at Rutgers University. They provided sage advice, a very valuable library, and more than five thousand clippings.

I am very grateful to my support staff, which always contributed first-rate work.

—Jill McManus, a skilled writer and a fine jazz pianist, ably conducted a score of interviews and dug important data out of several dusty libraries.

—Nancy Snyder and Scott Schwab, our West Coast wife-and-husband team, did formidable work in unearthing facts that turned hazy anecdotes into riveting stories; in addition, they recruited Bob Hayes and Cynthia Cooley, who provided essential insights into the disease of addiction.

—Charlton Price, Bob Rodgers, Tim Horner, and Marina Campbell also provided significant research help, and Gene Corey and Liz Kimberlin did excellent work against tight deadlines in transcribing taped interviews.

I am thankful to Gordon Jack for sharing with us the exhaustive research he did for a series of articles he wrote for the British magazine *Jazz Journal*. And Richard Palmer, Alain Tercinet, and Ron Kirkpatrick—authors of the three extant books about Stan Getz—provided especially rich insights into the music and the man who made it.

I am grateful to Patty Clark and Glenn Creason of the Los Angeles Public Library, Martha Gregory of the Tulsa Public Library, Tom Porton of James Monroe High School in New York, and the staffs of the New York Public Library Telephone Reference Service and the Bronx County Historical Society Library; they unearthed important data about pivotal events in Stan's life. And I appreciate the efforts of Jack Brown and Rod Baum of Rare Records in Teaneck, New Jersey, in providing, time after time, truly rare recordings at a moment's notice.

And finally, I wish to express my gratitude to my agent, Helen Rees, for her constant encouragement and wise advice, and to my editor, Paul Bresnick, who displayed great skill and patience in piloting me to the successful completion of this book.

CONTENTS

STAN GETZ

A PRINCE OF THE EAST BRONX

GOLDIE GETZ was so exhausted she could not scream anymore. She was into her thirty-fifth hour of labor, and she was weakening, and the doctor felt that he had to intervene to save her and the child. But first he wanted to talk to Al, her husband.

"I'm going to have to go in with forceps, or I could lose both of them, your wife and the baby. I wanted you to know about it, using the forceps."

"Yes, yes, anything," Al mumbled. When they arrived at the hospital two days before, he was lighthearted, but the hours of waiting had worn him down, and now he was sick with fear. His thoughts about Goldie were constantly jostled by the recollection of that awful day nine and a half years before when they told him that his mother Becky had died

1

giving birth to his brother Benny. Al felt a little sicker every time he thought about his mother lying there helplessly, bleeding to death.

The doctor worked furiously, and in less than an hour, on the morning of February 2, 1927, delivered Goldie of a baby boy, Stanley. Goldie was fine, but the baby had suffered a bloody mishap. His head was so large that the forceps had almost torn off one of his ears, and the doctor had to use sutures to reattach it.

A week later, as they were about to leave the hospital—St. Vincent's in Philadelphia—the cashier told Al, "Your wife and son can go, but you can't leave until you pay us fifty-two dollars for reattaching that ear."

"Fifty-two dollars? That's too much. You can keep him," Al quipped before paying the bill.

Stanley was greeted as someone special by both the Getzes and Goldie's family, the Yampolskys, because he was the first-born grandchild in either clan and a male. His younger brother Bob described the impact of his arrival: "It was a big event when Stan was born. They came from all around, and Stan lived up to being the crown prince . . . the shining prince of both entire families."

Both the Getzes and the Yampolskys had left the Kiev area in the Ukraine in 1903—reacting as Jews to the virulent pogroms of that time. They did not know each other in the old country, and they followed different paths to Philadelphia, their American destination.

Al's father, Harris Gayetskis, and Harris's wife, Becky, struggled across Europe, taking odd jobs to earn their way westward. They finally made it to London, where they lived in the Whitechapel district and where Harris owned a small tailoring shop. Al (named Alexander Cecil) was their first child, born in London on July 24, 1904. He was followed in London by Phil (named Pincus) in 1906 and another boy, born in 1908, who died during an epidemic in 1912.

Harris had two brothers and a sister who were prospering in Philadelphia, and they convinced him to join them there. He tried to obtain passage on the maiden voyage of the Titanic in 1912, but fortunately he could not get a booking on that "unsinkable" liner. He brought his family to America on another ship in 1914.

Harris settled in one of a row of four houses built by a brother in West Philadelphia, then a burgeoning neighborhood being filled by a growing middle class. His brother's house flanked his, and other family members lived nearby. Harris made a good living as a tailor and designer of women's clothing in New York, the center of the garment industry. He was earning a hundred dollars per week as early as 1924, considerably more than he could have made in Philadelphia. He never moved to New York, however, because he enjoyed living close to his kinfolk. He traveled between the two cities by train, staying in a New York rooming house from Monday to Friday and coming home for the weekends.

All members of the family shortened their name from Gayetskis to Getz on arriving in America. One of Harris's brothers, Nathan, subsequently made another switch. To obtain a job with the Third Avenue Elevated Railway Company in Manhattan, an organization not partial to Jews, he changed Getz to Harris. Nathan's son became a doctor, which prompted Stan's uncle Benny to say, "We finally attain the dream of every Jewish family, a doctor, and he doesn't even have our name."

Al's father was an austere, remote man who was never close to his children. Two years after Becky died, he married another woman, who died three years later from cancer; three years after that, he married Pauline, who brought up Benny and who survived till 1947. Harris died in 1960 at age eighty-three.

Goldie's father, Sam Yampolsky, came directly from the pogroms of the Ukraine to Philadelphia in 1903 with his wife Shifra. He had been a sergeant in the Czar's army and had quit after refusing an offer of a captaincy conditioned on his conversion to Christianity.

He made his home in the Meadows, a dirt-poor section of southwest Philadelphia near what is now the international airport. Until the late 1930s, the Meadows was semirural; people grew vegetables in open fields and kept chickens and goats and cows. Many of the houses lacked indoor plumbing, and most of the streets were unpaved. The population was working-class immigrant—Jews, Italians, Irish, and Germans struggling to survive.

Goldie, Sam's eldest child, was born on February 16, 1907, and a son, Meyer, arrived the following year. The young children suffered a terrible loss when their mother, Shifra, died in an influenza epidemic in 1910.

Two years later, Sam married Eva, a widow whose two sons, Joe and Harry, were roughly the same ages as Goldie and Meyer. Eva was too poor to support her boys and was forced to place them in a Jewish foster home. They remained there when she remarried and bore five of Sam's children, and they did not emerge until after adolescence. It appears that Sam would take only his own progeny into his home.

Goldie could never remember a time when she didn't have work to do. As the eldest of the children at home, she took on—without benefit of washing machines, vacuum cleaners, detergents, or dishwashers—a heavy load of household chores: washing, boiling, and drying countless diapers, cleaning up after dinners for nine, baby-sitting, mopping and sweeping and dusting. In addition, she made frequent visits to Joe and

Harry. Though not related by blood, she took a greater interest in them than anyone else in the family. Goldie particularly liked Joe, a bookish, affectionate child who was emotionally disoriented in his institutional surroundings. Goldie's half sister, Shaindel Bleshman, remembered:

> She worked at the five and dime—they made like five dollars a week in those days—and she would go to see them in the foster home. . . . She felt for them. Because my mother was very normal with five or six kids, and she wasn't about to be traveling anyplace, Goldie used to go like every other weekend. She'd buy them ties. A tie in those days cost ten to fifteen cents. And she'd buy them something to keep pencils in, a little case for fifteen cents.

Sam Yampolsky scraped out a living as a junk dealer, providing only the barest necessities for his large brood. He was a bon vivant whose fondness for alcohol, stylish clothes, and flirting with the ladies never abated until his death at eighty-seven in 1958.

Shaindel Bleshman has described him:

> My father was too heavy for light work and too light for heavy work. My father did not like to work. He liked to be dressed up, nice and clean all the time, and then he would play cards with the women. I never heard of him having any affair. Could have been, I won't deny that. He was handsome and could dance up a storm.
>
> When he was young, in the Russian Army, he would come home on furlough and say, "Hello, give me a kiss," and leave and go to the house where all the booze was, and the girls, and dance. And what a dancer. Fantastic.
>
> And smart as could be. What a whip he was. And talk. We used to call him the philosopher. Here comes the mayor! Here comes the judge! He read everything that was ever written. He knew everything about the law. And about religion and stuff like that.

Sam had a more ominous side. He was a frequent drunk, and an angry one. His wife and children were constantly on guard against random bursts of violence involving fists, knives, chairs, anything he could get hold of. The family was in constant turmoil as the daily struggle to put food on the table for nine hungry people was played out against a backdrop of rage and abuse.

Goldie carried with her a love for her father but also deep resentments for the anguish and physical pain he inflicted on the family. And she could never truly forgive him for what happened to Meyer, her full brother and the sibling who was dearest to her. One day in his middle teens, Meyer decided he could take no more abuse and chaos and ran away from home. The family never heard from him again, and Goldie was deeply wounded; she grieved for him as if he had died. In later years, she would feel the same kind of anger with her father as she grieved at the fate of her stepbrother Joe, who became psychotic as an adult after he left the foster home, and her half brother, Louis, who became an alcoholic.

Goldie left high school early to take a salesclerk's job at Woolworth's. She was becoming a beautiful young woman, but she had little time or energy to flirt with the neighborhood boys who had begun to take notice of her. Most nights she fell into bed exhausted after her long day at the store and her chores at home. Her only serious pastime was going to the movies, where for a few hours at a time she could enter the fantasy worlds of Valentino or Pickford or Chaplin.

Al Getz always seemed several steps behind his brother Phil, who was younger by two years. Phil—the charmer, the go-getter, the organizer— snagged a good job with a printing firm when he was only fifteen and then got his boss to hire Al, who had just dropped out of high school. And it was Phil who helped build the Stevensville Hotel in the Catskills for its proprietor and secured summer jobs there as waiters for Al and himself.

Al and Goldie met in the Catskills in the summer of 1925, introduced by Al's aunts, sisters of Harris who lived in the Meadows near the Yampol- skys. He was twenty-one, taking a break from the print shop; his duties as a waiter were less than onerous, and he had plenty of time to hang out with his pals and to flirt with the girls. Goldie was eighteen, happy not to be at Woolworth's, standing on her feet for hours at a time, thankful that she could spend a couple of weeks lying in the sun by day, laughing at the comedians and dancing to the bands at night.

Goldie had become a classical beauty. Her full, black hair framed a pert, upturned nose, perfectly formed lips closing over a slight overbite like the forties film star Gene Tierney, and large, soft eyes. All the fellows wanted to date her, and her first pick that summer was Phil Getz. For a while she was fascinated by his cocky self-assurance and energy, but soon she found herself more strongly drawn to his gentle, happy-go-lucky older brother. Al was sweet and kind, so different from the harsh males she had known, so different from her gruff father, always smelling of whiskey and lashing out at somebody. Besides, the Getzes were a nice middle-class Jewish family from West Philadelphia; Al was definitely a good catch.

Goldie was in her prime marriageable years, and marriage seemed a shining liberation from her life at home and at work. Al, totally dazzled by her beauty, was smitten at once. They were soon engaged.

Goldie and Al were married on Christmas Eve that year, and Goldie immediately quit work. It was 1925, and young Jewish women became housewives. It reflected badly on your husband if it appeared as if he could not support his family on his own. Goldie never took a paying job again.

When Stan was born thirteen months after the wedding, Al was mired in the lowest echelons of the printing business, earning barely enough to bring his wife and son back from the hospital to a tiny apartment above a store in West Philadelphia. Soon after, he moved his family to a similar flat in the Meadows a few blocks away from the Yampolskys. Stan, a golden blond, blue-eyed child, was doted on by his mother's clan and by the families of Harris's sisters, who lived close by.

Goldie soon realized that her husband would always have difficulty making a living. His bosses couldn't trust him with complicated jobs because he made frequent mistakes, and he was content to drift through his days at the shop doing simple tasks. Goldie looked in vain to Al for the drive and ambition that could pull the young family out from the shadows of poverty.

Al's situation worsened after the crash of 1929. As the vise of the Depression tightened, it squeezed thousands of jobs out of the printing industry. Before the crash Al's pay was marginal, but the work was steady. Now he was unemployed most of the time. He and Goldie could not afford even such a minor luxury as a night at the movies.

Their second child, Robert, arrived at the very bottom of the Great Depression, on October 30, 1932. It was a time of severe distress, when U.S. production and employment reached their lowest levels.

With another mouth to feed, Al's reserve of hope was almost exhausted. His brother Phil was making a decent living in New York and urged him to move there. Al reasoned that things could not get any worse than they were in Philadelphia; in the summer of 1933, he brought his family to a cold-water walk-up on Manhattan's Lower East Side. With Phil's help he found sporadic work, but his prospects did not improve appreciably, and he soon moved to a cheaper place in the East Bronx.

After the IRT subway line crosses under the Harlem River heading north from Manhattan into the East Bronx, it emerges above ground as an "el," an elevated railway, and blights everything in its path with noise, darkness, and dirt. It slices relentlessly through the length of the borough and, on its way, courses along Southern Boulevard for a mile and a half.

The Getzes lived midway through this stretch in a tenement on Minford Place at 170th Street, twenty yards west of Southern Boulevard. Al had rented a "railroad flat," a row of tiny rooms strung together like railroad cars. On Minford Place, the Getzes found themselves amidst a teeming stew of Jewish, Italian, Latino, and black families who, like themselves, were scratching out an existence at the lower margins of Depression America.

If you lived in the East Bronx in the 1930s, you spent much of your life out on its streets, and you rarely went elsewhere. Very few possessed the resources or the inclination to explore the world outside its boundaries; every place else was "out there," somewhat strange and alien.

Traveling away from the neighborhood was a major occasion for the Getzes, even if it meant venturing only a mile to Yankee Stadium, on the western edge of the Bronx. Goldie would scan the newspapers for the times when the Yankees allowed ladies in free, a "Ladies' Day," and she would announce it to the boys, and their excitement would build as the day approached. The three of them would make an excursion out of it, packing large lunches and catching an early trolley so they could watch batting practice before they settled down at game time for the serious rooting, cheering wildly for Joe DiMaggio, Lou Gehrig, Lefty Gomez, and their other heroes in the pinstriped uniforms.

Journeying to Manhattan was of a different order of magnitude. Bob Getz recalled:

> That was a completely other world from the East Bronx to Manhattan. We couldn't even go to Manhattan without getting dressed up. It was an occasion. A couple of times my parents took us to shows at Radio City Music Hall and the Strand. I remember going to see Jack Benny in some movie, then the stage show. A big thing for us.

Minford Place and 170th Street has been a low-rent location since 1904, when the el was built above an existing trolley line. To this day, the trains hurtle by every four minutes with a clatter that rattles windows, furniture, and anything else that is not nailed down. And until 1948, when they were replaced by buses, the trolley cars added their voices to the cacophony as they clanged along and screeched to a stop every two blocks. Stan could never get used to the noise or the acrid railway smells that assaulted his nostrils or the grimy darkness that blanketed the street beneath the el structure.

The Getzes lived only a block from the sweeter smells and sounds of Jennings, the neighborhood's market street. The tenements of Jennings were crowded with small ground-floor shops, and the pavement was covered with wagons and pushcarts. Food prices were written on brown paper bags mounted flaglike on slats, and in case you hadn't read them, the vendors shouted things like "Get your fresh flounder, caught this morning—ten cents" and "Sweetest peaches—six cents a pound." Adding to the din were the buyers ("High cash for old clothes—I want your old clothes, ladies") and the service sector ("Get your knives sharpened—sharpen your scissors today").

The great majority of the carts were horse-drawn, and they drew flocks of sparrows, which would pick slivers of undigested grain from the horse turds steaming on the pavement. The bony steeds spent the hours on Jennings methodically chewing the oats in their feed bags or staring stoically into space.

Finger food was plentiful. There was Sam the pickle man with a pickle for a nickel, and the sweet potato man doling out steaming hot potato halves slathered with butter, and the Good Humor man and the Eskimo Pie man and the guy making Italian ices by pouring green lime or bright orange or lemon liquid over shavings that he scraped from a block of ice.

Goods from the stores spilled out onto the sidewalks, racks of suits (with two pairs of pants—fifteen dollars) jostling with bolts of cloth wrapped around cores of cardboard and slatted boxes piled with tomatoes or apples or string beans.

The noisy good spirits of Jennings were deceptive. Toughs were waiting to pull you into alleys to mug you for as little as a dime, and Stan and Bob always had to be alert when Goldie gave them money and sent them out to shop for her; they were robbed several times.

If Jennings was rugged, Southern Boulevard was almost a war zone. Its dank caverns were patrolled by assorted goons, and it was known as a prime recruiting ground for "Murder, Inc.," the Jewish killer-for-hire gang headed by Lepke Buchalter and Gurrah Shapiro. In the gloom under the el, you could find prostitutes of any persuasion, or you could search out a "pad" where for five dollars you were supplied with heroin, the equipment for shooting up, and a room to "fix" in. And if you possessed stolen auto parts or other contraband goods, you would quickly be directed to a grimy storefront where you could fence them.

Minford Place, though only two blocks long, had its own caste system.

The northern block housed some middle-class families and was the site of a large, prosperous synagogue. The southern block, where the Getzes lived, was scruffy and poor, and possessed a storefront synagogue located beneath an apartment in a two-story building only eighteen feet wide. The Getzes worshiped at the storefront. Today it houses the Iglesia Christian Gabaon, a Latino Pentecostal church.

Al was indifferent to religion, an attitude he inherited from his father, who never insisted that Al be bar mitzvahed. The ceremony had been planned for September 1917, but it was canceled in the grief and confusion following the death of Al's mother, Becky, on August 25. It was never rescheduled. In most Jewish families at the time, not having a bar mitzvah was considered a major deprivation.

Goldie took a more serious attitude toward religion than her husband. Each week she performed "bench licht," the sabbath lighting of the candles by the mother of the household, and she insisted that her boys be bar mitzvahed. And she was very sensitive about their Jewish identity. Once one of her friends told her that Bob looked like a priest in a photo where he was wearing a dark turtleneck with a white collar, and Goldie became so angry that she wouldn't talk to the woman for six months.

Although they always embraced their Jewish identity, neither Stan nor Bob took Jewish religious teachings seriously. Between them they had four wives, all of whom were Christian, and seven children, none of whom were brought up in the Jewish faith.

For recreation Stan and Bob had Crotona Park, two blocks to the north. Although only about a fifth the size of Central Park in Manhattan, to the boys it seemed very large, a cool, cavernous leafy enclave with a man-made lake and an oversize swimming pool. The first time Bob headed for the pool, he was mugged at knifepoint for the dime admission, but both boys enjoyed swimming so much that they became regulars in spite of the dangers. They would run full tilt from their hot, oppressive apartment, hurriedly toss their dimes to a lugubrious attendant, and leap directly into the cool waters, where they splashed and swam for hours at a time.

Swimming became one of the true and lasting passions of Stan's life. As an adult, if he was near a large body of water, he would usually find a way to strip down quickly and leap into it. And the temperature did not matter; the colder the water, the more he enjoyed it.

Crotona Park also gave Stan a chance to exercise his entrepreneurial instincts. For a couple of summers, he earned extra cash by buying sunflower seeds in bulk on Jennings, packaging them in small bags and selling the bags for two cents apiece in the park. He would usually swim in the morning and peddle his wares in the afternoon, when the park was more crowded.

After a day cavorting in the park, Stan dreaded returning to the dark and cheerless railroad flat, where the only fresh air you breathed had to enter through the front and back windows; there was no side ventilation. Cooking odors lingered in the middle rooms and clung tenaciously to the upholstery and the curtains.

The summer heat waves brutalized apartment dwellers in the 1930s and the 1940s, when the only air-conditioned buildings were movie theaters. When the heat and the humidity engulfed New York, the mayor routinely lifted normal restrictions and allowed hundreds of thousands of people to sleep in the parks and on the beaches.

Goldie and Al felt that sleeping outdoors was too dangerous and undignified, and the family fought temperatures that often exceeded 100 degrees in their flat with a patchwork of feeble solutions—setting up a fan to blow air over a large chunk of ice, taking turns sleeping on the fire escape, showering three or four times a night.

The emotional climate in the flat would often heat up as well, as Goldie's disappointments festered and Al struggled to keep food on the table. Bob Getz remembers the tensions between his parents:

> They were always depressed. My mother was frustrated and didn't feel as if she were getting a fair shake, that life was miserable and treated her poorly; and my father was to blame. And he felt to blame.

As Al continued to fumble through life and his guilt mounted, he became more dependent and wraithlike. Bob Getz's ex-wife Pat was struck "by his lack of being there in any way, shape, or form. Al was a figment. I mean he was like this nebulous creature. He was so ineffectual."

Visits to the home of Phil Getz heightened the antagonisms between Goldie and Al. It was an article of faith among American Jews in the 1930s and 1940s that sincere effort would be rewarded, that if you worked hard, you and your family would rise economically and socially. Al's brother Phil was one of those who rose. He had quickly built his own thriving printing business and become a wealthy man.

Trips to his spacious home in the prestigious suburb of Glen Cove, Long Island, became increasingly stressful as Goldie compared Phil's opulence with her grim surroundings in the East Bronx and thought about what might have happened if she had pursued Phil rather than Al that romantic summer in the Catskills. Bob Getz recalls:

> Every time we came back from visiting Phil and his wife, Bessie, on Long Island, my mother would be depressed or angry. And there was always some fight. . . . I began to realize that it didn't do my mother any good to go visit the rich uncle.

Back in their railroad flat, Goldie imposed a strong instinctive solution to the family's problems—tough, autocratic rule by her. She called all the shots, as Al, Stan, and Bob trailed meekly in her wake. She was their stern guide and their protector, and she played her roles with gusto.

Stan took particular pride in the bravado and guts she displayed in dealing with hostile strangers, and as an adult loved to tell the story about Goldie and the bill collector in the derby hat.

While Stan, age six, clung timidly to his mother's leg, Goldie listened patiently as the bill collector stood at her front door and berated her for being a deadbeat. After he finished, she said, "You know, mister bill collector, you're pretty ugly. And I have a good way you can improve your looks."

"Yeah, how do I do that?"

"Take off your derby hat and take a shit in it. Then put it back on your head. You'd look much better with brown curls."

Then she slammed the door in his face and marched back into the apartment with her young son trailing proudly after her.

As Goldie became more disappointed with the hand that life had dealt her, she applied increasing pressure on Stanley, her prince, to succeed. She was convinced that by nurturing his talents and seeing them blossom, she would find the rewards that had for so long eluded her.

Even when Stan had only one shirt, Goldie washed and ironed it every evening so that he would make a good appearance at school. She prepared special lunches for him and religiously reviewed his homework to insure that it was complete and correct.

Goldie took much of the joy out Stan's schoolwork by setting unreasonably high goals. It happened over and over again with tough arithmetic or grammar problems; he would be filled with anxiety until he worked his way to a solution, and then true satisfaction would elude him. Unless he received a rare perfect grade, he would feel in some way wanting, because he hadn't achieved the perfection that Goldie demanded. Throughout his life Stan caused himself much unhappiness because he held himself to excessively high standards of performance.

Goldie didn't know exactly where Stan's talents lay, but she was sure that he possessed special gifts. He was consistently near the top of his class in school, and at the end of his sixth grade year in the fall of 1938, his marks and his IQ levels were so high that he was chosen for the Special Advancement Program. This meant that when he entered junior high in January 1939, Stan would complete both the seventh and eighth grades in one year by doubling up his courses; he would leap a year ahead of his contemporaries. When Goldie heard that Stan had been taken by the program, she told everyone whom she knew that she was certain he would become a doctor or a college professor.

His shining success would atone for the loss of her mother and her brother Meyer, the years and years of toil, her abusive father, the disappointments with Al, the wretchedness of Minford Place; her prince would erase the pain of the past, justify the struggles of the present.

She made it clear to everyone that Stan was her prince. And it was equally obvious that Bob could not attain this special status. He recalls:

> Stan was handsome, he was intelligent, he was personable. And then, five and a half years later, I came along. . . . Because of the economic structure of the family at the time, I think that I was a mistake. In any case, it was inopportune for me to come along. . . . I always felt out of place, because there was no question that Stan was just this extra special person that God put on this earth, and he happened to have fallen into the Getz family.

When the family could afford only a scrap of meat for dinner, Goldie decreed that it would go to Stan. Then she, Al, and Bob silently ate their beans and potatoes as they watched Stan put away the lone lamb chop or hamburger. He felt intensely guilty about being singled out for privilege in this way, and the memories of these meals pained him throughout his life.

Stan and Bob were more deeply pained by Goldie's practice of hitting them about the face and head when her frustrations overflowed. Being hit in the face was terribly humiliating for the boys, far worse than being hit in a more conventional place like the backside, and there was the added affront that usually they didn't deserve their punishment. Bob remembers, "My mother would hit me, smack me in the face, not because I did something wrong but because I upset her or was in her way."

One night Stan unconsciously earned Goldie's wrath when he walked in his sleep, went to the kitchen, and shat in the sink. He remembered for the rest of his life the walloping he received from her the next morning.

Of course, Stan could not openly express the anger and hurt he felt when he was hit unfairly, nor could he articulate his feelings of inadequacy in trying to meet Goldie's need that he redeem the wrongs she had suffered and assure her a happy future. These were impossible goals for a child to achieve, but Stan could not know that then. He just soldiered along, being a proper son and doing his schoolwork as best he could.

Goldie was anxious when Stan began junior high, worried that he would falter under the double course load. But his grades held up, and she was more certain than ever that he would become a doctor or a professor. She hadn't reckoned, however, on Borrah Minevich.

FROM MINEVICH TO BIG TEA: A MUSICAL JOURNEY

FROM THE AGE of six onward, Stan had been drawn to musical instruments as iron filings are drawn to a magnet. Whenever his family visited friends who owned a piano, he would pester the adults until they allowed him to play. He would then, with no hesitation, play perfectly by ear all the new tunes he had been hearing on the radio. Stan's interest pleased his parents because he was a shy, brooding kid whose enthusiasms were few. So they encouraged him when he conducted Metropolitan Opera performances while standing in front of the radio on Saturday afternoons or stayed after school to listen to band rehearsals or spent hours learning to hum Benny Goodman solos by heart.

Stan was constantly nagging them to buy him an instrument of his own, and Goldie kept discouraging him, telling him they couldn't possibly afford it. But he felt a surge of hope one spring day in 1939 when a variety group, Borrah Minevich's Harmonica Rascals, gave a concert at his junior high auditorium. Not only did they play exciting music but they were offering students the opportunity, for the remainder of the week, to join the Junior Harmonica Rascals. Membership cost one dollar—fifty cents for a harmonica and fifty cents for a series of summer lessons.

Stan knew that his parents couldn't afford to buy him a conventional instrument, but he believed that a harmonica plus lessons for one dollar might be within their range. When Minevich's canvasser came to their house, Stan mounted an all-out sales pitch with Goldie, and she succumbed. The next afternoon, Stan at age twelve was in possession of his first musical instrument.

The sound of the harmonica filled the apartment at all hours of the day. Stan worked out mouth-organ versions of big band arrangements like Woody Herman's "Woodchopper's Ball" and Goodman's "King Porter Stomp," memorized many popular and folk tunes, and mastered the blues scales. At the end of the summer, he earned an invitation to perform in a concert at his school.

For the occasion of his first ever public performance, Goldie dressed him in a pair of immaculate, carefully ironed white duck slacks; they were quickly stained yellow as Stan peed nervously while playing "O Susanna! Don't You Cry For Me." But he was determined to have his say, and he wouldn't stop playing as the stain grew larger and his mother cried and the audience laughed. He finished with a flourish before walking damply off the stage.

As Stan later recalled, his growing musical skills soon came to the attention of the school bandmaster:

> The physical training instructor at the junior high school was also the band conductor. He had a concert to play in two weeks and he needed a bass player. One day we were doing exercises, and he looked at me and said, "Hey you, come here. I'm going to teach you to play the bass part in the Minuet in the E Flat Symphony by Mozart." He took me upstairs and showed me the fingering.
>
> I went home after school lugging this bass. We lived in a very small apartment, and my mother opened the door and said, "It's either you or the bass. There's only room for one of you."

But Goldie relented, and Stan performed the Mozart piece flawlessly. He continued playing the bass in the school band for several months, learning how to blend in with the other instruments, to time his entrances and exits, to extract a resonant tone from his own instrument. In the structured band environment, Stan discovered several important things about himself—he could sight-read better than anyone else in the group, he had a photographic memory for music, and he had a perfect sense of pitch and a precise feel for rhythm. In other words he possessed musical gifts which are missing in ordinary mortals.

In addition, he found an arena where he could make his parents, and particularly Goldie, proud of him. He was too skinny and short to excel at athletics, and he was starting to lose interest in formal subjects such as English and algebra, but he could become a standout in music if he worked at it. He felt certain of that. And he felt certain of something else; he loved playing. He would practice for hours at a time and not lose his sense of enjoyment.

Stan also knew for sure that he disliked the bass, which for him had two serious drawbacks. First of all, since he bit his nails to the quick, his fingers bled all over the shiny mahogany sound board when he played. And secondly, the bass functioned largely to provide a rhythmic and harmonic undergirding in the arrangements. With his newfound talents, he longed to play a melody instrument; he let everyone within earshot know this.

Al heard Stan's pleas and, by scrimping on lunches, saved thirty-five dollars to buy him a secondhand alto saxophone; it was badly dented and sported corroded patches which were turning green and keys that moved very stiffly. Al gave it to Stan on February 16, 1940, Goldie's thirty-third birthday and two weeks past Stan's thirteenth birthday.

For Goldie and Al, Stan's musical talent represented a ticket to prosperity, the pathway from their dank tenement to a brighter, easier world. But for Stan it was entirely different. When he put the saxophone to his mouth for the first time, he knew for certain something that had stirred only faintly in him before: Music was his vocation, his lifelong passion. He would say much later:

> My life is music. And in some vague, mysterious and subconscious way, I have always been driven by a taut inner spring which has propelled me to almost compulsively reach for perfection in music, often—in fact, mostly—at the expense of everything else in my life. Happiness to me is only a byproduct of this constant reaching and reshaping.

Stan and the horn became inseparable. As he remembered:

In my neighborhood my choice was: be a bum or escape. So I became a music kid, practicing eight hours a day. I was a withdrawn, hypersensitive kid. I would practice the saxophone in the bathroom, and the tenements were so close together that someone from across the alleyway would yell, "Shut that kid up," and my mother would say, "Play louder, Stanley, play louder."

Stan managed to wheedle enough quarters from Goldie to take weekly lessons at a neighborhood music school run by an excellent teacher named Bill Sheiner, and he busied himself there with learning the other saxophones (soprano, tenor, and baritone) and the clarinet, a related instrument. The tenor sax, with its rich sound in the middle register, became his favorite.

One of Stan's main goals in the summer of 1940 was to insure that he be assigned to the main building of James Monroe High School when he matriculated there the following winter. He had to learn yet another instrument to achieve this.

Monroe was so overcrowded then that classes were held in six different buildings—the main one plus five deteriorating annexes. Stan was determined to avoid the annexes because the main building housed the orchestra studios, the swimming pool, and the gym.

He found his opportunity when an older friend who played first bassoon in the orchestra told him that the second bassoon chair was vacant. The bassoon is a reed instrument like the saxophone, but it is more difficult to play because the musician must control the vibration of two reeds rather than one. Stan borrowed a bassoon from Monroe during the summer vacation by putting down a five-dollar deposit and during the ensuing months taught himself how to play it well enough to pass the audition in January for the second chair. When he arrived at Monroe, he was known as the kid who could play all the reeds.

As one would suspect, Stan's music grade during the fall semester, his last at junior high, rose from ninety to one hundred, and his average in his other subjects dropped from seventy-eight to seventy.

Most of the alumni of the 1940s now look back on their days at James Monroe with fondness; they particularly remember a cadre of caring, hardworking teachers who fostered a lively, intellectual atmosphere despite the fact that Monroe was the most populous high school in the country at that time. More than 80 percent of the five thousand students were Jewish. There were about twenty blacks, and the rest of the kids were pretty evenly divided between those of Italian and Northern European stock.

Most of the students came from middle-class areas; kids from Stan's working-class neighborhood were a distinct minority. Goldie went to great lengths to distinguish Stan from his frequently grubby neighbors and was obsessive about dressing him impeccably. The habits of those days became deeply ingrained in him, and he was compulsively neat about his clothing throughout his adult life.

Stan, arriving at Monroe the week of his fourteenth birthday, found the music program to his liking; it covered a lot of territory, and the instruction was excellent. He completed three semesters at Monroe; during his last two, three of the six courses he took for credit were musical: theory, orchestra, and band. His average in these subjects was ninety-five; in the other three—English, chemistry, and French—it was fifty-eight.

He began every day with orchestra rehearsal. The orchestra had the same instrumentation as the New York Philharmonic and, with more than a hundred members, was roughly the same size. It played works by Mozart, Brahms, and other giants of the classical repertoire; Gilbert and Sullivan operettas; and marches (it doubled as the marching unit at athletic events). Stan was one of a small cadre of orchestra members whose superior skills qualified them for the band. This group, which played dance music, practiced late every afternoon.

Albert Becker, Stan's principal music teacher and the conductor of the orchestra, immediately recognized that Stan was extraordinarily gifted and dedicated; he provided many hours of free private instruction to his prize student. When Stan was only a sophomore, Becker started work on getting him a college scholarship to the first-rate Juilliard School.

After his first semester ended, Stan secured a summer job at a small, second-rung Borscht Belt hotel in the Catskills. He wore three hats: He worked as a musician, a busboy, and a wisecracking MC for the nightly stage shows. He always hated talking before an audience, and the experience as an MC strongly confirmed to him that his future lay in music rather than comedy.

When Stan returned to Monroe for the September 1941 semester, Becker pressed him to audition for the prestigious All-City High School Orchestra. He won acceptance easily. Membership gave Stan an opportunity to work with the cream of the city's teachers and young musicians, and the privilege of studying with a member of the New York Philharmonic. The Philharmonic paired Stan with Simon Kovar, a world-class bassoonist. The All-City Orchestra rehearsed on Saturday mornings and gave a half-dozen concerts during the school year.

At this time Stan started playing sax professionally in a wide variety of settings—fraternity parties, Sunday mambo matinees, Saturday night hops, bar mitzvahs. His average take was three dollars, and he felt very happy that he could in a small way ease the financial burdens of his hard-pressed parents. An aunt of Stan's remembers a time when Al wanted to give him a dime for subway fare to and from a gig. Stan insisted on taking only a nickel because he knew he would find the fare home in his night's pay.

He gave as much as he could to his parents, but he had one goal which involved putting away money for himself—the purchase of a tenor saxophone, his chosen instrument. By his fourteenth birthday, he had saved enough to buy a decent secondhand model.

Soon after he bought the tenor, Stan met Shorty Rogers, who later became an outstanding jazz trumpeter, writer, and arranger. Shorty remembered a remarkable encounter which led to a lifelong friendship:

> Although we lived close to each other, I never met Stan until we both were called to do a dance hall gig at the Chester Palace in the Bronx. We were playing stock arrangements: Count Basie things, Glenn Miller, Benny Goodman. There's a lot of reading involved.
>
> I'd been with the band several times; I knew my parts pretty well, and I notice there's a new guy unpacking a saxophone, so I asked who he was. The reply I got was, "His name is Stan Getz, he's fourteen years old, he studies with Bill Sheiner, and he's been playing with bands four months."
>
> And I thought, "Four months. Who can learn to read all this stuff?" It's like someone giving you a newspaper in Paris, another language, and in four months you can be fluent and read the whole paper. I'm sitting pretty close behind him, and I said, "I'm going to glance at my parts, but with the other eye, I'm going to watch this new kid."
>
> I listened, and to my amazement he never made one mistake. Then we did a Glenn Miller thing, "In the Mood," and he stood up and played Tex Beneke's solo ... with the same sound and everything. And I said, "What's going on with this guy?" And then we played "One O'Clock Jump." He did Lester Young's solo. Just perfect.

Al and Goldie became used to Stan arriving home at breakfast time because after most of his gigs, he would seek out jam sessions where he could play jazz, improvised music. Later he spoke of improvisation as a way of conversing:

It's like a language. You learn the alphabet, which are the scales. You learn sentences, which are the chords. And then you talk extemporaneously with the horn. It's a wonderful thing to *speak* extemporaneously, which is something I've never gotten the hang of. But musically I love to talk just off the top of my head. And that's what jazz music is all about.

Stan was totally immersed in music by the time he turned fifteen in February 1942. He was forever rushing—instrument case in hand—to rehearsals and concerts, lessons with Kovar or Sheiner or Becker, dances and parties, jam sessions. In the two short years since Al had given him his first saxophone, he had acquired a wonderfully rich musical education, and he was approaching a professional level of skill. He had loved all of it, but what he loved best was talking with his horn "off the top of his head," improvising.

By the fall of 1942, Stan's courses in French, English, and chemistry had become an unwelcome interruption to his burgeoning career. He missed many classes, and when he did show up, he frequently nodded off because he had played a late gig the night before. His average in his three academic subjects plummeted, and it didn't disturb him at all.

He began to earn recognition by older musicians as a solid big band performer, and one day in December 1942 one of them took him down to the Roseland Ballroom to try out for the band of Dick "Stinky" Rogers. After a quick run-through, Rogers offered him a job at thirty-five dollars per week. That was the easy part. The tough part was to convince Goldie and Al that he should drop out of school to become a full-time musician. Stan gnawed anxiously on his nails as they argued about it through the dinner hour and beyond. In the end they said yes; thirty-five dollars per week was too alluring. It was more than Al was making when he could get work, which wasn't very often.

Playing with Stinky at Roseland meant that Stan had made his mark as a professional; it was a quantum leap up from frat parties and bar mitzvahs. It also meant that he had to join the musicians union. He applied for membership immediately, adding two years to his age on the application.

The attraction at Roseland had always been dancing. The cavernous ballroom, which was located just off Times Square on Fifty-first Street, had catered to dancers of every stripe since 1919—couples as well as males who paid thirty-five cents for three turns around the floor with a taxi dancer. Stinky specialized in comical scat vocals, but he used those numbers sparingly as a change of pace from the smoothly romantic dance tunes his audience had come to hear. Stan was disappointed that he was not playing in a jazz-oriented band, but he was happy that he could hold his own with the seasoned crew which Stinky had assembled.

One night a couple of weeks after Stan had joined his band, Stinky poured himself a beer and stretched out on a couch as he relaxed in his dressing room between sets. His moments of repose were abruptly ended as a small man in an overcoat hurried into the room and handed him a piece of paper. The man was a truant officer, and the piece of paper was an order directing Stinky to fire Stanley Getz, the fifteen-year-old tenth-grade dropout who was in his employ.

At nine o'clock the next morning, Stan slouched in his seat and sourly ruminated on the first setback of his fast-moving career as he watched his French teacher cover a blackboard with verb conjugations. What could he possibly do with French verbs? Music was his life now, and he wanted to get on with it.

He also wanted to get on with helping Goldie and Al. He had felt very proud when he gave his mother his first thirty-five-dollar paycheck, and although the truancy system was to blame for his current predicament, he did not see it that way; he felt that he had let his parents down. He nearly cried when he told them that the stream of paychecks had ended; they looked totally crestfallen.

Stan's acceptance into Local 802 of the musicians union, on January 14, 1943, only sharpened his desire to move ahead with his career, preferably with a big band that played jazz. He put out the word to all his friends in the business, and he started frequenting places like the Nola Rehearsal Studios.

If you were a jazz musician in the 1940s, the Nola Studios, on Fifty-seventh Street down the block from Carnegie Hall, was an important place to hang out. Vincent Nola, a former opera singer and vocal coach, had built a thriving business in the warren of studios he rented out above an opulent Steinway piano showroom. All the big bands rehearsed there, and the hallways were filled with musicians swapping stories, drinking coffee out of paper cups, tuning up their instruments, reading trade papers like *Variety*, *Down Beat*, and *Metronome*.

On an afternoon in late January, a friend who played saxophone in Jack Teagarden's band told Stan to drop by during a rehearsal at Nola because there was a job available. The draft was sucking musicians out of Teagarden's group as fast as he could hire them; more than half of the band's complement of seventeen had joined the armed forces in the previous four months; to make matters worse, one of the sax players had been forced to quit because he was injured badly the previous night when his wife hit him in the face with a pitcher. Stan's friend had piqued Teagarden's interest when he told the bandleader that Stan not only played the sax very well but was three years below draft age.

A job with Teagarden would be an additional quantum leap upward for Stan. Teagarden—dubbed "Big Tea" by the media—was a major artist, the man who had pioneered the trombone in jazz and a wonderful, original singer. And his band was continually on the road, not easily reached by the New York truant authorities.

When Stan was introduced to Teagarden, he encountered a man of strong physical presence, a tall, solidly built Texan with jet black hair combed straight back and prominent cheekbones set in a wide, flat face. Teagarden's manner belied his looks, however, and he greeted Stan in an amiable southern drawl, saying, "Here's a horn, Gate. Sit in with us and read the fourth sax part." Teagarden called almost everyone Gate.

At first Stan was nervous about playing for a man he and every other young jazz musician idolized, but his exceptional sight-reading skills carried the day, and he sailed through the arrangements without an error. When he looked up after three tunes, Big Tea was smiling.

The bandleader pulled his most seasoned sax man over for a short whispered conversation and then turned to Stan and said, "Okay, Gate, seventy bucks a week. Get your tuxedo, dress shirt, and toothbrush. We're leaving Penn Station for Boston tomorrow morning."

The subway ride to the Bronx seemed to take forever, and Stan sprinted the two blocks from the station to his home. Al was there alone because Goldie was visiting her father in Philadelphia.

Stan knew this was a stroke of luck. Convincing Goldie that he should leave school for the job at Roseland had not been overly difficult, but talking her into letting him travel all over the country with a gang of hard-living nomads would definitely be a chore.

Al was a pushover. He said:

> Your mother won't like this much, but go ahead. I'll calm her down. The truant officer won't like it at all, but he won't find you. Christ, Stan, seventy bucks a week. I can't make that in two weeks. And I haven't had a job in a month anyway.

By the time Goldie returned to the Bronx, Stan was en route to St. Louis and sending home forty dollars each week. And he was firmly ensconced in the band after amazing Teagarden by memorizing in two days all his parts in the arrangements.

A month after Stan joined his group, Teagarden stepped off the bandstand at the Chase Hotel in St. Louis and was surprised to find himself face-to-face with a truant official demanding that he send Stan back to New York and James Monroe High. Big Tea moved the confrontation to a nearby bar and pleaded long and hard to keep the kid. The truant officer eventually laid down two conditions: Teagarden had to become Stan's legal guardian (with the consent of Stan's parents), and he had to promise to give Stan his school lessons every week. Following a flurry of long-distance calls, Stan's parents signed one set of papers in the Bronx and Teagarden signed another at the Chase, and the deal was done. Stan remained with the band.

Teagarden never gave Stan any formal schooling, but he provided his young ward with a Ph.D. in improvised music; Teagarden was a jazz master. He was also a prodigious drinker. "He taught me a lot about bending my right elbow," Stan later told a reporter.

MILES DAVIS said that the history of jazz can be encapsulated in four words: Louis Armstrong Charlie Parker. These men are the two unquestioned geniuses of the music. At the risk of oversimplification, they can be likened to Cézanne and Picasso. Armstrong and Cézanne created new art forms, and Parker and Picasso exploded the forms outward to express their full, dazzling possibilities.

While Armstrong strides as a giant across the jazz landscape of the 1920s, the music developed with amazing rapidity during that decade only because he had a handful of brilliant cohorts who understood clearly what he was doing and built enduringly on his foundations—men like saxophonist Coleman Hawkins, pianist Earl Hines, and Teagarden on trombone. Hawkins and Teagarden transformed what had been essentially comic vaudeville instruments into reputable vehicles of jazz expression.

Teagarden was bathed in music from his birth in a Texas cotton town in 1905. His mother, his sister, and his two brothers were professional musicians, and his father, a cotton gin engineer, led the town band and played cornet. Teagarden's mother started him on piano at age four and introduced him to the trombone when he was seven.

The black music Teagarden heard as a child affected him profoundly; he could never get enough of it. He would sneak off to black revival meetings to immerse himself in the sound of gospel, and he sought out itinerant blues shouters when they came through his town and local field hands to hear the work songs they sang when they picked cotton. He was untainted by racism, a remarkable virtue for a son of the Confederacy born in the early 1900s.

Teagarden began his professional career at age thirteen accompanying his newly widowed mother as she played piano at a silent movie theater. Family poverty forced him on the road in 1920 when he was fifteen, and for the next seven years he barnstormed the American Southwest and northern Mexico in bands with names like Peck Kelly and his Bad Boys, Willard Robinson's Deep River Orchestra, the Youngberg-Marin Peacocks, and Doc Ross and his Jazz Bandits.

This was the Prohibition era, and these bands played in roadhouses, speakeasies, and dance halls where bathtub gin and rotgut liquor flowed like a great river. Teagarden was almost killed when three gunmen sprayed bullets all over a San Antonio speakeasy in 1921. The owner went down, and as Big Tea tried to pull him to safety, seven slugs tore into the man's body and killed him. Teagarden's life was spared because the body had served as a shield.

At age seventeen, in 1922, Teagarden heard Louis Armstrong playing on a riverboat, and the two were introduced. Armstrong remembered the occasion as an encounter of two soul mates whose bonds transcended race:

> The time of those river boats, we'd just put into New Orleans and on the levee was a cat named Jack Teagarden wanting to see me. . . . He was from Texas, but it was always, "You a spade, and I'm an ofay. We got the same soul. Let's blow."—and that's the way it was.

Teagarden's life was forever changed. He understood for the first time the tremendous possibilities of his adopted profession and resolved to learn everything he could from Armstrong.

Thereafter, he carried Armstrong records with him wherever he traveled. He memorized his idol's solos, and, upon hearing that dry sands preserved artifacts forever, buried a recording of Armstrong's "Oriental Strut" in the western desert. He didn't record with Armstrong until 1929, when they made the widely anthologized "Knockin' a Jug" during one of the first racially integrated sessions.

Teagarden had perfect pitch (he could tell what key an airplane engine was whirring in) and lips of iron. One creates notes on the trombone by changing the position of one's lips and by moving the slide. When Teagarden was given his first instrument at age seven, his arms were too short to move the slide to its farthest positions, and he had to develop extraordinary lip strength and control in order to play all the notes. Throughout his career he used, of the seven standard slide positions, only the three closest to the body.

And his dynamic range extended from a whisper to a roar. Stan remembered a 1943 engagement at a movie theater in San Antonio:

> We were sitting behind the sound track. In those days, there was just a huge speaker behind the screen, and we were behind that, ready to go on with the stage show. Before we went on, there was a trailer for a movie with Tommy Dorsey's band, and you could hear Tommy playing "I'm Getting Sentimental Over You," his theme song. And Teagarden picked up his trombone and played it with him. His sound was so big it drowned out the whole huge speaker. That's just one small aspect of what he could do. He was tremendous.

Teagarden's technical skills were not the greatest of his gifts. Jazz is above all an improviser's art, and he was a master improviser, both with his horn and with his voice.

Big Tea consistently created beautiful melodies with an infectious swing, a bred-in-the-bone blues feeling, and a natural lyricism. Everything he played reflected an easy, laid-back mastery. And although his means were cool, the emotions he conveyed were hot. The critic Gary Giddins has this to say:

> Listen closely to Teagarden and there is always the shock of cogitating, feeling humanity. . . . Teagarden was never as provocative or versatile a vocalist as Armstrong, but he could emote as much feeling. . . . He haunts the music with his individuality. He was a player who expresses himself with honesty and immediacy every time he raises his horn to lips.

The element of Teagarden's art that most deeply affected young Stan was his guardian's powerful lyricism. Gunther Schuller, the Pulitzer Prize–winning composer and educator, is also struck by Teagarden's lyrical gift, which he believes grew from a unique vocal impulse.

> Teagarden was the first to bring to the trombone an essentially vocal-lyric style . . . a remarkable breakthrough achievement. Teagarden was also a remarkable and wholly unique singer, undoubtedly the best and the only true jazz singer next to Billie

Holiday, Cab Calloway, and Louis Armstrong (whom he, unlike dozens of others, did *not* imitate). Moreover, Teagarden's singing and trombone playing were virtually interchangeable.... The trombone's capacity for sliding, bending notes finds its exact parallel in Teagarden's singing in the manner in which he slithered through a song, the way he slurred over consonants, inflecting notes to form seamless lyrical shapes.

THROUGHOUT HIS LIFE, Stan acknowledged his musical debt to Big Tea. In 1964 he told a reporter, "In my early years, working with Jack Teagarden had the most affect on me. That was a very good introduction to professional music for me. Teagarden was a great musician. His playing is timeless—and it's logical." And in 1971 he said, "Can you imagine me, sixteen years old and sitting on the bandstand with him leading? ... We did maybe 260 jobs in the year, more or less one every day, and we drove two or three hundred miles to each in Jack's big Chrysler convertible. That was some training."

The training was particularly rich because, in addition to teaching by example on the bandstand, Teagarden conducted an almost continuous musical seminar when the band was traveling. He loved to talk shop, and when he wasn't too badly hung over, he was eager to help the younger musicians. He often created special study projects; he was, for instance, fascinated with the advanced harmonic ideas of pianist Art Tatum. So he transcribed note-for-note Tatum's best solos from records and analyzed them in detail with Stan and his other young charges.

Coaching new talent had been a pleasant counterpoint to Teagarden's often painful experiences as a bandleader. He had launched his orchestra in 1939, well into the big band era, and as a latecomer was forced to take secondary bookings. A naive and disorganized businessman, he allowed costs to skyrocket, and he passed through bankruptcy when his first band failed in 1940. Stan played in his second band, which always scrambled for bookings and secured few long engagements. The group barely stayed in the black and crisscrossed the country endlessly, subsisting mostly on one-nighters.

In 1943, at the height of World War II, the big bands grappled continuously with transportation problems. Gasoline was rationed, train and airplane schedules were sharply curtailed, and automotive parts were in extremely short supply. For long trips the band traveled by train and, in rare instances, by airplane. Usually they took to the road in two vehicles:

Teagarden, Stan, and two others rode in the Chrysler convertible, and the rest followed in a bus.

The vehicles broke down frequently, and the first man into a pair of coveralls and under the hood was Big Tea. The third passion of his life, after music and booze, was machines. He was constantly inventing them, tinkering with them, repairing them.

Life on the road numbed the entire Teagarden entourage with fatigue. The band drove in all types of weather over roads that were frequently slick or icy—scarred two-lane blacktops that ran through every Main Street in America. No interstates existed in 1943. The buses were cramped and reeked of sweat and stale cigarette smoke and were not air-conditioned.

Typically, the musicians would finish an engagement about 1:00 A.M., load up the bus, ride for six hours, unload, check into a hotel without air conditioning, and try to sleep until late afternoon. Then they would eat food that was almost always greasy and bland, set up for the gig, and play. And stumble out again into the blackness to repeat the routine for perhaps the two hundredth consecutive night.

The travels with Big Tea provided Stan with an opportunity for tremendous musical growth, and he made the most of it. That was the upside. The downside was alcohol.

Teagarden's thirst was monumental. There was booze wherever he went—in the cars and the trains, behind the bandstands, in the hotel rooms. When Stan arrived at Penn Station to join the band, one of the musicians gave him a pint of Scotch as a welcoming gift before Stan even stepped on the train.

It fell frequently to Stan, as Teagarden's ward, to haul his guardian up to bed when he passed out, to concoct exotic remedies when he arose with a hangover, and to make sure he was reasonably sober when he stepped onto the bandstand.

Stan found that the liquor that Big Tea and everyone else encouraged him to consume brought him relief from the stress and fatigue of the road. It also brought him a feeling of euphoria that he found increasingly impossible to resist. After a couple of nips, Stan would feel so terrific that he couldn't bear to lose the high. Each drink begat another to fuel his happy feeling, and he would quickly lose control as a relentless compulsion to prolong the pleasure took over. Although he would not come to understand this until much later, Stan was a classic example of a man whose history and genetics had programmed him for addiction. By the summer of 1943, he was getting drunk almost every night.

Stan acquired another addiction in 1943—nicotine; he began consuming a pack of cigarettes every day and continued to do so for the rest of his life.

Stan felt secure about his music but scared and vulnerable about himself. Although his face was usually a cool, impassive mask, beneath it lived a tense, frightened slum kid whose belief in his own worth extended only to his saxophone. He was confused about his male role models: his father, whose failures forced Stan on the road at age fifteen, and his guardian, a great and generous artist who couldn't stop drinking. Under the circumstances, Stan chose to "love the one you're with." While Al was scuffling from one printing job to the next in New York, Stan was on the road in the back seat of the Chrysler convertible getting plastered with his idol, Big Tea.

In spite of the boozing, Stan's skills improved. Teagarden noticed, and occasionally he would let Stan improvise a solo. Teagarden would say, "Take one, Gate," and Stan would edge forward shyly and stand, blue eyes intensely focused, holding the saxophone straight up and down, feeling the band surge behind him as for thirty or sixty seconds he sang to the dancers through his horn. Stan soon learned to tell when he had stirred something in them, and then he would feel a rush of happiness. He sought that rush almost every night for the rest of his life, and he usually found it.

Big Tea suffered an attack of ptomaine poisoning in Texas in early October 1943. Tired, ill, needing to dry out, and barely solvent, Teagarden decided to cancel his remaining engagements and regroup in southern California, where he and his wife had recently bought a house.

He took Stan with him, and Stan immediately fell in love with southern California. After the violent slums of the East Bronx and the grueling regimen of the road, the land of perpetual sunshine, palm trees, and wide open spaces seemed liked paradise. Stan knew quickly he wanted to settle there, and he told Al and Goldie that as soon as he found steady work, he would send for them.

To survive in Los Angeles, Stan had to solve an immediate economic problem: a California union regulation prevented him from working a steady local gig for ninety days. He was forced to take the only nonmusical job of his life, at starvation wages, as a salesman in a men's clothing store. Fortunately, the union ban did not apply to one-nighters by a national touring band, and Stan was able to supplement his salesman's pay by playing from time to time with a reconstituted Teagarden group and by appearing with them in musicals produced by Universal Pictures.

Nevertheless, he was forced to share a four-dollar-per-month room with another saxophone player, and his diet consisted mainly of Grape Nuts Flakes and apples. And booze. He resented not being able to play regularly and was anxious about his economic future, and he drank even more than when he was on the road with Big Tea. The alcohol released his frustration and anger, and as the nights wore on, he became testy and belligerent. His friends frequently found themselves extricating him from incipient brawls with barflies and bouncers.

In January, when the union restriction ended, Stan landed a short gig with Bob Chester's popular dance band at the Trianon Ballroom and then signed on with Dale Jones's six-piece Dixieland group, which served as the backup band at the premiere ballroom in the country, the opulent Palladium in Hollywood. Jones remembered Stan from the time they had played together with Stinky Rogers at Roseland the year before, and he was assured by Teagarden, one of his long-time associates, that Stan's playing had improved tremendously in the intervening twelve months. After Stan breezed through a couple of numbers, Jones knew that this was true.

Stan's prospects for steady work looked so good that in late January he bought cross-country railroad tickets for his parents and his brother. He had become the undisputed family breadwinner at the age of seventeen — and he had a serious drinking problem.

THE PRESIDENT AND THE NEEDLE

AL, GOLDIE, AND BOB arrived stiff and cranky from the five-day trip, and they weren't used to the brilliant sunshine which hit them as they emerged from cavernous Union Station in downtown Los Angeles. They blinked and shielded their eyes as Stan told them the bad news: He had run into a wall of bigotry in his attempts to find them a permanent place to stay. He later recalled, "They still had ads in the *L.A. Times* for renting apartments reading 'No children, no pets, no Jews.' We lived in the back of a barbershop until we found a Jewish building owner."

What they could afford to pay the Jewish building owner did not provide much shelter because Al had secured only a marginal job running presses and setting type at *The Hollywood Citizen News*. Bob Getz remembered their digs:

We lived in one room, my mother, my father, and I. They had a Murphy bed that came down and they slept on it, and I slept on a little cot. And that's all it was. One room and a kitchen and a bathroom. It was at 5347 Monroe in Hollywood right near Santa Monica and Western.

In spite of their cramped quarters, Bob felt liberated. Like Stan, he was totally smitten with California, overjoyed to put the grimy tenements, the muggers, and the thundering el trains behind him. He recalled:

For the first time in my life, I could be outdoors most of the time. I loved it. I wasn't weighed down with heavy sweaters or overcoats and galoshes, and I ran all over the place. There were so few high-rises you could see the sky in all directions, and it was always sunny.

Bob was enrolled in junior high school on February 7, 1944, and threw himself into the athletics program. He found that he was a talented baseball player, and most days he would spend hours on the ball field before dragging himself home exhausted just before dinner.

Al and Goldie could not find happiness in California. They missed almost everything they had left back east: schmoozing with their old neighbors, good lox and bagels, raucous family get-togethers, the bustle and noises and smells of a "real city" like New York or Philadelphia. But they felt they had no choice; they didn't want to be three thousand miles away from their favorite son and breadwinner.

Stan had quickly built a reputation around Los Angeles as an able big band sideman, and when Stan Kenton, whose band was based there, lost two sax players to the draft in February 1944, he asked Stan to join him at $125 per week. He accepted immediately. The band spent roughly three months each year in the Los Angeles area, and the generous salary meant security for Stan and the family.

In addition, the new job gave Stan an opportunity to gain serious recognition in the music business. In contrast to Teagarden, Kenton's fortunes were on the rise in early 1944. After years of struggle, everything was coming up roses for the thirty-three-year-old bandleader.

KENTON HAD LANDED a thirty-nine-week contract in September 1943 with the Bob Hope Pepsodent toothpaste show on NBC radio and was reaching a national audience of twenty million people every Tuesday night. Because Hope performed at a different Army or Navy base each week, the band received priority transportation and numerous opportunities for local exposure. Kenton usually booked three or four one-nighters in the vicinity of each base Hope had chosen and was thus able to build fan support in communities all over the United States.

When the band returned to Los Angeles, Kenton was assured of at least one long engagement every year at the Palladium, where he had a contract extending into 1946.

And in September 1943 Kenton had begun an association with a newly formed record company, Capitol, which gave him strong and sympathetic backing. Kenton's producer there was one of its three owners, the songwriter Johnny Mercer. Mercer provided Kenton with a first-class studio facility and technical staff, and he made an unusual deal with him: Kenton assumed a major workload as a roving promotion man for the company, and in return he was given almost total artistic freedom.

Kenton's personality was virtually a polar opposite of Teagarden's. Although Kenton enjoyed a drink, he was a workaholic, not an alcoholic (much later he would be both). Described by a biographer as "a lifetime product and prisoner of the Puritan ethic," Kenton played the piano, composed, was his own principal arranger, and managed the details of the band's tours and radio shows. And he spent whatever was left of his time fulfilling his agreement with Mercer—promoting himself and other Capitol artists with deejays, record outlets, newspapers, magazines. Trumpeter Buddy Childers remembered Kenton's solitary road regimen as the other musicians traveled in a bus:

> He got in his Lincoln and drove to the next town, and when he got there he went to one broadcast after another, to all the disc jockey shows in town, and he plugged the dance that we were doing that night and then he showed up. We were fresh, relatively fresh; we had some sleep. Stan just showed up and did it, and then did the same thing the next night . . . stopped to sleep about every third night. Or grab a few hours here and there. . . . And that's why the band survived—through the sheer force of his magnetism and his personality. He force fed the music to the people.

Kenton's musicians were his true family, and he sacrificed three marriages for his band. He held periodic staff meetings where the musicians could air their complaints, and he made a strong effort to treat them equitably. Whereas Teagarden's aesthetic was rooted in the blues of black

America, Kenton found his inspiration in the concert halls of Europe. He took a year off in 1937 to study European harmony and his theme song, "Artistry in Rhythm," featured a strain by Ravel and a Chopinesque piano solo. Other tunes used motifs from Wagner, Stravinsky, and Debussy; in fact, in 1964 Kenton recorded an entire album of material from Wagner's operas.

Kenton's growing appeal was based on a new approach to big band music, an approach built on masses of sound. Kenton's group was to the average big band of 1944 what the 1970s heavy metal pioneers were to the average rock band of their era—loud, bruising, and powerful. The sound was built mainly by the brass, with a phalanx of trumpets blasting and screaming over thick bottom chords from the trombones. The rhythms pounded rather than swung, and the saxophone players had to blow very hard to hold their own in the mix; alto saxophonist Al Harding recalled, "We were the loudest band; we were louder even than the guys today with the amplifiers. It was a physical effort to play in that band."

Kenton's conducting style fit perfectly with the band's dramatic music. In performance he was as theatrical as any modern-day rock idol. He looked like an incarnation of Ichabod Crane: He had flaxen hair, a narrow, angular face, immense hands, and long arms and legs that hung from a very skinny six-foot-four frame. The music energized him into frenetic movement. Driven by the beat, he would bound and stride about the stage, his gangly limbs gyrating wildly. And when a number built to a climax, his face would assume a rapturous expression, and he would grunt ecstatically as he threw his head back and thrust his arms skyward like a football referee signaling a touchdown.

Kenton was a middling improviser whose true passions were composing and arranging; the full band was his instrument. He wanted to create a new classical music incorporating jazz as one of several elements, and he was impatient with demands that his band play swinging music for dancers. He told reporters:

> When it comes to music for dancing, bands like Lombardo, Kaye, and Carle are tops. Our band is designed for creating moods and excitement. Our band is built to thrill. . . .
>
> Some of the wise boys who say my music is loud, blatant, and that's all, should see the faces of the kids who have driven a hundred miles through the snow to see the band . . . to stand in front of the bandstand in an ecstasy all their own. . . .
>
> Whenever you play dance music, it serves a function. It be-

comes a utility; you have to worry about the tempos and what you're going to play for people. But when you're playing for listening, you're free.

STAN JOINED the band that was "built to thrill" in late February 1944 when the group left Los Angeles for south Florida to begin a sweeping tour of twenty service camps. As usual, he memorized all the arrangements in two days, and, in a fit of teenage chutzpa, on the third day placed his music stand behind him.

As Kenton strode out to give the first downbeat, he saw the gap in his sax section and said to Stan, "What's the idea?"

"I don't need it. I've memorized everything."

"You might not need it, but we want a picture here in front. We don't want people looking at your shoes."

Stan fought back tears and immediately returned the stand to its place.

The band received an important boost when Anita O'Day joined on April 28, 1944. One of the best jazz singers ever, she is still active. Anita brought with her a strong following, having been a star with Gene Krupa, and she broadened Kenton's audience appeal significantly with her light, swinging approach to songs.

She remembered her first encounter with an ambitious seventeen-year-old sax player soon after she joined Kenton:

> This fellow came back stage to me and said, "Hi, Anita, I just joined the band."
>
> And I said, "Hi, good luck in whatever you do," you know. . . .
>
> About two days later . . . he says, "Would you ask Stan to let me take a solo, please? I want to just take a little solo."
>
> "Okay, I'll ask Stan." So, I forgot.
>
> The third night goes by and the fourth night, this new saxophone player comes by and says, "You said you were going to ask Stan if I could take a little solo—anywhere."
>
> I said, "I'll do it right now." I went over to Stan and I said, "You know this little kid that joined our band, whatever his name is. . . . He's always practicing."
>
> And he says, "Tell him he can play the second eight (bars) of the second chorus—on number twenty-six."
>
> Big deal! I go back, I get to tell him. He loves me, he's allahing

me, he takes his horn out. . . . Stan says, "Twenty-six," and the guy looks over at me and I say, "This is it, it's you." His first solo in life, I think. He was only seventeen.

The number is moving, the first chorus is over, I said, "Get ready. . . ." He's up there already standing. And finally it's his turn. . . . And he goes dah do dah do dah do dah do. How hot can you get? Dah do dah de dah do dah do. Very boring. His eight bars are over and he took a bow and sat down. That's Stan Getz, folks.

May 20, 1944, marked both Anita's recording debut with the band and Stan's first ever studio date. He had never gone into a studio with Teagarden because the musicians union was on strike against the record companies during his stay with the organization; that Teagarden band can be heard today only on air checks from Armed Forces Radio Service broadcasts, and these recordings contain no solos by Stan.

Anita had difficulty meshing her aesthetic with Kenton's. As she has written:

> In 1944 it wasn't totally true that if you didn't swing you didn't mean a thing. There were Dixieland bands, sweet bands, the Midwest's Million Dollar Corn Bands and all kinds of novelty orchestras. But swing was the thing and Stanley (Kenton) just wasn't into it. . . . In swing, or 4/4 time, everyone finds the downbeat—one—and goes from there. But for anything written in up-beats such as Stanley's "Opus in Pastel" the band didn't come in on *one*, it came in on *one and*. Now that's great. New. Different. Whatever. But I defy you to tap your foot to it because you can't tap *up*. And for me, singing to it was just as hard as dancing to it.

And Kenton's unswinging drummer made matters worse for Anita. Before their first recording session, she told Kenton:

> We can't cut it with that pan banger you've got. How about letting me bring in a good swing drummer just for the session? He agreed. So I went club hopping. . . . In this one joint I came upon Jesse Price, who had his own group and was really blowing.

She talked Price into joining the session, and one of the songs, "And Her Tears Flowed Like Wine," became Kenton's first big hit, reaching number four on the pop charts and selling four hundred thousand records. Anita argues, "To this day, I believe the tune succeeded because Jesse was an affirmative drummer."

Price joined the band after the record date, becoming its second black member. The other black, whose skin was light, frequently passed as a Cuban and would take "vacations" when the band toured the south. But Price's skin was unmistakably black, and this resulted in a short career with Kenton. Price quit after six weeks because racists within the band made life intolerable for him. He said afterward that although Kenton had treated him without prejudice man-to-man, the bandleader just did not have the will to face down the racists.

Stan continued to get high on booze, drinking himself unconscious almost every night. A coterie of heroin users in the band noticed this and enjoyed tempting him with stories of the superior transports of a heroin high.

Stan showed some curiosity, and when one of the older junkies persisted, he began to waver. One night, as the bus was barreling along a seemingly endless strip of blacktop, Stan's tempter told him that he had purchased some terrific dope and asked Stan to follow him to the back. When they got there, he spooned some powder from an envelope and told Stan to snort it.

Stan followed instructions, and he experienced that first-ever rush that junkies cherish for the rest of their lives—a burning in the sinuses and then a surge of pure pleasure starting in the stomach and moving into the head and the limbs. For junkies the heroin euphoria is far stronger than anything they experience with alcohol. And there is something more: All their anxieties and fears leave them, and in their place is a feeling of tranquil power; they feel as if nothing hurtful can touch them.

Stan sought the feeling several times during the next couple of weeks, and then he decided he wanted to boost it: He injected some and felt a more intense euphoria than he had the first time. When he laid off for a day, he became terribly sick; he was hooked.

Stan continued to function almost normally as a musician. Heroin knocks you out during the immediate "nodding" period following injection; the amount of time spent nodding depends upon the size of the dose and the health of the user, but it doesn't usually exceed forty minutes. The junkie awakens in an alert, energetic state and will function that way until he needs another fix—usually eight hours later.

To lead a quasinormal life, the junkie needs three things each day: his money, his connection, and his fixes. They become his first priorities, his obsessions. The great tenor sax player, Dexter Gordon, who was a heroin addict for several years, believed that the anxious grind of obtaining his drugs hurt his playing more than the drugs themselves:

Technically speaking, I don't think it helps you any. It in itself
doesn't impair your facility any. Getting hung up in the pursuit
of it, getting so involved so that you don't have the drive and
interest . . . this is what it did to me.

Stan had no problem with his junkie necessities. His salary was ample,
and connections in the drug underground turned up to supply the band
at every stop on the tour.

Stan continued to play his parts impeccably, but he had to blow harder
because the band was becoming brassier and noisier. In June, arranger-
trumpeter-trombonist Gene Roland signed on and added fifth trumpet
and trombone parts to the usual four-part scores. Kenton liked the louder,
fuller sound so much that he made it a permanent fixture thereafter,
becoming the only big band leader to use ten brass instruments.

In the midst of all the Kenton noise, Stan felt that he was learning
little. He became nostalgic for the days with Teagarden, when every one
of Big Tea's solos taught him something, and he began to look for other
mentors. As he searched, it became clear that his own greatest gift was
to create melodies, and this realization drew him to the work of the most
sublime melodist in jazz history, Lester Young.

From the early days in the Bronx, Stan had known about Lester, but
he had been too busy learning his craft to listen to him carefully. Now
he was ready to enter Young's musical world in earnest. The other Kenton
musicians began to question Stan's sanity when he would listen ten consecutive times to a record featuring Young. And they were convinced that
he had gone off the deep end when he played Young's solos note-for-
note for hours until he had them down perfectly.

YOUNG, born in Mississippi in 1909 to a family of professional black
musicians, was fortunate to spend vital years of development in the two
seminal cities of American jazz: New Orleans and Kansas City. As histo-
rian Phil Schaap points out, Lester's New Orleans childhood was filled
with wonderful music:

The key aspect of Lester Young's New Orleans childhood is the
fortunate placement of a musical genius in the birthplace of jazz
while that music was in its most creative period. Lester fell in
love with hot music. Swinging rhythm thrilled him. The drums
held a special attraction. Lester followed the New Orleans black

brass ensembles as they marched and played through the streets of the city. . . . Lester doubtless heard every significant New Orleans jazz man, including Baby Dodds, Paul Barbarin, Freddie Keppard, King Oliver, Kid Ory, and the teenaged Louis Armstrong.

During his teens and early twenties, Young played with his father's band and others throughout the Southwest and Midwest. In 1933, at the age of twenty-four, he settled in Kansas City just as that city was entering its golden jazz era. Inspired by the blues and by white saxophonist Frankie Trumbauer, he arrived there with a freshly developed lyrical approach to improvising.

His talents came to full flower in Kansas City, mostly in association with Count Basie's band; he first played with Basie in 1934 and joined his group permanently in 1936, staying until December 1940. The band achieved national prominence in 1937 and traveled extensively thereafter. After leaving Basie, Young usually performed as a leader of his own small groups. Between 1937 and 1941, Young made a series of classic small-band sides with Billie Holiday, and he and Basie recorded with Benny Goodman.

Billie gave Lester a nickname that became permanent. As she wrote:

I always felt he was the greatest, so his name had to be the greatest. In this country kings or counts or dukes don't amount to nothing. The greatest man around then was Franklin D. Roosevelt, and he was the President, so I started calling him The President. It got shortened to Pres.

Lester returned the favor by giving Billie her lifelong nickname, Lady Day.

During the formative years of jazz in the 1920s, Coleman Hawkins did the same thing for the saxophone that Jack Teagarden did for the trombone: He took a novelty instrument used mostly for comic effect and transformed it into a vehicle for expressing the full range of emotion. Hawkins's aesthetic dominated saxophone playing until Young burst on the scene with his first recordings in 1936. Pres challenged the accepted wisdom in three vital spheres: harmony, sound, and rhythm. And his innovations were so revolutionary that they changed not only the way jazz saxophone was played but also the way all jazz instruments were played.

The chords of a song provide the spine or structure of its harmony. When a chord is notated on the sheet music, it says to the interpreter that the tones of that chord will be the "comfortable" ones until the next chord appears. For example, the song "All of Me" begins with a C6 chord—comprising C, E, G, and A—that prevails for eight beats or two bars. The four C6 tones are thus for eight beats the "comfortable" ones, and the other eight notes in the scale are, in varying degrees, dissonant or "uncomfortable." (Western music is based on a scale of twelve notes. On the piano they appear as five black keys and seven white ones.) In other words, the C6 chord is a tyrant which dictates the harmonic parameters of "All of Me" until the next chord is introduced at the beginning of the third bar. It is an E7—E, A flat, B, D—and it dictates a new set of comfortable and uncomfortable notes for the next eight beats. It is then replaced by an A7 chord, and the process continues until the end of the tune. The full sequence of chords sets the contour and flavor of the entire song.

Before Young, the prevailing method of improvisation was based on exploring the ramifications of the chords, including both their comfortable and uncomfortable notes. The great exemplar of this style was Coleman Hawkins, who would interpret a song by mining thoroughly the tonal possibilities of its chords sequentially from beginning to end.

Pres treated the chords in a radically different way. He did not see them as ends in themselves; rather, he used them as a backdrop to the new melodies he was creating. The chords were no longer essential building blocks; they had become a framework for melodic invention. Pres would propel himself horizontally across the chords, etching his melody notes boldly against the harmony.

Young's brother Lee talked about his approach:

> He would say it confines you too much if you know it's a D flat 7. You start thinking of only the notes that will go in that chord, and he'd say that's not what he would hear. He wanted to play other things and make it fit. And he did.

Pres created a new sound to embody the free, lyrical quality of his ideas. The prevailing Hawkins style employed a gruff, swaggering, macho sound. Young's tone was pure and luminous, not gruff. He did not swagger; he floated over the chords and the beat.

As Young's harmony was freed from the domination of the chords, his rhythm was freed from the domination of the beat. Much of the power and beauty of his music stems from the unexpectedness of his rhythmic choices. He imbued everything with a tremendous sense of swing, but he was constantly changing the placement of the beat, delaying it, nudging it forward, shuffling it along until it emerged explosively at just the right moment.

Berkeley musicologist Louis Gottlieb has commented:

> Lester Young was *the* master of metric shifting. There are count-less instances in his solos where he obliterates the difference be-tween strong and weak beats, and strong and weak *halves* of the beat. I will never forget the first time I heard "I Never Knew" in a record store in Washington, D.C. I thought the record had slipped a groove [when he turned the beat around in the middle of his third chorus].

John Lewis, who played with Pres in 1950 and 1951 and who has been the director of the Modern Jazz Quartet since 1954, summed up Young's approach clearly:

> If you have a melodic design that is strong enough you can build on that design and on the accompanying rhythm patterns without relying on any particular harmonic [chord] progression. This is especially true if there is enough rhythmic character. Lester Young has been doing this for years. He doesn't always have to lean on the harmonic pattern. He can sustain a chorus by his melodic ideas and rhythm. The chords are there, and Lester can always fill out any chord that needs it, but he is not strictly dependent on the usual progression.

What Pres did was a good bit like sculpting. Let us liken a song to a conventional clay sculpture of a woman's head, quite beautiful in itself, which we present to Picasso to work on. He will flatten it here, stretch it there, tuck it, punch it, puncture it until he has created something more expressive, more deeply human than what he started with.

That is what Pres did with countless songs. Wanting to shape a story with each solo, he would never embark on an improvisation until he knew every word of the lyrics. The song might be complex like "A Ghost of a Chance" or simple like "Clap Hands, Here Comes Charlie." No matter. He sculpts them and transforms them, rolling out phrases of star-tling originality as he links them together into fresh melodies that embody an impeccable musical logic. When he finishes an improvisation, its struc-ture seems both beautiful and inevitable, and you want to cheer, or cry, or both.

And it was all done in a cool, offhand, almost languid manner. The

energy of artifice was concealed. As Pres spun out his masterful melodies,
you "never saw him sweat."

Young's approach never fully supplanted that of Hawkins—primarily
because it required more melodic talent. The gifted melodists like Stan
followed Young's lead, but those who did not possess great lyric resources
found Hawkins's style more congenial.

The more Stan studied Young's music, the more he loved it, the more
it became part of him. He was affected both by its melodic beauty and
its emotional immediacy. As he told reporters in later years:

> He was the first tenor saxophone player I heard play melodically,
> to make beautiful melodies. The saxophone is actually a transla-
> tion of the human voice, in my conception. All you can do is play
> melody. No matter how complicated it gets, it's still a melody. I
> never tried to play like Pres, but I so loved his conception of
> music that maybe some of it seeped into me. It's supposed to be
> that way. A lot of people have influenced me. You don't try to
> imitate it; you digest it. Because you love it so much, some of it
> comes out. . . .
>
> Pres was very respected, and he was a stud. But when he picked
> up the saxophone he still wore his heart on his sleeve, and as
> soon as he came in he showed how much of a human being he
> was. He played right out. There was no hate in his music, even
> though this was at a time when racial things were really bad. . . .
>
> After the thirty years or so I've been in music, he still comes
> through as a guy who wasn't afraid to show what he felt in his
> playing, instead of hiding his heart under a bunch of hate and a
> bunch of notes.

While Stan sat quietly when listening to Young's solos, he couldn't keep
from laughing when he heard stories of his idol's linguistic legerdemain.

Pres was an innovator in language as well as music, creating his own
unique vocabulary. White people were "grays," and he described his own
light skin as "Oxford gray." When he approved of something, he had "eyes
for it," and "no eyes" indicated disapproval. Spongers were "zoomers" and
"needle dancers" were heroin addicts. If he felt uncomfortable in a social
situation, he would say, "I feel a draft." "Did you wear a hat?" meant
"Did you have sex?" An attractive woman was "pound cake," "Bing and
Bob" were the police, and his "tribe" was his band. If he asked, "Can
Madame burn?" he meant, "Can your wife cook?" To fail was to be
"bruised." When he said to a pianist, "Have another helping but tone

down your left people," he meant, "Take another chorus but play more softly with your left hand."

YOUNG'S CONCEPTS liberated Stan's imagination as nothing had before, and during the summer of 1944, his improvising skills improved remarkably. He kept pestering Kenton for more solo time, but Kenton put him off by insisting that all the major sax improvisations be taken by Dave Matthews, a solid player with fifteen years as a big band musician. When Matthews left in August 1944, Stan intensified his pressure, cornering Kenton at rehearsals to show off his rapidly improving skills. His improvisations had by this time become so good that Kenton could not deny him, and he decreed that Matthews's solo assignments be split among Stan and two other sax players.

Stan's first improvisation on record can be heard on an Armed Forces Radio air check from December 19, 1944. He shares a chorus with tenor saxophonist Emmett Carls on the song "I Know That You Know." The big, brassy Kenton arrangement almost overwhelms the bright little show tune, and Carls, coming on first, plays a heated Hawkins-style solo using an extremely hoarse tone.

Stan's improvisation is like an island of calm in the agitated sea of brass, and his Pres-like sound is so light that he and Carls seem to be playing different instruments. His solo, built around a long descending phrase right out of Young's bag, possesses an assured logic and a lilting beauty. It is a far cry from his faltering debut effort, which Anita O'Day had derided just seven months before.

Stan's playing continued to improve, and soon after his eighteenth birthday on February 2, 1945, Kenton anointed him as the band's premier sax soloist. Emboldened by his new status, Stan asked Kenton about using some of Young's concepts in the band's arrangements. When Kenton denigrated Young's music as too simple, Stan couldn't believe it. It was Kenton's music that was simple, not Young's, and Stan was stunned and angry that Kenton could not perceive this; he now knew that his days with the band were numbered.

In late April 1945, as the group rolled into Chicago to begin a two-week engagement at the Sherman Hotel, he quit. Having been the leading sax soloist in one of the top bands in America, Stan was not concerned about finding work.

BENNY, FOUR
BEBOP,
AND
BEVERLY

WORD OF STAN'S defection from Kenton spread quickly among musicians, and bandleader Jimmy Dorsey soon knew about it. He was, like every World War II bandleader, fighting the ravages of the draft, and when he heard that a sax player of Stan's caliber was available, he hired him immediately. Dorsey was touring the Midwest and heading for Los Angeles, so his travel plans suited Stan perfectly. He joined Dorsey when the band arrived in Chicago from Indianapolis to replace Kenton's group at the Sherman Hotel on May 11, 1945.

Dorsey, born in 1904 to a Pennsylvania coal miner who led a local band, was one of the young white musicians drawn in the early 1920s to the Chicago of Louis Armstrong and Earl Hines and their cohorts. Along with people like his brother Tommy, Benny Goodman, Hoagy Carmi-

4 5

chael, and Gene Krupa, he was inspired by the hot black music pouring from the speakeasies and dance halls of Al Capone's domain. His father had schooled him well, and he soon found lucrative employment playing alto sax and clarinet in the bands of Paul Whiteman, Red Nichols, and Vincent Lopez.

In 1934 he and Tommy launched a big band, but a year later they separated because of a series of belligerent outbursts by Tommy that culminated in Tommy's walking off the bandstand one night after an argument about the tempo for a dance number. After the breakup each brother found wide popularity with a band of his own as their kind of hot swing music swept the nation after 1935. By the time Stan joined him in 1945, Jimmy's music had cooled off considerably, and his success with audiences was based upon a blend of smooth dance tunes, intriguing interplay from his female and male singers, and Latin numbers with an infectious beat.

Stan was not challenged by Jimmy's music, but he was happy with his relaxed, congenial leadership, and he knew that Jimmy would bring him home to Los Angeles in a matter of weeks. Stan was also happy to discover that it was easy to find heroin connections along the route west and after he arrived home.

Following an engagement in San Diego, Stan left Dorsey in July for his first gig as a leader, fronting a trio with pianist Joe Albany and former Kenton drummer Jimmy Falzone at the Swing Club in Hollywood. Albany did not play conventional swing piano; he was a pioneer of the new bebop style that was just beginning to revolutionize jazz. In choosing him, Stan showed that his ears and mind were open to the most progressive concepts in jazz in 1944.

The Swing Club gig lasted less than three months because in October Stan accepted an offer to join Benny Goodman's band while it was on tour in Canada. Stan quickly discovered that he had signed on with an organization in turmoil.

Goodman, after almost ten years as the top star of American pop music, had startled his fans by disbanding in March 1944 because of a dispute with his booking agency, MCA. But he soon found that he was unhappy on the sidelines and, despite the fact that the dispute had gone unresolved, organized a new band in March 1945.

Nearly all the members of his old contingent were either in the armed forces or working happily with other bands, and the new group was staffed almost entirely by unseasoned musicians. Their playing lacked cohesiveness and bite, and Benny quickly began experimenting with his personnel in an attempt to recapture the old magic. He had meager success, as sax player Danny Bank told Goodman's biographer Ross Firestone:

> Benny hired and fired relentlessly. He kept looking for the band and couldn't find it. During the year and a half I was with him I must have met forty saxophone players. They passed through the band like a parade. I rehearsed them, played their auditions, and then I saw them leave. And there were about the same number of brass players. . . . We would have one band for as long as three or four weeks, then there would be a new body, and everyone had to get used to each other all over again.

Stan arrived in the middle of this turbulence and almost immediately created some of his own with an outbreak of teenage chutzpah not unlike the music-stand incident with Kenton. Popsie Randolph, the "band boy" or road manager, remembered the occasion:

> Once in London, Ontario, we were playin' and Benny was up there with Liza Morrow, who was singin' with the band. Stan Getz was with us, and for a gag he wrote out a crazy sign on the back of some music and hung it up on the stand. We laughed, and Benny saw it, and sorta laughed too. But later that night he said, "Popsie, get rid of him."

Fortunately Benny changed his mind; he liked Stan's playing too much. Since Benny was a charter member of the Lester Young fan club, he adored Stan's solos, and he was delighted with the way Stan's swinging and powerful playing lifted the entire sax section.

BENNY GOODMAN was a millionaire before his thirtieth birthday, but he grew up in unheated Chicago tenements with ten siblings, and he frequently knew hunger as a child. His parents were East European Jewish immigrants who kept a kosher home, and his father was forced to supplement his meager earnings as a tailor by shoveling pig lard in the stockyards; his mother was illiterate.

Benny was born in 1909, a generation before Stan, but they shared the same escape route from poverty: They became outstanding musicians as teenagers. Benny started playing clarinet at age ten, quickly showed precocious skills, and was making forty-eight dollars per week in a dance band by the time he was fourteen.

Benny was obsessed with attaining musical perfection. Except when he was ill, he practiced several hours every day until he died at age seventy-seven. His daughter Rachel remembered:

> My father was an extremely self-absorbed man. This self-absorption, it enabled him to go where he needed to go. It also drove everybody else crazy, because it shut the rest of the world out. . . . I remember shortly after my mother died, coming to see him and he seemed so alone, except there was the clarinet next to him, and I thought: That's it, that's his biggest companion. The clarinet was his real best friend.

Benny's self-absorption made him very absent-minded, as collaborator Terry Gibbs recalled:

> He never could remember your name. One time we were rehearsing and his wife, she came in and said, "Benny, should I bring the musicians some toast?" He said, "Not now, Pops." He couldn't remember his wife's name. It got to the point where everybody was "Pops" to him—women, children, dogs, fire hydrants; everything was "Pops."

Benny's early models were people he heard in the Chicago speakeasies: Louis Armstrong, Bessie Smith, white clarinetists Leon Roppolo and Frank Teschemacher, and black clarinetist Jimmy Noone. As he matured, he was strongly influenced by Jack Teagarden and Lester Young, and recorded with both of them. Benny's improvisations lacked the lyrical originality and the humanity of these two men, but they were excellent nonetheless. He infused his long quicksilver lines with a hot, joyous urgency, and his infectious sense of swing got an entire nation up and dancing.

Goodman was the first pop millionaire created by electronics. He organized a band in late 1934 specifically to play on a once-a-week Nabisco radio show, *Let's Dance*. This program featured three bands every Saturday night on NBC: Kel Miller's for "sweet" dance tunes, Xavier Cugat's for rhumbas and other Latin rhythms, and Benny's for hot jazz. *Let's Dance* gave its audiences three hours of live music in each of the four American time zones, and its complicated logistics dictated that the show play to eastern audiences starting at 10:30 P.M. their time and to West

Coast audiences starting at 9:30 P.M. Pacific time. In order to accomplish this, the musicians were forced to work for five consecutive hours in New York, and Cugat's band, which was also playing at the Waldorf-Astoria Hotel, had to be shuttled by a fleet of taxis three times each night between the hotel and the NBC Studios.

Benny was woefully short of material for the show and reached out to a number of writers. Several responded, but one man, Fletcher Henderson, provided the arrangements which proved to be crucial to Benny's success. Henderson, alongside Duke Ellington, had created from the black musical consciousness of the 1920s the basic big band aesthetic which has prevailed to this day. It supplanted that of the weak-kneed dance ensembles that preceded it. Henderson's arrangements featured masses of reeds and brasses harmonizing powerfully with each other, fascinating interplay between improvising soloists and the band as a whole, and a driving beat created by a tightly knit four-man rhythm section.

Henderson's own band, spotlighting such soloists as Louis Armstrong, Coleman Hawkins, and Ben Webster, had floundered in 1934 after an exciting, innovative twelve-year run. Goodman started *Let's Dance* by using existing Henderson arrangements and then drove Fletcher to produce three new ones each week during the show's six-month run. Ross Firestone has recognized the importance of their partnership:

> . . . Through no fault of his own, Benny was the beneficiary of a dozen years of experimentation, development, and gradual perfection of a style of big band arranging that was to give him the identity he needed.

To his credit, Benny never stinted in his praise of Henderson. More than a half century later, he dedicated his last television special to Fletcher, saying, "The fascination with his arrangements was endless. I really thought he was a genius."

The *Let's Dance* show was abruptly canceled in late May of 1935 because a strike had closed down all the Nabisco factories. In a desperate move to keep the band alive, Benny's managers booked him into an August engagement at the Palomar Ballroom in Los Angeles with one-nighters and a four-week stay in Denver along the way. The pay was so bad that they could not afford a bus, and the musicians had to drive their own cars. Most of the ballroom owners insisted that Benny emphasize his "sweet" arrangements, and the tour was a dismal flop; he almost closed it down in Denver.

The band played to a surprisingly full house at its first California stop in Oakland and then moved on to the Palomar, where it opened on August 21, 1935. The audience was apathetic during the first set as the band played "sweet" arrangements. Then sparks began to fly. Ross Firestone describes what happened:

> The band was still dying, slowly this time, by inches. As they prepared for the next set, one of the sidemen—it might have been Bunny Berigan or maybe Gene Krupa—told Benny, what the hell, as long as they were going down, they might as well go down swinging. Benny nodded his head and broke out the Fletcher Henderson arrangements. . . . Benny recalled, "To our complete amazement half of the crowd stopped dancing and came surging around the stand. . . . That was the moment that decided things for me. After traveling 3,000 miles, we finally found people who were up on what we were trying to do, prepared to take our music the way we wanted to play it. That first big roar from the crowd was one of the sweetest sounds I ever heard in my life, and from that time on the night kept getting bigger and bigger. . . .

Three reasons, all rooted in the radio medium, account for the Palomar success. First of all, *Let's Dance* started in prime listening time—9:30 P.M.—on the West Coast, an hour earlier than in the other time zones. Second, the band was loose and thoroughly warmed up when it started performing for Pacific audiences two hours after it began playing its East Coast segment. And finally, popular California disc jockeys had been ardently plugging records that the band made just before it left New York. In other words, radio had created an army of California fans before the band arrived there.

The explosion at the Palomar propelled Benny forward on an astonishing arc of success as his "swing music" (a PR man's term) swept the country, and he became a cultural liberator of major proportions. Like Elvis Presley a generation later, he brought to the kids of straitlaced, white, middle America a hot, orgiastic black music that drove them wild. Unlike Elvis, Benny was the least likely candidate one could imagine for an American pop icon—an introverted, absent-minded, bespectacled, Jewish musical perfectionist. But he loved hot music, and he could play it to a fare-thee-well, and that's all that mattered.

The frenzy that Benny ignited built momentum in late 1936 and into early 1937. It began to peak on March 3 when the band opened at New York's Paramount Theater opposite a somber film about witchcraft, *Maid of Salem*, starring Claudette Colbert. When the band arrived at 7:00 A.M. to rehearse for the opening show, the streets were filled with kids lined up to buy tickets, and when the musicians faced the audience for the first time at 10:30 A.M. after the movie ended, the sold-out audience was on its feet cheering and screaming. Benny remembered:

> When we got on the stage the first time, the audience was in such hysteria and so enthusiastic we couldn't play. So, we just sat there for four or five minutes and said, "When you get through applauding, well—we'll play." We looked at them as if they were the show and we were the audience.

The crowd was quiet for a moment as Benny gave the downbeat, but it was soon cheering and screaming again as the band alternated hot numbers like "Bugle Call Rag" with ballads such as "Stardust"; midway through the performance, as the band roared through the loud, up-tempo "Riding High," hundreds of people surged out of their seats to crowd the stage and many others began jitterbugging in the aisles. The fervent dancing continued until the end of the show, and the noise didn't subside until the movie started again. Ross Firestone has written about this event:

> The Goodman Orchestra's brief forty-three-minute-sojourn on the Paramount stage was some kind of breakthrough that topped, and was different from, all its previous successors. What started out as just another stage show had turned into a kind of celebration of the spirit, a love feast of communal frenzy that was, as *Variety* observed, "tradition-shattering in its spontaneity, its unanimity, its sincerity, its volume, in the child-like violence of its manifestations."

The hysteria continued throughout 1937 as screaming and dancing in the aisles became a liberating ritual for middle-class kids wherever the band performed. This engendered a negative reaction from assorted clergymen, pundits, and other guardians of propriety. The director of the New York Schools of Music conducted experiments that, he claimed, showed that "when boys and girls were left alone, they conversed as usual if classical music was played, but started necking freely as soon as the music was changed to swing." Benny's associates were rattled by this sort of thing and sought a way to confer cultural and moral legitimacy upon his music. Then the publicist for his radio show came up with an excellent idea: present the band in concert at Carnegie Hall, a venue which—in the late

1930s, considerably more than now—was regarded as a bastion of musical propriety, a temple of art and culture.

The concert took place on January 16, 1938, and its results exceeded everyone's expectations. Tickets sold out quickly, and more than a hundred seats were placed on the stage to handle the overflow crowd. More important, it achieved for jazz a status equal to "higher" art forms such as opera and symphonic music. As critic James Lincoln Collier has written:

> The whole point was that it took place in Carnegie Hall. The publicity value was incalculable. So far as most people knew, this was the first concert of swing—the first jazz concert—and it was Benny Goodman who had put it on, thereby proving that jazz was art.

The music—which featured Lester Young, Count Basie, Basie's trumpet star Buck Clayton, and three Ellingtonians in guest cameos—reached a climax in a roaring twelve-minute version of the hypnotic "Sing, Sing, Sing." When it was over, the crowd cheered and applauded for five minutes, coaxing an encore—"Big John's Special," one of several Fletcher Henderson arrangements featured that night.

The concert was recorded, but the transcriptions languished in Benny's offices and homes until 1950, when his sister-in-law found them in a closet of an apartment she had taken over from him. He retrieved and listened to the recordings for the first time, found them to be exciting, and convinced his record company, Columbia, to issue them. The two-LP set became one of the most popular records in jazz history; over one million copies have been sold, and it is still in print today. Thus has the legacy of Fletcher Henderson been perpetuated.

Benny not only brought black music to white America but he brought black musicians to it as well. In early June 1935, soon after *Let's Dance* was canceled, Benny had jammed with black pianist Teddy Wilson at a party in Queens, New York, and felt a deep rapport with him. "Teddy and I began to play as though we were thinking with the same brain," he would say later, "It was a real kick." Before leaving on the Palomar tour a few weeks later, he brought Teddy into the studio with Gene Krupa and recorded four joyous, swinging sides. The Benny Goodman trio, which created some of the most enduring jazz of the thirties and forties, had been born.

On the trip back east from the Palomar, the band solidified its success with a triumphant six-month engagement at the Congress Hotel in Chicago, where it performed concerts in addition to its regular nightly dance gigs. The promoter urged Benny to bring Wilson from New York for a concert on April 12, 1936, and after an initial bout of indecision, Benny agreed.

It had been okay for whites to make music with blacks in the studio, where the audience couldn't see them; it was quite another thing to do it in public on a concert stage. Racial mixing had never been tried by a major band, and sentiment against it in 1936 was strong and visceral.

Benny's decision was an act of courage; he risked losing a large chunk of his audience just as he was tasting the fruits of success after years of struggle. His status as a pop icon carried the day, however, and the concert was a great success. Soon after, Wilson joined the band for good.

Goodman's interracial enterprise created tensions for the band in most cities that it visited, and care was always taken to avoid antagonizing bigots. Wilson and subsequent black band members like Lionel Hampton usually traveled separately from the white musicians and were often forced to stay at different hotels.

The road to bandstand equality remained a rough one well into the civil rights revolution of the 1960s. Billie Holiday quit the Artie Shaw band in 1938 after she was asked to take the freight elevator at the Hotel Edison in New York so that she would not offend the sensibilities of the white clientele, and trumpet star Roy Eldridge almost suffered a nervous breakdown from the daily humiliations he endured while playing with Gene Krupa in 1941. During a southern tour in 1950 Charlie Parker had to palm off trumpeter Red Rodney, the only white member of his group, as a black man. The very fair-skinned Rodney was billed as "Albino Red." As late as 1959, when one of Ella Fitzgerald's four accompanists was white, NBC Television and its sponsor, Bell Telephone, broadcast images of Ella with a black accompanist but refused to picture her with the white musician.

IN 1945 Benny was still preaching the gospel of Fletcher Henderson and black big band music, and Stan Getz felt very much at home with him. To Stan, Benny Goodman, the perfectionist and musical taskmaster, was the model of a big bandleader. As he told reporters in later years:

> I was in his band at eighteen, a fresh kid, and to watch him rehearse a band was something. His ears and musical knowledge, his taste at picking tempos, and choosing guys with good sounds for his bands. So wonderful. . . .

Great musician, Benny Goodman. His conception of sound
was very superior. There wasn't one horn player in all the fourteen
horns that had a bad sound. To get into his band you had to
have a good sound. And it was a joy to play in the saxophone
section that really clicked on all cylinders.

Another thing, he used to rehearse the band without the
rhythm section to see who really could swing. . . . And I thought
that was great.

And he admired Benny's commitment to musical excellence:

Benny was a great leader, a very centered man who didn't care
if we were on a radio broadcast, say the *Coca-Cola Spotlight
Broadcast*, where it's coast-to-coast. . . .

Well there's no such thing as dead air time; you do not have
dead air time. It's a no-no. Well he'd be thinking of the tempo
for the tune, and even though he knew he was supposed to go
into it, he would not beat it off until he had the right tempo,
which could be a minute or a minute and a half. He was a very
dedicated man to his music, Benny Goodman.

How do I rate a guy like that? Like I rate Jack Teagarden.
Benny and Tea were my first major influences.

The Goodman band came down from Canada to New York City in late
October 1945 for a two-month stay. It used New York as its base of operations as it traveled to a series of Army camps during most of November,
and on the twenty-eighth of that month, it began an engagement at the
Terrace Room in nearby Newark, New Jersey, where it played to capacity
crowds until December 23.

The two-month New York sojourn gave Stan an in-depth exposure to
bebop, the revolutionary form of jazz that soon dramatically changed the
way he played and the way he thought about his music. Although Joe
Albany had given Stan a taste of bebop with the Swing Club trio in 1944,
nothing had prepared him for the explosive power of the new music
as he listened to its acknowledged genius, alto saxophonist Charlie
"Bird" Parker, at the Spotlite Club on Fifty-second Street. Stan remembered:

Benny Goodman was doing only Army camps. We'd fly to them
in an Army plane. Three, four times a week. And the rest of the
time I'd be on 52nd Street to hear this amazing music. And I

was bowled over by it. . . . Once every 20, 30, maybe 50 years a guy will come along like Charlie Parker that's really avant-garde. When he played, people said, "That makes sense and it's new." And what he created opened up avenues still being explored. . . .

When I first heard Charlie Parker, I couldn't believe it. He was so ahead of his time. Also free. . . . He was just great.

Stan was fortunate to encounter bebop in its first great flowering. The revolution had started in 1940, and its innovations had blossomed during the next four years; the first important records were made in 1944, and then, in late 1945, all the essential pieces came together.

In fact, Stan might have heard Parker on the day that he created one of the shining masterpieces in jazz history. On November 26, 1945, Bird recorded six tracks for Savoy Records in New York. All of them were exceptional, but "Koko," an improvisation based on the song "Cherokee," was in a class by itself. The three-minute duration of the 78-rpm record put severe limits on the length of improvised solos. On "Koko," however, Parker had room to improvise two double-length choruses because Savoy's owner wished to avoid paying royalties to the composer of "Cherokee" and dispensed with the playing of the melody. Parker's virtuosity and inventiveness dazzle as he creates beautiful and varied melodies at a nearly impossible tempo exceeding three hundred beats per minute. Critic Gary Giddins assessed the impact of the recording:

"Koko" was the seminal point of departure for jazz in the postwar era. . . . Parker takes off for two choruses of overwhelming originality as though he were putting everything he knew into this one performance, imposing his will on the music and the musicians, setting forth new precepts with redoubtable nerve. Though improvised at tremendous velocity, his solo is colored with deft conceits. . . . And his sound!—so deeply, profoundly human; fat and sensuous, yet jagged and hard; inflamed with a gleeful audacity.

This incandescent music, which Stan was hearing at the Spotlite Club, had its origins in the dissatisfaction with the swing aesthetic that a small group of black musicians had begun to feel five years before.

ALTHOUGH MANY contributed, the bebop revolution had five principal leaders. One of them, Benny Goodman's guitarist Charlie Christian, died

of tuberculosis in 1942. The other four were Parker, trumpeter Dizzy
Gillespie, pianist Thelonious Monk, and drummer Kenny Clarke. The
revolution was rooted in the frustration these men felt when they could
not express their emotions with the rhythmic and harmonic materials at
hand in the early 1940s. So they radically transformed these materials.

The most fundamental changes were rhythmic. The beboppers had all
listened to Lester Young and, following his lead, they made rhythmic
displacement an integral part of their music. And they changed the fundamental role of the drummer from a timekeeper to a voice in the ensemble
equal to that of the horn players. They replaced the insistent timekeeping
beat of the bass drum with a shimmering, fluid pulse, played by the
drummer on a cymbal. Over this light pulse, the improvisers indulged in
the utmost rhythmic freedom. They created angular, asymmetrical phrases
of varying length, placing their accents wherever they would delight or
surprise. And the drummer, with his free hand and his feet, created poly-
rhythmic effects to blend with the lines that the soloists were playing.

Before bebop, jazz harmony (with notable exceptions such as Duke
Ellington and Art Tatum) was at about the level of mid-nineteenth-century
classical music. This frustrated the beboppers; they were determined to
use any and all combinations of notes available in Western music, and
they opened harmonic floodgates. Though they did not model themselves
on the classical composers, their music encompassed the dissonances of
Stravinsky, the brooding chords of Debussy, and everything in between.
During four years of experimentation, they moved jazz harmony from
Brahms to Bartók.

In order to expand their harmonic resources, they were forced to place
great emphasis on chordal structure; they achieved many of their effects
by augmenting chords with dissonant notes, substituting new, more complex chords for written ones, and changing chords more frequently to
speed up the harmonic pace of a tune. While they became deeply involved with chords, they did not forget the lessons of Lester Young; they
remained open to his rhythmic concepts and his practice of playing free
melodies across the harmony.

The main accomplishment of the beboppers was to expand radically
the resources available to the jazz improviser, and young musicians such
as Stan were prime beneficiaries. Instead of the purely primary colors of
the swing palette, they were now able to choose from an entire rainbow
of musical hues.

The revolution was hatched in several places, but its main venue was
a Harlem nightclub called Minton's. Henry Minton, the proprietor, was

a sax player and an official of the musicians union, and he made his place a musicians' hangout. He employed former bandleader Teddy Hill as musical director, and Hill in turn hired Clarke and Monk as the nucleus of the club's band. Gillespie was usually on the road with Cab Calloway and other big bands, but when he came to New York, he hooked up immediately with his fellow rebels. Parker, who was freelancing all over New York, sat in regularly.

Hill gave his musicians the freedom to play anything they wanted. He thought it would be good for business, and he turned out to be correct, as customers—including Benny Goodman—flocked to Minton's to hear the new sounds.

Bebop burst out of Harlem in 1944 and found a new home midst the teeming club scene on Swing Street, Fifty-second between Fifth and Seventh avenues in midtown Manhattan.

With the exception of the very large Hickory House, the now legendary clubs—the Onyx, the Three Deuces, Jimmy Ryan's, the Famous Door, Kelly's Stables, the Downbeat, the Spotlite—were not designed for the claustrophobic. They were low-ceilinged, windowless saloons squeezed into the twenty-foot-wide ground floors of what had been brownstone residences. The bar inevitably ran half the length of a sidewall, and the bandstand shared the rear wall with the entrance to the restrooms. The bandstand could comfortably accommodate five or six musicians but was frequently required to do service for more; when the fourteen-piece Basie aggregation played the Famous Door, the men were squeezed together like rush-hour subway passengers, and the music blasted the audience with gale force.

The Swing Street jazz fans squinted at the bandstand through a haze of cigarette smoke as they sat at tables the size of large soup plates and rubbed shoulders with drug dealers, hipsters, hustlers, and pimps (customers were often serviced by prostitutes in the men's rooms). Cocktails were seventy-five cents, a beer cost thirty-five cents, and the bar patrons had to hold their glasses tightly because the bartenders loved to run up their tabs by replacing half-finished drinks with fresh ones. The musicians usually drank between sets at the White Rose Tavern, around the corner on Sixth Avenue; the drinks were cheaper there.

If you were a fan, you endured all the aggravation because the music was so good, and you never planned to hit just one club since every joint featured a star or two. On November 1, 1945, for example, Charlie Parker was at the Spotlite with a sextet featuring Miles Davis and Dexter Gordon, Billie Holiday had just replaced Art Tatum at the Downbeat, and Ben Webster and

Sarah Vaughan shared the billing at the Onyx. Pianist Erroll Garner held forth at the Three Deuces, and the Fletcher Henderson trumpeter Henry "Red" Allen was the headliner at Jimmy Ryan's.

With all this talent packed into two blocks, the musicians couldn't resist locking horns with their peers, and they constantly crisscrossed Fifty-second Street to sit in with each other. Shorty Rogers remembered Dizzy Gillespie:

> He was playing with Benny Carter, he was a sideman in the band, and he was so obsessed, thinking, "I want to play, I want to play." He'd get this hour intermission and he couldn't stand it. And I actually would see him walking down the street in the middle of the road dodging cars, with his horn, and he'd look in each club, like, "I can go in this one and sit in." And he would find a place and jam.

And drummer Shelly Manne recalled expanding his musical horizons on Swing Street:

> It was beautiful because you'd play all kinds of music. I remember one night playing with Diz at the Onyx, going across the street playing with Trummy Young at the Deuces, and then sitting in with Billie Holiday at the Downbeat. And then you could go into Jimmy Ryan's if you wanted to play. It was like a history of jazz on one street, for that time.
>
> It was really healthy for musicians.... Possibly, even thinking about all the music that's happened since, I think that was ... one of the most creative times in jazz.

STAN, a new kid on the block, had problems being accepted by the veterans, but he did make it with Ben Webster, and he met Lester Young in the bargain:

> In the old days on 52nd Street, I used to listen to the great musicians there: Ben Webster's quartet in one place, Erroll Garner in another, Parker in this club, and Billie Holiday in that.
>
> I was with Benny Goodman's band at that time, and I wanted to get in with this exciting music on 52nd Street. But no one would let me sit in. No one except Ben that is, a beautiful guy.

He knew I was keen and some nights he'd say: "All right, kid, get your horn." And I would blow with the quartet and enjoy that.

And then one night, after I'd played with Ben, there was Lester Young backstage. Pres, you know, had heard me and you can guess how I felt; I was eighteen years old at that time.

We met for the first time and I mumbled about what a great pleasure it was. You know Lester spoke in a language all his own. Well, he said to me: "Nice eyes, Pres. Carry on." He called me Pres; I'll never forget that.

After his initial encounter with bebop, Stan began to study the music of Parker, Gillespie, et al., but he continued to sound like Pres. The Goodman band cut three studio tracks on November 20, 1945; Stan has an eight-bar solo on one of them, "Give Me the Simple Life," and it is very much in Young's mode.

Young's influence is even more strongly felt on the first four tracks Stan ever made with a small group. The session took place on December 14, 1945, for Savoy, which had recorded Parker's "Koko" less than three weeks before and which was one of several shoestring independent labels born in the wake of the 1942–44 recording strike. The group, a sextet named "Kai's Krazy Cats," was led by trombonist Kai Winding, who was also in Goodman's band and had performed with Stan in the New York All-City High School Orchestra in 1941. The Krazy Cats included another friend from Stan's high school days, Shorty Rogers, and its drummer was Shelly Manne.

Stan is featured on the Irving Berlin tune "Always," and fashions a mature, beautifully sculpted solo. It is almost a universe away from his tentative efforts with Kenton less than two years before, and it shows that at age eighteen Stan could hold his own with any improviser in the big band world.

Stan is heard on a series of air checks and two studio sessions with Goodman in December 1945 and January and February 1946. He has solos on the tunes "Swing Street," "Rattle and Roll," and "Swing Angel," and he is still in the thrall of Lester Young.

Bebop music rubbed Benny Goodman the wrong way. He could never get comfortable with its jagged rhythmic changes, thick harmonies, and advanced dissonant chords. As Marian McPartland, one of Benny's longtime collaborators, has said:

As marvelous as Benny is, I did notice, however, his seeming lack of interest in rich harmonies. His music reflects this; he always has concentrated on the beat, rhythmic excitement, the melodic line. Lush voicings and chord changes evidently leave him cold. He seems to want the blandest possible changes behind him, and his improvisations are carried out strictly within this framework. It bothers him to hear an unfamiliar voicing.

Benny flirted with the new music throughout 1946 and 1947, and in 1948 fielded a hybrid bebop-swing band which featured sax player Wardell Gray and clarinetist Ake "Stan" Hasselgard. But his heart wasn't in it, and he ended his uneasy relationship with bebop when he closed that band down in December 1949.

Stan and Winding felt compelled to explore the new music, and because of Benny's attitude, they were forced to form a closeted bebop cell group within the band. Danny Bank remembered:

> The band had a number of youngsters like Kai Winding and Stan Getz who carried Charlie Parker records with them on the road and practiced playing bebop together in the closet very secretly. They were like a closed society.
>
> It was a great honor to be working for Benny Goodman, and I'm sure they played his music as best they could, but they were growing in another direction. Stan Getz was growing constantly. He was only about seventeen years old and already had a terrific talent.
>
> Sometimes Benny would poke his nose in the dressing room and listen to what they were doing; then he'd go, "Tsk, tsk, tsk" and walk away. He probably went out and bought some records, but it wasn't his metier at all. It's not easy to find a language on the clarinet, and it's very difficult to change your language in the middle of your life.

While Stan and Kai were practicing their bebop licks in private, the Goodman band was packing in the fans with the tried-and-true swing formulas. Although Benny and the jazz critics agreed that this band was never as good musically as the 1934–1944 aggregation, the fans didn't seem to mind. They filled the Terrace Room in Newark to overflowing in December of 1945 despite awful weather, and starting January 3, they broke all attendance records at the Meadowbrook Gardens in Culver City, California, causing the engagement to be extended a full week to February 3.

The band wasn't winning critical accolades, but Benny was. In January

Down Beat selected him as its favorite soloist and best bandleader, and *Metronome* named him clarinetist of the year. Both magazines placed the Woody Herman band in first place, with the Goodman contingent finishing well back in the running.

The band continued to do excellent business in February, playing to full houses at the Mission Beach Ballroom in San Diego. While there, Stan became obstreperous again and was almost fired, but Goldie helped him keep his job. Popsie Randolph, Goodman's road manager, remembered:

> I thought Stan was keen then, but he was a cocky kid, just a cocky little boy. A wise guy. . . . I don't know what it was all about, but Stan's mother and father were visiting him, and when Benny was ready to fire him, Stan cried and his mother cried and so Benny gave him another chance.

Back on Fifty-second Street, a couple of months before, Stan had met a kindred spirit in trumpeter Red Rodney, another eighteen-year-old Jewish Philadelphia native who was an incipient bebopper. Rodney had been playing with the Elliot Lawrence band and in New York had drawn the attention of Gene Krupa, who was finishing a run there at the Capitol Theater. Krupa began a two-month engagement at the Palladium in Hollywood on Christmas Day 1945 and on January 10 hired Rodney. A *Metronome* review of a February 11 broadcast took note of the trumpeter's talent:

> Most obvious change is the addition of that little dynamo, Red Rodney, who came in on trumpet from that Philly Elliot Lawrence band. Though uncredited on the air, his Dizzy work stood out in every number in which he soloed. He clearly will spark the band to even better things.

Stan and Red started hanging out together around Los Angeles, spending several exciting nights at a place called Billy Berg's, where a quintet led by Parker and Gillespie was introducing bebop to the West Coast. The two Philadelphians were soon given an opportunity to perform together. A promoter, capitalizing on the proximity of Goodman and Krupa in Southern California and their long and well-publicized relationship—first as collaborators and now as rivals—booked their orchestras into a "battle of the bands" concert at a ballroom in Laguna Beach, roughly fifty miles south of Los Angeles. The "battle of the bands" format was a common one during the swing era; it usually produced exciting music as the bands matched fiery soloists and high octane arrangements in competitive face-offs for audience approval.

Beverly Byrne, Krupa's eighteen-year-old female vocalist, noticed Rodney chatting with Goodman's handsome young tenor soloist as the bands were setting up, and after she heard Stan play a couple of beautiful choruses, she knew she had to meet him. She pestered Rodney at intermission, and he introduced them when the concert was over.

Beverly had been brought into the band by her brother, Buddy Stewart, who was Krupa's male singer. She had replaced Anita O'Day when Anita had abruptly ended her second stint with Krupa just weeks before. Anita left in the middle of a performance at the Palladium, suffering from physical and emotional exhaustion; two consecutive years on the road had burned her out.

Buddy Stewart, who was five years older than his sister, was an outstanding singer whom some mid-1940s critics considered on a par with Frank Sinatra. Buddy had started performing at age eight with his parents, Al and Mamie Byrne, a vaudeville song and dance team, and he had adopted Stewart as a stage name early in his career. He had worked his way through the bands of Glenn Miller and Claude Thornhill before finding wide recognition with Krupa. His rich, flexible baritone could handle romantic ballads and bebop scatting with equal aplomb; in fact, he and Dave Lambert recorded the first ever bebop vocal, "What's This," with Krupa in 1945.

Beverly, who also had genuine vocal talent, had come to visit Buddy in California following her graduation from a convent high school in Massachusetts. She was looked after back east by an aunt and uncle; her ties to her parents, who were continually on the road, were not close.

Beverly's strong, husky voice constantly surprised people, because she was barely five feet tall and weighed less than a hundred pounds. She was always singing and seemed to know every tune ever written, so Buddy had little trouble selling her to Krupa as a fill-in during the minicrisis following Anita O'Day's sudden departure.

Stan and Beverly stopped for drinks after the Goodman-Krupa concert, and their teenage infatuation was instant and total. She was pretty, perky, full of song, in awe of his talent, and adoring; he was smitten for the first time in his life.

Beverly was naive and easily led. She worshiped her brother Buddy and had blind faith in his judgment. Since he and his wife and both of Beverly's parents were alcoholics, she had little difficulty in accepting Stan's addiction.

Shortly after meeting Stan, she left Krupa as he found a permanent replacement for O'Day in Carolyn Grey, who had sung with Woody Herman and had placed third in the 1944 *Down Beat* poll. Beverly then became a fixture backstage at the Goodman performances, and after they were over, she and Stan would jam together at after-hours places all over Los Angeles.

When the Goodman band traveled to New York to start a seven-week run at the Paramount Theater on February 27, she followed. She didn't see too much of Stan because the band was logging in eighteen-hour days while doing an unprecedented forty-three shows per week; with its co-attraction, the Bob Hope–Bing Crosby movie *Road to Utopia*, the band easily broke the all-time record for the Paramount by grossing $135,000 during its first week.

Beverly busied herself looking for work and quickly found a job. Her friend Millie Cohen (who was performing under the name of Pat Cameron) was singing with the Randy Brooks band but wanted to quit because she wished to spend more time with her infant son. Brooks was at one of New York's top night spots, the Cafe Rouge of the Hotel Pennsylvania, and Millie arranged for Beverly to audition for him. He hired her on the spot.

Brooks was a powerful trumpet player who played expressively on both slow, romantic tunes and up-tempo flag-wavers. He had made his reputation as a leading soloist with the popular Les Brown band, and in his first year as a leader in 1945 broke the record at Roseland by staying for twenty-two consecutive weeks. His group featured bebop touches on its fast numbers and smooth, creamy arrangements on ballads. Brooks's career was cut short when he suffered a stroke at age thirty-three in 1950, and he died tragically in a fire in 1967.

For the first time since he had become addicted a year and a half before, Stan's heroin supply became erratic in late March. Since an addict's first priority is to secure his dope, he missed four performances while frantically rushing around New York trying to score. This was too much for Benny, and he summarily fired Stan.

He started scuffling and got himself a one-week gig with the Buddy Morrow band at Roseland; then Beverly talked Brooks into hiring him. Unfortunately, no recordings of Beverly exist with this band, but Stan is heard soloing on one April 12, 1946, track: "A Night at the Deuces," an up-tempo Brooks band original intended to transport the listener to the Three Deuces on Fifty-second Street. For the first time on record, Stan is boppish; there are traces of Pres, but the Parker influence predominates, and one can also hear touches of the hard-edged bebop sound of Dexter Gordon, whom Stan heard with Parker at the Spotlite.

Stan soon found himself working for the same record company as Dexter. Savoy went on a talent spree in May and signed up, for very little money, a raft of promising unknowns; they included a Yiddish singer, a Texas cowboy band, and Stan, Dexter, and Shorty Rogers from the world of jazz.

Excellent notices in the May issue of *Metronome* ("There's so much that's really great in the band. Randy's lead horn. Stanley Getz's big-bodied kicking tenor. . . . The beat in little Beverly Byrne's voice.") indicated that Beverly and Stan were heating up commercially, and in July they left Brooks for more prominent bands. She joined Claude Thornhill in New York as a summer replacement, and he signed up with Herbie Fields, who was in the middle of a four-month engagement just across the Hudson at the Rustic Cabin in Englewood, New Jersey.

Fields's group was a hard-driving swing band with no bebop flourishes, and Stan had no difficulty reverting to his earlier style. He impressed everyone the first day when he memorized the intricate sax part of a duet with the pianist and played it flawlessly. His predecessor, Herb Steward, was an excellent musician, but he had to rely on sheet music every time he undertook the piece. Stan's roommate in New Jersey succeeded in having himself assigned to another room when he protested that Stan was leaving packets of heroin lying about and was shooting up four times a day.

Savoy wanted Stan to cut a bebop quartet date for his first gig as a leader, and they recruited as his rhythm section the crème de la crème of the bebop movement: Hank Jones on piano, Curly Russell on bass, and Max Roach, who would go on to become the greatest percussionist in jazz history, on drums. Four tunes were recorded at the session, which took place on July 31: two up-tempo burners, "Opus de Bop" and "Running Water," a relaxed ballad, "Don't Worry 'Bout Me," and a minor-key tune taken at a medium tempo, "And the Angels Swing."

The rhythm section cooks; Roach energetically drives the whole session along, Jones is an example of bebop correctness, and Russell is resolute in laying down a solid foundation. Stan is not inhibited by his illustrious company. He more than holds his own, showing a mastery of the bebop idiom. In little more than six months, he had learned one of the most difficult grammars in all of music; each of his solos is good, but on "Opus de Bop" and "And the Angels Swing" he creates, with fluency and ease, improvisations of particular rhythmic and harmonic complexity.

As autumn arrived, Stan became homesick for sunny Los Angeles and his family. Beverly's employment with Claude Thornhill had ended, and he had become bored with the Herbie Fields arrangements. They both felt sure that they could make a decent living in southern California, and they pulled up stakes in New York and headed west.

They were still very much in love, and they were married in Los Angeles on November 7, 1946, a few weeks after they had arrived there; both were nineteen. The ceremony was performed by a magistrate with Goldie and Al in attendance. Bob Getz didn't make it because he was playing in a championship junior high football game; Buddy Stewart was back in New York with his wife and a newborn baby, and Beverly's parents were on tour somewhere.

WOODY'N YOU

STAN WAS TIRED of the road, and he wanted to stay put for a while with his bride. His drug habit was expensive, and steady jobs were hard to come by, so he and Beverly freelanced all over southern California to make ends meet. At first they could not afford a car, and they moved frequently to live near their gigs. For several weeks they stayed in a motel because it was within walking distance of the club where Stan was playing. And as trumpeter Shorty Rogers remembers, when they did find a legitimate home, it could be pretty bizarre:

> That period when he lived in L.A., I think he didn't have a car, and one place they lived I'd go by and hang out with them. It was a little apartment, but it was adjoining a motorcycle repair

shop, so you could imagine. . . . like the guys were fixing motorcy-
cles and gunning the engines, it was like living inside the engine
of an airplane or something. . . . But in the middle of the motorcy-
cles, Stan was practicing, sounding beautiful.

Recording dates were plentiful by early 1947, and Stan became part of a
group of talented young musicians who were much in demand in the
studios. Several of them would become his close associates during the
years ahead: writer-pianist Ralph Burns; pianist Jimmy Rowles; saxophone
players Zoot Sims and Herbie Steward; drummer Don Lamond; Stan's
old pal from the Bronx, Shorty; and his associate from the Kenton band,
arranger-trumpeter-trombonist Gene Roland.

In May and June Stan did seven broadcasts and a record session with
a Benny Goodman band, which only came together to work in the studios.
Benny was still entranced with Stan's talent, and he rehired him when
Stan promised to show up on time, ready to play. Sims, Rowles, and
Lamond also performed on these eight Goodman dates.

Stan and Rowles played in early May with an orchestra that was pulled
together for a single recording session featuring Woody Herman's vocals;
it was fronted by Herman's key writer, Ralph Burns. In July the two
musicians recorded with the orchestra of another of Woody's writers,
Neal Hefti.

Lamond was on the latter date, and he also joined Stan and Rowles for
a recording with a group called The Blue Rhythm Band. This contingent
contained several outstanding players, such as trumpeter Charlie Shavers
and saxophonists Lucky Thompson and Butch Stone, and their cut of
"Blue Rhythm Blues" features Stan's only recorded alto saxophone solo.
He later told a reporter, "I played alto because they needed an alto player
and I needed the money—it was that simple. I borrowed Herbie Steward's
horn." The listener wishes that Stan had picked up the alto more often,
because he played with absolute ease, creating highly original lines burnished by a gorgeous tone.

Stan was also recorded at a June concert in the "Just Jazz" series promoted by Los Angeles disc jockey Gene Norman. This featured a stellar
group that boasted Nat King Cole, the former Goodman and Herman
vibraphone star Red Norvo (Shorty Rogers's brother-in-law), drummer Louis
Bellson, and Charlie Shavers. On "Body and Soul," Stan is heard in a
beautifully structured, lyrical solo that shows great maturity and poise.

Recording work was plentiful, but performance gigs were hard to come
by. Stan played briefly during February at the Meadowbrook Gardens in
Culver City with the big band of Vido Musso, a sax veteran of both

Kenton and Goodman. On a live recording of a boppish Gene Roland arrangement of a tune called "Cozy Blues," we hear solos from Roland on valve trombone and from Musso and Stan. Stan's Pres-inflected bop lines contrast clearly with Musso's heavy, Hawkins-style sound.

The Getzes' ability to obtain gigs improved in the spring of 1947, when they bought a Model A Ford. The Model A, which had been discontinued back in 1932, was the most dangerous American car ever built because the gas tank sat between the engine and the driver; but that didn't daunt Stan and Beverly because they bought it so cheaply and it used very little gas. Stan remembered:

> We had a Model A club. We all had Model A Fords. I bought mine for $68.00. It was a four-door sedan, and it had wings on the hood. Don Lamond had one. Herbie Steward had one. . . . And we'd find places to play that weren't about work, they were just jam sessions. We played jazz although there weren't any jazz jobs. We supported our families by working some dumb jobs. . . . We didn't get work playing jazz music. We got work playing rhumba bands, Mickey Mouse bands, dixieland bands . . . then after work we'd get together for jam sessions.

The Getzes also used the Model A to indulge Stan's great passion, swimming. Most afternoons they were at the beach at Santa Monica playing in the surf and soaking up the sun. The Lamonds were frequent companions, and Don remembers a traumatic event:

> Yeah, Stan loved to swim. He saved my kid's life one time. My boy was two years old, and we were just sitting there talking . . . and we looked up and my kid was headed into the biggest wave you ever saw. And Stan jumped up and ran and he grabbed him before my wife could even get to him.

Stan and Beverly often drove to Shorty Rogers's house in Burbank because Shorty had organized a "rehearsal" band there. Rehearsal bands, which have a long history in jazz, are nonpaying groups created by their leaders to work through new concepts and arrangements. Sometimes they make it to commercial engagements; most of the time they do not. Shorty remembered:

> I started to write some charts. It was a chance for me to try some things in the very formative stages of my writing. So it was a good

thing for me. Herbie Steward and Stan and I and Arnold Fishkin, the bass player, set it up. And Don Lamond played drums.

In July the entire rehearsal group, less Lamond, became the majority of Butch Stone's Septet at a place called the Red Feather in Inglewood. Stone had left Les Brown's big band, where he had been a popular singer and a baritone sax player, to front a group for the first time in his life. He featured Shorty's arrangements and won a rave review in *Down Beat*; it said in part:

> Stone is living up to or surpassing the expectations of even the most enthusiastic of his well-wishers. Butch has the best new small band in this territory. It's a bop outfit that swings every tune with dynamic control and commercial softness that pleases those who come to dance without offending the true jazz listeners. . . . Butch has surrounded himself with a gang of young musicians who fit excellently. . . . They, especially trumpeter Shorty Rogers who arranges most of the material, excite on their solos with sufficient technique and ideas. . . . If MCA can't and don't do big things with this musically and commercially great unit, it should go back to the trained seal acts.

In spite of the critical acclaim, the Stone gig did not cover the rent, and Stan and Herb Steward took a second job with an unusual unit that played at a place called Pete Pontrelli's Spanish Ballroom in East Los Angeles.

Its leader, trumpeter Tommy De Carlo, had a contract with Pontrelli but no arrangements and no band, and he turned to his friend Gene Roland to fill the gaps. Roland had an extensive library of arrangements and a group of seasoned musicians because he had been working with rehearsal bands on a fresh concept for a couple of years.

Roland had been fascinated with the sound of four tenor saxophones playing in close harmony, and he had first organized a rehearsal band to develop this idea back at the Nola Studios in New York in early 1946. The saxes were Lester Young disciples—Stan, Al Cohn, Joe Magro, and Louis Ott—and they were joined by a rhythm section and by Roland on valve trombone. The group never made it commercially, but they created a unique, light sound played mostly in the higher part of the tenor's range. The lower notes of the alto and the higher notes of the tenor overlap, and in many of the arrangements, Stan played tenor parts that were entirely in the alto's range.

Roland created a new rehearsal band in 1947 in Los Angeles using

Stan, Steward, Zoot Sims, and Jimmy Giuffre as the sax section. He knew Stan from New York, and Stan brought Steward and Sims into the group. And Roland and Giuffre went back a long way; they had been roommates at North Texas State College, had played together in an Air Force band during World War II, and had reconnected in Los Angeles in 1947. Giuffre remembered:

> Gene wrote and contacted me and he came out to Los Angeles. He told me he had this sound. So, we got that group together, and we played a few gigs, and rehearsed with a wire recorder. . . . Having four tenors blending with each other, they were just like syrup.

The four tenors shared an aesthetic bond because each was a disciple of Lester Young. Zoot Sims has talked about Young's inspiration:

> We were all influenced by Lester. Listen to the records that he made with Basie. Nobody's got what he's got. He's still the daddy.

Steward's style was even closer to Young's than Sims's, and Stan adored Herb's playing. Don Lamond remembers:

> I went over to the Red Feather one night to hear the Stone group, and Stan looked up at Herbie like he was Jesus Christ. He said, "I wish I could play like that. Each note he plays is a jewel."

The four saxes went into Pontrelli's with De Carlo leading and playing trumpet, Roland playing piano and anchoring the rhythm section, and Beverly Getz singing.

The saxes sounded almost as one as they played the long, flowing lines of Roland's arrangements; they were a true ensemble. And for jazz listeners, there was a wonderful extra dividend: Each was a consummate improviser. The customers at Pontrelli's didn't hear very much of the group's exciting jazz, however, because most of the time the band played mariachi tunes. The ballroom was in the heart of a Mexican neighborhood, and the great majority of its patrons came to hear their native music. Zoot Sims remembered:

> That was a funny gig. It was a Mexican ballroom. East Side L.A. It was Mexicans, and we played Mexican stocks. We'd play their music, which we didn't mind doing. I didn't mind it, but then

we'd slip in our own music, and they didn't mind it, so it worked out fine. And I used to take two street cars to get there. One street car and then a transfer.

Ralph Burns came down to check out his friends in the group one night in late July, and their jazz numbers blew him away. He couldn't wait to tell his boss, Woody Herman, who was organizing a new band. Woody dropped by a few days later and was so impressed that he decided to hire all four sax players—Giuffre as a writer and the other three as musicians.

WOODY HERMAN always had music in his life. As he told his biographer, Stuart Troup:

> I was listening to some kind of music constantly, from the beginning. My father, Otto, was a terrible ham. He saw in me the possible fulfillment of his love for show business, and he worked with me, teaching me songs, from the time I first remember seeing him. It wasn't long after I learned to walk that he was also coaching me to dance. He would have loved working on the stage, instead of as a shoemaker at the Nunn-Bush factory in Milwaukee.

Woody was born on May 13, 1913, in Milwaukee, the only child of adoring parents—Otto, a third generation German American, and Martha, a Polish immigrant who also, when times were tough, worked in the Nunn-Bush factory. Woody was fastidious about his clothes, and Otto always made certain that his son wore handmade footwear fashioned by the best craftsmen at Nunn-Bush; sometimes Otto made them himself. The family was Catholic, and Woody was an active communicant all his life.

Otto found singing and dancing engagements at Milwaukee theaters for Woody when he was six, and soon after Woody's eighth birthday, he enlisted him in a kiddie vaudeville act that toured the upper Midwest. The next year he started Woody studying the clarinet and the saxophone, and pretty soon his son was playing Chicago vaudeville houses billed as "The Boy Wonder of the Clarinet."

The music of Duke Ellington and, to a lesser extent, Coleman Hawkins and Jack Teagarden captivated Woody and convinced him at age fourteen that hot jazz—not vaudeville—was his calling. His parents were chagrined at first because they believed that jazz was an economic dead end, but they acquiesced when they understood their son's total dedication to the music.

After a four-year apprenticeship, mostly with the Tom Gerun Band on the West Coast, Woody in 1934 joined a big-league aggregation, the Isham Jones Band, at the princely salary of $125 per week; he was twenty-one, and was called upon to sing as well as play clarinet and saxophone. Jones, who played both piano and saxophone, was a major success as a band-leader and a songwriter. His record of "Wabash Blues" sold two million copies, and he had grown rich from the royalties on such songs as "It Had to Be You," "I'll See You in My Dreams," "On the Alamo," "The One I Love Belongs to Somebody Else," "You've Got Me Crying Again," and "There Is No Greater Love."

When prosperity dictated to Jones that he retire during the summer of 1936 at the age of forty-two, Woody and five other band members took over the organization as a cooperative enterprise. The group chose Woody, with his vocal skills and show business expertise, as their leader. While the cooperative was being organized, Woody was married on September 27, 1936, to Charlotte Neste, a showgirl he had met in San Francisco six years before when they were both seventeen. Their marriage flourished until Charlotte's death in 1982.

The reconstituted band opened on November 6, 1936, at the Roseland Ballroom in Brooklyn and had moderate success for the next two years as it tried to forge an identity independent of Isham Jones's. Toward the end of 1938, the cooperative decided that the blues was its forte, and henceforth the organization was known as "The Band That Plays the Blues."

The band made good on its name as it recorded the following blues between 1939 and 1941: "Woodchopper's Ball," "Dallas Blues," "Dippermouth Blues," "Bessie's Blues," "Chips' Blues," "Chips' Boogie Woogie," "Jumpin' Blues" "Blues Upstairs," "Blues Downstairs," "Casbah Blues," "Bishop's Blues," and its theme song, "Blue Flame."

The blues is a twelve-bar form made up of three distinct four-bar sections—A, B, C. The thirty-two-bar popular song is made up of four eight-bar sections in the following sequence—A, A, B, A. In addition to its true blues numbers, the band waxed such thirty-two-bar popular songs masquerading as blues as "Blue Dawn," "Blues on Parade," "Blue Prelude," "Farewell Blues," and "Blues in the Night."

The blues policy proved commercially successful as "Blues in the Night" and "Blue Flame" attained hit status, and "Woodchopper's Ball" became a megahit, a million-seller. Woody subsequently recorded "Wood-chopper's Ball" six more times, and altogether the tune sold five million records for him.

Woody reinvested his gains from the band's success and steadily bought shares from his co-op partners; by 1942 he owned 100 percent of the organization. By this time he and Charlotte were the parents of Ingrid, who was born on September 3, 1941.

Woody's greatest quality was his willingness to take chances aestheti-cally, to grant a large degree of artistic freedom to the people working for him. As he told an interviewer late in his life, "There will always be exciting times for anyone who's in a position to be experimenting and doing new things, new music and so on. That's the lifeblood of the whole thing."

Once he had attained both financial success and total control of his band, he felt free to deviate from the blues format. "With the personnel changes caused by the draft," he remembered, "we began to play differ-ently, and I was looking for different kinds of arrangements. . . . I felt that we were in a rut. We weren't progressing. Among those I turned to were Dave Matthews . . . and Dizzy Gillespie, who wrote three or four pieces for us."

Thus, in 1942 Woody became the first big bandleader to show an inter-est in the nascent bebop movement. In 1944 Dizzy named one of his most famous compositions, "Woody'n You," for Herman because, as Dizzy explained, "he liked my writing so much." The tune was very popular among beboppers, and Woody's groups performed it for many years but never recorded it.

In late 1943 Woody's band received a crucial infusion of fresh talent when Ralph Burns, bassist Chubby Jackson, and singer Frances Wayne jumped from the Charlie Barnet orchestra, because they believed they would find more artistic freedom with Woody. Of the hundreds of men and women who worked for Herman during his fifty-one years as a band-leader, he put Burns at the top:

> His arranging ability is beyond anyone's concept as far as I'm
> concerned. There's no one that ever really touched him. I think
> he's my biggest success . . . Of all the people that I've known
> through my bands, he has gone the farthest.

A flood of new talent followed Burns, Jackson, and Wayne during 1944 and transformed The Band That Plays the Blues into something entirely different. It started when trumpeter/arranger Neal Hefti defected from

Barnet in January; he was followed during the next six months by guitarist Billy Bauer, drummer Dave Tough, tenor player Flip Phillips, trumpeter Pete Candoli, and trombonist Bill Harris. Candoli was another Barnet defector, but the rest came from other bands.

Jackson, Tough, Bauer, and Burns provided an unshakable underpinning from the rhythm section, and Burns was an excellent soloist. Phillips, Candoli, and Harris were powerful improvisers who wished to take chances with the new musical ideas swirling around the jazz world in 1944, and Burns and Hefti fueled their desires with innovative writing. Chubby Jackson recalled:

> Ralph Burns was a genius of an arranger and a composer, very deep. Neal Hefti had a lighter flavor, but he could bounce your nose off. So we had the thrill of a very heavy symphonic, classical guy who would write gorgeous things, and another who would bounce you into the next state.

George Simon gave the band a new name when he concluded an ecstatic September 1944 review in *Metronome* with the following sentence: "Yes, this is a truly great all-around band, this Woody Herman Herd." As he later explained, "I called it the Herd because I was a frustrated sports writer and I used to do alliterations: the Herman Herd, the Goodman Gang, the Dorsey Dervishes. . . . The Herd was the only thing that really stuck."

Woody had an infectious, rough-hewn singing style and handled romantic ballads and raucous, rolling blues numbers with equal skill. A middling improviser on clarinet and alto sax, he realized his limitations and never got in the way of his brilliant young charges. Whereas almost every Goodman arrangement featured Benny, Woody was content to slot a chorus or a half-chorus into the mix with his other soloists.

Phillips was a versatile player. He would be lush and seductive on a ballad and then work an audience to a frenzy with his aggressive shouting on a hard, swinging number. Harris was one of the most exciting jazz trombonists ever. He played with great power, prompting a colleague to say that "he could blow metal fatigue into the horn," and he consistently created original and unpredictable melodies. Candoli had great range on the trumpet and delighted in playing high-note fanfares on the rousing, up-tempo tunes.

The outstanding characteristic of the Herd was a happy, muscular exuberance. As one critic put it, the band was "wild and yet disciplined, loud, completely musical, irreverent, and very funny to hear and to see."

You could never take the vaudevillian out of Woody, and he encouraged Candoli to leap on stage in a Superman costume to play his high-note barrages, Jackson to dance—wearing ballet slippers—with his bass and to shout rowdy encouragement to the soloists, and the entire trumpet section to dance mini-Rockette routines.

The public responded enthusiastically, and the band was rushed into a weekly CBS radio show for Old Gold cigarettes; it ran from July 26 to October 4, 1944. The speed with which the show was put together resulted in the Herd being paired incongruously with Allan Jones, a movie baritone whose singing style came out of light opera rather than jazz. In spite of this anomaly, the show was a success and the band reached a broad new audience.

It made its first truly Herd-like recordings in August and September, waxing tunes like "It Must Be Jelly, 'Cause Jam Don't Shake Like That," "Red Top," "Four or Five Times," "Sweet Lorraine," and "Is You Is or Is You Ain't My Baby?" The last tune gave listeners a true idea of what the Herd was about as Phillips, Candoli, Harris, and Herman produced powerhouse solos in an exciting setting provided by Burns.

Another important soloist, bebop trumpeter Sonny Berman, joined the band in February 1945, just in time to participate in one of the Herd's most celebrated recording sessions. The tracks of "Apple Honey," "Goosie Gander," "Northwest Passage," and "Caldonia" captured the Herd in full flight with soaring improvisations by each of the leading soloists. The exciting trumpet-section passage on "Caldonia" is actually a transcribed Dizzy Gillespie solo. For a change of pace, the band waxed a Burns arrangement of "Happiness Is a Thing Called Joe" featuring a warm reading by Frances Wayne. All of these recordings sold well, and "Happiness Is a Thing Called Joe" became a major hit.

Some of the most celebrated tunes were created collectively as "head" arrangements. Chubby Jackson remembers:

> On one-nighters, Woody would often leave in the middle of the last set and we would make up head arrangements. "Apple Honey" ... "Northwest Passage," those were made up by the rhythm section playing four to eight bars to get into it. Then Flip Phillips would start to play, endlessly. Meanwhile, Neal would add figures. Then Bill Harris, and finally the ensemble. The next night I would say to Woody, "We got one for you." ...
>
> Little by little we were adding our own flavor. Woody never stopped us. He would be the coordinator. ... We started to realize we were able to show as much genius as the boss wished.

The band only got better during the rest of 1945 as vibraphonist Red Norvo and trumpeters Conte Candoli (Pete's younger brother) and Shorty Rogers signed on, and Dave Tough (who had a severe alcohol problem) was replaced by Don Lamond, a versatile drummer whose style fit the band perfectly.

In August the band made a beautiful recording that became a big hit; it was "Bijou," a seductive Latin theme written by Ralph Burns that showcased the dynamic and expressive improvising skills of Bill Harris. This was followed by the good-natured "Your Father's Moustache" in September and a dynamic flag-waver, "Wild Root," in November. This last tune was named for the hair cream company that sponsored the radio show that the band took over in late October shortly after its Old Gold engagement ended. The Herd signed up for thirty-nine weeks, and it became the first band in several years to have a show all to itself; the added exposure helped it set attendance records at ballrooms and theaters wherever it played.

Igor Stravinsky was impressed by the freshness and inventiveness of the Herd, and in early 1945, through a friend, broached the possibility of writing something for the band. Woody originally dismissed the idea as a long shot, so he was very surprised when several months later he received a telegram from Stravinsky saying, "I'm writing something for you. It will be my Christmas present for you and the band."

The piece was called "Ebony Concerto," and during the Christmas season Stravinsky came to New York to rehearse the Herd. The setting was unorthodox; they used a hall at the Paramount Theater where the band was doing six shows a day, and they worked during the eighty-minute breaks between performances. Woody remembers:

> He was completely intrigued with the band and said, "Woody (pronounced 'Voodjya'), you have a beautiful family." No one will ever know what turned him on or what his reasoning was, because the piece was extremely subtle. . . . I spent a lot of time with him socially later on and he explained to me that it had been a challenge for him to write for us. He had of course written Stravinsky and not jazz.

Stravinsky was particularly impressed by Shorty Rogers, saying, "I can listen to Shorty Rogers's good style . . . for stretches of fifteen minutes or more and not feel the time at all, whereas the weight of every 'serious' virtuoso I know depressed me beyond the counter action of Equanil in about five." Shorty returned the compliment by writing a piece called "Igor" for the Herd.

The *Metronome* and *Down Beat* poll results, published in January 1946, confirmed that 1945 had been a banner year for the band. The Herd as a whole and three of its stars—Bill Harris, Flip Phillips, and Dave Tough—won first place emphatically in both contests. Chubby Jackson triumphed in the *Down Beat* poll and took a close second with *Metronome*.

The Herd introduced "Ebony Concerto" to a full house at Carnegie Hall on March 25, 1946. The concert also marked the premiere of the first three movements of a four-movement suite by Ralph Burns entitled "Summer Sequence"; he had by now given up the piano chair in the Herd to work full-time at writing and arranging. "Summer Sequence" is a more successful Herman piece than "Ebony Concerto" because it is totally in the jazz idiom; it sets a series of beautiful Burns melodies against subtly shifting backgrounds by the horn sections. "Ebony Concerto" and the unfinished "Summer Sequence" were recorded on August 19, with Stravinsky conducting his work.

Neal Hefti and Frances Wayne had been married in 1945 and in early 1946 decided to leave the road for a more sedentary life in Hollywood. Shorty Rogers came to the fore as a writer with Hefti's departure and contributed "Igor" and two other tunes to a recording session in May by a nine-piece offshoot of the Herd. This session is marked by several sparkling improvisations by Sonny Berman and by the return of pianist Jimmy Rowles, who had played briefly with the band before being drafted in 1943.

Woody was flush with money in the summer of 1946, and he paid $70,000 cash for the spectacular Hollywood Hills home of Humphrey Bogart and Lauren Bacall. The Hermans bought all of the furnishings except the washer-dryer, which Bacall insisted on keeping, because they were in short supply after the War. For years afterwards, the Hermans used napkin holders and other knickknacks monogrammed "B and B"— for Bogie and Baby. From the street the house looks like a one-story bungalow, but when you enter you discover that it is quite sizable as it descends three flights along the side of a canyon; you are also dazzled by the stunning view of all of Los Angeles.

To the outside world Woody, Charlotte, and Ingrid, ensconced in their beautiful Hollywood digs, seemed like the ideal show business family. But Woody and his bride knew that their personal world was in grave danger; Charlotte, driven by loneliness with Woody on the road forty weeks per year, had become addicted to a combination of alcohol and a barbiturate called Nembutal. Woody remembers:

I was disturbed by it, but there wasn't a great deal I could do [on the road]. Like anyone with a drinking problem, she had many excuses. I even threatened to take a walk. But it was an empty gesture; we were very tight. . . . I decided that the only way I could help was to go home. So, I broke up the band. . . . It had nothing to do with dissension in the band or anything like that. I was destroying Charlotte.

Just before the Christmas holidays, after a dance at the University of Indiana, Woody stunned his musicians by closing down one of the greatest and most successful jazz bands in history. He arranged for generous severance pay, and then he headed back to the Hollywood Hills.

Charlotte and Woody started a rigorous schedule of Alcoholics Anonymous meetings, and Charlotte got psychiatric help as well. While they were struggling to conquer Charlotte's addiction, they were hit with the terrible news that Sonny Berman had died of a drug overdose on January 16, 1947. He was only twenty-two.

Soon Woody settled into an unaccustomed domestic routine:

Being off the road was a situation I hadn't known since I was eight. It was appealing to eat dinner with my family, play with my daughter—carrying on with her out in the yard and throwing her into the bathtub.

To keep his hand in professionally, Woody did a weekly California radio show singing with Peggy Lee in front of a band led by her husband Dave Barbour, opened a booking office with his former road managers, recorded vocals with Dinah Shore and with a Ralph Burns orchestra, and ran a Saturday morning disc jockey show. The latter drew too many fans; Woody was forced to quit when rival deejays reacted to his popularity by refusing to play his recordings.

As Woody remembered, he and his band manager, Abe Turchen, turned to gambling to supplement their incomes:

Abe decided to bet West Coast baseball. This was hard to do, even if you're a winner, but that's how we lived for a good six months. He averaged between $750 and $1,500 a week, and we split it. . . . I couldn't take it, 'cause the bookmaker was always handing him an envelope at the end of each game, and that was about the time Bugsy Siegel got bumped off.

Charlotte made rapid progress, and by the summer of 1947 was sober and in a state of recovery that she maintained for the rest of her life.

WOODY WAS RESTLESS, despite his varied activities, and when he went out to hear music, the urge to lead a band again possessed him strongly. He recalled:

> One night, some friends and I went out to a little joint on Sunset near Vine Street. Phil Moore, a pianist and arranger, was leading a little group there that included trumpeter Ernie Royal. When I heard Ernie play so fluently at the top of the horn, it gave me the hots for music again.
>
> Trying to make something different was always in the back of my mind. You hear a great player or two and the idea is replanted, as long as I could do it without having to return to what I already did. The family problems were taken care of, and I felt I had to do something productive again. . . .
>
> When I heard Ernie and what he could do with such ease, I decided to get me a band. I just asked him if he wanted to come and join, and he said, "Yeah, that sounds all right." I said, "I'll put together a band then." . . . Ralph came out to help me put it together.

Burns quickly re-recruited Shorty Rogers, Don Lamond, alto sax player Sam Marowitz, and trumpeter Marky Markowitz from the Herd, and bassist Walt Yoder and guitarist Gene Sargent from The Band That Plays the Blues.

Then he and Woody conscripted another new man, an inventive, twenty-three-year-old baritone sax player named Serge Chaloff. Chaloff had made a nationwide reputation for the ease and speed with which he played complex and lyrical bebop lines on his cumbersome instrument. Despite a classical background—his father played piano with the Boston Symphony, and his mother taught at the New England Conservatory of Music—Chaloff turned to jazz at age twelve and became a professional four years later. He achieved wide popularity while showing a mastery of the bebop idiom with the Boyd Raeburn, Georgie Auld, and Jimmy Dorsey bands in 1945 and 1946.

Soon after Chaloff signed on, Burns heard the four saxes playing Gene Roland's arrangements with the De Carlo group at Pontrelli's. He couldn't wait to get Woody down to the Ballroom, because he felt strongly that the four men would work together productively with Chaloff.

When Woody agreed and hired the De Carlo crew, he and Burns possessed the nucleus of an exciting new band. They had an entire sax section with Getz, Sims, Steward, Marowitz, and Chaloff, three excellent trumpeters in Rogers, Royal, and Markowitz, three-quarters of the rhythm section with Lamond, Yoder, and Sargent, and three inventive writers in Burns, Rogers, and Giuffre. Soon after, they added a fourth writer, saxophonist Al Cohn, Stan's friend from Roland's 1946 New York rehearsal band.

They had hired a full complement of players by early September and went into rehearsal two weeks later. Ernie Royal was the only black. Among the late hires were Jerri Ney, a female singer who also played the vibraphone, and two excellent trombone soloists, Earl Swope and Ollie Wilson.

The creation of the new Herman band meant the end of the Butch Stone and De Carlo groups. Stone returned to Les Brown, with whom he works to the present day, and De Carlo continued to freelance around Los Angeles. Roland was rehired by Kenton, where he stayed for the following decade; he worked for Woody in 1956 and 1957, and then returned to Kenton for another four years.

Woody knew exactly what kind of music he wanted his new band to play. The 1944–46 group had strong boppish elements, but its swing and blues heritage predominated on most of its numbers. The new aggregation, which was quickly dubbed the Second Herd, was an all-out bebop band. Woody remembered:

> The Second Herd was organized with the full intent of going straight ahead with bebop. . . . The bebop evolution had become the core of our music. We gathered invention and diversification not only with the charts of Al Cohn and Jimmy Giuffre, but from the provocative sound of our reed and brass soloists. . . . Shorty Rogers, who helped with a lot of things in the First Herd, was writing terrific bebop charts.

Stan was excited about playing in a bebop setting, and he knew at the start that he was in convivial company. He recalled:

> From the very beginning that band was something special. I remember our first rehearsal at a place on Santa Monica Boulevard. Ralph Burns came in with a brand new, pretty difficult chart on

"Lover Come Back to Me"—about five pages worth; it overlapped
the music stands. And that band read it down and swung it without a moment's hesitation. . . . It sure makes you want to blow
when you've got those cats with you. You hear the right sounds
all night; finally the right sounds come out of you.

Stan did not know it at the time, but the inventiveness and the high-
caliber musicianship of his Herman colleagues soon challenged him to
new heights of creativity.

FOUR BROTHERS   SIX

THE SECOND HERD performed in public for the first time at the Municipal Auditorium in San Bernardino, California, on October 16, 1947. During the next two months, it sandwiched long engagements in Salt Lake City and St. Louis among a string of western one-nighters as it worked on its book of arrangements in preparation for a series of recordings in late December.

The musicians union had decreed a strike against the record companies starting January 1, 1948; the previous one had dragged on for twenty-seven months in 1942–44, and during the last weeks of 1947, all the bands were streaming into the studios to beat the year-end deadline. Vocalist Jerri Ney had proved inadequate, and Mary Ann McCall, who had sung with the First Herd after Frances Wayne left, returned for the recording sessions.

The band entered the studio feeling good about a *Down Beat* review of a December 18 one-nighter in Chicago that began, "Within one year from this date Woody Herman will have recaptured everything he gave up in 1946, plus more. Mark these words. This Herd can very easily become the greatest thing that has happened in American music." It was impossible to live up to this hyperbole, but with its first recording session the Second Herd established a powerful and exciting identity.

The band recorded fourteen songs between December 22 and December 31; eleven were released, five became hits, and one was so distinctive that it gave the band a second name. The five hits were composed by four writers, illustrating the depth of talent Woody had assembled.

The first, "I've Got News for You," is built around a Shorty Rogers orchestration of a blues solo by his idol, Charlie Parker. Shorty revered Parker.

> When Bird came on the scene . . . it was just as shocking as in the Bible: everything was dark, and then the light appeared for the first time. . . . And I considered it a great privilege to have been alive at that time to say, "There's a new guy, his name is Charlie Parker. You have to hear him. And when you hear him you just get blown through the walls." Just going out into new discoveries, uncharted areas of musical explorations.

The entire sax section plays the Parker chorus, and the three men from the Pontrelli crew create a lilting sound as they blend smoothly with Chaloff and Marowitz. Woody sings the lyric and Royal takes a spirited trumpet solo.

Stan and Chaloff get their first opportunities to solo as Herdsmen on the second success of the session, "Keen and Peachy," a straight-ahead swinger by Burns and Rogers as arranged by Burns. The saxophonists power their way through the tune with exuberant ease. The third hit was "The Goof and I," a boppish number written and arranged by Al Cohn and distinguished by a driving Chaloff improvisation.

The most important tune recorded during the December session was "Four Brothers," Jimmy Giuffre's first contribution to the band. An absolutely distinctive sound is created as Marowitz sits the number out, Stan takes the melody lead, Chaloff plays an octave below him, and Sims and Steward harmonize in between. For less skilled musicians a blending of three tenors and a baritone would sound muddy and heavy, but these four create a light, lyrical texture as they play Giuffre's Pres-like song. The melody statement is followed by brilliant solos played in succession by Sims, Chaloff, Steward, and Getz, and the record ends with each of them playing two-bar breaks before a fanfare by the entire band.

Their creation was soon called the "Four Brothers" sound; it was widely imitated, and the name the Four Brothers Band became as well known as the Second Herd in describing this Herman aggregation.

On the same day that the Second Herd recorded "Four Brothers," it waxed the fourth and final part of "Summer Sequence" with a short, poignant solo by Stan. Ralph Burns had completed this segment more than a year after he wrote the first three segments for the First Herd. The two songs were among the Herd's most frequently requested numbers and brought Stan wide attention for the first time.

With "Keen and Peachy," "Four Brothers," and "Summer Sequence IV," we hear for the first time Stan's fully formed style. He no longer sounds like Lester Young or Charlie Parker or Dexter Gordon; he is his own man. His apprenticeship, which began with Jack Teagarden almost five years before, has ended, and he has become a mature artist at age twenty.

The first thing we notice is Stan's sound. A sax player constructs his sound from several elements: the way he grips and manipulates the mouthpiece with his teeth, tongue, and facial muscles (his embouchure), the reed and mouthpiece he chooses, the volume and velocity of the air he propels through his horn. Every jazz master has created a distinctive sound; a Miles Davis or a Lester Young or a Ben Webster has only to play a handful of notes, and we know who it is.

Stan's sound broadened and deepened in the ensuing years, but by late 1947, it had attained its distinctive textures. He retained the airy buoyancy of Pres but overlaid it with a hoarseness, a Jewish ache, which gave poignancy to almost everything he played and which penetrated to the listener's marrow. And, in order to express a wide range of emotion, he became a master of dynamics; he could now move from a whisper to a shout in a single phrase.

In these Second Herd recordings, we hear that a Pres-like emphasis on melody has become the foundation stone of Stan's aesthetic. He has broadened the expressive range of his playing by mastering the expanded vocabulary of bebop, but he has put that vocabulary firmly in the service of melody. He would never waver from this practice.

Stan was fond of telling a story about Lester Young and Sonny Stitt. Stitt, a close friend of Stan's, was a bebop sax player who was very proud of his ability to work his way through complex chord changes at lightning tempos. Once when he and Stan and Pres were touring together in a bus during the mid-1950s, Stitt was showing off these skills as he reeled off chorus after virtuoso chorus. When he finished, he asked, "Pres, what do you think of that?" Young replied, "That's all very fine, Lady Stitt, but can you sing me a song?" Stan always sang a song.

A month before Stan's December recording session, Al and Goldie, who could never get used to California, returned to New York with Bob. During their entire California stay, the three of them never moved from the one-room Hollywood apartment with the Murphy bed. After a short stopover in Queens, they headed straight back to their East Bronx neighborhood and moved into a tenement on Hoe Avenue two blocks from where they lived before.

The return from his beloved California demoralized Bob. He enrolled at James Monroe High School in January 1948 but never spent much time there. He usually played hookey, riding the subway down to Forty-second Street and spending his afternoons watching grade-Z action movies there.

During January Jimmy Raney, a wonderful guitarist, joined the Herd, and Al Cohn took Herb Steward's place. Cohn was an excellent recruit for the Four Brothers. His playing was as inventive as Steward's, but more robust. As Red Rodney related, Woody did not take to him immediately:

> Al Cohn loved Woody. But it took a while for Woody to like him. He had Zoot and Stan, and all of a sudden Al comes in, who was not as flamboyant as either of the other two. But musically, every time Al played a solo, the trumpet section and the trombone section would lean forward to listen. It didn't take Woody long to recognize Al's greatness.

Cohn's arrival with the Second Herd began an association with Sims that lasted for thirty-seven years. He and Zoot co-led several excellent groups between 1957 and Sims's death in 1985.

Cohn was renowned for his one-liners. He defined a gentleman as "someone who knows how to play an accordion, but doesn't." He once turned down the offer of a Danish beer called Elephant by saying, "I drink to forget." A fellow musician asked him how he felt as he suffered through a hangover one morning in Italy, and he replied, "Like a million lire." When a friend told him that he was going back to school to study Jewish history, Al asked, "What would you like to know?" And one night when a bartender inquired, "What will you have?" he answered, "One too many." After finishing an album with twenty-four mandolin players, a friend questioned, "Where did they find all those guys?" "Well," said Al, "all day today you couldn't get a haircut in Jersey City."

Herb Steward quit the Second Herd because he had become disgusted with the heavy drug use in the band. Roughly half the musicians were addicted, and when Al Cohn replaced Herb, each of the Four Brothers was a user. This could create dangerous situations, as Stan recalled:

> I remember playing one time with Woody's band at this afternoon concert. Nine acts of vaudeville and a trained bear. The bear came on, and I mean, this bear had to be nine feet tall. And the band came out, and the two on each side of Sam Marowitz — the lead alto player who was very strait-laced, no drugs, no drinking — were Serge Chaloff, Zoot Sims, Al Cohn, and me, all stoned. The bear was doing this thing with the trainer, and at one point the bear came around and his arm went over the saxophone section. He could have killed the five of us, but only Sam Marowitz ducked. The rest of us were too stoned to even know that the bear was near us.

Heroin use had become almost a rite of passage among young jazz musicians in 1948, and one reason was the example of Charlie Parker. The fact that Parker — whose genius had become a beacon to everyone in jazz — was a hard-core heroin addict reinforced the musicians' urge to use the drug. If Henri Matisse had been a user, it is probable that many young painters would have tried heroin.

The resident dealer and ringleader was Serge Chaloff, who was to heroin what W. C. Fields was to liquor. Woody recalled:

> It was no secret that we had quite a few junkies in the Second Herd. It never became a serious problem on the bandstand, although sometimes guys missed a bus or otherwise had trouble getting to a gig on time. But the drugs didn't appear to cut into their musical ability, which is why I put up with it as long as I did. . . .
>
> On the bus, the guys who were hooked sat in a section of their own. Serge Chaloff would hang a blanket to separate his group from the rest of the band and would distribute the goodies.
>
> I was concerned about the drug problem, but my overriding focus was to produce good music. . . . I don't think anyone ever accomplished or proved anything by saying, "You're involved in narcotics. Get out of my band." If a person has ability, he must have a chance to show his ability.

Once, after Woody bawled Serge out when the drugs made him sound lethargic in performance, they went to an after-hours bar. Woody remembered what happened next:

> They were seven deep at the bar . . . and finally I get a couple of drinks, and it's hot in there, and I'm sweating, and somebody's got their hands on me, and I hear, "Hey, Woody baby, whadya wanna talk to me like that for? I'm straight, baby, I'm straight." And it's Mr. Chaloff . . . We were jammed in there, packed in, and . . . I peed down Serge's leg.

Woody finally became fed up with Serge and tried to fire him while the band was playing at a Boston dance hall that overlooked the Charles River. At intermission, Serge called Woody over to a window overlooking the river and asked, "What do you see out there, Woody?"

"A lot of water."

"Look more closely."

"Well," said Woody, "there's some litter floating around."

"That litter," said Serge, "that's the baritone sax parts of the arrangements. Now you can't fire me; I'm the only person in the world that knows them by heart." Serge had saved his job.

Serge finally kicked his heroin habit in 1955, and his future looked very bright. But soon after making a brilliant LP in March 1956, he was stricken with an irreversible cancer. He performed courageously from a wheelchair until shortly before his death in July 1957 at age thirty-three.

The band stayed on the West Coast during early 1948. After completing a film short for Universal, it moved into the Palladium for a six-week engagement that ended on March 15 and that broadened its audience due to a CBS radio hookup. It then headed east where it settled in for seven months.

Stan and Beverly had never nested anywhere in the Los Angeles area for more than a few weeks. But now she was pregnant, and they decided to find a permanent residence. They wanted to be together during Beverly's pregnancy, so they followed the Herd back east, taking a small apartment in Cambria Heights in Queens, New York.

Down Beat's lead concerning the Second Herd's opening at New York's Hotel Commodore on April 20 said that "Woody Herman returned to Gotham in a blaze of glory." Because the recording strike continued, our only evidence of the band's music during this engagement are four Armed Forces Radio Service air checks. One of them catches Stan in top form playing two liquid choruses on a Gerry Mulligan tune, "Elevation."

The Herd moved directly from The Commodore to The Capitol Theater on Broadway, where it was teamed with a fluffy Van Johnson-June Allyson comedy, *The Bride Goes Wild*, from May 20 to June 17. This engagement was marked by a vaudeville stunt in which the musicians began their rendition of Khachaturian's "Sabre Dance" brandishing cardboard knives and ended it with the knives buried in each other's backs. The band was strengthened when Bill Harris came back to the trombone section during the Capitol gig and when Chubby Jackson returned on bass in mid-July.

Bob Getz escaped from the East Bronx by hanging out backstage with the band, and toward the end of the run, Stan got him a job as an usher at the Capitol that lasted a few months. Bob recalled:

> I'd stand in front with my little smart uniform and say, "For the best available seats, kindly use the grand stairway in front. For the best available seats, kindly use the grand stairway in front." Over and over and over again. That was my job. Those theaters were grand palaces.

Soon afterward, Bob was introduced to drugs by Serge Chaloff and Stan.

> I went to Asbury Park [New Jersey] when they were playing there and Stan was busy one afternoon and Serge, who I had just met, took me to the movies. We sat in the balcony and he takes out a pipe and starts smoking grass. I didn't know what it was, but after two whiffs I realized that it was something different.
>
> I got scared. I couldn't wait to get back, and I told Stan. He looked at Bev and said, "Bob, it's time we told you the facts of life." And Stan turned me on. That was my first taste of marijuana. And it was several months later when I got my first taste of heroin. Not from Stan.

Beverly's sister, Bobbie Byrne, moved in with Stan and Beverly in Cambria Heights soon after graduating from high school in June and quickly found a job in Manhattan. In the evenings she would frequently drive Stan to and from work because Beverly was afraid that the drugs might cause him to fall asleep at the wheel.

After a series of one-nighters in the East and Midwest, the Second Herd returned to New York on October 24, 1948, for an engagement at a bustling cellar club called the Royal Roost on Broadway between Forty-seventh and Forty-eighth streets. The Roost, which had started as a fried chicken joint, became the temple of bebop in the spring of 1948, when promoter Monte Kay and deejay "Symphony Sid" Torin sponsored weekly concerts featuring Bird, Miles Davis, and Dexter Gordon. The concerts became so popular that the owners adopted a seven-nights-a-week jazz policy.

Symphony Sid, a tireless proselytizer for bebop who billed himself as "the all-night, all-frantic one," incorporated a live hour from the club every Friday night on his disc jockey show on station WMCA; this was accomplished with a remote microphone hookup that allowed Sid to host the entire show from his studio. Between April 1948 and April 1949, when they moved to a larger place called Bop City, he and Kay brought to the Roost such stars as Bird, Dizzy, Pres, Miles Davis, Kenny Clarke, Max Roach, the Count Basie band, Dexter Gordon, Flip Phillips, Dinah Washington, and Ella Fitzgerald.

Sid had a deep New York baritone, and his broadcasts were sprinkled with Yiddishisms: Dinah Washington was his "verblundet" one, and he would threaten an unruly spectator with "Watch out, or I'll go Sephardic on you." His commercials were adamantly hip: "When Fate deals you one from the bottom of the deck, fall by the Sunshine Funeral Parlors. Your loved ones will be handled with dignity and care, and the cats at Sunshine will not lay too heavy a tab on you."

He always introduced the artists over the strains of a tune Pres wrote for him, "Jumping with Symphony Sid," and he said things like, "We're taking our microphone down to the house that bop built, the Royal Roost, the Metropolitan Bopera House, where the music is in a real knocked-out groove, and you can relax until 4:00 A.M. digging the gonest sounds of pure progressive jazz. To start things jumping, here's Woody Herman's fabulous Second Herd with 'The Goof and I.' "

The band's reputation in the jazz world had been growing, and the Roost was crowded with musicians on opening night. The Herd followed an engagement by Dizzy's big band, and Dizzy, Stan Kenton, and most of Kenton's orchestra were among the spectators. The attendance of these heavyweights sparked the Herd to peaks of creativity. *Down Beat's* headline read, "With Practically No Weak Spots, Herman Herd Gives Magnificent Performance," and the reviewer wrote:

> The most startling thing about listening to this band is that you have to go back to 1938 and Count Basie's opening at New York's Famous Door to find a parallel example of a band selling its personal enthusiasm about playing to the customers as this one

does. . . . Standout attraction by far was the superlative drumming of ex-Washingtonian Don Lamond. Terry Gibbs, young bop vibist, justified early raves with a hair-raising display of ideas and technique. Bill Harris played excellent trombone as usual. . . . The reeds, paced by the baritone of Serge Chaloff and Stan Getz's hardtone staccato tenor ideas, not only were loaded with ideas, but also had a unity of conception which gave their playing a wonderful rhythmic smack.

The Second Herd reached its zenith artistically during the Roost gig, which lasted four and a half weeks until November 24, 1948. The band had received a creative boost with the addition of three more fine soloists—vibraphonist Terry Gibbs and pianist Lou Levy in September, and trumpeter Red Rodney in October; and a year of playing together had given the group a cohesiveness and a cocky self-confidence that shone through everything it played. Rodney remembered:

It was a great band, every chair. It was just a tremendous orchestra, section by section. The soloists and spirit-wise; the band was spirited. . . . It was a lot of camaraderie in the band, friendship. . . . Musically, we cut everybody else. Any band that came near us. We were just so proud. This is Woody Herman. How could you compare with us?

The record ban was continuing, and our evidence of the band's creativity comes from air checks of five Symphony Sid and three CBS broadcasts.

Stan excels, playing mature, lyrical solos on both slow and fast numbers, and Woody gives everyone an opportunity to stretch out because he does not face the three-minute time limit imposed in the studio by the 78-rpm disc. On one rendition of "Keeper of the Flame," there are thirteen solos by twelve different musicians.

One day after the Roost opening, Stan made a bootleg quintet recording for an obscure label called "Sittin' In With." His sidemen included Charlie Parker's pianist Al Haig, whom Stan called "the best accompanist in the business," and guitarist Jimmy Raney. Among the tunes they recorded was "Diaper Pin," which Stan wrote in anticipation of the imminent birth of his first child. Three days later, on October 28, 1948, Steven Paul Getz was born at Misericordia Hospital on Manhattan's East Side.

Beverly and Steven returned from Misericordia to Cambria Heights, where Bobbie Byrne and Bob Getz became the resident baby-sitters. Bob had dropped out of high school and had begun a three-and-a-half year addiction to heroin, and sometime during 1947 or 1948, Beverly had started using the drug also. Bob remembered the scene:

> When the kid came, I was there for Stan, because he was on the road or working late in the clubs. I lived there a lot—anything to get out of the Bronx and out of my mother's and father's reach. . . .
>
> We used drugs together. . . . I had this face like a perpetual juvenile; they used to send me down to Harlem to score for them. I had this red club jacket with a zipper, and I looked like a choir boy. . . .
>
> My parents didn't even know that Stan was doing all that stuff, so I bore the brunt of it. I remember my mother slapping me one night when I came home with my eyes popping out of my head. She said, "You're high, you bum," and she slapped me. And she said, "Look at your brother. He's involved with those people all of the time, and he doesn't do that."
>
> Beverly was my closest friend. I loved her.

Al and Goldie's troubles with Bob were compounded by the self-induced collapse of Al's business. Al, his brother Benny, and a third man had opened a small printing shop soon after Al had returned from California a year earlier. The business struggled, and sales were very anemic toward the end of 1948. Benny spent ten-hour days hustling for orders and was constantly frustrated by the lack of energy and motivation exhibited by his two partners. The end came when he returned to the shop in the middle of a particularly trying day to find Al and his other associate playing cards. Benny was so angry that he engineered the immediate liquidation of the business, and Al was forced to become an hourly worker again.

Goldie's trials with Al and Bob would sometimes cause her upper body to become rigid. Bob Getz remembered one of these incidents:

> She would have these times where her nerves would tense up so badly. I remember once, I must have been sixteen at the time, we were up in the Catskills. The doctor came in and saw my mother like that and said, "Stop it, Mrs. Getz, stop it." And I said, "What's this guy talking about?" And she stopped. That was the first time I was led to understand that my mother had psychological stressful dysfunction. Before that, I thought it was due to high blood pressure.

When the Roost engagement ended in late November, Stan took leave of the family for several months as the Herd went on tour. Its first stop was the Empire Room in Hollywood, a nightclub created for Woody, because the other southern California venues like the Palladium were all booked for the holiday season. Woody's manager got together with Gene Norman, the disc jockey and promoter whom Stan had played for the previous year, and they found a place on Vine Street that had been the Hollywood Breakfast Club; they cleaned it up, renamed it the Empire Room, and opened on December 7. Gene Norman remembered:

> That was like I'd died and gone to heaven. To hear that band every night. . . . We went on the air New Year's Eve coast-to-coast, and what a thrill. I was in my mid-twenties, and here I was in my own nightclub presenting the Woody Herman band.

Ava Gardner, who had recently divorced Artie Shaw and was already a major star, loved the Second Herd. She became smitten with Stan, but he was too busy arranging his heroin supplies to pay any attention to her. Terry Gibbs recalled:

> Ava Gardner was running after Stan Getz. He sloughed her off all the time at the Empire Room. She would come in every night to get Stan. He'd walk over to her and say, "Hello," and out of the corner of his eye he'd see a friend and run over to his friend and leave Ava.

In spite of its artistic success, the Second Herd was stumbling commercially—and for three main reasons. First of all, the basic market conditions that nurtured the big bands were disappearing as much of the listening population moved to the suburbs, began to watch TV, and used their new cars to explore the American countryside; Benny Goodman was fronting his last permanent band, and Tommy Dorsey, Harry James, Gene Krupa, and other major leaders had shut down. Secondly, the recording ban, which had kept the Herman crew out of the studios for almost a year, limited their public exposure. And finally, the wider public, except in centers of hipness like New York, was not ready to embrace bebop. Woody explained:

> The audience that could understand "Apple Honey" couldn't relate to "Lemon Drop" or "Four Brothers." Musically, the bebop route was magnificent, but businesswise it was the dumbest thing

I ever did. Those pieces didn't really succeed, except with a small percentage of our listeners, until the mid-1950s.

The band opened strongly at the Empire Room, but business tailed off toward the end of the engagement.

The recording ban ended on December 14. Woody, who had recorded with Columbia before the strike, quickly signed a more lucrative contract with Capitol. To celebrate, the Second Herd played a basketball game on Christmas Day against the Capitol All-Stars at the Hollywood YMCA. The Herd lost, 49–31; Stan scored three points.

The Herd couldn't wait to get into the Capitol studios on December 29 and 30 to end their year-long recording drought. They waxed six tracks, three of which were vocal numbers: a seductive Burns arrangement of Ellington's "I Got It Bad (And That Ain't Good)," which spotlights the husky, vulnerable quality of Mary Ann McCall's voice; a relaxed, comic tune by Woody, "I Ain't Gettin' Any Younger"; and "Lemon Drop," a blistering bebop number featuring a wordless vocal by the trio of Gibbs, Jackson, and Rogers.

Stan has prominent solos on two shouting, up-tempo Shorty Rogers instrumentals in which the band is driven inexorably by Lamond and Jackson: "That's Right," a blues, and "Keeper of the Flame," a new tune written over the chords of an old one, "I Found a New Baby."

On the sixth number of the session, Stan created an indelible jazz classic that also became a runaway pop hit, "Early Autumn." Stan had pestered Woody for months for a new tune that would showcase his ballad skills, and Woody assigned the task of writing it to Ralph Burns. A year earlier, following Stan's solo near the end of the "Summer Sequence IV" recording, Ralph had the Four Brothers play a lush, romantic line which seemed to stick in everyone's memory. This became the main strain, the A part in the A-A-B-A sequence, of "Early Autumn." After the tune is laid out by the Four Brothers and Woody, Terry Gibbs takes a short improvised solo.

Then Stan steps up to play one of the most beautifully conceived expressions of romantic yearning in all of American popular music. Everything fits perfectly: his caressing sound, his creation of a haunting improvised melody, his relaxed manipulation of the rhythms. The solo connected powerfully with the romantic fantasies of postwar America and started him on the road to stardom.

"Early Autumn" became an immediate hit with live audiences, but the record was not released for several months, and Stan's improvisation did not reach a wider public until then.

For the rest of his life, people would ask Stan if he was especially inspired when he created his famous solo. But to him, it was just another day at the office:

> The fourth movement of "Summer Sequence" was just something tossed in front of us, an afterthought by Ralph Burns ... and there was a solo on my part. And then "Early Autumn" was another record date. . . . Ralph designated that he wanted me to have the solo on that. So I played that, and it's just a record date. So, there are no visions of grandeur.
>
> You know I've heard the "Summer Sequence" solo maybe three times in my whole life. Because I don't possess my own records. I don't remember what I played on it.
>
> "Early Autumn" I've heard, because it's played on the radio enough for me to hear it. And it's okay. It's a nice solo. But, I don't get it. I don't understand why it was such an earthshaking thing. It's just another ballad solo for me. . . . My music is something that's done and forgotten about.

Audiences loved it, and they clamored to hear more from the handsome young tenor player. Stan soon became the "first among equals" of the Herd's soloists. Terry Gibbs remembered:

> Woody's a smart man. And you gotta put it where it's at, who's going to break up the audience. And Stan could play. . . . Woody had a hard job pointing to a guy. Who do you point to? If you want a tenor saxophone solo, you don't know who to point to. I mean, you just got to take a man and point. And Stan Getz had the hit ... so he pointed to Stan.

Chubby Jackson had gotten married during the Empire Room engagement, and soon after it ended on January 3, he decided to leave the band and settle down in Los Angeles. He was replaced by the brilliant former Ellington bassist, Oscar Pettiford. Jimmy Giuffre finally became a "Brother" in January when he replaced Zoot Sims, who left to join Buddy Rich. And soon after Giuffre came on board, he and his fellow Brothers got to play with Dizzy Gillespie for the first time. Dizzy and the Herd were stranded in Salt Lake City in a snowstorm, and Dizzy's group was stuck in Denver. Dizzy accepted Woody's offer of his band, they co-led the Herd, and the engagement was salvaged.

The *Metronome* poll results for 1948 were published in January, and

Stan made an appearance for the first time, placing tenth on tenor; Brothers Sims and Cohn finished seventeenth and twenty-seventh, respectively. Charlie Ventura, a Hawkins stylist who had made his reputation with Gene Krupa, was the winner. The Herd came in third behind the Kenton and Gillespie aggregations, but two of its members, Serge Chaloff and Bill Harris, took firsts; Woody was cited for "the comeback of the year."

By mid-February, Stan had been with the Herd for almost eighteen months—longer than with any other band—and he was tired of the road. On Valentine's Day he was so shaken by a road tragedy that he made up his mind to quit the Herd. He remembered the incident years later:

> My wife had had our first child, and I wanted to get off the road. We had been traveling with Woody for about a year and three quarters. I wanted to be with her, work in New York, or something.
>
> What instigated it, though, was something that happened when we were leaving Chicago. We were going to play at the University of Illinois at Champaign-Urbana. It was the first night of a tour with Nat Cole, and we were driving down there on a cold, cold day with lots of ice on the road. Everybody else went on the bus, but Ralph Burns had a new yellow Ford convertible, and he and Serge Chaloff and I decided to drive down together.
>
> The traction on the Ford wasn't good enough, though, so we had to stop at this little town and phone the manager of the band. He arranged to have the express train to St. Louis flagged down at the local station so that we could get to the job.
>
> It took this train about half a mile to stop, and when we got on, I noticed everyone on the train looked at us in a very bad way. Ralph later found out that the brakeman had gotten off the train to see why it had been stopped and had slipped on the ice and fallen under the wheels of a local train. He was decapitated, and he was, like, two weeks away from retirement.
>
> Well, when I heard about that, something happened inside me. I felt so bad that I just lost heart and decided I was going to leave.

Stan left the Herd at the end of March 1950 and began to freelance around New York. He made several excellent small group records with Herdsman such as Gibbs, Rogers, Sims, Cohn, and Raney, and in quartet and sextet settings with the pianist Al Haig. Most were produced by a young enthusiast named Bob Weinstock, and one tune, "Long Island

Sound," became a hit—in part because Symphony Sid pushed it hard on his deejay show.

As this dialogue between critics Loren Schoenberg and Dan Morgenstern attests, Stan's playing on the "Long Island Sound" session was particularly masterful:

> Schoenberg: You have essentially a virtuoso conception of the saxophone, but it's one of the first virtuoso conceptions that's not a heavy one. It's not a hitting-you-over-the-head kind of virtuosity. By this time, he's so light and airy, and yet he whips out all these runs and fast things. It's really amazing.
>
> Morgenstern: He's so relaxed and yet his command of the instrument is so astonishing. He is truly a virtuoso. And at the same time he's always telling a story, and he's always swinging, and he's always playing a melody, and singing.

Recording dates were plentiful, but finding steady club work was difficult. Stan even took a job with a band in a May Day parade; it was a tough gig, because the group was vilified by right-wingers. He remembered:

> I needed the ten dollars. The people were throwing pieces of wood at us and spitting at us. We came to Thirty-fourth Street and had to turn right and go down Eighth Avenue. By that time, there was a lot of abuse being directed at the band, and the trumpet player, as we turned right, kept marching straight and said, "To hell with the ten dollars."

Stan organized an exciting all-star big band that included Zoot Sims, Gerry Mulligan, Tommy Potter, Roy Haynes, outstanding composer-trombonist Johnny Mandel, and powerful bebop pianist Billy Taylor, but the only serious booking they found was a week in August at New York's Apollo Theater. Stan always spoke of his opportunity to lead this group as a special privilege.

Economic conditions prevented him from ever again leading a big band, and he regretted it greatly. Throughout his life Stan liked nothing better than to blow in the middle of a sax section driven by a swinging rhythm section and surrounded by surging trumpets and trombones; whenever he encountered a big band, he would beg the leader to let him sit in. A couple of years before he died, he was asked what he would choose to do if he could fulfill one dream, and he replied, "I'd like to have my own big band and travel with it first class."

Stan's scuffling ended abruptly soon after the Herman recording of "Early Autumn" was issued in July. The disc quickly built momentum and by late August was a major hit; disc jockeys played it incessantly, people crowded into the record stores to buy it, and couples all over the country were slow dancing and making out in Chevys and Fords to its strains.

Stan was catapulted to stardom. He was flooded with offers to perform and quickly booked a series of lucrative gigs. The format he chose was the familiar jazz quartet featuring a horn soloist with rhythm—drums, bass, piano—accompaniment.

Soon he bought his first house in Levittown, the archetypal postwar suburb. After the move, his brother Bob continued to escape from the East Bronx to spend many nights with Stan and Beverly, but her sister Bobbie left them to take an apartment in Manhattan.

Stan was saddened to hear that financial losses had forced Woody to disband the Second Herd after a December 4 concert in Oklahoma City. He had dropped $180,000 during its two-year life.

Woody regrouped and led exciting big bands until a few months before he died in 1987. Of perhaps 150 big bands that flourished during World War II, only three are steadily on the road today: Herman's, Ellington's, and Basie's; their founders are gone, and they are led by younger men. Kenton's band made it until his death in 1979, when he decreed in his will that it not survive him.

Getz always had fond memories of Woody and his days with the Second Herd:

> Woody was a great guy to us, probably the fairest man I ever worked for. He was so egoless and democratic. . . . Putting guys together—Woody's great at that. And once he puts them together, he knows how to develop each guy's musical personality. . . . He adored standing up there, listening to good musicians play. . . . That was the best band I ever played on. It had the most remarkable musicianship, and it was literally an uncontrollable herd of young stallions. Woody could hardly keep the reins on the horses.

An invitation to play at the opening of New York's Birdland club on December 15 was proof that Stan had arrived among the jazz elite; he would perform in a show that featured both Lester Young and Charlie Parker. Birdland, which was named for Parker and called itself "The Jazz Corner of the World," was originally scheduled to open in August, but the owners—the same people who had operated the Royal Roost and later

Bop City—had problems obtaining their liquor license, and the premiere was delayed until December.

Birdland occupied a large cellar on Broadway between Fifty-second and Fifty-third streets that now houses an elaborate strip joint. It was bigger than the Roost or Bop City; legal occupancy was 273 people, a figure greatly exceeded on good nights.

After you paid a ninety-eight-cent admission at a ticket window halfway down the staircase, you descended into the club itself and then let your pocketbook dictate which of three sections to head for. If you chose the bar, which was along the left wall, you were expected to buy at least one drink. On the opposite side of the room were booths and tables, where you were subject to a cover charge and could order drinks as well as badly cooked "down home" food like chicken and ribs. In the center was the bandstand, and between it and the bar were the "bleachers," where your ninety-eight-cent admission paid for the whole evening's entertainment. You had to arrive early to grab one of the few chairs there; most bleacherites stood.

The walls were covered with striking life-size black-and-white photos of jazz giants such as Parker and Gillespie, and on opening night canaries sat in cages behind the bar. They lasted only a few weeks before the heavy smoke killed them.

Symphony Sid set himself up in a glass booth at the rear of the club and did his entire midnight-to-4:00 A.M. broadcast for station WJZ from Birdland. Three hours were devoted to records, and one was broadcast from the bandstand.

The emcee at Birdland was a black midget from Alabama named Pee Wee Marquette who had a penchant for green velvet suits with extra-wide lapels and all-white formal wear with tails. He was renowned for his cigarette lighter. Bassist and writer Bill Crow remembered:

> Pee Wee had one of the first adjustable butane cigarette lighters on the market. He used it to ostentatiously light the large cigars he sometimes smoked, but he carried it mainly as a service to patrons at Birdland. To compensate for his height he would adjust the lighter for maximum flame length. It was an unnerving experience in a dark nightclub to put a cigarette in your mouth and have a two-foot flame suddenly shoot up from waist level with Pee Wee leering hopefully at the other end.

Pee Wee had a voice so shrill that it could almost break glass, and he would garble the names of the performers unless they paid him off. Once

Lester Young, angered by Pee Wee's persistent demands for loot, called him "half a mother-fucker."

The ambitious opening show on December 15 took the listener on "A Journey Through Jazz" guided by William B. Williams, a popular disc jockey. Four bands and three soloists illustrated the principal jazz styles of the era. Max Kaminsky's Dixieland group led things off and then accompanied the first soloist, Kansas City blues shouter and trumpeter Oran "Hot Lips" Page. He was followed by Lester Young's quartet, which used Kaminsky's pianist, Dick Hyman, and Basie's great drummer, Jo Jones.

The next soloist was Harry Belafonte, in the precalypso jazz phase of his career; he led into a scorching set by Charlie Parker with a quintet that included Red Rodney on trumpet, Al Haig on piano, Tommy Potter on bass, and Roy Haynes on drums.

Stan, backed by Haig, Potter, and Haynes, was the third soloist. As Hyman remembered, he acquitted himself well:

> He knew what he wanted, and he was harmonically perfectly organized. And those long lines were so gorgeous—always with passion, not just rattled off.

Stan was followed by the last group of the evening, the sextet of the blind pianist Lenny Tristano, which featured the young sax stars Lee Konitz and Warne Marsh. Tristano's music was a dense, personal offshoot of bebop, which Birdland billed as "the music of the 1950s."

"A Journey Through Jazz" was both a commercial and critical success and ran through January 1, 1950.

Another firm indication that Stan had reached the top rung of jazz was his selection to play in an all-star Carnegie Hall concert on the evening of Christmas. Audience members were given an aural banquet which rivaled any gastronomic feast they had consumed earlier that day. The concert—promoted by Symphony Sid, Monte Kay, and writer Leonard Feather and emceed by Sid—featured a breathtaking array of talent: a septet with Miles Davis, Serge Chaloff, Sonny Stitt, trombonist Benny Green, Max Roach, bassist Curley Russell, and the greatest of the bebop pianists, the magnificent Bud Powell; Stan teaming up with Kai Winding, Al Haig, Tommy Potter, and Roy Haynes; Sarah Vaughan with her trio; Lenny Tristano's sextet; and Charlie Parker playing at his highest level with his quintet.

The music, preserved on a disc (Jass-CD-16) compiled in 1989 from widely scattered bits of tape, bristles with youthful energy and daring; Tristano, age thirty, was the oldest person on stage that night.

As Gary Giddins wrote in 1989:

> What did people think when they filed out of Carnegie Hall Christmas night 1949? Did their feet ever touch the ground? Did they think it would go on like that forever?

The polls in January 1950 confirmed Stan's newfound stardom. *Metronome* named him the number one tenor player for 1949 and, along with Lee Konitz, "Musician of the Year." The magazine's writer could not contain his enthusiasm:

> The acclaim for Stan Getz was universal last year, and it is growing this year as this yearbook went to press. Not since the big years of Coleman Hawkins and the succeeding success of Lester Young has a tenor man hit musicians so hard and reached so firmly into the hearts and heads of jazz fans ... Fortunately for his growth as a musician and his rating with other musicians and fans, his records as a leader and a soloist with little bands on little labels maintain the same quality of sound and reinforce the fine impression of his "Early Autumn" side.

Stan leaped from tenth to second in the *Down Beat* poll, and he and winner Flip Phillips were chosen as the two tenors on the magazine's all-star band.

Stan was twenty-two years old, at the top of his profession, living in a brand-new suburban home with a beautiful young wife and a healthy year-old son. But his first priority every day was insuring his heroin supply.

A NICE BUNCH OF GUYS

SEVEN

STAN FREELANCED successfully during the 1950s with an ever-shifting array of musicians and in a variety of formats. He performed both as a leader and a sideman in big bands, cooperative small bands, quartets, quintets, sextets.

In 1950 he was playing all over the Northeast, but Birdland, where he performed several times, became his base of operations. Morris Levy, the proprietor of the club, was convinced that Stan had star drawing power, and on January 6 brought him into the studio for his new company, Birdland Records, which he owned with two other men.

Stan played on the January 6 session with his preferred accompanists at the time, the rhythm section of Al Haig, Tommy Potter, and Roy Haynes; these three men were a working unit that backed up other soloists such as Charlie Parker, Harry Belafonte, and rising tenor star Wardell Gray. The quartet waxed a fast bebop number and four romantic standards; Stan played freshly and sensitively throughout, but without the bite that had made "Early Autumn" such a compelling statement. The quartet also backed—on two ballads—Junior Parker (born Arthur Daniels), a protégé of Charlie Parker who sang in the lush baritone style of Billy Eckstine.

Four days later, Stan cut two sides as a member of the *Metronome* All-Stars. The magazine had recorded a band of its poll-winners every year since it began the voting in 1941, and it donated the revenues from the discs to the musicians union's unemployment fund and other charities; the musicians played for nothing.

The winners for 1949—who included Dizzy Gillespie, Kai Winding, Lee Konitz, Serge Chaloff, Lenny Tristano, and Max Roach—played two tunes, and Stan is featured on one, "Double Date." The record earned the highest rating from the rival magazine *Down Beat*, whose reviewer said, "Unlike most all-star dates, these two sides make musical sense. Congratulations to *Metronome* for having turned them out."

As expected, *Metronome* co-editor Barry Ulanov wrote enthusiastically about Stan's work:

> Herewith, . . . some comment on the continued evidence of achievement and improvement.
> *Item*: The playing of Stan Getz at Birdland and on our All Star session at Columbia a few weeks ago. It's been obvious for several seasons that Stan could produce a lovely sound, that he was a decorative enhancement of any group to which he belonged. His solos on "Early Autumn" and the last side of "Summer Sequence" showed how touching his tone could be. He has, of late, added idea to expression: his sets at the club and his contributions to our sides moved outside the conventions of familiar melodic lines. To your list of the few first-rate add Stan.

While Stan was making all-star records, his brother-in-law Buddy Stewart was struggling. Buddy left Charlie Barnet's orchestra in the summer of 1949 and during the months following barely survived as a single on the East Coast. In late January he booked a gig in California, where his wife and son were living, but he didn't have the money to get back there.

A friend, Dick Zalud, remembered seeing him in Charlie's Tavern in New York:

I was at the bar having a beer, and he sidled up.

"Listen," he says, "I've got to get to California. Can you help me, can you give me a couple of bucks, you know, just to get . . ."

I said, "Gee, you know, I'm scuffling, Buddy, I don't . . ."

And the next night I saw him again in Charlie's. He said, "Everything's cool, I got a ride. Everything's O.K. I'll see you."

And we all said goodbye to him. That was it.

A few days later, on February 2, Buddy was killed just outside Deming, New Mexico, when the car veered off the road; his traveling companion was injured but survived. Charlie Barnet immediately began raising money for Buddy's family, sending the following telegram to *Down Beat* and other publications:

> Buddy Stewart was tragically killed today in New Mexico in an automobile accident, leaving his wife Jerry, and small son Shawn, destitute and penniless. It is imperative that those of us in show business who knew Buddy, loved him, and enjoyed his wonderful talent, help in raising funds to take care of his burial and the immediate problems of his wife and baby. Please send a check or money order immediately for whatever you can to: Mrs. Jerry Stewart, 4342 Gentry Avenue, North Hollywood, Calif.

The New York jazz community responded to Barnet's appeal by holding a benefit at Birdland from which the Stewart family received all the admissions money and a percentage of the drink receipts. Charlie Parker, Dizzy Gillespie, Lester Young, Ella Fitzgerald, Harry Belafonte, Lenny Tristano, Charlie Ventura, Al Cohn, Stan, and John Coltrane—virtually unknown at age twenty-three—were among the many musicians who participated in the six-hour event.

Beverly Getz was shattered by her brother's death. Her sister Bobbie explained:

> He was five years older than her and he was her backbone. She lost her guiding spirit when he died in 1950. She was crushed. Bev would always follow someone else's lead. That's why Buddy's death was so important. He gave her a strong lead.

When Buddy was alive, Beverly had someone other than Stan whom she could turn to, whose opinion she respected. Now she was totally in her husband's orbit, and she drifted more deeply into drugs.

A cooperative band with Miles Davis, Bud Powell, Max Roach, trombonist J. J. Johnson, and bassist Curly Russell was one of several groups Stan was working with in early 1950. A February 18 Birdland broadcast of this unit (with Tadd Dameron substituting for Powell and Gene Ramey for Russell) survives. Four of the five numbers are long and complex arrangements similar to the work Davis was doing at that time with his *Birth of the Cool* nonet. The fifth selection is "That Old Black Magic," a ballad showcase for Stan where the two other horn men, Davis and Johnson, sit out. Jack Chambers, a biographer of Miles, has written that the co-op had voted to give Stan the "leader's" privilege of soloing alone on this tune because he had won such wide acclaim as a master of the ballad.

Chambers also wrote about Stan's relationship with Miles:

> The prospect of Davis and Getz working cooperatively in a band might fire the imagination of any jazz historian, because both men are notoriously prickly personalities, accepting no nonsense, real or imagined, from any quarter. That alone would seem to guarantee a difficult relationship, but they seem always to have held one another in the highest regard, perhaps because they share a melodic gift that leaves them with very few rivals. Davis says, "I like Stan because he has so much patience, the way he plays those melodies—other people can't get nothing out of a song, but he can. It takes a lot of imagination, that he has, that so many other people don't have." Their mutual respect comes through clearly in the few recorded minutes that have survived from the hours they spent working together in 1950.

It was at this time that critics anointed Stan and Miles as leaders of what they called the "cool" school in jazz. Miles had pioneered the concept as early as September 1948 when he brought his *Birth of the Cool* nonet into the Royal Roost for a two-week engagement opposite the Count Basie band. Basie, along with several other musicians and critics, liked the group, but it failed commercially. The nonet booked only one more club date, but Miles persevered in the recording studios, waxing twelve sides on January 21 and April 21, 1949, and March 9, 1950. The personnel differed on each session, and only Miles, Lee Konitz, Gerry Mulligan, and tuba player Bill Barber played on all three dates; Max Roach performed on two of them.

As Miles related, what drove his group was a desire to return to hummable melody:

Birth of the Cool became a collector's item, I think, out of a reaction
to Bird and Dizzy's music. Bird and Diz played this hip, real fast
thing, and if you weren't a fast listener, you couldn't catch the
humor or the feeling in their music. Their musical sound wasn't
sweet, and it didn't have harmonic lines that you could easily hum
out on the street with your girlfriend trying to get over with a kiss.
Bebop didn't have the humanity of Duke Ellington. It didn't even
have that recognizable thing. Bird and Diz were great, fantastic,
challenging—but they weren't sweet. But *Birth of the Cool* was
different because you could hear everything and hum it also.

Stan didn't have a specific aesthetic agenda like Miles, but his incredible gift for creating melody, his translucent sound, and his relaxed mastery
caused the critics to put him at the center of the cool school. As Barry
Ulanov wrote in *Metronome* in June 1950:

... there is little doubt among devotees of today's jazz that the
tenor is properly sounded only by Stan and those who follow in
his tonal tradition.
"Cool" is the adjective which best describes that sound, "cool,"
inevitably overworked because it seems such a precise description
of the almost indescribable. The great change in jazz effected in
the last couple of years has been a revolution in thermodynamics,
a new conception of the relation between heat and the mechanics
of making music. The change, the new conception, the revolution, all are best illustrated by the playing of this youngster....
This year his polished authority on his instrument is the undeni-
able and highly attractive center of cool jazz.

The cool appellation was a convenient one for the critics, and it stuck
to Stan for several years, but it did not do justice to his work. He fought
the cool label in the press, and he demonstrated in his music that it was
inappropriate. He told *Metronome* in the autumn of 1950:

I can play different styles and appreciate styles; I'm not trying to
shove any style or sound down people's throats. It's fun swingin'
and getting "hot" for a change instead of trying to be cool. I don't
want to become stagnant. I can be a real stompin' tenor man.

Stan expressed the widest range of emotions—from icy coldness to searing
heat—in his music, and the hot side of his soul is evident in many of

his recordings of this period. Examples include his solos recorded on August 17, 1950, with the big band he led at New York's Apollo Theater and the quartet sides he cut on December 10.

The latter date was Stan's first at Roost Records with producer Teddy Reig, an old hand who had presided over Stan's first gig as a leader in 1946 as well as Charlie Parker's "Koko" session. The December 10 session also marked the recording debut of Horace Silver, whom Stan had discovered a couple of months before and who has gone on to a distinguished career as a band leader, soloist, and composer. Stan had traveled as a single to Hartford, Connecticut, to play at The Sundown Club, and the owner provided him with a local rhythm section consisting of Silver, Walter Bolden on drums, and Joe Calloway on bass. Stan was so impressed by Silver's spirited, innovative playing that he signed up the whole trio. Horace remembered:

> I had been saving my money to go to New York, and I tried to do this two times but without enough gumption to make the move. I was apprehensive about the prospects. Stan said he liked my playing and followed through with his promise to hire the entire trio. I dearly owe it to him for leading me into the jazz world. I was and always have been impressed with how deeply Stan loved the music. Master musicians like Stan, Diz, and Miles love it so intensely they are like children when they get together and share energies about the music.

Another outstanding musician whom Stan hired in late 1950 was guitarist Jimmy Raney. He had felt a special kinship with Raney from their first encounter at a Chicago jam session in 1945 when Stan was with Benny Goodman; from the start he wanted to form a group with the guitarist. Stan's enthusiastic recommendation helped Raney win his job with the Second Herd in 1948, and they collaborated happily in small band recording sessions in 1948 and 1949.

But they did not find an opportunity to create a working group until Stan was able to secure a Bop City gig for which he added Raney to his quartet with Horace Silver's trio. Stan and Raney enjoyed the engagement so much that they vowed to make serious efforts to seek other similar bookings; thus was born one of the most fruitful partnerships of Stan's career.

Stan won the *Metronome* poll again for 1950 and for the first time topped the *Down Beat* voting. He recorded another *Metronome* All-Star date on January 23, 1951, in the company of such seasoned collaborators as Davis, Roach, Winding, Chaloff, Konitz, and Terry Gibbs; the outstanding new winner was pianist George Shearing. Charlie Parker had won on alto, but his manager, Norman Granz, vetoed his participation, because Granz believed that playing for nothing was not in Parker's interest; he reasoned that even if the revenues from the date went to charity, *Metronome* benefited more than the musicians did from the large amount of free publicity generated by the sessions. These All-Star tracks are not effective because, in contrast to their 1950 counterparts, none of the soloists is allotted enough space to say anything meaningful.

Granz, who was in 1951 the premier American jazz impresario, planned his first-ever European tour for March, but at the last minute financial hassles with European promoters forced him to cancel. The promoter for the Swedish part of the tour had been very impressed by Stan's recordings, and he reached out across the Atlantic and signed him to play the dates that had been canceled in Sweden. The promoter also recruited the veteran New Orleans clarinet and soprano sax star Sidney Bechet from Paris, where Bechet had become a pop icon and where he had taken up permanent residence. Swedish rhythm sections were provided for the two visitors for the week of concerts that was planned.

The reception Stan received on arriving in Sweden on March 18 deeply affected him, and he talked about it often in later years. As he stepped off the plane bleary-eyed and scruffy after the sixteen-hour flight, he saw on the tarmac a sizable, cheering group led by an important-looking man who was wearing a homburg and holding a bunch of red tulips. Stan turned around to see if he was being followed by a movie star, but there was no one there; the reception was for him. After years of low-key arrivals, he was being treated like a celebrity for the first time. His initial feeling of bewilderment and joy persisted as he was feted and accorded the dignity due a major artist during his entire week in Sweden.

It wasn't an easy week, because he ran out of heroin and suffered from withdrawal; photos taken in Sweden show him looking drained and almost cadaverously gaunt. Despite his travail, however, the junket was musically and commercially successful; Stan even found time to record eight tunes with Swedish musicians. These men were highly professional, and one of them, pianist Bengt Hallberg, showed great promise as an improviser. The talented, drug-free young Swedes stirred in Stan for the first time the feeling that he might struggle free of his addiction. But he was back in the United States on March 26 and immediately began shooting up again.

While addiction continued to hold Stan captive, his brother Bob ended three years on heroin in the spring of 1951. Bob had drifted through those years getting high with his friends and with Stan and Beverly, dropping in and out of high school but never completing the eleventh grade, almost earning a criminal record. He later recalled a traumatic bust:

> My fifteen-year-old girlfriend and myself both got busted in a pad—Teddy's Pad, on Southern Boulevard. You go and you pay a few bucks and you'd get fixed. I was busted and I got beat up by one of the Federal men who didn't take kindly to my trying to protect my girlfriend from his rifling through her pocketbook.
>
> They took pictures of the entire place, and there was a picture of me with blood and tears rolling down my face. And I had my hands wrapped up. This girl Lynn had these big, big beautiful blue eyes, like a deer, like a doe. . . .
>
> They let me go later, and I never got a record.
>
> Several months after, a co-editor of *Life* magazine came up and tried to convince my parents to allow that picture to be put on the cover of *Life* magazine. My parents never really had a good sense of what to do in those circumstances, and they went to my father's brother. He said, "Absolutely not." And it was probably a good thing.

Bob tried to kick his habit several times, but he did not possess sufficient motivation to stay off for good until he found, by chance, an apprentice acting job in Connecticut which gave him a purpose in life beside getting high. And getting clean was made easier for him when Al and Goldie finally left the criminal milieu of Southern Boulevard and found a small apartment on Union Turnpike in a lower-middle-class neighborhood in Queens. His parents also did what they thought was best in the circumstances; they provided Bob with lots of alcohol. He remembered:

> When this acting thing got rolling, my parents would stock the refrigerator with beer and have schnapps up in the closet. They bought their first TV set . . . to keep me at home. And then it was drink, drink, drink. I never even realized that there was a similarity or relationship between drugs and alcohol. I switched from drugs to alcohol and I became a rather functional person, but I really couldn't think of life without getting high for a long, long time.

While Bob was kicking heroin, Stan was busy at Birdland and elsewhere and was booking a satisfying number of engagements with Jimmy Raney.

He took Jimmy into the studio for Teddy Reig of Roost Records on August 15, 1951, to cut five tracks with Horace Silver, drummer Roy Haynes, and bassist Leonard Gaskin.

Raney, who came from Kentucky, had the lanky frame and the long, angular face of the southern farmers who stare out of the Depression photographs Walker Evans made for the Farm Security Administration; like Stan, he was a melodist who could create lithe, relaxed improvisations even at the fastest tempos, and he possessed an uncanny ability to anticipate Stan's musical ideas. Stan adjusted his mouthpiece and his embouchure to adapt to the sonority of Raney's guitar, and the two of them played unison and contrapuntal lines as if they were opposite sides of the same heartbeat.

Each of the five August 15 tracks is only three minutes in length to allow issuance on both the 78-rpm and the LP (33-rpm) formats, but the musicians make the best of their solo opportunities. They play one standard, Jerome Kern's "The Song Is You," and dig into four new tunes, including one by pianist Silver. All are taken at brisk tempos set unerringly by Haynes, and Stan, Raney, and Silver are highly energized. Stan's playing is particularly hot and aggressive, and he and Raney enjoy some lively counterpoint on "The Song Is You." The tracks were issued as *Chamber Music by the Stan Getz Quintet.*

Silver left the unit a few weeks later, because he wanted to settle down in New York and participate in its bubbling jazz scene. He was much in demand and quickly found work as a single and with leaders such as Terry Gibbs, Art Blakey, and Coleman Hawkins. His place in the quintet was taken by Al Haig, who was one of Raney's closest friends. Haynes and Gaskin also wanted to move on and were replaced by Tiny Kahn and Curley Russell, respectively.

On September 9, while Beverly was giving birth to a second son— David Allen—at the Misericordia Hospital in New York, Stan and the quintet were in Chicago playing to rave reviews at the Blue Note Club. *Down Beat*'s headline read "Fresh Ideas, Crack Men Make New Getz 5 Great" and its reporter wrote:

> Stan Getz's quintet sounded great in its Blue Note two-weeker. Jimmy Raney, Curley Russell, Al Haig, and Tiny Kahn make up as good a rhythm section as you'll find in jazz today, and Stan, at ease in front of such swinging support, was playing at his highest level.
>
> With Jimmy's guitar being used like a horn, usually playing unison a third away from Getz's tenor, the group gets a big,

cohesive sound, and is also in a position to do some experimenting. On the chords of "Cherokee," for example, Raney has written
a canon-like line. . . . Tiny, too, is doing some writing.

    Several bookings are in store for the combo . . . so the threat
of being forced to break up for lack of work is small. And all that
suits us just fine, for Stan finally has some men with him whose
backing makes him extend himself. Result: one of the best small
groups we've heard in many months.

Teddy Reig decided that he would next record the quintet "live," and
he chose as his venue the Storyville Club in Boston. George Wein, who
owned the place, had used the name Storyville for a succession of night-
spots that he ran in the Boston area before he struck gold with the Newport Jazz festival and its successors; he booked the quintet opposite Billie
Holiday and her trio, and he and Reig turned on the recording machines
the night of October 28, 1951. The resulting LPs were released as *At
Storyville, Volumes 1 and 2.*

Jazz producers had begun to realize the creative possibilities of extended
improvisations on the recently introduced LP record, and—writing off the
78-rpm market—Reig told the soloists to take several choruses on each
number. They recorded thirteen tunes in sixty-seven minutes that night,
or more than five minutes per tune; the longest cut lasts well over
seven minutes.

The Storyville recordings capture Stan at one of the creative peaks of
his career. He plays with brawny intensity, and the empathy he feels with
his colleagues constantly pushes him to flights of inspired melody. Raney
keeps pace with unflagging invention and lyricism.

    Ten of the thirteen numbers are played at tempos from medium fast
to blistering. "Parker 51," written by Raney and named for his friend Ray
Parker, is taken at 344 beats per minute—a faster pace than even Charlie
Parker's "Koko." The coordination shown by Stan and Jimmy playing
intertwining lines on this number is so precise that the two men are like
pilots on the Navy Blue Angels daredevil team doing barrel rolls wing-to-
wing at six hundred miles per hour. Their performance perfectly illustrates
the point critic Stanley Crouch made when he wrote about:

    . . . how much jazz teaches us about the relationship of the brain
    to the motor areas of the body. The conception and the execution
    of quality ideas in a mobile environment—giving order to the
    present—is probably jazz's greatest contribution to our under-
    standing of human potential.

Drummer Tiny Kahn, whose three-hundred-pound heft belied his fluid dexterity, is outstanding throughout. He pushes the unit along with authority, he takes imaginative solos, and his time never wavers. Haig and Kotick provide solid support, although Haig occasionally falters when his fingers cannot execute his ideas at the faster tempos.

Stan sat in with Billie Holiday every night during their joint Storyville engagement, and he can be heard on a broadcast air check gracefully accompanying her on October 29, 1951.

In early 1952, Johnny Smith, a friend of Stan's who played guitar at the NBC radio and TV studios in New York, told Stan about an opportunity for steady work there. Stan saw a chance to come off the road and recharge his batteries, and he took the job. The move meant less income, he told *Down Beat*, but he enjoyed the variety of settings at NBC, and he was keeping his jazz options open:

> I can imagine some guys finding this kind of work dull, but to me it's great. On "The Kate Smith Show," for instance, I had to play baritone, tenor, clarinet, and bass clarinet. On "The Jane Pickens Show" I play clarinet only. Once I even played some jazz clarinet.
>
> The other night I did "The Cameo Television Theater Show." I was the only musician on it. There I was, all by myself playing bass clarinet. I had to create some themes, mood music to hold the sequences together. . . .
>
> One of the nice things about this job is that I get to hear the NBC Symphony at work. I'd like to play bassoon in the Symphony. I'm going to start playing bassoon on the pop programs as soon as I've studied some. . . .
>
> I can still play plenty of jazz dates. I have a deal to work Birdland six months out of the year, and if I take an offer that comes in to play the summer on the French Riviera, I can take a leave of absence from NBC.

On March 11, 1952, Stan took part in a Roost studio date with a quintet headed by Johnny Smith; Don Lamond was the drummer. They recorded four tunes, and one of them, the title track "Moonlight in Vermont," became Stan's biggest hit since "Early Autumn"; once again he had created a caressing melody etched with an aching tone which connected right on with the romantic longings of the American public. The tune was played at a slow tempo; Smith took most of the solo space and provided a lush chordal setting for Stan's choruses.

The bright promise of the NBC job tarnished quickly, and a couple of months after the "Moonlight in Vermont" session, Stan quit the network. Years later he told *Down Beat*:

> It was just horrible. I was more like a technician than a musician—just press the right button at the right time, that's it. I used to double on all sorts of things; I'd play clarinet, bass clarinet, alto, tenor, baritone. After about three months of it, I began taking bookings with the quintet—I think Jimmy Raney was on the band at the time.
>
> I would work from 12 to 5 on the Kate Smith show, an afternoon television spectacular, and then catch a plane for Rochester or wherever. So I was working seven nights and five days a week, flying back and forth every day. Or if we worked, say, in Atlantic City, where there's no plane, I'd drive . . . four hours there and back. After a while I just got fed up and gave up the studio work.

"Moonlight in Vermont" flew out of the record stores during the summer of 1952, and Stan was besieged with bookings. He began earning more than $1,000 per week. Aside from a small sum he spent each week to subsidize his father in a new business, a small specialty print shop, he didn't have much to show for it. His and Beverly's addictions had become so expensive that they would drive six hours round-trip between Levittown on Long Island and Philadelphia to score cheap heroin. At a crest in popularity, Stan was in fact digging a deep financial hole for himself; he was not paying the IRS the taxes he was withholding for his musicians.

The club owners insisted that he perform "Moonlight in Vermont" once each night; aside from this he was free to play whatever he liked. Most of his bookings were for the quintet with Jimmy Raney, and when he wasn't playing his favorite standards such as "These Foolish Things," "Strike Up the Band," and "Stella by Starlight," he featured tunes by Jimmy, Horace Silver, and other young composers such as Johnny Mandel and Gigi Gryce.

Stan worked as a single in California from mid-August to mid-October 1952, and for one week substituted for Gerry Mulligan while Mulligan was trying to kick his drug habit; the Mulligan group was a pianoless quartet that featured trumpeter Chet Baker. Eliminating the piano intrigued Stan, because it allowed the sonority of the horns to be heard more clearly.

Stan returned to the East Coast in late October, and soon after hired three new musicians—Bill Crow on bass, Frank Isola on drums, and

Duke Jordan on piano—to form what was to be his last working unit with Rancy.

Crow remembers that he was shaken up by two aspects of Stan's personality—his promiscuity and his addiction:

> He always had five or six girls. I remember on my first job with him in Boston, I couldn't believe the skill with which he manipulated all of these women. He had girls that he knew in Boston, there was a girl who had flown up from New York to be with him, and then Beverly came up in the middle of the week.
>
> He had them all in different rooms in the same hotel, and one night they were even all sitting at the table in front of the bandstand while he played. And each of them thought that she was with him. I don't know how he managed this. I was absolutely flabbergasted.

And Crow found that heroin made Stan a difficult boss:

> Heroin had a different effect on Stan than it did on most junkies I knew. The others just became passive and distant when they were high. Stan had a pleasant disposition when he was sober, but when using drugs he could be awash with maudlin sentiment one minute and cold, distrustful, and cruel the next. Discussing him with friends at Jim and Andy's bar one day, Zoot Sims said, "Yeah, Stan's a nice bunch of guys!"

Crow recalled two instances when Stan's addiction brought him close to death. The first occurred as a result of a run-in with the police:

> Stan came up out of Birdland. He ran up to 110th Street and copped from the street corner connections that he used to cop from. Did up his little bit and rushed down and made the first set at Birdland.
>
> Comes upstairs. His car was parked not far from Birdland on Broadway, and a couple of narcotics officers grabbed him. They're sitting in the car with him. Stan was very good at copping pleas, he had a baby face and he knew how to beg and plead and sound like someone who was very innocent, someone who had just fallen into evil companions and all that. And the baby shoes were hanging on his mirror.
>
> A lot of guys saw him get grabbed by these two guys, and see

him sitting in the car, and they assumed that they are going to take him to jail. The word is all around downstairs at Birdland within fifteen minutes. That kind of word travels fast.

So, he actually talked them into releasing him—as though he was a first offender and a loving husband, who was in terrible trouble if his wife found out, his little kids and all that—and so these guys took pity on him and let him go with a stern talking-to.

He gets right in the car and drives back up to 110th Street. Now the word has already preceded him up there that he just got busted, and everybody makes the assumption that the only way he could have gotten away was to have fingered his connection.

Usually what would happen in a case like that is they would sell you some poisoned heroin and that would be your punishment. They called that a hot shot. And a guy who told me this story from the 110th Street end said it was just by the intervention of another guy who said, "Don't do it, Stan's okay," that he wasn't murdered.

Stan's second brush with death occurred when he and Bill dropped in on a party to visit with Stan's old schoolmate, a man named Blackie. Bill remembered that when he decided to leave, he found Stan in a basement rec room with four or five other men:

He was leaning on the pool table, tying up his arm and getting ready to shoot up some heroin. I said, "Come on Stan, don't do that. It's time to go home."

"I'll be right with you," he frowned. "I just want to do up one more little taste."

He injected the drug, loosened the tie on his arm, turned pale, and collapsed on the floor. Blackie quickly rolled him over on his back.

"He isn't breathing!"

"Oh my God," yelled the host. "Get him out of here! I don't want no stiff in my house!"

"Push on his ribs!" I shouted. "Artificial respiration! He's turning blue!"

Blackie pumped his chest while I pried his mouth open and pulled his tongue forward. After a few tense moments, Stan made a strangling noise and sucked in some air. His color returned, and he began breathing on his own again.

RIGHT: Stan's mother, Goldie Yampolsky, was a teenage beauty when this photograph was taken circa 1924. *Photograph from the Collection of Beverly McGovern.* BELOW: Al and Goldie Getz on December 24, 1925, the day they were married. He was twenty-one and she was eighteen. *Photographs from the Collection of Bob Getz.*

LEFT: Stan takes five at age two—1928. *Photograph from the Collection of Beverly McGovern.*
BELOW: Stan and his brother, Bob, caught in a happy moment in 1935. Stan was eight and Bob was three. *Photograph from the Collection of Bob Getz.*

LEFT: Al and Goldie Getz striding down a New York street during the early 1950s.
Photograph from the Collection of Beverly McGovern.

BELOW: Stan stands proudly in his prayer shawl on his Bar Mitzvah day—1940.
Photograph from the Collection of Beverly McGovern.

The Jack Teagarden band posing—in January 1944—for a publicity photo at Universal Studios, where they were performing in a musical film. Teagarden is holding his trombone at the center of the picture and Stan, age sixteen, sits at the right end of the first row. *Photograph from the Collection of Frank Driggs.*

The sax section of the Stan Kenton band rises for a musical fanfare at the urging of its leader—who stands at the far right—during the summer of 1944. Stan is the second sax player from the right. *Photograph from the Collection of Frank Driggs.*

Lester Young, the "President" and Stan's idol, is backed by Count Basie's band as he solos in shades at Catalina Island, California, in 1939. *Photograph from the Collection of Frank Driggs.*

Stan soloing with the Benny Goodman band during their highly successful engagement at the Terrace Room in Newark, New Jersey, in December 1945. Benny is seen in the background accompanying him. *Photograph
from the Collection of Frank Driggs.*

ABOVE: Woody Herman and the Second Herd, the "Four Brothers" band, performing at New York's Commodore Hotel in May 1948. Serge Chaloff solos as fellow brothers Stan, Al Cohn, and Zoot Sims (front row left to right) sit it out. Guitarist Jimmy Rainey sits to Stan's right. The seated singer is Mary Ann McCall. *From the Collection of Frank Driggs.* LEFT: Beverly Byrne, Stan's first wife and the mother of his three oldest children, Steve, David, and Bev, in a 1946 publicity still when she was a vocalist with the Randy Brooks band. *Photograph from the Collection of Beverly McGovern.*

A December 1949 poster of Birdland's successful opening show, described as a "Journey Thru Jazz 1920-1950." The show, coming soon after Stan's blockbuster hit recording of "Early Autumn," signaled his acceptance among the jazz elite as he shared the bill with giants such as Lester Young and Charlie Parker. A young Harry Belafonte was also featured. *From the Collection of Dick Hyman.*

Stan loved big bands, but to his regret he had only one opportunity during his career to lead one. It featured Gerry Mulligan, Zoot Sims, Billy Taylor, and Roy Haynes and performed at New York's Apollo Theater in August 1950. Stan looks weary in this shot taken in the alley behind the theater. *From the Collection of Frank Driggs.*

An unidentified fan sits between Stan and Charlie Parker in this photo from the early 1950s. Behind them are Latin jazz stars Mario Bauza and Machito. *Photograph by Hilda Grillo. Collection of Beverly McGovern.*

Stan with Miles Davis at a *Metronome* All-Star recording session on January 23, 1951. Ralph Burns, who wrote "Early Autumn," the song that catapulted Stan to stardom, stands between them. *Photograph from the Collection of Frank Driggs.*

RIGHT: Stan and Jimmy Raney during a quintet gig at Boston's Storyville Club on October 29, 1951. *Photograph by Bob Parent, courtesy of Don Parent.* BELOW: Stan gave Horace Silver's career a big boost when he hired him out of an obscure Hartford, Connecticut, club in 1950 and provided him with his first opportunity to record. This 1961 photo captures the intensity Horace always brings to his music. *Photograph by Chuck Stewart.*

When he opened his eyes, he scowled at Blackie and said, "Man, get off me! You're getting my suit all dirty!"

"Motherfucker! You were dead!" yelled Blackie, jumping to his feet. "I've been pumping air into you! You were blue, man! You were dead!"

Stan got up and brushed himself off. He gave everyone a surly look and said, "Well, I bet I'm higher than any of you."

Stan's habit did not prevent the quintet from finding plenty of club work in the Northeast and booking the occasional concert. They took part in Duke Ellington's Twenty-Fifth Anniversary Celebration at Carnegie Hall on November 14, 1952; this event also featured Charlie Parker with Strings, the Ahmad Jamal Trio, and guest soloists Dizzy Gillespie and Billie Holiday.

Overwhelming ticket demand dictated an additional midnight concert, and more than five thousand people attended the two shows, one of which was recorded. Stan's quintet was given a generous forty minutes on stage at each performance. Their second set—which was recorded and released as *Stan Getz Quintet at Carnegie Hall*—included the obligatory rendition of "Moonlight in Vermont"; whereas the Roost recording was mostly Johnny Smith, this version is all Stan and is taken at a faster, more swinging tempo. They also played surging, stomping versions of Gershwin's "Strike Up the Band" and Raney's "Parker 51." Stan dedicated the latter to Ben Webster, who had come to fame with Ellington and who was in the audience, and he calls it "Cherokee" for the tune whose chords formed the basis of the "Parker 51" line.

The most important long-term consequence for Stan of the "Moonlight in Vermont" disc was that it led to a contract with Norman Granz. Granz had been impressed with the emotional power of Stan's playing and the sensational sales of the recording, and he signed Stan to an exclusive contract with his Clef label starting on December 10, when Stan's Roost contract expired.

Stan was excited to join Granz's entourage because Clef had much wider distribution than Roost and considerably greater resources for promotion; in addition, an affiliation with Granz held the promise of joining his lucrative tours with outstanding musicians. The autumn 1951 tour, for example, had featured Ella Fitzgerald, Gene Krupa, Lester Young, Roy Eldridge, Flip Phillips, Bill Harris, Illinois Jacquet, Ray Brown, Oscar Peterson, and Hank Jones.

NORMAN GRANZ, a gangling, unfailingly energetic man, is both a bleeding heart liberal and a ruthlessly effective capitalist. From the beginning, his primary motivation has been to achieve racial justice. As he told *Down Beat* in December 1951:

> My aims should be listed in this order—first, sociological. To promote tolerance and the elimination of racial discrimination; second, pure business, or to put it as plainly as possible, to make money; and third—and last, mind you—to sell jazz.

His jazz career began in 1943 at age twenty-four when he was a film editor at MGM. He was indignant that Los Angeles jazz clubs admitted only white patrons, and he began renting the clubs on off nights to stage jam sessions for integrated audiences. His confidence received a major boost when, on July 2, 1944, he organized a successful benefit concert at the Los Angeles Philharmonic Auditorium for the Sleepy Lagoon Defense Fund; the Fund had been organized to provide legal aid for a group of young Mexicans who had been sent to San Quentin prison after someone was killed during the so-called "zoot suit" riots in Los Angeles.

The concert drew two thousand people and featured Nat King Cole, saxophonist Illinois Jacquet, guitarist Les Paul, pianists Joe Sullivan and Meade Lux Lewis, and clarinetist Barney Bigard. Illinois Jacquet drew the most attention; according to *Down Beat*, he "had the kids wild with the screaming high notes of his tenor sax." The music critic of the *Los Angeles Times*, who was strongly biased toward classical music, declined a personal invitation from Granz with the statement that it would be "beneath her dignity" to cover such an event.

The success of the Sleepy Lagoon show emboldened Granz four weeks later to promote another one at the Philharmonic Auditorium. It was a straight commercial entertainment starring Count Basie's band and Joe Sullivan, and it netted a tidy profit. Soon Granz was staging monthly concerts; he dubbed them "Jazz at the Philharmonic" (or JATP).

He then hit on the idea of making an extra profit by recording his concerts. The big distributors believed that issuing recordings with shouts and applause by the audience was outlandish, and the only person willing to touch the initial JATP recordings was a decidedly minor distributor named Moe Asch. The first disc sold about 150,000 copies, and subsequent ones were more successful; Asch went broke due to bad decisions unrelated to JATP, but Granz's fortunes took off.

The widespread popularity of the recordings encouraged him to book his artists for national tours. After a false start in 1945, the tours met with mounting success beginning in 1946. The musicians he chose played in a directly emotional, visceral way. As Granz told reporters:

> My concerts are primarily emotional music.... I could put on as cerebral a concert as you like, but I'd rather go the emotional route. And do you know, the public's taste reflects mine—the biggest flop I've ever had in my life was the tour I put on with some of the cerebral musicians like Dave Brubeck and Gerry Mulligan.
>
> Jazz is so alive that it makes *you* feel alive.... I think that music should make you happy. It should have energy, a lot of energy. When I hear Oscar Peterson, Roy Eldridge, Dizzy, or Benny Carter, I'm swept up in a marvelous burst of energy and good feeling.
>
> Roy [Eldridge] is so intense about *everything* that it's far more important for him to dare, to try to achieve a particular peak— even if he fails in the attempt—than it is to play it safe. That *is* jazz.

Granz paid his musicians top dollar, and he was vehement about social issues:

> I felt that it made no kind of sense to treat a musician with any kind of respect and dignity onstage, and then make him go around to the back door when he was offstage. We were battling not only anti-black discrimination, but discrimination against all jazz musicians. I insisted that my players were given the same respect as Leonard Bernstein or Heifetz, because they were just as good— both as men and as musicians....
>
> We still have to make some concessions to prejudice here and there, but these concessions are gradually becoming fewer and fewer. One of these days, we'll all put up together in the best hotel in Atlanta and no one will think anything about it.

And the musicians loved him. As Dizzy Gillespie said:

> The importance of JATP is that it was the original "first class" treatment for jazz musicians. With Norman, you traveled first class, stayed in first class hotels, and never played anywhere there was segregated seating.

GRANZ WAS EAGER to get Stan into the studio, and he produced the first quintet session for his label on December 12, 1952, only a couple of days after the Roost contract expired. He wanted to spotlight Stan as a ballad player, and he got his money's worth.

Stan, featured throughout, creates at least four gemlike solos on the eight well-known romantic tunes Granz chose for the date; Raney is relegated to the role of accompanist. Stan spins out a voluptuous array of sounds on the five slow numbers, and he tells particularly compelling stories of vulnerability and loss on "Body and Soul" and "Stars Fell on Alabama." This is the kind of music one imagines Gatsby and Daisy dancing to on the terrace overlooking Long Island Sound. The two songs taken at fast tempos—"The Way You Look Tonight" and "Lover Come Back to Me"—are given romping interpretations that stand among Stan's best work with Raney.

The quintet owed Teddy Reig at Roost another session, but it found itself in a bind because it could not schedule the date until December 19, nine days too late to avoid a contractual conflict with Granz; Reig solved this problem by entering a false day of record, December 5, with the union. Whatever the date, it was a sad one for Reig, because Stan was far and away his best-selling artist, and "Moonlight in Vermont" was his only runaway hit.

To capitalize on the success of "Moonlight in Vermont," Reig had Stan record three ballads, and to promote Birdland and insure airplay by Symphony Sid, he chose as the fourth track George Shearing's "Lullaby of Birdland." Raney plays beautiful unison lines with Stan and lays down emphatic accompaniments for him, but he has virtually no solo space; Stan's balladeering is impeccable.

On December 29, 1952, twelve days after the Roost date, Granz brought the quintet back to the studio to record four sides—three more romantic songs and a sprightly new tune by Gigi Gryce, "Hymn of the Orient." Stan and his men maintain the same high standard that they established on the first date for Granz.

The 12 tracks recorded for Granz on December 12 and December 29 were originally issued as 78's and were later put together as an LP, *Stan Getz Plays.*

Toward the end of the December 29 session, Raney took Stan into the men's room and told him he could no longer work with him. Raney, who was not a user, abhorred Stan's drug scene with his pushers and hangers-on, his daily anxieties about supplies, and his paranoia about the police. Stan was crushed by Raney's defection, and he tried strenuously to woo him back. He jeopardized his relationship with Granz by appearing illegally on a Raney-led Roost session on April 23, 1953, where he adopted the pseudonym "Sven Coolson." Stan originally wished to use the pseudonym "Djuh Berrih" for Chu Berry, a deceased sax player whom he admired, but the producer favored "Sven Coolson," and he prevailed.

Raney remembered a time when Stan asked him to return, swearing that he was clean and that there wouldn't be any further problems with drugs:

> I got in town and went up to the hotel, knocked on Stan's door, and I could see when he answers the door that he's stoned. And I say, "Oh, Stan, I thought you told me that it was going to be different."
>
> And Stan is saying, "No, no, man, I'm not on anything. I've got this terrible headache and I took some prescription drugs . . . and I've been up all night and I'm really tired," and blah, blah, blah.
>
> And I said, "Come on Stan, don't give me that crap. I can see that you're stoned."
>
> "No, really, Jimmy," and he goes into this long song and dance, and I finally say, "Stan, when I walked in, I saw you push your works underneath the magazine over there."
>
> And Stan gets real angry and says, "Then why did you let me sit here and lie to you for an hour?"

The "Sven Coolson" date spotlighted three tunes by Raney and Thelonious Monk's "Round Midnight" and were included on an LP called *Early Stan.* For the first time since the Storyville session, the quintet was not constricted by the three-minute time limit of the 78-rpm record, and the men used their freedom to good advantage. In contrast to the two Granz sessions and the last one for Roost, Stan was not the featured artist. He and Raney were again equal partners; they both soloed at length and they indulged anew in delightful unison and contrapuntal passages.

In 1990, Mosaic reissued—in a boxed three-CD set—all the Getz-Raney quintet sessions which were originally made for Roost and Granz; an excellent essay by Bill Crow accompanies the CDs.

After Raney left the group, Stan wanted to continue with a quintet, but now he desired a different sound. When his drummer, Frank Isola, suggested using valve trombonist Bob Brookmeyer, Stan jumped at the idea.

Brookmeyer's long, flowing improvisations promised to be very compatible with Stan's, and Bob was an outstanding composer and arranger. He played with the group for a week in early January 1953 and then left to fulfill a six-week commitment to Woody Herman.

Stan hired composer-trombonist Johnny Mandel to fill in until Brookmeyer could rejoin him in early March. He used the interlude with Mandel to adapt his playing to the timbre of the trombone. As he had with Raney's guitar, Stan changed his mouthpiece and his embouchure to blend his sax sound with that of another instrument.

Stan looked forward to Brookmeyer's return, and in early February he told *Down Beat* that he planned to create a sextet by adding himself and Brookmeyer to Gerry Mulligan's pianoless quartet with Chet Baker. Stan described this dream band with intensity, telling the reporter that:

> I'm going out to the coast and when I return at the end of February, I intend to bring with me Gerry Mulligan and Chet Baker. . . . With guys who can blow as much as Gerry, Chet, and Bob, the band should be the end. All three of them will write for the band.

Mulligan, whom Stan had not consulted, became so alarmed when he read this that he fired off a statement which *Down Beat* printed in its next issue. It said in part:

> I don't know what Stan has in mind here when he talks about adding me and Chet to his combo, joining me, or whatever it is, but it's not for me. . . . For years I stayed in the background and wrote arrangements for many bands. Now, in the quartet, I have something that is all mine. I can see no reason for sharing it with anyone.

Stan defused the controversy with a statement a month later in *Down Beat* in which he blamed his interviewer for turning a "pleasant speculation" into a "pretty pat thing." Stan closed by saying:

> The important part of the idea was the musical structure that could be built and the fact that I have access to bookings and a major record label that would be to Gerry's advantage, and he has originality in music that it would groove me to work with.

That's all! That's it! So, take me off your list of leaders with
evil designs on young talent.

Stan's dream band died there, but three years later Mulligan created a
pianoless sextet with Brookmeyer, Zoot Sims, and trumpeter Jon Eardley,
whose sound was close to what Stan had in mind.

Stan brought a fresh quintet into the studio for Granz on May 16, 1953;
the only holdover from his previous Granz session was Bill Crow. In
addition to Brookmeyer, the new men were John Williams on piano and
Al Levitt on drums; they had both signed on with Stan in January. The
tracks were in the three-minute, 78-rpm format. Granz chose the Rodgers
and Hart show tune "Have You Met Miss Jones?" plus three songs by
Brookmeyer, but—supervising from the control booth—he was imperious
about Brookmeyer's titles.

After the first recording, he called out, "What's the name of that one?"
" 'A Rustic Dance,' " said Bob.
"Great. Let's call it 'Rustic Hop.' "
Following the second tune, Granz asked again for the name.
" 'Trolley Car,' " Bob answered.
"We got a good mix on that one," said Norman. "Let's call it 'Cool Mix.' "
Brookmeyer, just twenty-three and cowed by the lanky impresario,
laughed and accepted the new titles.

Brookmeyer did not improvise as lyrically as Raney, and he didn't have
the same near-mystical rapport with Stan that Raney did, but he had more
fun. On these four tunes he and Stan engaged in joyous, rollicking musical conversations playing counterpoint, and they blew infectious riffs
(short repeated phrases) beneath each other's solos. The four tracks were
issued as 78's, and "Rustic Hop" is currently in release on the CD *The
Artistry of Stan Getz*.

After the May 16 Granz session, Stan went to California with a quintet
that included Brookmeyer, Isola, Williams, and Teddy Kotick. Williams
remembered the coast-to-coast trip with Stan and Kotick in Stan's car:

> I'd assumed that we ought to leave Monday if we were going to
> open Friday three thousand miles away. But Stan, as always, had
> better things to do on Monday, namely some lovely young lady.
> That happened with him in every city we played. . . .
>
> It was about five o'clock on Tuesday that we finally pulled out
> of Washington. Thankfully there was a friendly little druggist in
> Washington who was a real jazz enthusiast—he particularly loved

Louis Armstrong, as I recall—and with the help of his amphet-
amines, we made it to LA in about sixty hours of driving time.

Stan and his men had sufficient bookings to support themselves into
September, and they freelanced when there was no work for the group
as a unit; Stan found opportunities to play with Jimmy Giuffre and Shelly
Manne and was recorded live on June 12 with the Mulligan quartet,
joining Chet Baker on trumpet, Joe Mondragon on bass, and Larry Bun-
ker on drums. Stan was once more filling in for Mulligan as he struggled
with his addiction; soon after, the struggle took a sad turn when Gerry
was jailed for a narcotics offense.

Stan fell in love with California again, and in July he moved Beverly
and their two boys to a house he rented in Laurel Canyon, north of
Hollywood. The house literally clung to the side of the canyon and was
a strenuous sixty-eight steps above street level.

As Beverly and the kids settled into their new home, the quintet settled
into a club called Zardi's for a seven-week engagement beginning July 21.
Zardi's had rapidly become the number one jazz club in Los Angeles after
manager Ben Arkin changed its policy from Dixieland to modern jazz.

Granz brought Stan's quintet into the studio on July 30 and August 15
and 22, 1953; they waxed eleven tunes for an album called *Interpretations*.
Unlike his previous recordings on May 16, these were destined for 33-rpm
LPs, and the musicians could stretch out; the tracks covered seventy minutes in all. The longer format allowed Stan and Brookmeyer to extend
their happy contrapuntal conversations and to deepen a musical friendship
that Stan characterized in this way:

> We seem to be on the same wave-length musically and personally.
> We complement each other naturally, even though my tenor and
> his valve trombone are in the same register and have the same
> timbre. We have the same yearning for fresh, uncluttered, me-
> lodic improvisation.

On August 3, 1953, Granz inserted Stan into one of his all-star lineups
for the first time—a group that included Count Basie, Buddy Rich, Wardell Gray, the *Down Beat* poll winner Buddy De Franco on clarinet, and
veteran alto sax stars Benny Carter and Willie Smith. Granz set the musicians up in a jam session, a format he often favored because he loved to
give his soloists lots of room to spread their wings. The musicians blew
freely on "Lady Be Good" for twenty minutes and on two blues for twelve
and fifteen minutes, respectively. Then each horn player chose a ballad

to play in a romantic medley; Stan picked "Willow Weep for Me." Stan more than held his own in this company, creating fresh and sinewy improvisations on all four numbers. The tracks were issued as *Norman Granz Jam Sessions #3 and #4*.

Stan was deeply saddened on August 20 when he heard that Tiny Kahn had died the previous day from a heart attack while vacationing on Martha's Vineyard. Kahn, who never touched drugs or alcohol, had suffered a mild attack two months before. His obesity had contributed to his condition, and he was on a corrective diet when he died; in those days before heart surgery, this seemed to be his only path to recovery. Stan, Tiny's best friend, Terry Gibbs, and other contemporaries believed that Tiny's creativity as a composer and arranger equaled that which he brought to the drums. Stan was unstinting in his praise:

> He's one of my favorite drummers of all time.... Tiny would musically get underneath you and lift you up. Most drummers batten you down from the top. And he wrote as well as he played. He personifies the saying "the good die young." He was just the best.

In spite of the quintet's growing musical rapport, their bookings petered out when they finished the Zardi's engagement on September 7. Stan went on tour as the featured soloist with the Stan Kenton band and its singer, June Christy. Williams and Kotick returned to the East Coast, and Brookmeyer and Isola freelanced in California.

After he returned from the Kenton tour in October, Stan gigged mostly in California in groups with Chet Baker, but in early December he was able to put together a week at the Hi-Hat in Boston with Brookmeyer, Kotick, Duke Jordan, and Roy Haynes.

The day he returned to California, December 9, 1953, Granz matched him up in the studio with Dizzy Gillespie and a rhythm section consisting of Oscar Peterson on piano, Herb Ellis on guitar, Ray Brown on bass, and Max Roach on drums for an album named *Diz and Getz*.

The intensity of Stan's playing indicates that he felt especially challenged going mano-a-mano with a heavyweight of Dizzy's stature. *Down Beat* described their encounter as "a high-energy face-off between two masters who push each other to the limit"; this is evident on their first number, "It Don't Mean a Thing (If It Ain't Got That Swing)," which is played at a pace that Stan described as "the fastest tempo in captivity." Dizzy leads off with a blazing solo, but Stan gathers himself and maintains the temperature with a passionate outing of singular muscularity. And

Stan returns thrust for thrust as they exchange four-bar phrases at the end of the number. The men play three ballads on the date, and on "The Talk of the Town," Stan achieves a peak of poignant lyricism which even Dizzy can't reach. With this session Stan confirmed to Granz and the world that he was a complete saxophone player, equally adept at up-tempo wailing and romantic balladry.

After the breakup of the quintet with Brookmeyer, Stan was able to regroup and secure both a mid-December engagement at Zardi's and a lucrative Detroit booking over the Christmas holidays with a brand new quintet featuring Chet Baker on trumpet and Jimmy Rowles on piano.

Stan was glad that he had moved the family back to California—especially after they determined in October that Beverly was pregnant again. They were happy to replace the kids' snowsuits with T-shirts and shorts and to eat barbecue in the backyard in shirtsleeves in December. Norman Granz was recording Stan with the elite of the jazz world, and good bookings were easy to come by. They were as content as a junkie couple could be with an income equivalent to $160,000 in 1996 dollars; they had a reliable heroin connection and were able to stay high all the time, even as they watched their boys romp in the woods by their house or in the sand and surf of the Pacific.

BUSTED   EIGHT

ZARDI'S WAS CRAWLING with narcs on the night of December 18, 1953. At that time in Los Angeles, heroin use had not yet spread to affluent Bel Air and Beverly Hills or to the middle-class suburbs. It was limited to the jazz community and a few notorious ghetto areas. The narcs concentrated on four or five street corners in the black and Mexican neighborhoods and on a handful of jazz clubs; Zardi's, located on Sunset Boulevard, was one of them.

Ben Arkin, Zardi's manager, had to be pleased that he had booked Stan for this pre-Christmas week. His quintet with Baker and Rowles was filling the place every night. Rowles was the only member of the group who wasn't using heroin.

Stan had grown careless about narcs after nine years of using and no arrests. Rowles recalls:

One time they called me in the back and Stan says, "Here, hold this. Put your hand out, I want you to hold something for me." I put my hand out, and he poured a whole bunch of heroin packets into it. The place is loaded with fuzz, and I'm standing back there holding all the evidence. I looked at them, and these guys were fighting over how much dope they were going to get. So I said to the bass player, "Hey, give me your hat," and I dumped the stuff there, and I left.

Stan may have been careless, but he was not blatant enough to shoot up in the club. Rowles remembers:

Stan would get me to drive him around to service stations between sets so he could find his little box with his works in it. I'd be sitting in my car, and he'd be looking around over in the bushes behind the Shell station somewhere in Hollywood, and he'd go in the men's room and lock the door and fix himself and come back out. Then I'd have to stop at another place where he would hide the little box again. I'd have to remember where it was so he could come back there and get it.

It was 3:00 A.M. on December 19 when Stan slid into his car after the last set. He soon took a right off Sunset and climbed into the steep, narrow turns of Laurel Canyon. Fatigue had overcome any instinct toward paranoia, and he failed to notice the sedan that was following him.

Within ten minutes he had parked in front of his home on Laurel Pass, climbed up the sixty-eight steps to the front door, and let himself in. He had barely taken off his jacket when he heard a knock and a male voice saying, "We need your help. We ran up behind you as we were parking, and our bumper locked up with yours." Stan grabbed a loaded .32 revolver, opened the door, and pointed it at the three men standing there. LAPD Detective John O'Grady identified himself as a narcotics officer and drew his own gun, and Stan immediately put down the .32.

Beverly was half asleep, but she could make out the words "narcotics officer" and, as the detectives pushed their way into the house, she ran to the bathroom with what the officers later said looked like a small bundle of heroin. Despite an order to stop, she flushed the bundle down the toilet.

When Stan was confronted with the needle marks on his arms, he admitted to taking a pop that night and was hustled down to the station house. In 1953 in California, just being a user was a crime, and Stan was booked for "vagrancy, drug addict" and released on a $1,000 bond. The police decided not to charge him with "being an addict in possession of a deadly weapon" or to charge Beverly with obstructing justice.

The next morning the *Los Angeles Times* ran a headline that read, "Musician Stan Getz 27 Jailed in Dope Charge." Above it was a photo of one of the arresting officers examining Stan's .32 as Stan looked on stiffly. The headline in the *Los Angeles Herald-Express* announced "Top Jazz Musician Nabbed in Dope Raid on Hollywood Home—Needle Marks on Arm Told," and the *Hollywood Citizen-News* ran one in extra large type reading, "Dope Officers Disarm Hollywood Band Leader."

Stan pleaded guilty on January 20, 1954, after a judge denied his request for a postponement to allow him to perform on a Norman Granz tour in Europe. The judge ordered Stan to return on February 17 for sentencing, adding that "in such cases, a ninety-day sentence is generally the minimum." He directed that Stan's jail term start as soon as he was sentenced.

Stan felt comforted that despite his troubles, his fans still loved him. Both *Metronome* and *Down Beat* announced in January that Stan had won their polls again.

On January 23 Granz recorded Stan doing easy, relaxed interpretations of four standard tunes in a session which contrasts starkly with his previous high-energy outing with Dizzy Gillespie. Accompanist Jimmy Rowles has some sparkling moments on piano, but drummer Max Roach and bassist Bob Whitlock have little else to do but keep time. The tracks, originally released as 78's, were, in 1988, tacked on to the CD reissue of *Stan Getz Plays*.

For his last gig before incarceration, Stan signed on with promoter Gene Norman for an eight-day West Coast tour starting with two sold-out Los Angeles concerts the night of Friday, February 5. Norman knew Stan's work well; he had recorded him in concert in 1948, had managed the Empire Room in Hollywood when Woody's Second Herd played there in 1949, and had for five years played Stan's recordings frequently on his disc jockey show. He had decided to put two groups on the road together: a quintet led by the blind piano star George Shearing and a combo featuring three Lester Young disciples on tenor sax: Stan, Zoot Sims, and Wardell Gray, a rail-thin black man with a fluent, bluesy approach to improvising. Norman saved money by contracting with local promoters to provide the piano-bass-drum accompaniment for the three tenor players in the cities along the way.

Stan and Shearing were the stars of the tour, and the newspaper advertising reflected this. Their names appeared in type four times as large as those of Sims and Gray.

Wardell Gray had made his reputation crossing musical swords with Dexter Gordon in emotional, up-tempo "tenor duels," and Gene Norman decreed that the sax players climax their set every night with a scorching fifteen-minute, three-way battle using the tune "Indiana" as their vehicle. They challenged and prodded each other to escalating heights of originality, and the crowds loved it.

Stan didn't want to go cold turkey in jail, so he decided to kick his habit during the tour. He thought he could ease the rigors of withdrawal by using barbs (barbiturates). He switched to this drug from heroin on the third day of the trip, Monday, February 8.

Stan had functioned very successfully and creatively for nine years as an addict in a highly competitive profession. He used all his wiles to ensure his three daily necessities—his money, his connection, his fixes—and he was forever alert to threats to his routine.

Heroin cuddles the junkie in its arms and whisks him away from all the pain of being himself, from all the depression and guilt, the self-doubt. And the obliteration of pain is only half of what the drug delivers. It also makes the junkie feel powerful and confident and in control. His horn sounds great, his hair is perfect, that chick will be his tonight. Heroin had been Stan's friend, his family, his lover for nine years. Now he was alone. It was gone, and there was nothing to replace it but the anguish he had been running away from.

Mercifully, Stan didn't fall from heroin's embrace all at once. The drug lingered in his system for a while, and the barbs helped to mask the reality of what was happening to his mind and body. But as the days passed, his distress mounted and the barbs began to make things worse rather than better.

Except in the euphoric moments after the junkie fixes and the short period of "nodding out" that immediately follows, he is alert and acutely attuned to what is going on around him. Barbs scare and disorient him because, in order to work, they must put him into a drowsy twilight zone far from his usual state of awareness and control. And the barbs were causing Stan to lose his feisty alertness just as his body was starting to revolt in earnest.

On the third day of withdrawal, Wednesday, the physical symptoms hit him with sledgehammer power. His stomach was knotted with cramps, his skin burned to the touch, and every bone and muscle pulsed with pain. Stan responded by reaching ever more greedily for the twilight zone by swallowing more barbs and adding whiskey to the mix.

He spent the fourth day of withdrawal in a Portland, Oregon, bar, drinking and popping barbs. Portland was the next-to-last stop on the tour, which ended the following evening in Seattle, Washington.

Immediately after the Portland show, a driver whisked George Shearing away to Seattle in a car. Stan delayed the departure of the other men, who milled impatiently around a small bus which had been chartered for them. He was forced to lie down for twenty minutes to allow a fierce attack of cramps to subside. They left at 11:30 P.M.

Stan fell asleep as soon as he boarded the bus, but he was up again quickly. He darted nervously up and down the aisle and launched a shrill verbal attack on an innocent victim—Toots Thielemans, a Belgian member of Shearing's group and the only man ever to make the harmonica a legitimate jazz instrument. Toots, who played excellent guitar as well, doubled on that instrument with Shearing.

Toots was sitting quietly when Stan lurched toward him and grabbed at him and cried out, "The worst insult you can give a musician is to call him insensitive, and you're very insensitive, Toots." Zoot Sims quickly intervened and pulled Stan back to his seat as Stan yelled, "You too, Zoot. You're insensitive, too." Zoot had become Stan's protective older brother and maintained that role for the remainder of the trip. Everyone else in the bus understood what was going on, and Zoot's actions calmed them.

Stan now insisted that they stop for food and booze, and they found a Chinese place just south of the Washington border. He ate something, knocked down two double shots, and returned to the bus with a water glass full of whiskey. He drank it and went chest to chest with Al McKibbon, Shearing's very large bass player. Stan looked up into McKibbon's face and yelled, "You're black, man, but you don't know anything about rhythm." McKibbon, a gentle and scholarly man who outweighed Stan by about fifty pounds, held him at arm's length saying, "Come on, Stan, stop this. You've got to stop this."

Zoot intervened again and returned Stan to his seat. He found a pillow in an overhead rack and whacked Zoot with it till it ripped and a cascade of feathers filled the small bus. Then he slumped in his seat and slept fitfully for four hours till they arrived at the Olympic Hotel in Seattle around 7:20 Friday morning.

When he awoke, Stan experienced a spasm of nausea and his whole body trembled. His head ached, his back ached, everything ached. How was he going to make it through the desperate hours of this day, the next day? He felt trapped in a suffocating web of weakness and pain.

As he dragged himself from the bus, he noticed that a drugstore was open across the street from the hotel, and he made a decision. He was going to get some morphine, a relative of heroin that has the same effect. Just one shot would transport him to a sunny pinnacle where all this pain and misery would disappear, and he would feel beautiful and princely again.

The other men hung around on the pavement to gather up their baggage, but Stan moved swiftly to the reservation desk, checked in, and took the elevator to his room.

Just as swiftly, he was downstairs again. He crossed the street and at 7:40 A.M. entered the drugstore. Mrs. Mary Brewster, the forty-four-year-old cashier and the store's most trusted employee, had let the four fountain ladies in at 7:00 A.M. to start preparing food, and she had opened for business a half hour later. Stan was her first customer.

He held his right hand in his windbreaker pocket with his forefinger simulating the barrel of a gun and told her, "Give me a capsule of morphine. Don't scream. If you do, I'll blow your brains out." Two customers came in and Stan stood by nervously as Mary served them. She managed to whisper "stickup" to one of them, who left and called the police. Then she turned to Stan and said, "Let me see your gun." This totally unnerved him, and he turned and left the store; Mary watched him run back across the street into the hotel.

When Stan returned to his room, he telephoned Mary to apologize. By this time Patrolman Earl Fisher, responding from his squad car to an "armed holdup in progress" radio alert, had entered the store. He picked up an extension phone and listened in.

Stan told Mary, "I'm sorry for the crazy thing I did. I've never done anything like that before. I'm not a stickup man. I'm from a good family. I'm going to commit myself on Wednesday."

"Why don't you commit yourself today?" asked Mary.

"I can't. If I don't get drugs, I'll kill."

Mary told Stan that there was a doctor in the store who wanted to talk with him, and she signaled Fisher to speak. He remembered:

> I thought he'd get suspicious if I used a name like Smith, so I said, "This is Dr. Fishbein. Is there anything I can do to help you?" He started giving me his life history and then I said, "What room are you in, and I'll be over." And he told me. There were other cops in the store now, and I put my hand over the phone and told them to get someone the hell over to the room.

By this time there were a dozen policemen milling around the hotel, and two of them were sent up to arrest Stan.

After he hung up the phone, Stan was flooded by an anguish which welled up behind his breastbone and seared his entire being. He wanted to die. He felt like scum, utterly filthy. He could never undo the disgrace he had brought on his family. He had grievously wounded Goldie; she had suffered so much, and she had cared for him through all the hungry, hard, ugly times. He didn't deserve to live. He swallowed all the barbs he had left—a fistful, a fearsome amount.

The police found Stan walking in the hallway outside his room. They cuffed his wrists behind his back and brought him down to the street, where newspaper photographers took pictures. One of the photos, showing Stan looking out the window of a squad car wide-eyed and filled with fear, ran on the AP wires and was carried by newspapers throughout the country.

Stan's legs felt like Jell-O as he sat and spoke quietly during his questioning at the local jail. When he told the detectives he had fallen into a drug habit only six months before, they laughed because they knew that the deeply scarred needle tracks on his arms meant years of addiction. But he rambled on, telling them:

> I'm a good guy, a family man. My wife's expecting our third kid soon. I love my two boys. I'm no bum, no stickup artist. As soon as I got back to the room I called up the lady on the telephone and apologized for what I had done. Does this look like the way a stickup man acts?
>
> I admit it was a stupid, rash act, but as far as being a thief or a stickup man, I'm from a good family and wouldn't do a thing like that. I've been fighting to get off heroin, and I just got desperate when the barbs didn't work. I'm going down to L.A. next week to do time, and then I'll be clean for life.

The detectives finished with him at about 10:40 A.M. and locked him up in a cell. It had been three hours since the stick-up attempt.

During a routine check of his cell thirty minutes later guards discovered Stan crumpled on his cot unconscious. The prison doctor found Stan's breathing and pulse dangerously shallow and rushed him immediately to the emergency room at Harborview County Hospital.

The final fistful of barbs had brought Stan's respiratory system close to a shutdown; in other words, he was choking to death. The doctors performed an emergency tracheotomy; they cut a hole in Stan's throat, stuck a tube through it into his windpipe, and pumped oxygen into his lungs and drew saliva and phlegm out of them. The procedure saved Stan's life. A short vertical scar below his Adam's apple served as a permanent souvenir of the ordeal.

The hospital was so crowded that Stan's bed was placed in a hallway, but he couldn't tell the difference for two days; he didn't awaken from his comalike sleep until noon on Sunday. When he opened his eyes, he saw the tube leading into his throat, an IV device in his arm feeding him nutrients and medicines to ease the rigors of withdrawal, and a cop standing guard nearby. He felt totally exhausted. The only visitor he received that day was the hospital rabbi making his rounds. Stan felt comforted when the rabbi held his hand and they recited a couple of prayers together in the old familiar Hebrew. His spirits were further buoyed when a nurse brought him a pile of encouraging telegrams, phone messages, and letters. National publication of the AP wirephoto had elicited a wide sympathetic response.

The next day Stan was strong enough to talk to reporters. Tears ran down his cheeks as he sobbed and told them he would break the narcotics habit, "not only for the sake of my wife and children, but for my Dad and Mom." Then he said:

> I started fooling around with the stuff a few years ago, but I didn't get the habit until about a year ago. It's awfully hard to explain why I did it. . . . It seemed to close everybody out and I could concentrate better on my music in a world of my own.
>
> I was voted tops in *Down Beat* and *Metronome* five consecutive times. I played with the tops—Woody Herman, Benny Goodman, Jimmy Dorsey, Stan Kenton. . . . I was making about $1,250 a week. The stuff was costing me $70 a day. It took everything I had. Of course, I was helping out Dad—set him up in a little creative print shop in New York. I was helping out my wife's folks too.
>
> I think I can make it now. I know I can, because I've got to, for my wife and kids. My wife's expecting a baby any day now.

Stan neglected to tell the journalists that his wife was as deeply addicted as he was.

That afternoon an assistant district attorney came to his bedside with good news. He told Stan that he had been booked as "a habitual user of narcotics" and not for the more serious crime of attempted robbery. After he explained that Stan would be released on a $1,500 bond the following day to fly to Los Angeles to begin his jail term there, he made him sign a document promising to return voluntarily to Seattle at his own expense to face the charge there.

Two days later a Los Angeles judge looked down from the bench at Stan and flayed him verbally. His lecture reflected the 1950s assumption that moral inadequacy was at the root of addiction; it was not until a decade later that very persuasive medical evidence showed that it was a disease and official attitudes began to change. The judge said:

> You have talent, family and a good background, but despite an income of a thousand dollars a week, you are not only broke but your family is living under deplorable conditions. They are sleeping on the floor while you travel in luxury spending money on yourself—and doing what comes naturally.
>
> You're a poor excuse for a man. If you can't behave yourself, someone else is going to have to look after you. Getting something up that backbone of yours is the problem. It's time you grew up.

The judge sentenced Stan to six months in jail plus three years probation, adding that "anything less than 180 days would be a waste of time."

The Seattle prosecutor decided to drop his charge against Stan after he learned of the length of the Los Angeles sentence.

Fortunately, Stan was directed to start his prison term in the jail ward of the Los Angeles General Hospital, where doctors would help him through the final stages of withdrawal.

On Stan's third day as a prisoner, February 19, Beverly Getz was rushed to Los Angeles General, where she gave birth to a daughter, Beverly Patricia. She was assigned a bed on the eighth floor, five floors below the ward where Stan was being kept under armed guard.

THE ABYSS

NINE

THE FIRST THING the guards did with Stan after he was moved from the hospital to the Los Angeles County Jail was to make him strip. Then they threw him into a filthy shower room, where they forced him to wash with the coarse yellow soap that they used on the walls and floors of the cells. Before he could towel off, they hit his body with a caustic disinfectant which they shot from spray guns, and every one of his pores burned. As he huddled in pain, the guards gave him a towel, a set of ill-fitting clothes, a pillow, a dirty mattress that smelled of urine and vomit, and a tattered old blanket.

Stan dressed and they took him to his cell in a section of the jail called the hype tank which was reserved for "hypes"—the narcotics prisoners. The tank was run with fists of iron by two "trusty" prisoners who maintained their power by paying off the guards. The trusties controlled and made profits from everything, including the food. Once a week, when stew was served, they would take the day's ration of bread and all the meat from the pot. They would eat what they wanted, and then sell sandwiches to the other prisoners for fifty cents each. Vendors were allowed in the cell block to sell cigarettes and books and candies, and the trusties would buy up all the five-cent candy bars and sell them to the other prisoners for fifteen or twenty cents each.

Stan thanked God that the judge had sent him to the hospital, where the doctors carefully weaned him of dope, because every day he watched prisoners kicking the habit alone in dank cells where the lights were never turned off. They were a pitiable group—their skin burning, their bodies convulsed, their stomachs throwing up anything they tried to eat.

The trusties administered or sanctioned beatings to any prisoners whom they believed had crossed them. Stan, who was assigned to a floor-sweeping detail, made himself as unobtrusive as possible and obeyed all his orders quickly and quietly. By lying low, he rarely incurred the wrath of the trusties and suffered only a few beatings.

Back in Laurel Canyon, Beverly was selling off furniture and shepherding the small amount of money that she and Stan had saved, spending it on drugs and food only. Beverly's friend Pat Cameron, the singer who had gotten her the job with the Randy Brooks band in 1946, remembered those times:

> She became completely addicted. . . . She had that addictive personality. . . . I lost contact with her. . . . Stanley's in jail and I see her picture in the paper holding baby Beverly . . . and I say, "Oh, my God." And I tracked her down. She was in terrible shape. . . .
>
> I went to Hollywood in '54; my marriage broke up. . . . I was pretty screwed up at that time myself. I was walking around with a broken heart and a broken home. She helped me and I helped her. We were both on, you know—the time that Stanley was in jail. I had this thing and she had the baby.
>
> We were together. I was with her about four months. March, April, May, June. . . . With the three kids—taking care of them and eating a lot of graham crackers and marshmallow whip. Oh, God. One time we had that for three days straight. We had no money for food. We were really scuffling. . . . Not working.
>
> She was in very bad financial shape and the electric was cut off. My boyfriend would bring . . . loads of ice to keep the milk

cold. Up those sixty-eight steps to their place. Finally, Norman Granz really came through.

Beverly had gone to Granz and explained her plight, and he put her on a weekly allowance until her husband was released.

Stan felt as if he had been dropped off in paradise when roughly four months into his sentence, the authorities transferred him from the hype tank to a minimum-security prison farm in a San Fernando Valley town north of Los Angeles called Saugus; the L.A. County Jail was overcrowded, and they moved nonviolent first offenders to farms like Saugus as soon as they could. Stan put on weight and acquired a tan working in the fields and looked healthy when he emerged from jail on August 16, 1954, exactly six months after his incarceration.

While in prison, Stan wrote a letter to *Down Beat* about his addiction. He was responding to a letter from a Seattle high school junior that said in part:

> Someday I hope with all my heart to become a professional musician. I like jazz better than any other kind of music. I have been wondering just how many Stan Getzes there are in music. I think he is a very fine musician. Why did he turn to dope? I would like to see anyone caught selling dope *killed*.
>
> It must be terrible to be a dope addict. I feel sorry for them, and I also feel ashamed of them as musicians. . . . I wish someone would clean up the music business, especially the jazz field.
>
> Is there just a few [addicts in music], or are there many? I want to be a musician in the worst way, but I don't want to be playing next to a dope addict. What can be done about this problem?

Stan answered the student in a letter published in the April 21, 1954, *Down Beat*. Like the speech of the Los Angeles judge who had sentenced him, it reflected the 1950s assumption that addiction stemmed from a lack of morals. Stan described his abortive holdup and his suicide attempt and then wrote:

> God didn't want to kill me. This was his warning. Next time I'm sure he won't let me live. As I lay there alive, not wanting to live because of what I had done to my loved ones and all the people who had tried to help me, the nurse came in with a good many letters, telegrams, and phone messages—all saying the same thing.

They told me not to despair, that they admired my music, that I should pray as they were praying for me, and most important, that they forgave me.

I was never what you might call a religious person, beyond being Bar Mitzvahed (confirmed in the Jewish faith), but those people showed me that there is a God, not above us but here on earth in the warm hearts of people. . . .

I realize what I have done has hurt jazz music in general. To say I'm sorry is not nearly enough. I can't blame what I've done on the pressures of creative music in this country. Tell this boy from Seattle that it's pure and simple degeneracy of the mind, a lack of morals and personality shortcomings I have that he doesn't. Tell him that the really good musicians are too smart to mess with it, and don't need it anyway.

I have much more to write . . . but we are allowed only three pages a day.

My best to you,
Stan Getz

The months in jail at age twenty-seven were the first ever as an adult that Stan had spent in a sober state. The alcoholism of his maternal grandfather and his maternal uncle Louis indicates that he had a genetic predisposition toward substance abuse, and he had become addicted to alcohol at fifteen and to heroin at seventeen; when most of his contemporaries were at the local gym shooting hoops, he was on the road shooting dope.

Stan's adolescence and early adulthood were spent in an anesthetized fog where healthy emotional development was impossible; he never got in touch with his true feelings because the liquor and the heroin masked them from him. And he had no mentors to help him over the emotional shoals everyone encounters between fifteen and twenty-seven; his parents were far out of their depth in dealing with his problems, and they had turned him loose at fifteen to an alcoholic guardian in a profession where alcoholism and drug addiction were endemic.

In jail Stan discovered that when he was sober he would be gripped by an almost intolerably painful depression. He wanted a quick cessation of the pain when he was released, and he found it by returning to what he knew best—anesthetizing it with heroin or alcohol.

He drank freely, but he became very careful about how he used heroin. To avoid the fresh needle marks on his arms which would mean rearrest, he snorted the drug instead of injecting it. And he attempted to avoid readdiction by "chipping"—going on three- or four-day binges; the body is not normally enslaved to the drug until the eleventh or twelfth day of consecutive use.

Stan's depression was intensified by the chaotic conditions he found at home. Drifting from one fix to the next, Beverly was overwhelmed by the needs of her three rambunctious young children. Most days she would herd them into the living room, where they would sit for hours in dirty clothes eating junk food and watching TV. Stan was able to provide some help when he was at home, but he knew that his assistance would be sporadic because, to make an adequate living, he had to be on the road for months at a time.

Everything one can say about Stan's stunted emotional development one can also say about Beverly's—except that genetically she was probably more predisposed to addiction than he was; both her parents and three of her siblings were substance abusers. And as she and Stan lived with their children in drug-dominated chaos, they careened around blindly with little hope of outside help; in those days there were few institutions which had even a rudimentary comprehension of their problems. Now the substance abuser has the benefit of decades of massive research on the disease that—we have now recognized—touches one in ten Americans, and he or she can turn to a panoply of treatment centers and techniques. In 1954 the abuser's only forms of solace were stern-faced lecturers who attributed the whole problem to moral decadence or a tiny number of professionals and Alcoholics and Narcotics Anonymous practitioners who were groping toward an understanding of the disease. In addition, with Stan on probation, he and Beverly were afraid that if she sought help, the courts would take the children away from them.

Stan wasted no time getting back on the bandstand after he left the prison farm, joining Chet Baker's quintet at the Tiffany Club in Los Angeles within thirty-six hours of his release. Three days later he appeared, backed by Baker's group, at an all-star concert which also featured Max Roach, Zoot Sims, Buddy DeFranco, Red Norvo, and Cab Calloway. The event attracted more than six thousand people to the Los Angeles Shrine Auditorium, and Stan received a tumultuous ovation, far longer and louder than that accorded the other musicians; his fans were telling him that they forgave him for everything and were happy to have him back.

In early September Stan brought a quartet into Zardi's for a two-week engagement, and in October embarked with a quintet on his first ever Norman Granz tour, which was called "Modern Jazz Concert." Its format differed from Granz's JATP junkets, which featured loosely organized jam sessions built around individual stars. "Modern Jazz Concert" spotlighted four groups playing their standard repertoires; there were no jam session segments.

The Duke Ellington Orchestra and the Dave Brubeck and Gerry Mulligan quartets joined Stan's group in the talent package. To create the quintet, Stan again recruited Bob Brookmeyer, and musically the two men picked up where they had left off ten months before. The tour was a box office success and was marked by back-to-back sold-out concerts the same night in Newark, New Jersey, and New York's Carnegie Hall and by a performance before seven thousand people at the Shrine on the final night of the junket, November 8, 1954.

The quintet's set at the Shrine was recorded, and it produced enough material for one-and-a-half albums. Granz brought the group into the studio the next day to record enough extra cuts for a two-album release, *Stan Getz at the Shrine*. Because of contractual obligations, he was forced to use Frank Isola on drums in the studio session after Art Mardigan played them at the Shrine concert. Stan's partnership with Brookmeyer had reached a point where both men were totally relaxed in each other's company, and they delight the listener with musical conversations conducted with great imagination and an easy swing.

After the Granz tour ended, Brookmeyer wanted to move on again, and Stan brought trumpeter Tony Fruscella into the vacant brass spot. Fruscella, who played in a wistful, lyrical style much akin to Chet Baker's, fit in easily with Stan's aesthetic. The new quintet headed east on November 15 to play until February 10, 1955, in Buffalo, Baltimore, Boston, and New York. They then planned a one-month break—while Stan undertook a tour as a single for Birdland owner Morris Levy—to be followed in March and April by three weeks at Birdland and two weeks at Storyville in Boston.

When Birdland opened in 1949, most show business experts believed it would have the average nightspot life span of three years, but it celebrated its fifth anniversary on December 15, 1954, in robust health. As *Down Beat* pointed out, "The polytonal aviary has hosted an average of 5,000 guests a week for the past five years with a total of more than 1,300,000 birdlovers having dropped in since 1949."

The club celebrated with a show highlighting Sarah Vaughan and her trio, the George Shearing quintet, and the Basie band featuring Lester Young; klieg lights illuminated the Broadway facade, Steve Allen did a portion of TV's *Tonight Show* from the packed, smoky basement, and the Mutual Broadcasting System aired the proceedings on coast-to-coast radio. Each of the groups was required to promote the club by playing Shearing's "Lullaby of Birdland" at least once that night.

The fifth birthday celebration was a prelude to Morris Levy's one-month "Birdland Stars of 1955" tour, which was scheduled to visit twenty-four cities. For the tour, Levy asked Stan and the Erroll Garner Trio to join the three groups that played the anniversary show. Levy wanted Stan to perform as a single backed by the Basie orchestra, and on December 16, the night after the birthday bash, Stan left his quintet and joined the band at the club to work on the arrangements for the tour.

He was excited to be performing with Basie, whose orchestra had played Birdland almost as often as he had. The Count had shrunk his band to a seven-man combo for a short time in 1950 when so many of the big bands were dying, but he soon came charging back with a full unit, thanks largely to the writing of Neal Hefti, Woody Herman's old cohort. By 1954 Basie was at the top of the heap again, and most critics now believe that the 1954–1959 band ranks with the Count's 1936–1942 outfit as his best ever. In 1955 the group swung with crackling power, and any jazz soloist at the time would have given his eyeteeth to be backed up by that roaring aggregation. Stan told a reporter that "playing with Basie for a jazzman is the equivalent of a classical musician playing under Toscanini. . . . You can imagine how I feel." And Stan was delighted that the band's other guest soloist for the junket was his beloved President, Lester Young.

The December 16, 1954, session was recorded as *Basie, Getz, and Sarah Vaughan at Birdland*, and the listener hears Stan working happily through the arrangements of the ballad "Easy Living," Neal Hefti's up-tempo "Little Pony," and a blues. We hear him and the orchestra playing the same repertoire in a concert recorded in Topeka, Kansas, ten weeks later on February 25 (released as *Stars of Birdland on Tour*), and the performances, as expected, are much tighter. Stan and the Basie musicians interact with great precision, and the band inspires him to solo with a fiery passion and energy. At both performances, Pee Wee Marquette introduces Stan as "one of the foremost tenor men of all time."

In December *Down Beat* announced that Stan had won their poll again; this moved him to take a full-page ad in the magazine featuring a touching photo in which he is seated with his sax in his hands and is leaning forward to accept a kiss on the cheek from his six-year-old son. Underneath, the copy reads: "To all the *Down Beat* Readers—Stevie joins me in thanking you for voting me the best tenor saxist of the year for the fifth straight time." In January, *Metronome*'s readers honored Stan for the sixth consecutive year, but this did not elicit an ad.

Granz recorded the quintet at Birdland on January 23 and in the studio eight days later. These are Stan's only recordings with Fruscella, and they reflect the relaxed musical rapport that the two men had quickly achieved. That rapport did not extend to their personal lives, however, and Fruscella's tenure with the group ended abruptly a few days later when Stan punched him in the face during a fight. Only one of the Fruscella cuts, "Round-up Time," is in release today—on the CD *The Artistry of Stan Getz.*

The "Birdland Stars of 1955" kicked off their tour on Friday, February 11, in Boston, played a Saturday night doubleheader at the Mosque Theater in Newark and Carnegie Hall in New York, and appeared the next night at the National Guard Armory in Washington, D.C.

Monica Silfverskiold, a twenty-year-old Swede who was studying foreign affairs at Georgetown University, attended the Washington concert with two fellow students. Full-figured and tall, she was stunning—Marilyn Monroe with class. Luminous eyes, fine cheekbones, and a full, sensuous mouth defined a classical Nordic face. Monica had never heard of Stan or his postjail comeback and was surprised to hear him greeted with the wildest applause of the evening before he even blew a note.

After the concert her friends took her backstage, where they conducted an interview with Stan for a student radio show. When they mentioned that she was a native of Sweden, he told her about his 1951 visit there. He described the man in the homburg with the tulips at the airport and became intensely emotional when he explained that her countrymen had touched him deeply by treating him, for the first time in his life, with the dignity of an artist.

As Monica and her friends left and headed for a taxi, Stan came running up behind them.

"Can I join you?" he asked. "I'm headed in the same direction."

Monica thought this was strange because Stan had no idea where they were going. He climbed into the front seat with his saxophone and turned and asked, "How would you like to join me at a jam session? Sarah Vaughan will be there. Count Basie and some of his people. Shearing."

The two men answered, "Okay, great," but Monica demurred.

"I can't. I must get back to where I live, the YMCA. I've already gone past my ten o'clock curfew. I'm sorry."

After they dropped her off, Stan was crestfallen. He was eager to introduce this beautiful young woman to the excitement of a jam session, but now he was stuck with the two men, in whom he had little interest. And no jam session had been planned. To cover his tracks, he had to get to a telephone and organize a session for Monica's friends to attend. As he was dropping coins into the machine, he promised himself that he would be in touch with her again soon.

Stan had spent less than a week in California since early October, and he was not scheduled to return there until after his Boston gig in late April. Beverly was lonely, she felt increasingly inadequate trying to cope with her addiction and the three kids, and a terrifying incident early that winter had soured her on living in Laurel Canyon. One day, as she was walking a trail in a deserted area near her home with her two small boys, she was attacked by a mental patient who tried to strangle her. The boys ran down the trail screaming and were heard by police who subdued the strangler. Beverly's throat was badly injured, and she was traumatized by the event.

Shortly after, she and Stan determined that she should move back to New York, where Goldie and Al could help with the children and where most of Stan's work was now originating. To save money, they decided that she should share a ride with a young man named Tom Killough, who was heading to Kansas City, Missouri, to hook up with a girlfriend. Killough was a somewhat unsavory character who was reputed to be one of Beverly's connections.

Stan made plans to leave the Birdland tour after an Omaha, Nebraska, concert on Saturday night, February 27, and then travel two hundred miles the next day to meet Beverly and the kids in Kansas City. Then he would take them the rest of the way to New York.

Killough and Beverly drove northeast across the breadth of Oklahoma that Saturday, expecting to arrive in Tulsa at about 6:00 P.M.; they planned to spend the night there before making the 250-mile journey to Kansas City the next day. They chose to travel on the recently opened Turner Turnpike—a straight-as-a-ruler toll road with a seventy-mile-per-hour speed limit—because it was the fast way to go; Route 66, the old Ozark Trail, ran parallel to the Turnpike and required no tolls, but it cut through every town along the way and took forever to negotiate.

David Getz, age three, sat between his mother and Killough as Killough drove at eighty across the rolling, grassy, monotonous plains between Oklahoma City and Tulsa; Steve, age six, sat in the back seat next to his one-year-old sister, whom the family had taken to calling "Little Bev" and who lay in a bassinet. The temperature was in the sixties, unusually springlike for late February, and Killough fought to stay awake as he moved through the hazy sunshine of late afternoon. As he passed north of the town of Stroud, fifty miles west of Tulsa, his eyes closed in sleep and the car veered to the right up a grassy shoulder. In a millisecond, its engine was split in two as it crashed into a vertical steel beam that was supporting an overpass taking another road north over the Turnpike.

There were no seat belts in 1955, and Killough, David, and Beverly were thrown with sickening force into the windshield, which shattered.

When a highway patrolman arrived a few moments later, he found David unconscious on the hood surrounded by broken glass, Killough slumped unconscious against the steering wheel, and Beverly in great pain pinned between the front seat and the dashboard. Steve, who was bleeding above his right eye, and Little Bev, with no outward signs of injury, were screaming in the back seat.

The five victims were taken to the General Hospital in Stroud—population 2,500—where they received emergency care and where preliminary diagnoses were made. Killough and David were in comas with smashed skulls and were given little chance to live; David's left side was paralyzed and his left collarbone was broken. His mother had fractured two vertebrae in her lower back and badly dislocated one of them, had broken her right forearm, had sustained numerous bruises and cuts to her head and body, and suffered numbness in her right leg and foot. In a sense, she was fortunate; if the vertebral fractures and dislocation had been slightly more severe, she would have become a paraplegic. Little Bev was unharmed, despite the fact that her bassinet had split in two. Steve had suffered a broken right arm (which was put in a cast at Stroud), a mild concussion, and a cut on his forehead.

The Stroud doctors succeeded in reaching Stan in Omaha at around 7:00 P.M. After he heard the news, he almost tore the telephone from the wall before breaking down in sobs. He tried frantically to book a flight that night to Tulsa, but found none available till the next morning. In his highly agitated state, he decided that performing in the Birdland concert would divert his mind from his troubles for a couple of hours, and he played the gig. Never a good sleeper, he lay awake all night chain-smoking and staring at the ceiling.

Because the small hospital in Stroud could not deal adequately with their severe injuries, Beverly and Killough were taken by ambulance to the St. John's Medical Center in Tulsa, where they were admitted at 10:20 P.M. St. John's, Tulsa's oldest hospital and its second largest, was a first-rate facility run by the Roman Catholic Sisters of the Sorrowful Mother. Steve and Little Bev were also taken to St. John's but were not admitted as patients; they were placed under the care of a nun who bedded them down for the night. The Stroud doctors wanted to send David to Tulsa as well, but his condition was so perilous that they decided to keep him till morning at least. He remained comatose.

Beverly's chart at St. John's shows that on admission she was in "poor health" with "pus in her kidneys" and that her nutrition was "fair." After putting her on the morphine derivative Demerol to dull her pain, the physicians placed a cast on her right arm and braced her lower back where the vertebrae had been injured.

When Stan arrived at St. John's around noon Sunday, February 28, he found Beverly slipping in and out of sleep from the effects of the Demerol. She couldn't turn her swollen and discolored face toward him because the back brace immobilized her torso, and she looked up at the ceiling as she squeezed his hand and spoke groggily of her ordeal. When she fell into a deep sleep, Stan looked in on Steve, who awoke from a nap long enough to acknowledge his dad, and Little Bev, who was gurgling happily in a crib.

Stan was told that David's condition was now stable enough to allow the doctors to move him to St. John's, but he was not emotionally prepared to see the pale, almost lifeless little figure they wheeled off the ambulance at 2:55 P.M. Stan's legs felt weak and his stomach went queasy when he viewed his son; the left side of David's body was rigid with paralysis and the right side was limp; a turban of bandages swathed his head, his face was purple with bruises, and a figure-eight dressing was wrapped around his chest to stabilize his broken collar bone. The admissions report described the boy as "semi-comatose and extremely critical," and he was placed under the care of the same doctor who was handling his mother. Stan was told that his son's only hope was an operation to relieve pressure on his brain, and he immediately signed papers authorizing such a procedure.

Stan arranged for Steve and Little Bev to be flown to New York where Goldie and Al would meet them, and he put them on a plane in the early evening. Then he returned to St. John's to David's bedside.

He later told a reporter that he sat that entire night by his terribly damaged son—kept barely alive by the tubes that ran in and out of him—and prayed and castigated himself for their troubles. Deep down, Stan was a frightened, insecure young man who—except when playing his horn—felt good about himself only when heroin or alcohol obliterated his fears and pain and made him feel confident and powerful. But not even these drugs this night could erase his despair and anguish as he sat and sobbed and prayed.

Stan explained to the reporter that he was sure that God was punishing him for his weakness and his sins; he cursed himself for allowing Killough to drive the family east, for enslaving himself and Beverly to heroin and booze, for letting his three kids grow up virtually uncared for in drug-dominated chaos, for the mangled bodies of his wife and son. If God took David, Stan would understand; he deserved it. He felt lost at the bottom of an abyss, and he did not know if he could ever climb out of it.

AN ANGEL OF DELIVERANCE

STAN CONTINUED his bedside vigil as the doctors waited another day and night for David to gain strength for the ordeal of surgery; he left his son's room only to smoke cigarettes and pace about in the corridor outside.

By Tuesday morning, March 1, 1955, the surgeons felt it was safe to proceed, and they cut a hole in David's smashed skull in order to get a good look at his brain. They found wedged between it and the bone on the left side "a huge subdural hygroma" (two shot glasses of blood and other fluids surrounded by a membrane). On the right side they discovered the cause of the child's paralysis: a fragment of bone that had been "driven down into the brain over the motor area." After they removed the bone fragment and the hygroma and other debris, they reconstructed his skull and sewed up his scalp. Aside from a short and predictable rise in his temperature to 103 degrees, his vital signs remained stable.

Stan stayed at his son's side until David finally opened his eyes two days later and sipped a few drops of water. As Stan ran to tell Beverly the good news, a nurse stopped him to say that Tom Killough had just died; despite an operation to relieve pressure on his brain, he had never regained consciousness after the accident.

By Sunday, March 6, David was able to swallow a bit of cream of wheat, but his paralysis continued and he could not talk. During the week that followed, he regained some movement in his left arm and leg and said a few words but could not create sentences.

The surgeons wished to fuse together several of Beverly's lower vertebrae to stabilize her spine and to enhance the healing of the fractures. Surgical and physical therapy techniques today get the patient back home and moving around three weeks after such an operation, but in 1955 the recovery process required several months of near immobility in a hospital. No one wanted to leave Beverly to fend for herself for months in a strange institution 1,300 miles from home, and Stan arranged to have her operation performed at the Hospital for Joint Diseases in New York. To prepare her for her journey, the St. John's surgeons on March 11 encased her in a body cast that extended from just under her armpits to her pubic bone, and they placed a fresh cast on her right forearm.

Stan was deeply saddened two days later when he heard on the radio that Charlie Parker had died the previous night in New York from lobar pneumonia—complicated by ulcers and cirrhosis of the liver. Two decades of hard living had taken a heavy toll; Bird was thirty-five, but the doctor who pronounced him dead thought he was dealing with the body of a fifty-year-old. Parker died while laughing at a juggler on the Tommy Dorsey television show; he was staying in the Fifth Avenue apartment of Baroness Pannonica de Koenigswarter, a Rothschild heiress and a renowned patroness of bebop; Thelonious Monk would die in another of her homes in 1982.

Stan was in awe of Bird's genius, and remembered him as an intelligent, witty companion who loved to laugh. They had enjoyed each other's company many times and occasionally had scored dope and shot up together. Stan felt that Clint Eastwood's 1988 biographical movie *Bird* was very one-sided in concentrating almost exclusively on the depressing, self-destructive aspects of Parker's personality.

Stan flew Beverly and David to New York on Monday, March 14, and deposited them with Goldie and Al at their Queens apartment. That night he recorded two pieces with Gunther Schuller's Modern Jazz Society, an unusual group that was part of a new "Third Stream" movement in music. The Third Streamers wished to marry the best in the jazz and classical idioms to create a new third form. They did some intriguing work but did not exert a strong aesthetic influence because what they created took on the gauzy coloration of chamber music and lacked the visceral punch of jazz.

Schuller's group had a hybrid instrumentation, wedding a French horn (played by him), a bassoon, and a harp with more conventional jazz instruments such as a saxophone, a trap drum set, and a trombone. Stan managed a swinging solo against a background of seventeenth-century fanfares and counterpoint on "The Queen's Fancy" and took a couple of haunting choruses on the slow-paced, elegiac "Midsommer." Schuller's album was called *A Concert of Contemporary Music.*

Stan took up his long-scheduled Birdland engagement the next night and played there for two weeks with a sextet featuring two other horns, Brookmeyer on trombone and Phil Sunkel, better known as a writer, on trumpet.

After David emerged from his coma and the trauma of Oklahoma began to ease, Stan could not keep from his mind the image of Monica Silfverskiold, the beautiful Swedish Georgetown student he had met in Washington. During the Birdland gig, he called her, discovered that she was ill at the University Medical Center, and came down to visit her despite her protestations that he would be barred from the isolation ward she was in. The doctors were keeping her there because they were having difficulty diagnosing her illness; later they determined it was measles. Monica remembered:

> . . . At that part of the hospital was like a dragon nurse that would not let anybody come past. And somehow, I can't believe how, Stan charmed his way past. . . .
>
> He didn't have any flowers or presents, or anything, so he bought out the newsstand downstairs. . . . It was these publications that I would never in a million years have been interested in. He wasn't interested in them either, but he came with an armful of them. And I saw his face there, behind the glass thing, and it was surreal.
>
> I had asked the doctor who was treating me—he was from New York, from the Bronx—if he had ever heard of Stan Getz, because I had gone to this concert. And he said, "Yes. Bad news. Bad news. He's a terrible man, and he was just arrested and in jail."

And that was the first time I had ever realized why they had given him an ovation when he hadn't even played.

I couldn't put the two together—this thing that the doctor said, and Stan, who seemed like such a completely innocent, sweet, intelligent. . . .

Then he told me in that hospital setting, he told me his entire life—Beverly, jail. And he was remarkably open and candid. . . . I had never known anyone to be so completely candid. Swedes never tell you anything about their bad sides. Just their good sides.

MONICA'S LIFE had been utterly unlike his. She was an aristocrat, the granddaughter of Count Eric von Rosen, and a member of the privileged "jeunesse dorée," the golden youth of postwar Europe.

Her mother Mary grew up on the von Rosen estate—thousands of acres of farms and woodland and lakes surrounding Rockelstad, a castle with scores of rooms built circa 1640. Rockelstad had a medieval look because Count Eric, a huntsman and explorer whose temperament was romantic, had embellished it with imposing storybook towers. Mary had wed Dr. Nils Silfverskiold, a handsome orthopedic surgeon who was eighteen years her senior, in 1932; it was Nils's third marriage and her first. Monica was born in 1934, and a brother, Nils Peter, followed in 1937.

Monica's family had a colorful history in public affairs. Her father was an active Communist when he married her mother, and her grandfather Count Eric had the distinction of starting the swastika on its journey to Nazi Germany. It began one snowy night in February 1920 when the Count chartered a plane to Rockelstad; it was flown by a young commercial pilot who had been a highly decorated World War I ace, Hermann Göring. David Irving, the biographer of the future Nazi leader, has described the scene:

> After a bumpy, stomach-pitching flight, Göring landed expertly on the frozen lake next to the castle and accepted the Count's invitation to spend the night. He had always liked castles. Balloons of cognac in their hands, Hermann and Eric strolled through the great structure. . . . By coincidence, there were several swastika emblems embellishing the castle. . . . Hermann had never seen one before; Count Eric had discovered the swastika on rune stones in Gotland, and had incorporated this harmless Nordic symbol of the rising sun everywhere at Rockelstad—embossed on

the hearth and iron firedogs and on one wall of his shooting box in the grounds.

Göring discovered something far more important to him than the swastika that night in 1920 at Rockelstad; he found the love of his life, Carin, Countess von Fock, the sister of Count Eric's wife. The Countess—age 31—was five years older than Göring, the bored wife of a Swedish army officer, and the mother of a young son.

Soon after they were introduced that night, Carin took Hermann to the chapel of the von Rosen's private Edelweiss Religious Order that was nestled in the shadows of the castle. As they meditated in the still, cold darkness, the two of them experienced an almost mystical bonding. A few days later, he wrote her about those moments:

> It was so quiet, so lovely that I forgot all the earthly noise, all my worries, and felt as though in another world.... I was like a swimmer resting on a lonely island to gather new strength before he throws himself anew into the raging torrent of life.

They soon embarked on a love affair that scandalized the strait-laced Swedish upper classes of the early 1920s. Their passion was so strong, however, that it survived banishment by Carin's father, rebuke by Swedish society, and economic hardship.

The couple's lives were transformed when they met Adolf Hitler in the fall of 1922; he mesmerized them, and they became ardent Nazis. Carin obtained a divorce in December 1922 and married Göring on February 3, 1923. He quickly became invaluable to Hitler as he used his military experience to turn the Führer's ragtag SA militia into a potent private army. After Hitler took the salute of thousands of well-disciplined SA troops on parade on April 15, 1923, Carin wrote her son:

> After it was over, the Führer embraced the Beloved One (her husband) and told me that if he said what he really thought of his achievement, the Beloved One would get a swollen head.
>
> I said that my own head was already swollen with pride, and he kissed my hand and said, "No head so pretty as yours could ever be swollen."

As the Nazis struggled towards dominance, Carin was her husband's active helpmate—tending to his wounds in Austria after the failed "putsch" of November 1923, playing the political hostess in Berlin following his return in 1928, inveighing against "the revolting Jews," serving as Hitler's emissary to the Italian Fascists.

Carin died in 1931—worn down by bouts of tuberculosis, pneumonia, and heart disease—but she lived to see her husband on the brink of immense political power.

Göring remained friendly with Count Eric and clashed with the Count's son-in-law, Dr. Nils Silfverskiold, soon after Nils had married Monica's mother. In June 1933 Göring who was now the second most powerful member of Germany's government after Hitler, boasted to Nils at a dinner at Rockelstad that the Nazis would "gradually destroy" Germany's Communists. Nils, a zealous Communist at the time, was incensed and soon found an opportunity to strike back. He had come upon records of Göring's secret treatment for morphine addiction at a Swedish hospital in 1927 and handed the Nazi a political setback when he arranged for their publication.

More turmoil ensued with Göring four months later, according to David Irving:

> Göring flew up to Stockholm for four days to visit Carin's grave— it was two years since her death—and her relatives. Angry Communists protested that he was holding a "big Nazi get-to-gether" at Count von Rosen's castle, and the Communist daily newspaper *Folkets Dagblad* claimed he had "issued directives to his relatives on how the Swedish Nazis should set about ... introducing a Nazi dictatorship." ... Coming out of a Stockholm theater, he was jeered by an organized mob, who shouted, "Down with Göring, murderer of the workers!"
>
> Not in the most tactful style, he left on Carin's grave a swastika-shaped wreath.... The Communists trampled the flowers and painted a message on the gravestone: "Some of us Swedes take offense at the German Mr. Göring's violation of the grave. His dead wife may rest in peace—but spare us the German propaganda on her tomb."

This was too much for Göring, and he started planning the removal of Carin's casket from Sweden to Prussia. He built a granite mausoleum to receive her remains, and next to it he constructed a shrine—Carinhall— modeled after a hunting lodge on the von Rosen estate. Eric von Rosen helped with its construction and gave Göring a dagger "with its crossguard and pommel encrusted with jewels, its hilt fluted with ivory, its scabbard richly engraved with hunting scenes"; the weapon was inscribed, "A knife from Eric to Hermann."

Over the next twelve years, Göring transformed Carinhall into a bloated, vulgar baroque palace, but on June 20, 1934, when Carin's casket arrived there, it possessed a simple dignity. The reinterment ceremony was far from simple.

> Few pharaohs' wives can have been buried with more solemn ceremony. A special train bore the pewter sarcophagus across northern Prussia from the Swedish ferry to the railroad station where Göring and Hitler, both hatless and somber, awaited her arrival. At Göring's command, towns and cities along the train's whole route were cast into deep mourning. . . .
>
> The scene at Carinhall itself was like the setting for a Bayreuth opera. . . . Richard Wagner's rich funeral music throbbed and droned among the hazed conifers.
>
> Göring had invited Carin's relatives, along with hundreds of diplomats and politicians, to witness this moving evidence of how beholden he was to her memory. To the blare of hunting horns and trumpets and the answering bellows of Hermann's future trophies grazing in the forests, a dozen strong men groaned and strained to manhandle the sarcophagus down into the granite mausoleum. Afterward, Göring led Hitler down the steps alone.

That evening at Carinhall, Göring convinced Hitler that it was necessary to liquidate their principal enemies—mostly Nazis—and ten days later he and the Führer directed the systematic murder of their opponents in the infamous "Night of the Long Knives." This operation, in which eighty-four were killed by hit squads, solidified Göring's status as Hitler's number two man, a position he held until the disintegration of the Third Reich in 1945.

Göring stayed in touch with Eric von Rosen during World War II. In December 1939—three months after the conflict started—Göring sent peace feelers to the British government through Eric, and in November 1940 he used a letter to him to warn the Swedes to stay neutral and to assure the Finns that Germany would continue to back them against Russia. Eric's son and Monica's uncle, Count Carl Gustaf von Rosen, flew to visit Göring in Germany as the Third Reich was starting to collapse in August 1944, but he was denied access by Göring's staff.

The purpose of Count Carl Gustaf's visit is cloudy, especially since he had fought on the antifascist side in Ethiopia against the Italians in 1935. He identified himself politically as an "independent socialist" and had a colorful postwar career in aviation in Africa. From 1946 to 1956, he was

Chief of the Ethiopian Air Force, and in 1968 he flew humanitarian and military missions for Biafra in its futile attempt to secede from Nigeria. He was again in Ethiopia from 1974 to 1977, flying food to areas where thousands were dying from starvation. Where the terrain did not allow him to land, he would drop his cargo in so-called "food parcel bombings." Carl Gustaf was killed by a grenade during a guerilla attack in Ethiopia in 1977.

The marriage of Monica's parents did not survive World War II; they were divorced in 1943, and Mary was, for several months afterward, emotionally bruised by the rupture. She recovered her equilibrium, and in 1945 entered a successful marriage to a professor of pathology at Lund, Dr. Johann Ahlgren; Lund, which became Monica's home town, is the site of one of Sweden's two main universities and is less than an hour from Copenhagen, Denmark's capital. In 1947 the Ahlgrens had a son, Jan. Nils Silfverskiold also married again, to a woman considerably younger than Mary; they had two daughters.

MONICA PASSED her college entrance exams with flying colors at the age of eighteen, but she felt stultified in her native country.

> Sweden ... is so drab and so cold and, in those days it was terribly formal and students would be very academically oriented and speak in long syllables.... I was totally uncomfortable in that environment.

She was also disgusted by the heavy drinking which was the norm among Swedish undergraduates. She had in fact become a teetotaler, following an unpleasant encounter with alcohol at a French boarding school a couple of years before:

> I was going to try smoking and drinking wine one evening.... We bought two bottles of wine and bought all the chocolate croissants we could carry, and I've never been so absolutely ill in my life as I was after that.
> I remember lying in bed in the morning and the bed was kind of moving and I said to myself, "Why do people do this? It costs money, and you feel miserable," and I just made that decision. And I never smoked and never drank.... I was always quite well known for being a prude, and for absolutely refusing alcohol.

Monica's feelings of alienation led her to do a revolutionary thing for a mid-1950s European student; she opted out of the Swedish college system and chose to do her undergraduate work in America. At that time few Europeans followed this path because a European undergraduate degree was considered an essential first step on the career ladder there.

She had been vacillating between the study of foreign affairs and medicine and chose the latter when a friend of her father's helped her win a scholarship in aviation medicine at the University of New Mexico in Albuquerque for the fall of 1953. He was Dr. Randy Lovelace, a leader in aviation medicine who later became Director of Space Medicine at NASA. Lovelace ran a renowned clinic in Albuquerque which combined basic research, health care, and education; it had been founded by his uncle and bore the family name.

Monica moved in with his family and experienced much of the happiness that had eluded her in Sweden. She remembered, "Coming there to me was what you experienced as far as liberation. I felt for the first time that I can really be myself and not pretend, and it was just wonderful." She grew in many ways. She learned to fly and to ride in rodeos, and she explored the southwestern deserts and mountains. In addition to her courses in Aviation Medicine, she studied anthropology, Latin-American affairs, Spanish, and Portuguese.

After a few months, however, it became clear to Monica that she could not find fulfillment in medicine, and she decided to concentrate on her other main academic interest, foreign affairs. Her advisers pointed her to Georgetown's outstanding school in that discipline, and she quickly won a scholarship there, beginning with the September 1954 academic year. Seven months later she was in the university's hospital listening as Stan told her the story of his life. She was not yet twenty-one.

Compared to his junkie wife, Monica seemed to Stan like an incredible gift—a beautiful angel of deliverance who could lift him from the abyss he had fallen into. She was intelligent, idealistic, sophisticated, full of youthful energy. And a teetotaler in the bargain. He was dazzled. Before he left her bedside, he told her he would see her again very soon.

First he had to attend to Beverly's injuries. He brought her to New York's Hospital for Joint Diseases on March 23, 1955, and on the next day a surgeon fused her lower vertebrae together with bits of bone taken from her pelvis and placed her in a full body cast. He also reset and recast her broken right arm. He told her that he would keep her in the hospital in the body cast for several months to achieve full recovery.

On the night of April 2, Stan played in a standing-room-only Charlie Parker memorial concert at Carnegie Hall. The event lasted more than

three hours, and over sixty artists participated; they included Dizzy Gillespie, Thelonious Monk, Lester Young, Kenny Clarke, Billie Holiday,
Dinah Washington, Pearl Bailey, Sammy Davis, Jr., Lenny Tristano, Horace Silver, J. J. Johnson, Al Cohn, Gerry Mulligan, Bob Brookmeyer, Lee
Konitz, Charlie Shavers, and Kai Winding.

Monica had recovered from the measles the next time Stan visited her
in Washington. While he was there—within the space of a few hours—
she twice did something that he would never forget. Stan was driving her
through the countryside and swigging liquor from a bottle, and when he
put it down, she took it and poured its contents out the window. Later
that day, he and a friend were drinking heavily at the friend's house, and
she astounded them both by taking their bottle and pouring the liquor
down the toilet.

Monica was to encounter another intoxicating substance soon after
when she visited Stan in Boston, where he was playing with Brookmeyer
and the quintet:

> I saw the setting, and the way he lived, and I started to understand
> that he just came from a different planet. I remember being very
> impressed by Bob Brookmeyer. . . . He was so intelligent and had
> such a dry sense of humor and was so bright, but I was stunned
> that they were smoking pot quite openly, which was illegal, and
> Stan was on probation still. . . .
>
> It was just to me mind-blowing what these people were doing.
> All looking very young and intelligent and innocent, they were
> living a life that I just couldn't understand.

Monica may not have understood this life, but she continued to be
drawn to it. On a weekend in May a few weeks later, she went with Stan
to New York and Philadelphia to meet his family.

Shaindel Bleshman, Goldie's younger half sister, had come from Philadelphia to visit Goldie in late March, and it was obvious to her after a
couple of hours that Goldie was exhausting herself taking care of the
three children.

"You're pushing fifty, Goldie. You're going to walk yourself into an
early grave looking after those three," Shaindel said. "Let me have one
of them."

Goldie replied, "You can take anybody, but not the baby and Steven,"
and Shaindel drove home that afternoon with David in tow.

David's recovery was slow and difficult. He was forced to learn everything all over again—talking, walking, dressing himself, going to the bath-

room. And he would easily become disoriented; he wandered from Shaindel's home so often that they were forced to lock all the doors from the inside. Shaindel's husband Charlie pitched in, and their two children—Meyer, age twelve, and Lenore, age nineteen—adored David and helped enormously. David slept in Lenore's room, and she and her brother pampered him and spent hours helping him regain basic skills.

Monica was somewhat intimidated by Goldie's noisy, histrionic style, but she took easily to Shaindel, who had an earthy sense of humor and a relaxed manner. Monica totally won over Stan's kids as well as Lenore and Meyer. She was a glamorous figure to them, but she pitched in with mundane chores such as dishwashing and spent hours playing with the children. Stan couldn't believe that this classy, gorgeous, clean-living lady had walked into his life and seemed to be lighting a path out of its sordid chaos.

He told Monica that he adored her and that it was all over with Beverly. In a few days her semester at Georgetown ended, and before she flew back to Sweden, they promised each other that they would try to get together there before she had to return to Washington in September.

Then he told Beverly, immobilized in her body cast at the hospital, that he wanted a divorce and would make a decent financial settlement for her. He announced that he was going to California for the summer to appear in a movie and would see her in September. Beverly was devastated.

Universal Studios, in 1954, had a runaway hit with *The Glenn Miller Story*, which starred Jimmy Stewart, was produced by Aaron Rosenberg, and was written by Valentine Davies. Wishing to follow up on this success, they approached Benny Goodman to do the story of his life. Benny had been interested in such a project as far back as 1942, and when Universal assigned Rosenberg and Davies to the film and gave Benny total control over its musical content, he signed on. Benny wanted Tony Curtis to play the lead, but Universal surprised him in choosing Steve Allen, host of TV's *Tonight Show* and a jazz enthusiast.

Benny recruited Gene Krupa, Lionel Hampton, Teddy Wilson, Harry James, Ziggy Elman, and Martha Tilton to re-create their star turns with the great late-1930s band, and—for additional featured solos—he chose Stan, trombonist Urbie Green, and Basie trumpeter Buck Clayton. Stan had nonspeaking bits in two scenes and played the only two saxophone solos in the movie. The music is excellent, and the sound track album sold well.

The film was an amalgam of 1950s biopic clichés, stilted dialogue, and wooden acting and achieved modest success at the box office. The plot focuses on the romance between Benny and his WASP fiancée, a virginal Vanderbilt heiress played by Donna Reed; the dramatic tension is created when Benny's mama disapproves of the union because she believes that the social and religious chasm between the lovers is too great to be bridged. After much hand-wringing, mama comes around, and the couple is reunited at the Carnegie Hall concert of 1938. In real life Benny's mama didn't disapprove, Benny wouldn't have paid attention to her anyway, and his fiancée was a divorcée with three children.

Stan flew to California for a June 17, 1955, court hearing at which he was fined $250 for failing to make a report to his probation officer. On July 1 he arrived at Universal Studios for the first day of shooting on the Goodman movie. The pace of filmmaking was so slow that he had plenty of energy to perform in the evenings, and he put together a quintet to play at Zardi's and to record for Granz. Stan remembered:

> We were filming during the ungodly morning hours that Hollywood uses to grind out its products, and at night Lou Levy, Shelly Manne, Leroy Vinnegar, Conte Candoli, and I played at Zardi's. That music was infinitely more satisfying than the filming (most of which ended on the cutting floor, anyway) and we decided to record it. Since this quintet—all originally East Coast musicians endowing the music with an East Coast virility—made this recording on the West Coast, we called it *West Coast Jazz* as a joke.

Stan's playing is particularly virile on the up-tempo tune "Shine," where he gets carried away and unexpectedly takes eighteen hot choruses; he later told a reporter that it was "as easy as falling off a log." The pell-mell energy of "Shine" is nicely balanced on the LP by a contemplative, darkly hued reading of "Summertime." Stan also cut four sides in a quartet setting without Candoli, which were issued as a separate album, *Stan Getz and the Cool Sounds*; here a relaxed version of "Serenade in Blue" is outstanding.

Granz took advantage of Lionel Hampton's presence in California for the Goodman movie to team him up with Stan and Levy, Manne, and Vinnegar for the recording *Hamp and Getz*. Stan and Hamp inspire each other to especially inventive wailing on "Cherokee" and "Jumpin' at the Woodside," and then settle down for smooth, elegant interpretations of "Autumn in New York" and "Gladys." Later the same day, Granz teamed Hampton with Art Tatum and Buddy Rich for another fine LP.

During this busy summer, Stan went on an extended heroin binge and became addicted again. After the Goodman filming ended in late August, he looked forward to a few weeks of leisure before he was to begin his first ever JATP tour in Hartford, Connecticut, on September 16, 1955. He flew back east and then impulsively boarded a plane for Sweden. Monica had thought she might see him there that summer, but she expected reasonable advance warning and was surprised to receive a telegram from the plane's refueling station in Nova Scotia saying that Stan was arriving in Stockholm in a few hours.

She was appalled at his condition when he stepped off the plane. He was overweight, his face was swollen, and he was in the first nasty stages of withdrawal. Against her protestations he demanded to see a doctor to obtain access to drugs, which were illegal in Sweden. Monica took him to a neurologist cousin of hers, and he laughed Stan out of the office when he asked for a narcotics prescription.

He somehow managed to obtain drugs in Stockholm independently of Monica, and he continued using as they visited Rockelstad for a few days and moved southwest to the city of Gothenburg, where he played in a jam session in a private home on September 5. The following night, he performed at a concert in Malmö, Sweden's southernmost city.

Malmö is next door to Lund, which was the home of Monica's mother, Mary Ahlgren, and her husband and son; following the concert, Monica stayed with the Ahlgrens, and Stan checked into a Lund hotel. The next day, when Monica and Mary came to pick Stan up for lunch, he didn't respond to their calls from the hotel lobby. They had a porter force open the door to his room because they believed he had taken an overdose, and their fears seemed confirmed when they found him lying unconscious.

Monica had Stan admitted at a hospital in Lund by another of her medical cousins who was the head of the psychiatric department there. Stan's dangerously high temperature and his blood count told the doctors that he was not suffering from an overdose but an infection, and they soon determined that he had a critical case of staph pneumonia. He was allergic to penicillin, and they gave him high doses of other antibiotics to keep him alive. The physicians also maintained him on morphine, because they didn't want to subject his system to withdrawal while his body fought the infection. Nurses were in short supply at the hospital, and Monica and her mother exhausted themselves caring for him while he mumbled deliriously and hovered near death.

In the middle of this ordeal, another beau of Monica's, an American Rhodes Scholar, turned up. She remembered, "I just shut him off someplace, you know; it was really very sad." He quickly realized that Monica was expending all her energy on Stan, and—after hanging around for a few disconsolate days—he left.

Somehow, Monica got news of Stan's critical illness to Norman Granz, and he recruited Lester Young to take Stan's place on the JATP tour due to start on September 16.

In his delirium Stan kept calling for a powerful Jewish antibiotic, Goldie's pea soup, and Monica telephoned her about this. Goldie made a large batch and dispatched her son Bob to find dry ice to preserve it for the trip to Sweden. After a long search he found some in a dark shop under an el station in Queens, packed it around the soup, and sent it off by air. Unfortunately, the dry ice evaporated en route, and the soup was spoiled when it arrived in Sweden. No one ever related this to Goldie. To her dying day she told everyone that her pea soup had helped save Stan's life.

After a couple of weeks, the fever broke and the infection subsided. But before the doctors could release Stan, they had to transfer him to Monica's cousin's department to be detoxified from the morphine. Monica recalled:

> In those days I guess they didn't know much about how to do that, because they had to put him in a straitjacket. And he was wild. Dangerous. He was just mind-blowing. . . .
>
> He was totally awful, awful as a patient, and one morning he woke up, and he looked just exactly like I remembered he looked the first time that I had seen him. He had lost all that puffiness; he was calm, and he was humorous.
>
> That was really the moment that I thought that this could be somebody I could spend the rest of my life with. Because he was very romantic then. And that time that he spent in the hospital was just wonderful.

She bought him a phonograph and a batch of his favorite Sinatra records.

> I remember violets, "I Bought You Violets for Your Furs." He just loved all these songs. Romantic songs. And we would walk hand in hand through those parks. . . . I had to cancel my semester—which my parents were really upset about—in Georgetown. . . .

Upon his release from the hospital, Monica took Stan to Rockelstad, where he continued his recuperation.

> That was really when I fell in love. I was very apprehensive. Stan was the very determined pursuer. . . . I didn't want to hurt any-

body else. My mother and father had been divorced, and I never wanted to be in the role of another woman of any kind. It turns out that relationship (with Beverly) was already gone by the way-side for a long time. But I wanted to make sure. I mean there were three children there. I was only twenty, twenty-one. . . .

I had been given so much in Sweden—a really truly happy childhood and two truly wonderful parents—that I kind of felt that God put Stan in my way, so to speak. That nobody else could sort of salvage this situation. And maybe it was an overconfidence in myself at the time, but I truly loved him. I knew he loved me. . . . I didn't realize the enormity of the chemical dependency factor. I kind of thought—which many people did at the time—that love cures all.

Stan threw himself forcefully into the music scene as soon as he felt strong enough to leave Rockelstad. First he flew to Copenhagen to meet with Norman Granz to arrange a December 16, 1955, Stockholm recording session with Swedish musicians. When he returned, he played in a Stockholm concert and at a party sponsored by Philips Records for the Columbia record producer George Avakian. The British music magazine *Melody Maker* carried a large photograph of Monica looking adoringly at Stan at the Philips party; the caption described her as "a Swedish admirer" of Stan's.

Stan sounds like a man with lung problems on the December 16 date, which was released as *Stan Getz in Stockholm*. In contrast to the robust sound displayed on his August sessions in California, his tone is weak and breathy. He was also burdened by an inadequate rhythm section. Stan said of the drummer, "At least he didn't get in the way. Rhythm sections, especially drummers, are a problem for American musicians everywhere in Europe." And he wasn't happy with the pianist, Bengt Hallberg, either. "He doesn't permit himself to get excited when he plays jazz," Stan commented. "He's afraid of letting himself go that much. He's afraid he'll get hurt."

Stan's doctors were worried that his full musical schedule might permanently damage his scarred lungs, and they convinced him that his only chance for a full recovery was to spend several months recuperating in a warm climate. American sunbelt cities were ruled out because it was feared that Stan would too easily become addicted again there. Monica's maternal grandfather, Count Eric, had died in 1948, but he had established strong connections in East Africa that the von Rosen family continued to maintain. So it was decided that Monica take Stan to Malindi, a

Kenyan resort on the Indian Ocean. To preserve decorum, Monica's parents arranged for the couple to be booked separately in the only two hotels there.

After arriving in the Kenyan capital, Nairobi, it took them two days to travel the 225 miles to Malindi in primitive vehicles and in ferries pulled manually across rivers with chains. Once there, they lay in the sun and swam and snorkeled in the Indian Ocean, and they did the usual tourist things like observing wild animals in the jungle.

One day, as they were riding in a jeep through the jungle to a place called the blue lagoon, they came upon a film company, and a woman shouted, "Hey, Stan." It was Donna Reed, whom he had met on the set of *The Benny Goodman Story*. She was co-starring with Cornel Wilde in *Beyond Mombasa*, a decidedly mediocre action epic that involved a hidden uranium mine and a group of vicious killers. Donna and her husband, Tony Owen, a film executive, soon were spending most of their evenings in Malindi with Stan and Monica, and the couples grew to be close friends. Donna, who was thirteen years older than Monica, became something of a mother figure and adviser to her as their relationship matured.

Monica discovered a great deal about Stan at the African resort:

> I remember New Year's, that year, we spent in Malindi. It was the most romantic experience—beautiful hotel, the moon and the palm trees, and the whole thing. . . .
>
> In the beginning, he was drug free and we had a wonderful time. . . . One night he got hold of a doctor in the hotel and he asked him for barbiturates, sleeping pills. . . .
>
> The first incident I remember, we were downstairs in my hotel, Sinbad, and he started drinking, and he took these sleeping pills. I had a red dress with all kinds of little tiny, tiny buttons that took a long time to button. He took my dress and just ripped it like that, and all the buttons just flew.
>
> And I said, "What are you doing?" And he got some idea that somebody was looking at me funny and I was looking funny at that person. Just insanely jealous. And then he went up and took a razor blade and cut every single piece of clothing that I had, methodically, into shreds.
>
> I was suicidal. I just didn't know what to do. . . . I couldn't understand how that happened. You know how you do. You know—had I done anything? Had I provoked it? I was just devastated.

And I remember there was a wonderful couple who owned that hotel, and they said, "Get rid of him. Don't go anywhere near him. We'll see to it that you get back to Sweden somehow, safe."

But then Stan the next day was just devastated and apologetic and charming. . . . I was puzzled.

Monica and Stan then traveled to Mount Kilimanjaro, where a wealthy American oilman invited them to his home near the top of the peak. Whiskey was plentiful, and Stan drank too much and became violent again. Monica recalled:

The first thing he does is pick up the saxophone and just bash it against the trees. His favorite horn. And then I knew that it was going to be an evening of rampage. And then I remember just being afraid for my life. I just thought, I don't want to be here. And in the morning, this man realized that something was very wrong, so he had a private plane take us into Nairobi.

And we check into a hotel . . . and Stan disappeared, and he comes back from the pharmacy with all kinds of pills and a bottle of gin. And I just took the pills and poured them in the toilet with one hand, and the gin with the other hand, and all of sudden I see this fist just come flying into my face, and pieces of bone and blood everywhere.

And the next thing I remember, I'm in the hospital and they put Stan in a cage. And the Swedish ambassador came and they just said, "Should we let him out? What happened?" And I said, "I just don't honestly know what happened." . . . Of course, a passionless Stan was let out of his cage, and he was just devastated.

And I'd come back to Sweden with plaster all over my face, and we together constructed the story about an automobile accident, because we also had to explain his horn being absolutely crushed.

Soon after their arrival in Sweden, Monica and Stan announced their engagement.

A NEW DIRECTION

AFTER SHE AND STAN returned to New York from Europe in March of 1956, Monica wasted no time reorganizing the Getz family, which was still widely scattered. Beverly was staying with friends in Manhattan, David continued to live with Shaindel in Philadelphia, and Steve and Little Bev were camping out with Goldie and Al in Queens. The first task Monica set for herself was the rehabilitation of Beverly. Once she had reunited Beverly with her children in a stable household, she and Stan could move to California and start to build their own life together.

Beverly had been discharged from the hospital several months earlier and had made an excellent recovery from her injuries. She had lost some flexibility in her back, particularly when bending forward, but would suffer no other aftereffects and was in no pain. Her arm had healed more slowly, and she did not regain full use of it for several more months. As Monica remembered, Beverly's addictions presented more problems than her physical injuries.

> When I got back one of my projects, being superresponsible, was to try to help Beverly. . . . I was going to be this do-gooder, and I was going to fix everything and everybody. It was just my mission in life. . . .
>
> I was just so determined that she was going to have her children and Stan was going to give her a proper divorce and a nice settlement and he was going to take good care of her. That was his first obligation, and I was going to help her become a singer again. That's what she deserved. . . .
>
> She had eaten Dexedrines out of paper bags, so she had no teeth. They were like little rotten stumps. . . . And I made this appointment with the dentist. . . . And I made an appointment for her—at Elizabeth Arden—to get herself beautiful, and I got her gigs. . . . I was invested in trying to get Beverly on her feet. And she and I were really good friends.

Beverly often frustrated Monica because her erratic habits worked against keeping dentistry appointments or singing engagements. Beverly knew that she needed to pull herself together to mother her children properly, but her lonely battle against her cravings was proving long and arduous. Her bouts of sobriety were too often punctuated by Dexedrine binges; she would awaken at 3:30 P.M., take some Dexedrines to get going and continue to take them until late in the evening, when she would switch to heavy dosages of alcohol to get to sleep.

Beverly wanted the summer to straighten herself out and asked that her reunion with her children be delayed until the start of the school year in September. This presented Stan and Monica with an opportunity to spend some time with the kids. Unfortunately, because of an unusual New York City regulation, they were forced to spend it on the road.

During the mid-1950s, in order to perform in a New York establishment which served liquor, an entertainer needed a card issued by the authorities under the city's arbitrary and senseless cabaret law. Because of his Los Angeles conviction, Stan's card was revoked after he had played at the Basin Street club in May, and he was forced to find work on an extended tour that would take him to Los Angeles and San Francisco for most of the summer. In late June Monica scooped up the children from Shaindel and Goldie and took them to California, where they spent several pleasant weeks with her and their father.

They returned to New York in late summer, and Monica tackled her next project—making room for Beverly. She remembered:

> I got Goldie and Al a beautiful apartment in Forest Hills. They left the Union Turnpike apartment for Beverly and the children, a very nice little apartment. Left every piece of furniture. All the linen. Beverly didn't have a thing. . . . So here's this very nice little bourgeois setup.

Beverly, who had attained a tenuous sobriety over the summer, was often shaken when Monica visited Union Turnpike. Steve Getz recalled:

> Dad showed up with Monica, and Beverly, my mother, wasn't that impressed. . . .
>
> She was kind of angry at him for doing it, because in walked this . . . raging beauty. . . . It was like seeing Grace Kelly. It was like being in a room with Grace Kelly. . . . We all look at her and say, "Wow, look at this lady. . . ."

Steve also remembered a time when Monica brought him home late from an outing in a convertible:

> Movie star, convertible, ice cream cones, and hot dogs. . . . I remember we got back from that outing that afternoon, and I see my mother looking through the blinds, and she comes out like she's angry. She comes running down the stairs and opens up the door and she says to Monica, "Where have you been? Where have you been with my kid?"
>
> And you know, by this time I've spent five or six hours with Grace Kelly here, and I'm sort of beginning to like it a lot. I remember my mother, she's arguing and Monica's just saying, "Oh, I'm terribly . . ." playing the innocent one. "I'm sorry, time got behind us," and what have you. And all of a sudden my mother grabs my hand and starts pulling on me, yanking me. And Monica's got me by the other hand, so it's like a tug-of-war going on. . . .
>
> So she finally yanks me in the house and I remember going back in feeling sad to leave Monica and confused and it was weird. It was very vivid.

Steve's confusion ebbed when Monica and Stan left in mid-September; she headed for southern California to find a permanent home for the two of them, and he embarked on his first ever JATP tour. Monica was reunited with him a month later when the tour ended at the Shrine Auditorium in Los Angeles.

The tour marked the debut of both Stan and the Modern Jazz Quartet with JATP, and for Stan's segment Granz teamed him with three quarters of the Quartet (John Lewis on piano, Percy Heath on bass, and Connie Kay on drums) plus Dizzy Gillespie and sax player Sonny Stitt. Other artists featured on the junket were Ella Fitzgerald, Roy Eldridge, Oscar Peterson, Gene Krupa, Flip Phillips, Illinois Jacquet, Ray Brown, Herb Ellis, and Jo Jones. All the concerts ended with Stan, Gillespie, Stitt, Eldridge, Phillips, and Jacquet backing Ella in a rousing jam session version of "Lady Be Good."

Granz was so excited by the nightly high-energy jousting of Stan, Gillespie, and Stitt that he brought them into a Los Angeles studio on October 16, 1956—immediately after the tour ended—to create the album *For Musicians Only*. A stellar rhythm section—John Lewis on piano, Herb Ellis on guitar, Ray Brown on bass, and Stan Levey on drums—provides powerfully swinging support to the three horn players, who take all the solos. The men have ample opportunity to stretch out, because the numbers run from eight and a half to thirteen minutes in length.

As with Stan's first recorded encounter with Dizzy three years before, there is an intensely competitive air to the session. Stitt contributes strongly to this feeling; he sounds as if he wants to prove that he is the fastest gun in the West, and as Stan later commented, he pushed hard:

> With Stitt you've got to work. He doesn't let you rest. You've *got* to work hard, or you're left at the starting gate.

Stitt has a chance to show his mettle on two tunes played at Mach 2 tempo—"Bebop" and "Wee"—but Stan and Dizzy match him with solos of equal facility.

On the other numbers which are played at conventionally fast tempos— "Lover Come Back to Me" and the Russian folk tune "Dark Eyes"—Stan is spurred to performances that rank among the best of his career. He comes on like a keening Jewish cantor and is by turns slashingly sardonic, softly romantic, and fiercely lyrical. He expresses these emotions by exploiting the broad range of sounds that the saxophone can produce: achy cries in the high register, bubbling belches from the bottom of the horn, silky moans from the middle range.

Stan was happy to immerse himself in his work at the session, because he had just received distressing news from Goldie about Beverly and the children. Their situation had quickly deteriorated, because Tony Fruscella—the trumpeter who left Stan's group in January 1955 after fighting with him—had moved into the Union Turnpike apartment with them.

Fruscella's music was disciplined, but his life was chaotic and dominated by drugs and liquor. He grew up in an orphanage, was briefly married to Morgana King, who played Marlon Brando's wife in *The Godfather*, and spent the major part of his adult life in crash pads, hospitals, and jails. When he died from cirrhosis of the liver at age forty-two in 1969, an obituary said, "The usual background landscape would be strewn with a couple of wives, countless chicks, barbiturate containers, and empty bottles." Fruscella was using heavily and had gotten Beverly hooked again; he was also dealing drugs from the apartment.

As Steve remembered, Beverly and Fruscella often left the children unattended and without food:

> The refrigerator was totally empty, and I used to go downstairs and knock on the neighbor's door and ask for a can of soup so I could feed myself and my brother and my sister. All we used to do at that time was watch television; we stopped going to school.

Stan and Monica were planning an elaborate spring wedding at Rockelstad to coincide with a JATP tour, and they hoped to have Ella Fitzgerald sing at the nuptials. The news about Fruscella and the neglect of the children forced them to change their plans. Goldie convinced them that they now might have to mount an effort to remove the children from Beverly's care, and they each knew that no judge would give custody to an ex-convict on probation. They believed they would have a much better chance if Stan were married to someone with a clean record.

Stan hurriedly put together a financial settlement for Beverly and got her to sign a consent to a Mexican divorce. At that time Mexico required the physical presence of one spouse and a written consent from the other, and Stan flew to Juarez with the proper documentation on October 30, 1956; he obtained the divorce the next day.

When Monica told Donna Reed and her husband Tony what was happening, they offered to arrange a wedding in Las Vegas and serve as matron of honor and best man; Stan and Monica were delighted to accept, and when they arrived by plane in Nevada on November 2, Donna and Tony had already bought the rings. Donna helped Monica select a wedding dress, and the next day the four of them headed to a small

Lutheran church for the nuptials. The ceremony went happily, and they laughed when the rings were mixed up and Monica's wedding band could not be slipped onto Stan's thick finger. After the wedding Stan and Monica took up residence in a small apartment on Wilshire Boulevard in Beverly Hills.

On November 24, Stan made an outstanding quartet album—*The Steamer*—with his old Second Herd cohort Lou Levy on piano, Leroy Vinnegar on bass, and Stan Levey on drums. His performance almost reaches the level of the Gillespie-Stitt session of the previous month as he again weds musical intelligence with passion to create a series of dazzling tracks.

Stan's marriage spurred Beverly to a major effort at self-improvement. She sobered up in December and stocked the refrigerator, served regular meals, plied the children with Christmas presents, and decorated a tree. But drugs and alcohol seduced her again in January, and she became deeply addicted once more.

This prompted Goldie to send a message to Stan and Monica in Beverly Hills that could almost be heard without the telephone wires: "What are you guys doing out there sitting around in the sunshine? Your children are sitting in the dark starving to death. You've got to do something." Stan reacted by hopping the first plane to New York and taking a cab directly to the Union Turnpike apartment.

He had trouble getting someone to come to the door, even though it was 5:00 P.M. A woman in her underwear let him in, and when Stan entered, he found both Fruscella and Beverly passed out and the children sitting on the floor watching TV in dirty clothes. Stan cleaned up the kids and got them some food, but he left the apartment supremely frustrated because he knew that the courts were extremely reluctant to take children away from their mothers, no matter what the provocation.

Stan decided that he must stay in New York to keep an eye on the kids, and he checked into a hotel on upper Broadway in Manhattan. While there, he hired a skillful lawyer and mounted an appeal of his banishment by New York City from clubs that served liquor. He presented affidavits from doctors and psychiatrists that he was unlikely to become addicted again, and he submitted to a lengthy hearing. And as he was fighting the municipal bureaucracy in New York City, Monica was encountering that of the IRS in California.

Stan managed his finances bizarrely. He sent all his bills to his father, who would throw them into a valise; when a creditor became insistent about payment, Stan would call Al and he would extricate the bill and send off a check. But there was an all-important creditor whom Stan ignored almost completely; he never sent the IRS the withholding taxes he collected for the musicians in his groups, and he was behind in the payment of his own taxes. Monica believed naively that these were small, easily handled matters, and she marched blithely into the IRS offices to straighten out the bill. She almost went into shock when they calculated that Stan owed them more than $21,000, the equivalent of about $70,000 in 1996.

She turned to Donna Reed for help, and Donna found her and Stan a top-drawer law firm. When the lawyers looked at the IRS obligation and Stan's other debts, which came to another $21,000, they recommended that he seek a bankruptcy attorney in New York. On the advice of the New York attorney, Stan filed for bankruptcy on March 7, 1957; he listed assets of $86.11 and liabilities of $42,398.59. Among Stan's nongovernmental creditors were Norman Granz; hospitals, ambulance services, doctors, and nurses in Oklahoma and New York; and the bail-bondsman from his California arrest.

As in all bankruptcies, every debt but the IRS obligation was expunged, and the IRS hounded Stan unmercifully for its $21,000. They garnisheed his wages and turned up regularly on paydays to collect directly a large chunk of his income from the club owners.

Stan tried to economize by hiring gifted unknowns for his quartet and in the process fostered a unique talent, singer-pianist Mose Allison. Allison, who created a singular and enduring style by marrying Mississippi Delta folk blues with bebop, joined Stan in the winter of 1957 and made his recording debut on February 16 with the quartet. Allison was featured in every club set, usually doing numbers from his twenty-part composition called "Back Country Suite." He remained with Stan until late summer, when his own March recording of the suite became a hit, and he left to capitalize on its success.

Acting on a tip about Tony Fruscella's drug-dealing, narcotics detectives arrested him for possession at Beverly's apartment on April 9, 1957. A newspaper reported that "the shapely Beverly Getz answered the door, dressed in brief shorts and a halter." The detectives found 144 Dexedrine pills in Fruscella's pocket; he told them that an unknown person had given them to him at a party and that he took them to stay awake when playing late-night gigs. No one believed him, and he served six months on the possession charge. Beverly disappeared after the arrest, the cops contacted Stan, and Monica flew in the next day.

She encountered a mess at Union Turnpike; a closet was filled to the ceiling with empty liquor bottles, there were several large gashes in the walls, and the kitchen counter was piled with dirty dishes. As Little Bev watched cartoons, Steve and Stan rolled up their sleeves and washed the dishes, and David helped Monica scrub and mop. Stan had not washed dishes before as an adult; until then he had followed Goldie's decree that her prince should not sully his dignity by performing such a mundane household chore. That night he and Monica fell exhausted onto a couch in the living room, and the three children slept in what had been Al and Goldie's double bed in the only bedroom. Stan and Monica's dreams of starting a life together separate from the children were forever shattered; the small apartment was the first of many homes the five of them would share in the decades ahead.

On April 15, 1957, five days after they moved to Union Turnpike, Stan and Monica received some very good news: He had been issued a temporary sixty-day cabaret card and could work in New York clubs again. The case made Stan a hero for performers everywhere because the authorities studied his progress to determine whether to make the system more lenient, and when he stayed out of trouble, they loosened the reins considerably. A decade later they abandoned the cabaret card system entirely.

A few weeks later Goldie, Stan, and Monica were struggling in court to keep his three children out of a foster home. After strong pleas from Goldie and a social worker, a judge awarded custody to Goldie. She immediately delegated her maternal responsibilities to Monica, who was barely twenty-three years old at the time.

Although the cramped quarters at Union Turnpike tried everyone's patience, the children gradually became accustomed to an orderly and caring regimen there. The entire family became more relaxed when, three months later, they moved to a house with a back yard about eight miles away in suburban Great Neck.

Al and Goldie often came to visit, and she was shaken when she saw Stan happily performing household tasks at Monica's behest. Watching him wash his socks actually drove her to tears. "What has the world come to?" she cried. "I brought my son up so he should never have to wash his own socks. Stanley, don't do this. Don't do this." Goldie wasn't mollified when he explained that he was saving money because hotels on the road were constantly losing his socks in their laundries.

Monica's mother Mary also came to visit; she met Goldie and Al and lived amidst the bedlam created by three energetic kids and soon became distressed at the fatigue and stress she saw in her daughter's face. When she returned to Sweden, she generously sent Monica a household servant, an "au pair," to ease her burdens.

Beverly broke the suburban calm of Great Neck one afternoon when she stormed in on Monica and the children and shouted, "I want my kids back. Give me my kids. I want more money."

"Everything's settled with the kids. They stay here," Monica yelled back. "And Stan's paying you very good alimony." Then Beverly began hitting her with her purse and Monica grabbed one of her own and retaliated.

David was six at the time and Beverly was three, and both—as adults— have vivid memories of the large fair woman and the small dark one standing toe-to-toe whacking each other with handbags; it was the last time that they would ever see their mother.

Monica recalls the encounter differently; she doesn't remember the flailing handbags but retains a scary image of Beverly threatening her in the kitchen with a knife.

Steve ran to a neighbor's and called the police, and when an officer arrived, Beverly calmed down and told him, "Oh, I was just visiting," and left.

That frightening afternoon caused Stan to offer Beverly an attractive lump sum settlement in place of monthly alimony payments. Tempted by the prospect of ready cash, she accepted the deal and lived independently of the Getzes thereafter.

The mid-1950s saw the birth of the summer festivals that became very important jazz institutions in the decades ahead. In July Stan played in one for the first time—the fourth edition of George Wein's Newport Festival, the granddaddy of them all, and in August he participated in the North Shore Festival in Massachusetts and the New York Festival in the Big Apple.

The 1957 JATP tour kicked off at Carnegie Hall on September 14; this time Norman Granz pulled together the incredible saxophone lineup of Lester Young, Coleman Hawkins, Sonny Stitt, Illinois Jacquet, Flip Phillips, and Stan; then he added to the mix seminal bebop trombonist J. J. Johnson, trumpeter Roy Eldridge, the Modern Jazz Quartet, the Oscar Peterson Trio, and Ella Fitzgerald.

Stan was always teamed with J. J. Johnson for his concert sets; they had previously worked together in the cooperative band with Miles Davis in 1950 and on Schuller's "Third Steam" recording in 1955, and Stan respected J.J.'s talents highly; their JATP rhythm section comprised Modern Jazz Quartet drummer Connie Kay and Peterson's trio—Oscar on piano, Herb Ellis on guitar, and Ray Brown on bass.

Granz put Stan into overdrive as the tour progressed; between October 10 and October 28, 1957, he recorded him eight times—in the studio with

Peterson's trio, a Herb Ellis quintet featuring Roy Eldridge, a Gerry Mulligan quintet, and a large orchestra backing Ella Fitzgerald—and in three live concert settings, two with J. J. Johnson and one with Ella. In addition, Stan was a member of a JATP contingent which performed and was recorded aurally on Nat King Cole's NBC-TV show on October 15.

During this period in October, Stan was thrown into varied settings with a disparate group of competitive world-class artists, and he acquitted himself splendidly. Many fine jazz musicians would be proud if their career output contained as many gems as Stan produced in just nineteen hectic days.

The Peterson session—*Stan Getz with the Oscar Peterson Trio*—has the easy, laid-back quality of a group of old friends jamming in a back room after hours. Herb Ellis and Ray Brown provide impeccable backing as Oscar and Stan produce chorus after chorus of mellow, effortless swing. Stan later reflected:

> A terrific feeling prevails here. It is one of the most enjoyable recordings I ever made. How refreshing it is to play with these pros—no drums needed, nor missed.

The Ellis recording, a pianoless, all-blues date, is called *Nothing But the Blues*. Ellis, who shared a house with Jimmy Giuffre and Gene Roland at North Texas State College, has an earthy southwestern feel for the blues, and Eldridge insures that the session moves right down "into the alley" as he alternates guttural rasps with high register cries. Stan fits in beautifully as he leaves the complexities of bebop behind and wails plaintively in a traditional blues mode.

The *Mulligan Meets Getz* session produced several rollicking tracks on which the horn men prod each other to happy feats of inventiveness. They trade horns—Gerry playing tenor and Stan baritone—on half of the six tunes, and this gimmick adds nothing to the session since each man seems slightly uncomfortable with the other's instrument.

Stan's concert recordings with J. J. Johnson provided Granz with what he was always seeking—fresh, unbridled emotion expressed with imagination. Aside from pensive renditions of two ballads, the sessions display an ebullient joy and catch Stan and J.J. at their steaming, romping best; the performances are more reminiscent of Stan's high energy outings with Dizzy Gillespie than the laid-back session with Peterson.

The currently issued CD—*Stan Getz and J. J. Johnson at the Opera House*—covers an October 19 concert from Chicago's Opera House that was recorded monaurally and a performance from the Shrine in Los

Angeles on October 25 that was waxed in stereo; the Chicago concert provides six numbers for the CD, four of which are repeated at the Los Angeles session. On the four numbers that were recorded twice, Stan and J.J change tempos at the second concert, and they never repeat themselves when improvising; their fund of melodic ideas seems inexhaustible as they tear through two blues, a very fast rendition of "Crazy Rhythm," and a driving swing version of "My Funny Valentine."

Stan's interpretation of the ballad "It Never Entered My Mind" from the Chicago concert shows that his romantic sensibility had only deepened since the days of "Early Autumn" and "Moonlight in Vermont." The British writer Richard Palmer describes Stan's rendition accurately when he says:

> Getz produces one of his greatest ballad performances, tear-inducing in its pathos without ever remotely approaching the sentimental. It also manages to swing at the gentlest of tempi, a feat managed only by the great masters.

Stan's romantic side was on display again nine days later when he backed Ella Fitzgerald on four tunes as the only soloist with an orchestra playing lush string backgrounds; the album was called *Like Someone in Love*. He provided her with particularly emphatic support on "You're Blasé" and "What Will I Tell My Heart."

Nat King Cole was very relaxed with the JATP musicians on his October 15 TV show, and he obviously enjoyed jamming with them. Granz brought along the Peterson Trio plus drummer Jo Jones as the rhythm section and spotlighted Stan, Coleman Hawkins, Flip Phillips, Illinois Jacquet, and Roy Eldridge on the horns. Stan shares spirited solos with Eldridge on "I Want to Be Happy" and with Hawkins on "Stompin' at the Savoy" and backs Cole up on two other tunes. He looks slim and fit and slightly nervous on camera.

When he returned from the West Coast in November, Stan was greeted by the joyous news that Monica was pregnant. And this knowledge came to him against a backdrop of domestic stability; Steve and David were trotting off to school every day, Little Bev was getting used to regular hours and clean clothes, and the au pair was helping Monica cope with her assorted chores.

Monica's happiness with her pregnancy was dampened when she found out inadvertently, in a letter from a friend, that her father Nils had died three months earlier, on August 18, 1957, in Stockholm; he was sixty-nine and had been felled by a stroke. Monica wasn't properly notified because a gap had grown between Nils's fourth and last wife and his children by Monica's mother Mary.

Monica and Stan decided that she should have their baby in Lund in Sweden. Because they were uninsured and the IRS was grabbing every penny they could put by, they were afraid that they couldn't afford good obstetrical or postnatal care in the U.S. Alternatively, Sweden's socialized medicine program offered them the most generous medical and maternity benefits in the world at that time. In addition, Monica expected that she and her baby would receive extra attention at the Lund hospital because of her family's associations there.

Stan stayed with the family in Great Neck for a month because he was booked into a series of lucrative road dates from mid-December until mid-February. While traveling, he received the news that he had won the *Down Beat* and *Metronome* polls for the eighth and ninth times, respectively; the victories had become almost a year-end ritual.

While completing an engagement in San Francisco, Stan made an excellent LP, *Cal Tjader–Stan Getz Sextet*, with the vibraphonist Cal Tjader on February 8, 1958. Tjader, as a member of George Shearing's quintet, had shared with Stan the horrible Portland-Seattle bus ride the morning of Stan's aborted holdup, and he was an ethnic anomaly, a Swedish-American who specialized in Latin jazz.

Tjader was the leader on the date because, in an unusual move, Granz had farmed Stan out to Tjader's label for a fee. Stan contributed more than his horn, however, as he brought along two very talented discoveries of his—drummer Billy Higgins and bassist Scott LaFaro, both twenty-one at the time. Higgins has played with such giants as Thelonious Monk, Ornette Coleman, John Coltrane, Sonny Rollins, and Dexter Gordon during a brilliant career, and LaFaro touched peaks few jazz bassists have ever reached before he was killed in a 1961 auto crash while a member of Stan's quartet.

The album pays deference to both Tjader's Latinism and a wistful, lyrical element in his sensibility; the men work out at length on a samba, but they also take the opportunity to indulge their romanticism on three lovely ballads. LaFaro and Higgins provide rich, propulsive support throughout.

Stan stopped off in Chicago on his way east to make for Granz, on February 16, his first ever recording with Chet Baker, *Stan Meets Chet*. It was not one of their best outings; Stan's playing is up to par, but Baker lacks energy, and the pickup rhythm section never jells.

Stan relaxed somewhat after he came off the road; he gigged around New York until late April and then flew to Europe to participate with

Dizzy Gillespie, Sonny Stitt, Coleman Hawkins, Roy Eldridge, the Oscar Peterson Trio, Jo Jones, Lou Levy, and Ella Fitzgerald in the JATP 1958 tour of the continent. Stan made a studio recording in Paris on May 1 with Gillespie, Eldridge, and the Peterson Trio, which was used on the sound track of the movie *Les Tricheurs*, and the full JATP entourage performed its kickoff concert the following day. Norman Granz then broke Ella, Jones, and the Peterson Trio away on a separate itinerary, and the two groups were reunited for a June 16 concert at the Brussels World's Fair.

Monica closed up shop in Great Neck in June and headed for Rockelstad and Lund with the three children and the au pair. After the JATP tour ended with the Brussels Fair, Stan easily found gigs at European clubs and festivals. On July 13, while he was performing at the Cannes Festival, Monica gave birth to Pamela Mary Pauline Getz in Lund. Stan didn't see the baby for several more days, and when he did he was not in good shape. He had stopped along the way in England, where it was legal for doctors to write prescriptions for narcotics. He had found a cooperative physician and had gone on a short binge.

CHALLENGE AND RESPONSE TWELVE

THE GETZES spent several weeks at Rockelstad after Pamela was born, and Stan loafed through the long summer days when the sun didn't set until past midnight. He swam and sunbathed for hours at a time, took long walks through the piney woods, fished with Steve and David, played with the little girls. He had at last found tranquillity after five years of turmoil, and he was beginning to agree with Monica's growing conviction that they should take up residence in Scandinavia. These feelings were reinforced every time he went out to perform; he adored the European audiences, who treated him with an affection bordering on reverence. And he was relieved that each week he didn't have to face an IRS agent grabbing for his paycheck. He met his U.S. tax obligations, but in a more civilized manner; he mailed his payments to New York. He was also relieved that he was not being met at every turn by drug pushers; in 1958 Scandinavia was virtually drug-free.

By the time Pamela was christened on August 16, 1958, in the chapel at Rockelstad, Stan had decided to stay in Scandinavia. The logical place to settle was Copenhagen, less than an hour by car and boat from Monica's home town, Lund. Copenhagen, with a population close to 1.5 million, bustled with commercial and artistic activity; it made the other, far smaller Scandinavian cities seem provincial by comparison. And it was the home of the most successful jazz impresario in Europe, Anders Dyrup.

Through her academic connections, Monica's mother found the Getzes a lovely villa in a town outside Copenhagen named Kungens Lyngby. Originally an outbuilding to a royal residence, it faced a swan-filled lake and was situated in a quiet park. The calm of the place was shattered only when David teased the swans, and the powerful birds climbed onto the lawn honking loudly and chasing the children; the swans would invariably settle down when Stan appeared and played romantic songs to them on his saxophone.

Once ensconced at Kungens Lyngby, Stan and Monica became suburbanites again. He immediately secured work at the state-owned Copenhagen radio station, commuting in a small, newly acquired German car and by bicycle. The older children were enrolled in local schools, where they amazed Stan with the speed with which they picked up Danish; he found the language impenetrable, but it posed no serious handicap because the great majority of Danes spoke English.

Stan supplemented his income with appearances in other European cities where engagements were plentiful. One of his out-of-town gigs took him in January 1959 to Le Blue Note in Paris, where Lester Young was booked to follow him as the featured artist. Lester caught Stan's last show, and when Stan came off the bandstand, Lester greeted him with a broad smile and said, "You're my singer." Stan maintained thereafter that this was the greatest compliment he had ever earned. He never saw Pres again; years of heavy drinking had worn Lester down, and he died in New York two months later at the age of forty-nine.

Soon after Stan's encounter with Lester, Monica arranged a lunch at Copenhagen's leading hotel with Anders Dyrup to discuss the possibility of Stan performing for him.

Dyrup, an architect and the son of a wealthy paint manufacturer, was only thirty, but he had been active in the jazz world for a decade as a researcher, record producer, and manager and owner of clubs. He had spent several years in Louisiana helping scholar William Russell to record aging, pioneer New Orleans and Delta musicians such as George Lewis,

Jim Robinson, and Snooks Eaglin, and he was one of the three founders of Preservation Hall, the New Orleans performance site which flourishes to this day as a nurturer of authentic Dixieland music.

Dyrup's musical enthusiasms were not limited to traditional jazz, and he produced records under two labels—Storyville for Dixieland and Sonet for modern jazz. He had returned to Denmark from the U.S. in 1954 and was surprised and delighted when ten thousand people responded to his advertisements for a nonprofit jazz society, called Club Montmartre, which would sponsor concerts and other events and publish a newsletter.

After the society had operated successfully for four years in ad hoc venues throughout Copenhagen, he was emboldened to start a for-profit venture with the Montmartre name in a small, attractive space he purchased near the center of the city. As you approached the new location, you encountered a giant photo of Count Basie staring down at you from the wall of the building; aside from this icon, Dyrup provided no other evidence that you had arrived at his club.

Patrons were greeted by Dyrup's wife, Lotte, who also ran the excellent kitchen. The Montmartre seated only 120 customers, who sat on benches at rough-hewn wooden tables, and standees crowded into every other available space, doubling the body count. The room was dark and filled with the smells of food, beer, schnapps, and tobacco and candle smoke. The candles provided the only illumination, and they cast distorted shadows against the bright colors of the fanciful wall decorations that had been created by friends of Dyrup's, members of a painting and sculpture cooperative called "Six Plus Two."

Most of the clientele arrived in the hip European uniform of the day— the hooded loden coat. The women leaned toward Brigitte Bardot hairdos and tight skirts, while the men fancied beards, pipes, and corduroys. The audience took its jazz seriously, staring down anyone who dared speak while the musicians were playing.

When Monica sat down to lunch with Dyrup, he was celebrating the wildly successful opening of the new club—two weeks of standing-room-only business generated by clarinetist George Lewis and his traditional New Orleans group featuring trombonist Jim Robinson. She surprised him when she suggested that Stan play for him for a very reasonable fee, explaining that her husband now valued a calm, predictable life more than a high income.

Dyrup was delighted to hear this and quickly booked Stan to play with Mose Allison, who had been performing in Sweden, and two Danes on bass and drums. This arrangement lasted for only one set, because the Danes performed so ineptly. They were dismissed on the spot, and Stan and Mose played the remainder of the month-long engagement triumphantly as a duo.

Soon Stan settled into a regular Monday-to-Thursday gig at the Montmartre, reserving the weekends for engagements elsewhere in Europe. For the first time in his life, he had a steady job and didn't need to scuffle. As Stan told a reporter, he was pleased with his comfortable routine:

> I'm tired of competition. . . . Here, I have more time with my family. I don't make as much money as in the States, but it's cheaper to live here. And it's unhurried. I enjoy the relaxed way of living in Europe. I wanted to find peace of mind. That's hard to find in the States.

And he applauded the lack of racism in Denmark:

> In my opinion, people are more civilized here and there are no race problems. I should like to be alive in 500 years when we'll all be one race, all be mixed. I hate the racial thing.

Stan's first order of business at the Montmartre was to find good backup musicians, and he was elated to discover that premier American bassist Oscar Pettiford had recently expatriated himself to Europe and was looking for a place to settle down. The two men had played together briefly during the last few weeks of Stan's tenure with Woody Herman and for a New York quartet engagement in 1956 and had deeply respected each other's work.

Pettiford's main reason for leaving America was to find a more tolerant racial climate for his children, and he was delighted with the attitudes he encountered in Denmark. He was born in 1922 on an Indian reservation in Oklahoma: His mother was a full-blooded Choctaw, and his father was part Cherokee and part black. He was thus subjected to two kinds of prejudice in the United States, and he further inflamed the native bigots by marrying a white woman.

Pettiford had completed—in the early 1940s—the work of recently deceased trailblazer Jimmy Blanton in transforming the bass from a mere timekeeper into a melodic, improvising instrument. He became a prime mover in the bebop revolution, playing with Thelonious Monk at Minton's and coleading with Dizzy Gillespie in 1944 the first bebop band on Fifty-second Street. After four brilliant years with Duke Ellington and Woody Herman (1945–49), he found success during the 1950s on the bandstand and in the studios leading small groups; he also made important recordings with the bands of Monk and Art Blakey.

To Stan, Pettiford was manna from heaven. He had everything—prodigious technique, perfect intonation, an impeccable sense of time, and a far-ranging melodic imagination. The two men soon found a couple of competent musicians to round out a quartet for the Montmartre—American expatriate drummer Joe Harris, who was doing radio work in Stockholm, and Swedish pianist Jan Johansson. An air check of an October 25, 1959, performance by this quartet—released on the album *Stan Getz: Scandinavian Days*—is the only aural evidence we have of Stan's work with Pettiford. A spirit of joy pervades as the two masters drive each other through sparkling solos.

The Montmartre became a gathering place for touring American musicians—the JATP troupes as well as people like Art Blakey, Lee Konitz, and Kenny Clarke—and was packed almost every night. Monica and Pettiford's wife Jackie became caught up in the spirit of the place and were there constantly to help the Dyrups with promotional and management tasks.

Stan was scratched from the British part of the spring 1959 JATP European tour; the U.K. government denied him access to that country after they had obtained evidence of his drug escapade the previous summer during the week following Pamela's birth.

Stan tried to convince Norman Granz to intervene, but he refused. "I won't fight for you if you're going to get high," he told Stan at a meeting in Sweden. "You put all of us in a hole when you pull crap like that; you jeopardize the whole tour. Clean up your act." Stan cursed and yelled for half an hour, but he couldn't budge Granz, and he was forced to turn for help to the New York lawyer who had regained his cabaret card. The attorney, working with British counsel, prevailed once more, and Stan was allowed to perform in Britain again later that year.

Granz hired Sonny Stitt to fill in for Stan in England and then teamed Stan up with Sonny and Dizzy Gillespie as a concert unit for the remainder of the tour.

In August of 1959, Stan's ego received a boost when he took seventh place in an all-time, all-star jazz poll conducted by *Metronome*. The first six places went—in order—to Charlie Parker, Miles Davis, Gerry Mulligan, Lester Young, Louis Armstrong, and Dizzy Gillespie; Benny Goodman, Thelonious Monk, and Dave Brubeck followed Stan in the eighth, ninth, and tenth slots, respectively.

That same month Stan and Monica sent Steve off to Aiglon, a strict boarding school in Switzerland modeled after the "public" schools of England. Steve was particularly unhappy to leave because the Getzes had rented a spectacular weekend retreat for the summer—a large house in

Prince Hamlet's Elsinore facing on Ore Sund, the strait that separates Denmark and Sweden. Steve and David loved running down its broad lawn with their father to swim in the chilly waters, and they played hectic games of hide-and-seek in the nooks and crannies of the big dwelling.

As Anders Dyrup remembers, the place became a mecca for visiting jazzmen:

> Stan and Monica were the American jazz ambassadors in Copen-hagen, so whenever American musicians were around it was par-tying at their house in Elsinore—a twenty-room place with a little tower which had a music room of about 1,600 square feet.
>
> Monica was a very good hostess, and the musicians used to go up and have dinner and stay with Stan and relax before the concert. We always came late for concerts; I had a little Morgan Plus 4 sports car, and we had to race. Norman Granz got to hate us because we always came at the very last minute at 120 miles per hour.
>
> When they finished the concerts, they piled into Montmartre. I don't remember any concert by American jazz musicians in Denmark which didn't wind up in a jam session in Montmartre.
>
> And often after Montmartre they would go back to Elsinore. I had a boat at that time, and I had another house at the oceanfront about twenty miles south of Stan's house. And we went down to my boat and hoisted the sails and sailed up in the early morning sun and came up to his house, and sometimes swam ashore. All the instruments were brought up by taxi.
>
> I remember one morning, Jim Hall was on guitar, and Stan and Gerry were on opposite horns—Stan on baritone and Mulli-gan playing the tenor. They played for four or five hours in the early morning. We had some beautiful experiences there.

Despite the newly won stability at work and at home, the freedom from the tyranny of the needle, and the beauty of his surroundings, Stan could not escape his perennial psychic companions: pain and depression. Dyrup remembers:

> Stan was not always happy. He wasn't meant to be happy all the time. . . . There were incidents where he was low down, and Mon-ica and I would sit and comfort him all night. He never tried to hurt any of us, but he hurt himself from time to time. He got in moods where he was a difficult person to handle.

In the absence of drugs, Stan turned to alcohol to deal with the pain that filled him so often, and a visit from Goldie and Al triggered a particularly frightening drunken episode at a rented house in a town called Roomstead that they had moved to from Kungens Lyngby. Goldie's presence awakened in Stan all the conflicting emotions he had felt about her in childhood, emotions that drew the following comments from a psychiatrist who treated him near the end of his life:

> Goldie was a depressed personality and gave Stan, starting from early childhood, strong and constant signals that she counted on him to erase her depression. He tried to relieve her depression but couldn't because this is an impossible task for a child. As a consequence, he carried into adulthood guilt and remorse that he could never do enough for the most important person in his life; these feelings affected every one of his endeavors.
>
> His violence when drinking was a "breaking free" from the guilt and remorse that were his constant companions.

One night after dinner with Monica, the kids, Monica's mother, and his parents, Stan felt overwhelmed by the mixture of sadness and rage which seemed to be bursting through his skull. He tried to dull the rage with generous drafts of Scotch, but it kept building in him until he went outside, found a pile of bricks, and threw them one by one through every window in the house. Then he came inside and grabbed a poker from the fireplace and smashed all the plates in a collection of renowned Royal Copenhagen china owned by the landlord.

Everyone else locked themselves in a bedroom as Monica summoned the police. When they arrived with a couple of frightening-looking dogs, Stan was standing calmly in the living room contemplating his handiwork.

The police were more knowledgeable about his afflictions than Monica, and they put him in the care of a doctor who specialized in treating alcoholism. The physician prescribed Antabuse, the drug that causes violent illness if alcohol is taken within three days of ingesting it, but Stan shortly stopped using it, proclaiming that because he wasn't an alcoholic, he didn't need it.

In March of 1960, Granz sent two JATP units out to tour Europe. The first one featured Ella Fitzgerald, the Shelly Manne quintet, the Jimmy Giuffre trio, and Roy Eldridge; the second paired Stan in a quartet with a revolutionary group featuring two men whose work Stan admired greatly: the Miles Davis quintet with tenor saxophonist John Coltrane. This gave Stan his initial opportunity to hear firsthand some of the music which had been rocking the American jazz world since early 1959.

IN THAT YEAR revolutionary ideas that had been simmering beneath the surface of the jazz community exploded with great force. Fifteen years after the sophisticated chordal aesthetic of bebop had swept all before it, several adventurous artists were finding that the use of chords as the basis for improvising no longer provided sufficient stimulus for their imaginations.

For them the chords had become overly familiar signposts on roads that had been traveled far too many times. A veteran improviser like Miles Davis might easily, by 1959, have performed "All of Me" three hundred times, and each time he would have found that the harmonic movement of this tune was unvarying: As we have seen, the first six bars are defined by three chords that appear at two-bar intervals; each chord is the dictator of its two-bar time span and determines which will be the "comfortable" and "uncomfortable" notes for its segment; the harmony of the remainder of the tune is similarly defined by chords that never vary. When encountered for the three hundredth time, a chord sequence like this had—for some—become restrictive and boring.

The most important improvisers who grappled with this problem of imaginative stimulus during the late 1950s were Charles Mingus, Gil Evans, Cecil Taylor, Lenny Tristano, Miles Davis, John Coltrane, and Ornette Coleman. Coltrane and Coleman had the greatest immediate impact, and Coleman's approach, which came to be called "free jazz," was the most radical.

Coleman simply did away with all harmonic structures. His first record—*Something Else!!!!* cut on February 10 and 22, 1959—did not quite go that far, but it departed sufficiently from accepted chordal norms to sound quite startling at the time.

Coleman sometimes made a small nod to the concept of structure by providing a tonal center—a note or a cluster of notes—that the discerning listener could hear as the center of gravity of the piece. Otherwise, his improvisations grew from motif to motif without harmonic premises. As critic Ekkehard Jost has put it:

> Coleman invents, as he goes along, [motifs] independent of the theme and continues to develop them. In this way—independently of the chord progressions, let it be noted—an inner cohesion is created that is comparable to the stream of consciousness

in Joyce or the "automatic writing" of the surrealists; one idea
grows from another, is reformulated, and leads to yet another
new idea.

Coleman's concepts challenged the improviser as had no jazz aesthetic
before or since. In his music the improviser has nothing to fall back on
but his own ability to create—continuously—new melodies out of thin
air. Coleman was up to the task, a prodigious maker of song who brought
to his music a lacerating bluesiness which gave it a burning emotional
impact. On his chosen instrument, the alto sax, he was able to imbue his
tumbling melodies with a uniquely piercing human sound.

Gunther Schuller and John Lewis were so impressed by Coleman's first
recorded efforts that they brought him to a jazz school they were running
in Lenox, Massachusetts, during the summer of 1959. The work that
Coleman did there led to a November 17 quartet engagement at the Five
Spot, a dingy club located in the East Village on the Bowery, New York's
skid row.

Coleman brought with him three musicians—Don Cherry on trumpet,
Charlie Haden on bass, and Billy Higgins on drums—who had thoroughly
absorbed his principles. Their radical music electrified and polarized the
jazz community. No one—even its most vehement detractors—could deny
its raw power, and it remained controversial for several years thereafter.
During 1960 Coleman made several records culminating on December
21 with *Free Jazz* for a double quartet—Haden and Scott LaFaro on bass,
Higgins and Ed Blackwell on drums, Cherry and Freddy Hubbard on
trumpet, himself and Eric Dolphy on reeds—that solidified his position
as a major force in the music and gave his aesthetic a name.

During the same period Miles Davis and John Coltrane pioneered a
liberating approach to improvisation that was less radical than the total
freedom from harmonic structure espoused by Coleman. They took a
middle ground by using modes, which were less restrictive than chords,
as the basis of their system.

A mode is simply a scale, a set of notes played in sequence—for example, the five black notes on the piano keyboard (the sharps of C, D, F,
G, and A). Modes, which have been used for centuries in Western music
and provide the structure for forms such as the Gregorian chant, were
suggested as a basis for jazz improvisation by composer-percussionist
George Russell as early as 1953.

The key to Russell's concept was that the notes of the mode or scale
would dictate the harmony for extended periods—sixteen bars, for example. If the improviser were to choose the five black keys as his mode, he

would then be free to create any melodies he wanted from the mode notes throughout the sixteen-bar segment. Instead of eight or sixteen or even more chords in sequence defining his choices, he would base his improvisation on what was essentially one large chord made up of the five black notes.

Miles Davis became the first major jazz musician to be influenced by Russell's ideas, and in 1958 he composed a thirty-two bar tune, "Milestones," which was based on two modes; the first held sway for sixteen bars, the second for eight, and the first for eight again. He recorded "Milestones" with Coltrane on April 3, 1958, and both men felt liberated by the new harmonic philosophy. A few months later, Davis spoke of his fascination with scales (or modes):

> When Gil Evans wrote the arrangement of "I Love You, Porgy," he only wrote a scale for me to play, no chords. . . . When you go this way, you can go on forever. You don't have to worry about [chord] changes and you can do more with the line. It becomes a challenge to see how melodically inventive you are. When you're based on chords, you know at the end of 32 bars that the chords have run out and there's nothing to do but repeat what you've just done—with variations. I think a movement in jazz is beginning away from the conventional string of chords and a return to emphasis on melodic rather than harmonic variations. There will be fewer chords, but infinite possibilities as to what to do with them.

Davis continued to work on Russell's concepts, and on March 2 and April 22, 1959—just weeks after Ornette Coleman recorded *Something Else!!!!*— he created five selections for the first all-modal album, *Kind of Blue*. The title tune consists of five modes, each played as long as the soloist wishes; the second employs one mode in ten-bar sequences, a third follows the pattern of "Milestones" with two modes over thirty-two bars, and the fourth and fifth use modes based on blues scales.

For *Kind of Blue* Davis recorded with a sextet composed of Coltrane on tenor sax, Cannonball Adderley on alto sax, Paul Chambers on bass, Jimmy Cobb on drums, and Bill Evans on piano for four tunes and Wynton Kelly for one. Adderley and Kelly were not entirely comfortable with the modal aesthetic, but it inspired Davis, Coltrane, and Evans to a series of stunning melodic statements. The freshness and beauty of *Kind of Blue* hit the jazz world with great and immediate force, and soon many of the brightest young musicians were demanding to learn about the new creative approach; it attracted many more adherents than did Coleman's free jazz because most of the younger artists felt a need for some degree of structure to undergird their improvising.

Davis was the most intellectually restless of all the jazz innovators, and for him modality was a way station to further changes in harmony, form, and instrumentation during the 1960s and the 1970s. For Coltrane, however, modality released unprecedented creative forces and in a few short years made him a figure of historic importance.

Just two years before *Kind of Blue*, Coltrane's career was at a standstill following his dismissal from an earlier Davis group, where his addictions to heroin and alcohol had made him unreliable. The timing of his firing was unfortunate, because—with Davis—he was blossoming into an outstanding improviser after serving middling apprenticeships with the bands of Dizzy Gillespie, Earl Bostic, and the veteran Ellingtonian Johnny Hodges. In early 1957 Coltrane was thirty-one years old, had never been a leader on a record date, and was subsisting on occasional gigs in the studios and clubs of New York and Philadelphia.

Then three events swiftly transformed his life: First, in March of 1957, he went cold turkey at his mother's home to break—simultaneously and forever—his addictions to heroin and alcohol. Secondly, once his body was clean, he experienced a religious epiphany and became possessed by a deep spirituality that never left him. He wrote about this in 1964:

> During the year 1957, I experienced, by the grace of God, a spiritual awakening which was to lead me to a richer, fuller, more productive life. At that time, in gratitude, I humbly asked to be given the means and privilege to make others happy through music. I feel this has been granted through His grace. ALL PRAISE TO GOD. . . .
>
> May we never forget that in the sunshine of our lives, through the storm and after the rain—it is all with God—in all ways and forever.
>
> ALL PRAISE TO GOD.

And to complete his transformation, in April he came under the spell of a major musical intelligence, the composer-pianist Thelonious Monk.

A recording date on April 16 with a Monk unit so inspired Coltrane that he talked Monk into becoming his mentor. He soon became a frequent visitor to Monk's cluttered apartment just behind what is now Lincoln Center in Manhattan. Coltrane later described these sessions:

He'd play one of his tunes and he'd look at me. So I'd get my
horn out and start trying to find what he was playing. We'd go
over and over the thing until we had most of it worked out. If
there were any parts that I had a lot of difficulties with, he'd get
his portfolio out and show me the thing written out. He would
rather a guy would learn without reading, because you feel it
better and quicker that way. Sometimes we'd get just one tune
a day.

Monk was so impressed with his pupil that he made Coltrane a member
of his quartet for an open-ended engagement at the Five Spot beginning
in July 1957 and lasting for almost five months. As Coltrane recalled, he
went to school with Monk every night at the Five Spot.

Monk gave me complete freedom. . . . He also got me into the
habit of playing long solos on his pieces, playing the same piece
for a long time to find new conceptions for solos. It got so I
would go as far as possible on one phrase until I ran out of ideas.
The harmonies got to be an obsession for me. Sometimes I'd
think I was making music through the wrong end of a magnifying glass.
    Working with Monk brought me close to a musical architect
of the highest order. I felt I learned from him in every way—
through the senses, theoretically, technically. I would talk to
Monk about musical problems, and he would sit at the piano
and show me the answers just by playing them. I could watch
him play and find out the things I wanted to know. Also, I could
see a lot of things that I didn't know about at all.
    I think Monk is one of the true greats of all time. . . . If a guy
needs a little spark, a boost, he can just be around Monk, and
Monk will give it to him.

Coltrane was known for his marathon practice and study sessions from
the start of his career, but his commitment intensified during the Five
Spot engagement. Every day he would analyze audio tapes of the previous
night's performance and then work for hours on musical problems before
boarding the subway for his trip to the East Village.
    When the Five Spot gig ended in December 1957, Monk decided to
disband for a while and Davis rehired Coltrane—now a far better musician than he had been a year earlier; he continued to grow during 1958
and 1959 with Davis, and the theoretical foundations he had built with

Monk prepared him to cope with the modal concepts that Miles had brought to fruition with *Kind of Blue.*

Coltrane was ready to undertake important modal explorations on his own, but before that he was driven to create a chordal tour de force, the *Giant Steps* album; it contains six chordal tunes recorded on May 4 and 5, 1959, and a modal number waxed almost seven months later on December 2 to fill out the playing time on the LP.

Giant Steps showed that Coltrane had become possessed by a desire to transform sound into pure emotion. His incessant practicing gave him the physical prowess to attempt this daunting task, and his studies with Monk and Davis provided him with the necessary intellectual tools. And he projected his melodies with a massive, passionate sound, a more penetrating version of Coleman Hawkins's raw personal cry.

Coltrane wrote all seven songs on *Giant Steps*; the chordal numbers comprise two sophisticated blues and four harmonically complex tunes taken at fast tempos; the single modal piece is a tender, dreamy ballad. The title song, recorded at a manic speed, is the epitome of harmonic density with two chord changes per bar, and Coltrane plays a multitude of notes to examine all their implications. This kind of relentless exploration caused critic Ira Gitler to coin the term "sheets of sound" to describe what Coltrane was doing:

> I called his music "sheets of sound," because of the density of textures he was using. His multinote improvisations were so thick and complex they were almost flowing out of the horn by themselves. That really hit me, the continuous flow of ideas without stopping. It was almost superhuman, and the amount of energy he was using could have powered a space ship.

Miles Davis described the effect of *Giant Steps* differently:

> What he does is to play five notes of a chord and then keep changing it around, trying to see how many different ways it can sound. It's like explaining something five different ways.

Having made a major chordal statement with *Giant Steps* in May 1959, Coltrane embarked on a thorough exploration of modal harmony during the rest of that year and into 1960. By the time he and Davis and their quintet teamed up with Stan and his quartet for the JATP European tour in March of 1960, Coltrane was playing modal music with tremendous freshness, beauty, and power.

STAN HEARD THIS night after night and for the first time felt an urge to give up his comfortable life in Denmark and return to the fray in America. His constant striving for musical perfection always fed off challenges—whether it meant learning a demanding Benny Goodman arrangement, interpreting a soulful Ralph Burns song, mastering the complexities of bebop, or crossing swords with Dizzy Gillespie and Sonny Stitt in an up-tempo cutting contest. And the revolutionary music of 1959 and 1960 was challenging him deeply. He reflected that while Coleman and Davis and Coltrane were making epochal statements—*Something Else!!!!* and *Kind of Blue*—a year earlier in the States, he was recording with the likes of Bent Axen, Erik Molbak, and Ole Jorgensen in Copenhagen. And while his American confreres were building on their discoveries and growing artistically, he was spending most of his time helping Scandinavian musicians learn the principles of swing and bebop.

Oscar Pettiford was the only musical intelligence with whom Stan could consistently explore the American innovations, and his feelings of artistic isolation increased dramatically when Pettiford was suddenly taken away from him. On September 4, 1960, Oscar had complained of a severe sore throat after playing a concert at a Copenhagen art gallery. Fearing that he was suffering from a highly contagious strep infection and seeking to protect Oscar's three small children, his doctor admitted him to a hospital. His condition worsened rapidly there, and by September 6 he was almost completely paralyzed. He died two days later from an obscure viral meningitis; he was only thirty-seven.

Again Stan was filled with anger and pain, and again he drank. He couldn't face the world for several days and did not truly rally himself until October 1, when he played a benefit concert in Copenhagen that raised $4,600 for the Pettiford family.

With Pettiford gone, Stan became obsessively anxious about what his innovative contemporaries were doing back in America—particularly Coltrane, who had gone out on his own upon returning to the States from the JATP tour in April 1960. Stan's anxieties reached a new peak when he heard about Coltrane's October 24 recording of the album *My Favorite Things* featuring a modal rendition of the title tune.

"My Favorite Things" is a simple, sentimental Richard Rodgers song from the musical *The Sound of Music* which Coltrane further simplified when he reduced its harmonic content to two modes. Playing the soprano sax, an instrument he had recently added to his arsenal, Coltrane switched back and forth between the modes to produce torrents of surging, burning melody.

The hypnotic melodic lines of *My Favorite Things* beguiled the public, and it became one of the best-selling jazz LPs of all time; Coltrane had arrived in a big way. This was confirmed when for 1960 he dethroned Stan in both the *Down Beat* and *Metronome* polls; Stan had ruled at *Down Beat* for ten years and at *Metronome* for eleven.

His losses in the polls convinced Stan that he had to return home, and, against Monica's wishes, he booked passage to New York on the Swedish ship the *Kungsholm* for her, himself, and the two girls; Steve remained at the Aiglon boarding school in Switzerland with David, who had joined him there the previous August.

Stan knew that his playing had matured and become richer while in Europe, and—during the Atlantic voyage—he planned for himself three projects which would exhibit his still developing talents to the American public; he would put together a first-rate working quartet, he would record again with his musical soulmate Bob Brookmeyer, and he would commission Eddie Sauter—a brilliant writer and a friend since the Benny Goodman days in 1945—to write an extended work for him.

The family's arrival on January 19, 1961, was less than auspicious. A blizzard was raging, only one reporter came to the ship to greet them, arrangements for a temporary apartment in Manhattan fell through, and Stan's manager Jack Whittemore called to say that he had no immediate bookings because several planned engagements had been canceled.

Stan's cash reserves were very low, so he piled Monica and the two kids into a small hotel room and burned up the phone lines recruiting musicians for his quartet and pressing Whittemore to find him work.

The first gig Whittemore came up with was *Macy's and All That Jazz*, a late-January promotion for the retailer organized by Lionel Hampton. The free five-hour event at the flagship department store in Manhattan drew several thousand people and featured Stan, the old Benny Goodman Quartet (Benny, Hampton, Gene Krupa, Teddy Wilson), Basie singer Jimmy Rushing, Horace Silver, Dizzy Gillespie, J. J. Johnson, Gerry Mulligan, Arthur Godfrey playing banjo, Buddy Rich, and Jo Jones. Stan was teamed with Silver, Hampton, and Krupa and backed up Godfrey on "Twelfth Street Rag" and a blues; he was eager to show everyone that he was alive and well and played with great vigor.

The jazz world was stunned to learn in early February 1961 that Norman Granz had sold his record operations, which had been consolidated under the Verve label, to MGM for $2.5 million. Granz, who had moved to Switzerland in 1958, agreed to stay with the organization to run its European wing and to supervise selected recording sessions.

From Switzerland he arranged three recording dates for Stan. The first took place on February 13 and was a warm-up session involving Bob Brookmeyer. They tried out some new ideas, but did not feel ready to commit their talents to a commercial release and promised to get together again in a few months' time. The second and third were quartet dates: a session in Chicago on February 20 with local accompanists and one in New York on February 21 with Stan's new working group using a substitute drummer.

Stan had chosen for his new quartet his old associate Roy Haynes on drums; Steve Kuhn, a talented young musician who had played with Coltrane, on piano; and Scott LaFaro on bass. LaFaro, now age twenty-five, seemed to have limitless potential. His technical facility was so great that he played the bass as others would a guitar; he created subtle, propulsive variations on the beat that every subsequent bass player copied, and he had mastered all three jazz idioms: chordal, modal, and free. LaFaro had been recorded with Ornette Coleman on the *Free Jazz* session of December 1960 and on a quartet date a month later, had participated in several John Lewis–Gunther Schuller third stream recordings, and since early 1959 had worked in the trio of pianist Bill Evans, which produced a couple of LPs that have become jazz classics.

Haynes could not make the February 21 recording date, and Stan used an energetic young drummer, Pete LaRoca, in his stead. On the most exciting track of the session, the fast-paced "Airegin," the pianist, Kuhn, lays out for most of Stan's multichorus solo, and Stan's and LaFaro's voices mesh in a scintillating rapport similar to that which Stan had achieved a decade earlier with guitarist Jimmy Raney. "Airegin" can be found on the 1984 reissue album *Stan the Man.*

Stan's anxieties about his reacceptance by the American public festered as he waited for Whittemore to find him a major New York booking, and he would often kill a bottle of Scotch by early afternoon as he smoked incessantly and paced about the small house he and Monica had rented in suburban Westchester north of New York City.

In early March Stan played at clubs in Philadelphia and Chicago, but these engagements were treated by aficionados as warmups to the main event, which took place on March 23, 1961, at New York's Village Vanguard, America's oldest jazz club. The crowd filled the venerable wedge-shaped cellar and spilled out onto the narrow staircase leading to the street as the musicians, the fans, and the critics speculated about Stan's chances of weathering the challenge of reentry. Bill Coss of *Down Beat* described Stan's response:

> More than just music lovers crowded the Village Vanguard during the Getz New York re-debut. There were also in attendance the haters, musical and otherwise, who came to find out whether the young white man—who had long ago lengthened the already legendary and unorthodox Lester Young line into something of his own—could stand up against what is, in current jazz, at least a revolution from it. . . .
>
> The young man can, does—seems almost as if he always will—measure up.
>
> The still broad-shouldered, blue-eyed, bland-faced young man met musicians backstage, and they tried him with words and with Indian-hold handshakes of questionable peace and unquestionable war. The young man out front was his arrogant best, holding his audiences with strong quotations from his past and much stronger assertions of his version of the newest . . . sound. . . .
>
> There was a hush in the club, and that is so, because Getz is so eloquent a voice that words must surely fail.

Words didn't fail John Wilson of *The New York Times*, who wrote:

> Getz is playing with considerably more depth than he has in the past. Once he gets well into a solo, he is more probing and searching in his use of the saxophone. . . .
>
> Mr. Getz makes use of the full range of his instrument, kicking his ideas along with an occasional propulsive accent from the very bottom of the horn, leaving long, smooth-flowing lines with staccato phrases and frequently roughening his essentially lyrical style with a hoarsely caustic tone.
>
> He is a much more venturesome musician now than when he was last heard in this country.

Despite the critical acclaim, Stan drew sparse audiences during the months after the Vanguard engagement, discovering how quickly fans can forget you if you leave them for two and a half years. Following Miles Davis into a Hollywood club where Miles had done record business, Stan's quartet fared so poorly that the owner canceled the midweek shows and limited the performances to weekends. And Coltrane outdrew him by a large margin when they played rival clubs simultaneously in San Francisco.

Stan was doubly discouraged because he believed that his new quartet was one of the best groups he had ever assembled. The youngsters LaFaro and Kuhn, fresh from their work with Coleman and Coltrane, stimulated him with their new ideas and great skills, and the veteran Haynes proved night after night that he was one of the most imaginative percussionists in jazz.

Whittemore managed Coltrane as well as Stan, and he attempted to revive Stan's fortunes by booking the two men in double bills in New York and elsewhere. Coltrane got most of the applause, and this frustrated Stan, but he felt no bitterness toward his rival; the two men admired each other both personally and professionally. Coltrane told reporters, "We would all play like Stan Getz, if we could," and Stan commented:

> I'd come in early and listen to John during his set, and he'd be playing so beautifully in his style that he inspired me to push myself all that much harder when it was my turn to play. There was no cutting contest involved, though some critics and fans might have thought so. I was really pleased that the audience could dig both of us, two different tenor styles, because that's what music is all about—a lot of guys saying different things their own way, and saying something worth listening to.

Stan was getting enough work to pay all his bills, but the new MGM executives at Verve were beginning to panic about his ability to reconnect with his audience, and they pressured him to make a highly commercial album filled with romantic ballads. He fought them off because artistically he burned to make his collaborative recording with Eddie Sauter, a project that had come to be called *Focus*. The MGM people believed that the Sauter project had almost no commercial appeal but reluctantly acceded to Stan's wishes. As Stan related, he had given Sauter carte blanche:

> The *Focus* album came about because I had admired Eddie Sauter's writing for so long. I played his arrangements when I was on Benny Goodman's band in 1945. And he seemed so neglected. He was writing music for jingles and for television programs. I thought, "Why should a man this great have to do things like that?"
>
> So I asked him to write something for me.
>
> He said, "What?"
>
> I said, "I don't want any arrangements on standards, pop songs,

jazz classics, or anything. I want it to be all your own original music—something that you really believe in."

Stan and Sauter met several times as Sauter developed the idea of writing a seven-part suite for a small string orchestra built around the renowned Beaux Arts String Quartet. The piece could be played as a finished work by the orchestra, but Sauter left just enough room for Stan to add an extra improvised line by ear. The recording sessions were scheduled for July 14 and 28, 1961, with producer Creed Taylor, whom MGM had hired immediately after buying Verve from Granz. Taylor had been lured away from ABC, where he had created its successful jazz label, Impulse!

Stan gave LaFaro Sunday, June 25, off to make a trio recording with Bill Evans at the Village Vanguard; they created a superb album, the culmination of all the work LaFaro had done with the pianist for two years. Stan again gave LaFaro time off after a triumphant set with Stan's quartet on July 3 at the Newport/New York Jazz Festival; on this occasion LaFaro drove to the small city of Geneva in the north central part of New York State to visit his mother. Stan never saw him again. LaFaro, a notoriously reckless driver, was killed instantly on July 6, 1961, at age twenty-five when his car crashed into a tree in Geneva.

Stan drove to Geneva for the funeral, and as he returned he looked forward to a happier event, his daughter Pamela's third birthday party on July 13.

Goldie became strangely ill soon after she left Al at their Forest Hills apartment and traveled to Stan's house for the party. By the time she arrived, she could not keep her left eye open and her left leg felt weak. When she saw Stan's disturbed reaction to her countenance and the way she dragged her leg, she minimized her discomfort because she did not want to disrupt the party. She said, "Just let me lie down a little while. I'll be okay. I'm a little dizzy; that's all it is." She lay down on a couch as the shouting children milled around her spilling ice cream and soda, and she soon asked Stan to help her to the bathroom.

After he half-carried her there, Goldie fell unconscious to the floor, and he ran in terror to the phone to call an ambulance. He followed as they hoisted her on a stretcher into the vehicle and sat shakily beside her during the trip to a nearby hospital. Soon after they wheeled her into the emergency room, Goldie died of a massive cerebral hemorrhage at age fifty-four. A concussion suffered a few weeks before in a taxicab accident may have contributed to her death; her high blood pressure almost certainly did.

Stan telephoned Monica to tell her the awful news, and then he put a doctor on the line with instructions about getting Al from Forest Hills to the hospital. Stan had informed the physician that Al had developed adult-onset diabetes, and the doctor told Monica, "You medicate the father, because he's diabetic and he's liable to go into shock. And you don't tell him that she's gone."

"How can I not tell him?"

"You have to bring him here so he can be under medical care when he's told. Just say that she's seriously ill."

When Monica told Al that Goldie was very sick, he became extremely agitated and then almost collapsed. She made him take his medicine, and then they embarked on the nightmare journey to Westchester, which consumed more than an hour. Al ran from the car before it came to a full stop, and while Monica was parking it, she could hear through an open window his agonized wailing as he was told of Goldie's death.

Unable to face his own pain and remorse, Stan reacted to Goldie's passing by drinking himself into oblivion. He postponed his grief and anesthetized himself with Scotch throughout the funeral and the eight-day Jewish mourning period known as sitting shiva, and his sloppy attempts to participate in the mourning prayers brought him to the brink of fistfights with several of his relatives.

Acrimony also surrounded Stan's brother, Bob, who angered Al and the other family elders because he could not participate in the shiva ritual. Bob had flown east from his home in Los Angeles but could remain only for the funeral because the biggest project of his theatrical career thus far—an improvisational musical review he was producing and directing—was in its final week of rehearsal.

Steve and David were not told of Goldie's death until they were greeted at the airport during the next to last day of shiva as they returned from their semester at Aiglon. Steve remembered:

> Monica and Stan and our grandfather were there to meet the plane, and we were looking around for Goldie. You know, "Where's our grandmother?" And then my grandfather took me aside and whispered in my ear. We just missed seeing her by only a week.

Stan ended his binge after two weeks, because he knew he had to be in the studio for the *Focus* album on July 28. He was originally slated to record, with the string orchestra, four parts of the seven-part suite on July 14; the remaining three were scheduled for July 28. Goldie's death on July 13 prevented him from attending the first session, and—because the other musicians could not change their schedules—they went ahead and recorded the first four sections without him.

Stan thus entered the studio on July 28 with two handicaps; he was forced to record all seven parts of the thirty-eight-minute suite in one day, and he had to play through the first four sections alone wearing earphones to hear the tracks which the other men had previously laid down. The earphones created significant difficulties because they prevented Stan from hearing his own playing.

Stan told Creed Taylor that he never made a recording completely sober, and he asked his producer to bring bottles of Alka-Seltzer and Scotch to the studio; after fortifying his stomach with the medicine, he sipped the whiskey throughout the grueling session.

The seven movements of *Focus* are not mere background arrangements for tenor saxophone but self-standing compositions that combine to form a narrative work of great structural order. Sauter remembered:

> I conceived the composition as seven different fairy tales—that's what they are—as if Hans Christian Andersen were a musician. They're not songs as much as they are short stories. I decided on that, because Stan tells stories so well. He's a musical poet.

The suite begins with the highly percussive, slashingly melodic "I'm Late, I'm Late," the only track where Roy Haynes joins the ensemble; it then passes through three wistful, romantic sections, builds to a climax in the brooding and swingingly assertive fifth and sixth movements, and releases its tension in the restful calm of its seventh movement.

Stan had attended a few rehearsals, and he was given a sketchy outline as a musical roadmap, but otherwise he had no preparation for the *Focus* session. And he had planned it that way, because he believed that spontaneity of expression was essential to good jazz. As he told a reporter years later:

> You rehearse as little as possible and the less you concentrate, the better. That sounds silly, doesn't it? Have you heard of the alpha state? The best way to create something is to get into the alpha state. Alpha is what we call "relaxed concentration." For example, an accountant doesn't use the alpha—he just concentrates.
>
> The more you tighten up physically and mentally in jazz music, and maybe in most music, the worse it gets. That's why

first takes have a much better chance of sounding right. So you rehearse as little as possible.

You still have to be in love with the music, like you're in love with a new girl. And I don't think that you should call attention to the fact that you're recording. Turn the tape on and let it go.

Stan was deep into the alpha state on July 28, 1961, as he intuitively wove brilliant lines into the fabric of Sauter's compositions. He remembered:

I saw what he had written down but I still couldn't envision what he wanted. As soon as I . . . started to play, I knew what he wanted. The beautiful part was that it was exactly the vehicle I was looking for: new sounds, new freedom, and I was still able to be me.

Stan took a page from Ornette Coleman's book as he improvised freely on Sauter's motifs rather than his chord sequences, and he exhibited wonderful agility throughout as he varied his dynamics and rhythm to deepen the music's emotional content.

His improvisations on two takes of "I'm Late, I'm Late" were such excitingly contrasting interpretations of the same themes that Sauter decided to splice them together and double the length of that movement. Stan's warm, aching statement on the second segment, "Her"—dedicated to Goldie—is as touching as anything he ever created, and his treatment of the final movement calls to mind Matisse's *"Luxe, calme, et volupté"* in its languid beauty.

Stan had risen to the challenge of the times by creating an innovative work that was uniquely his and which expanded the horizons of jazz for all who followed him. He had met Coleman on his own ground with his motific improvisations, and although it was not their intention, he and Sauter had created the most fully realized third stream record ever made.

Focus was recognized as a major achievement when it was released, and it has stood the test of time. Critic Richard Palmer commented in 1987:

What impresses me now . . . is the audacity of Eddie Sauter's writing and Getz's sublime response to it.

In 1984 I wrote that "Focus" struck me as being in the class of Bartok, Schoenberg, and Stravinsky. The intervening years have done nothing to alter that opinion, except to add the name of Prokofiev. . . .

"Focus" is unique, I think, in its utter lack of compromise. [Sauter] was determined to write pieces that had continuity of thought and shape and thematic strength. In essence, this meant taking on classical writing on its own terms and forcing the jazz soloist to respond with no concessions to him whatever. As a result of Sauter's bravery and Getz's magnificence, "Focus" remains the only instance thus far when jazz met classical music and achieved something both unique and absolutely successful.

And for Stan himself, *Focus* occupied a special place among his works. He told a reporter a year before his death:

The record I'm proud of is *Focus*. That was one hell of an effort, to match up with those strings with no music written, but just a score transposed into my key. I listen to that record and feel proud.

Stan's success with the innovative material of *Focus* did not blind him to the fact that he would continue to find his most creative expression within the chordal format. He was not among those improvisers—such as Coleman and Coltrane—who found chordal structures lacking in stimulus, and he was far from alone in this; many great jazz musicians since the early 1960s have retained or adopted the chordal system.

When the dust had settled, the end result of the aesthetic battles of the late 1950s and early 1960s was to broaden dramatically the resources available to the improviser. Since then, the jazz musician has been able to choose among the chordal, the modal, and the free as soul and imagination dictate; some will even use all three aesthetics during the course of a single set in a nightclub.

Sonny Rollins, who most critics believe is the greatest improviser alive today, works almost exclusively within the chordal aesthetic. Joe Lovano, considered by many to be the heir to Sonny's throne, is comfortable with all three approaches, although most of his performances are chordal. The same is true of the younger stars in jazz—musicians like the Marsalis brothers, Joshua Redman, James Carter, Terence Blanchard, Jacky Terrasson, and Stephen Scott.

With *Focus*, Stan showed that he was equal to the innovative challenges of the time. He had validated his talent once more, and he would soon expand further the horizons of his art.

STAN'S BOSSA

CREED TAYLOR brought the obligatory bottles of Alka-Seltzer and Scotch to Stan's recording dates with Bob Brookmeyer on September 12 and 13, 1961, and Stan quickly eased his anxieties with the fizzy liquid followed by the clear brown one as he teamed up again with the trombonist whom he regarded as a prime musical inspiration. He had looked forward impatiently to the sessions because playing with Brookmeyer fulfilled the third and last of the artistic commitments he had made to himself when he crossed the Atlantic on the *Kungsholm* the previous January; the two horn men were backed up by Stan's working rhythm section of Steve Kuhn, Roy Haynes, and John Neves, the bass player who replaced Scott LaFaro, and the album was called *Getz-Brookmeyer 61*.

Stan and Brookmeyer had not recorded jointly for six and a half years, but the tracks sound as if they had been playing together every night for months. As Brookmeyer told a reporter earlier in 1961, his approach to improvising closely matched Stan's in its emotional directness:

> What you are producing should be a human sound. The metal instrument is just a thing you use. . . . A jazz man should be saying what he feels. He's one human being talking to others, telling his story—and that means humor and sadness, joy, all the things that humans have.

Throughout the album the two men engage in a completely unembarrassed communication of feeling, and they create a particularly moving dialogue on a ballad written by Brookmeyer called "Who Could Care."

Norman Granz touched Stan's life again a month later when he flew into New York from his home in Switzerland to stage a press conference at which he demanded that the contracts of all jazz artists contain a clause prohibiting performances before segregated audiences. He discounted the union, saying, "You can't expect the American Federation of Musicians to insist on such a thing, because it has segregation in its own locals," and he looked to the artists' managers for action. When the press conference ended, a committee of producers and writers was formed to meet with important managers; they got together first with Stan's manager Jack Whittemore, who helped them greatly. Although audience segregation did not end completely until the civil rights laws of the mid-1960s, Granz's initiative resulted in significant progress.

Stan saw little of his family during the remainder of 1961 because he toured continuously, and Monica returned to Lund in December to have a second child, which was expected in March. Steve and David were studying again at Aiglon, and Beverly and Pamela accompanied Monica to Sweden.

Stan received confirmation in December that he still faced a daunting task in regaining his fans; John Coltrane out-polled him by more than two to one in the *Down Beat* voting for 1961. *Metronome* produced no 1961 poll results because it ceased publication at the end of that year.

One night in December, as Stan was playing in a Washington, D.C., club, the guitarist Charlie Byrd and his wife, Ginny—who lived nearby— approached him. "I've got some terrific new Latin music I would like you to hear," Byrd said. "Ginny and I both think you'd sound absolutely wonderful playing it. Come over to our place for lunch tomorrow, and we'll listen to it." Stan accepted the invitation.

Byrd had started as a jazz musician in the late 1940s but devoted himself almost exclusively to classical music from 1950 to 1956, studying with the masterful Andres Segovia in 1954. Byrd was reluctant to marry the genres, and in performance he broke his sets into two distinct segments; after filling the jazz portion with swinging versions of tunes like "How Long Has This Been Going On?" and "In a Mellotone," he would dismiss his sidemen and play precise solo interpretations of works by composers such as Bach, Paganini, and Villa-Lobos. He had secured a near-permanent engagement at a convivial cellar club in Washington called the Showboat Lounge, where *Down Beat* called him "a big fish in a little pond." His wife, Ginny, helped manage his affairs and occasionally sang with his trio.

From March to June of 1961, Byrd, Ginny, and his group made a twelve-week State Department tour of Latin America. Byrd, who was musically curious, collected tapes, records, and scores of indigenous music in Venezuela, Brazil, Chile, Paraguay, Peru, and Argentina and was particularly impressed with a jazz-samba hybrid called bossa nova, which was growing in popularity in Brazil. He had heard bossa nova in several night spots and enjoyed sitting in and playing it with local musicians.

On returning to the United States, Byrd worked some bossa nova arrangements into his act but became frustrated when he could not convince any of the record companies, including his own (Riverside), to wax his Brazilian material. Byrd couldn't wait to play his bossa nova tapes for Stan because he believed that the warmly melodic music was perfectly suited to his lyric style, and he knew that Stan had far greater clout with the record companies than he did.

After they finished lunch, Byrd performed a couple of Brazilian tunes on his guitar and then played tapes featuring the two true heavyweights of bossa nova—guitarist João Gilberto singing his own songs and those of Antonio Carlos Jobim; Stan immediately fell in love with the music. Despite the simplicity of the arrangements, he was fascinated by the limpid tunes and by the relaxed but insistent rhythm, which entered his bloodstream with alarming ease. Improvising over this, he thought, would be a pleasure; the rhythmic pulse carries you irresistibly forward, like a gentle wave.

Stan told Creed Taylor of his enthusiasm for bossa nova and asked the producer if he could record with Byrd. Taylor, who saw modest commercial possibilities in such a project, agreed. At the outset they encountered musical difficulties; a session with New York musicians had to be aborted because they could not master the Brazilian rhythms, and Byrd reorganized the recording around the men who had accompanied him to Brazil. He rehearsed them intensively and by early February was ready to make the record.

On February 13, 1962, Stan and Creed took the air shuttle from New York to Washington and headed to a location chosen by Byrd because it had wonderful acoustics—Pierce Hall at the All Souls Unitarian Church in the northwest sector of the city. Stan was unfamiliar with the charts, but he quickly memorized them and during the next two hours laid down seven tracks with Byrd, two bassists, and two drummers. It was a casual session, quite relaxed compared to Stan's previous intense outings with Sauter and Brookmeyer. He and Creed left the church quickly, because they wished to catch a plane that would return them to New York in time for dinner. They succeeded.

As Jobim has explained, bossa nova means "new flair" in his native tongue:

> In Portuguese, a *bossa* means a protuberance, a hump, a bump. And the human brain has these protuberances—these bumps in the head . . . So if a guy has a *bossa* for something, it is literally a bump in the brain—a talent for something. To say that he has a *bossa* for guitar would mean he has a genius for guitar. So it has come to mean a *flair* for something. And *bossa nova* was a "new flair."

Jobim, João Gilberto, and their associates created their "new flair" by taking the samba, a hard-driving street dance music, and transforming it in two ways: They added sophisticated jazz harmonies, and they recast its simple, symmetrical rhythm into a subtle, asymmetrical one which flowed hypnotically. What they accomplished was similar to Duke Ellington taking a folk blues and building a complex, lyrical piece from it.

Their primary jazz influence was the "cool school." Most of Brazil's popular music in the 1950s struck them as bombastic and obvious, and the early 1950s harmonies of Miles Davis's *Birth of the Cool* nonet, Stan's quartets, and Gerry Mulligan's pianoless groups helped them to create a subtle and provocative alternative to the prevailing Brazilian style.

The samba is based on a symmetrical triplet rhythm—da DA da—which is repeated throughout a given piece. The bossa nova has an asymmetrical rhythm with three pauses built into it that gives the music a forward tilt and a lilting momentum. The beat goes—da DA (pause) da DA (pause) da (pause) da. It is the samba triplet repeated three times with the first two pauses taking the place of soft beats (das), and the last replacing a hard one (DA).

Jobim credited the rhythmic innovations to Gilberto:

The guy who brought us the beat was João Gilberto. In bossa nova, there were many guys involved, but João Gilberto appeared as a light, as a big star in the firmament, in the heavens. He became a focus. He was pulling the guitar in one way, and singing the other way. It created a third thing that was profound. . . . I believe that bossa nova is a distillery of the samba, a sophisticated branch of the samba.

If Gilberto was the rhythmic innovator, Jobim—with his great talent for creating melody—did more than anyone else to define the form and popularize it. According to his publisher, seven of his compositions have been performed more than one million times each on radio and TV.

Jobim's and Gilberto's rise to prominence began in 1958 with the almost simultaneous release of a record by Gilberto—singing his own "Bim Bom" and Jobim's "Chega de Saudade"—and of the highly successful international film *Black Orpheus* with music by Jobim and fellow Brazilian Luiz Bonfa. The reaction of Brazil's white middle-class youth to Gilberto's singing was comparable to their American counterparts' response to Elvis Presley a few years earlier. Gilberto and Jobim became heroes of a counterculture, and the kids were pleased when traditionalists became angry with the new music. Jobim remembered:

Naturally the purists got furious with us. For them, the samba is like a religion and they said, "This is not samba, this is jazz." They repelled everything.

Creed Taylor was not concerned with Brazilian arguments over nomenclature when he named the Getz-Byrd album *Jazz Samba*. As he recalled:

The marketing people slowed the release somewhat because they wanted to change the title. I said no. That's precisely what it was—a jazz samba, a marriage of jazz and samba. An American audience wouldn't know what a bossa nova was, but they could understand this literal description.

Jazz Samba comprises five happy, swinging tunes and two sad ones, and Stan projects both moods with energy and intelligence. The best of the happy numbers are Jobim's "Desafinado" and "One Note Samba," which benefit from Stan's virile and rhythmically compelling interpretations. On the darker tunes, "Samba Triste" and "Baia," he cries through his horn to express a sultry, yearning melancholy reminiscent of the most moving

passages in *Focus*. Byrd backs him skillfully and has exuberant solos on
"O Pato" and "One Note Samba" and a broodingly powerful one on
"Samba Triste."

Six weeks after the *Jazz Samba* session, Stan received the happy news
that on March 21, 1962, Monica had given birth in Lund to a healthy
son, Nicolaus George Peter Richard Getz.

He was further elated when eight days later *Down Beat* printed a highly
laudatory review of *Focus*. It was the second time in two months that one
of his albums had received the magazine's highest accolade: five stars.
The previous month the *Getz-Brookmeyer 61* album had been so honored.

Stan was surprised when the *Focus* review was followed on June 21,
1962, with a four-and-a-half star review of *Jazz Samba*. Stan liked the
music from the Byrd recording, but he viewed the results of the session
as modest compared to the major artistic achievement of *Focus*. He was
further surprised when *Jazz Samba* received copious airplay during the
summer and starting selling furiously in August.

Monica returned that month to help the family move into a new home
that Stan had rented. It was near their previous one in suburban Westchester, and it was larger because it had to accommodate the entire brood,
including the new baby and Steve and David, who had finished their
studies at Aiglon. Monica had felt overburdened facing a major house-
moving while coping with an infant son, and she left Beverly, now eight
years old, with her mother, Mary, in Lund. The two did not get along, and
soon Beverly, with Mary and Monica's consent, moved in with neighbors;
she rejoined the family in the United States in December.

While Monica was still in Sweden, Stan was reunited with his brother
Bob and was forced to cope with a crisis created by his father.

After an eight-day California courtship, Bob had recently married Pat
Willert, a tall blond model who rivaled Monica in beauty, and he had
returned to New York from Los Angeles to perform in a Broadway play,
Never Live Over a Pretzel Factory; Pat found abundant work in New
York, and they settled comfortably into a nearby suburban community in
New Jersey.

Al had also married, but with disastrous consequences. He had led a
lonely life in a single room in an upper Broadway hotel after Goldie died,
and he had wed the first woman who had taken an interest in him. Two
weeks after their marriage, when he overheard her on the telephone
plotting an assignation with another man, he left her, and she walked off
with his meager savings. Stan came to his aid and arranged a quick
annulment.

Creed Taylor had recorded several albums featuring a talented big band writer and leader named Gary McFarland and believed that he and Stan would work well together. After listening to some McFarland tapes, Stan became enthusiastic, and he went into the studio on August 27 and 28, 1962, fronting a McFarland orchestra; the resulting album was called *Big Band Bossa Nova*. McFarland, twenty-eight, was a protégé of John Lewis and an early admirer of João Gilberto. He had a natural feel for bossa nova, and he wrote muscular arrangements brightened by spicy dissonances and freshly varied dynamics.

He assembled for Stan a powerful group with such excellent soloists as Bob Brookmeyer on trombone, Doc Severinsen on trumpet, Jim Hall on guitar, and Hank Jones on piano. The album contains two pieces by Jobim, one each by Gilberto and Luiz Bonfa, and four McFarland tunes that sound authentically Brazilian. Stan reaches lyric peaks on McFarland's "Melancolio" and Bonfa's *Black Orpheus* theme, "Manha De Carnival," but the high point of the album is a rendition of Jobim's "Chega de Saudade" that begins with a haunting solo by Severinsen and moves on to a soulful and inventive dialogue by Brookmeyer and Stan.

Billboard magazine's charts of record sales have been the bible of the industry since 1958, and Stan was elated when *Jazz Samba* first appeared on the listing for pop albums on September 15, 1962, and "Desafinado" hit the charts for pop singles two weeks later; jazz recordings rarely sold widely enough to make it to the pop charts.

Stan played the Monterey Jazz Festival in California on September 21 and ignited the crowd by performing tunes from the *Jazz Samba* album with a quintet featuring his old cohort, Jimmy Raney, on guitar; Raney had agreed to sign on again because Stan had stopped abusing illegal substances. The next month Whittemore booked Stan and Charlie Byrd onto NBC-TV's *Perry Como Show* and into a sold-out two-week engagement at the Village Gate in New York.

Stan was getting rich from his pop success, and almost everyone was jumping on his bandwagon: Shorty Rogers, Herbie Mann, Sonny Rollins, Coleman Hawkins, and Cal Tjader were among two dozen musicians who released bossa nova albums during October 1962.

Stan anticipated eagerly his next major booking, a November 21 Carnegie Hall concert, because it would allow him, for the first time, to meet and perhaps play with Jobim and Gilberto. The event was sponsored jointly by *Show Magazine* and Audio Fidelity Records, which had acquired the copyrights to many of the important bossa nova compositions. The sponsors obtained the help of Brazil's foreign office and Varig, its national airline, and contracted to bring more than twenty artists to New York for the event.

Jobim and Gilberto were reluctant to come because the arrangements were chaotic and the pay was low; they gave in at the last moment to pressure from the Brazilian government and media and flew to New York, where their worst fears were realized.

The concert was a disaster. Stan was never paired with Brazilian musicians; too many mediocre groups were booked; chaos frequently reigned on stage, and the sound was terrible because the microphones—placed to maximize the recording for Audio Fidelity—did not carry the music well to the people in the hall. The audience had difficulty hearing them, but the performances of Jobim and Gilberto were the high spots of the evening; the Audio Fidelity recording released more than a year later demonstrates that they played with a special warmth, freshness, and grace. There is no record of Stan's performance because Verve would not allow Audio Fidelity to put him on wax, but critics wrote that he performed well, soloing with Bob Brookmeyer in front of the McFarland big band and with a quartet.

The Brazilian government was so embarrassed by the Carnegie Hall fiasco that a couple of weeks later they sponsored, on their own, two well-organized concerts at the large Village Gate nightclub in New York. Jobim and Gilberto were at last able to present their art to an American audience in a dignified and congenial setting, and they gave compelling performances. Stan was unhappy that midwestern tour obligations prevented him from participating, but he was almost overwhelmed by the enthusiastic crowds who came to hear him.

Bossa nova had become a national craze during the last weeks of 1962. Dancers jammed night clubs to sway to its beat, almost every position on the radio dial pulsated with its sound, any album with the two magic words in its name was grabbed off the shelves of record stores, and novelty manufacturers flooded the market with items such as bossa nova T-shirts, bossa nova dancing dolls, and bossa nova Day-Glo posters. The irrationality that accompanies any craze helped fuel public demand, and the mostly happy music with the hint of melancholy and the infectious rhythm reflected the buoyant optimism of a seemingly invincible America led by a handsome couple who lived in Camelot.

It is not surprising that Stan had ignited this craze, that he had a bossa, a flair, for bossa nova. Jobim, Gilberto, and its other progenitors were like his musical brothers, listening to his records and developing—a continent away—their own variant on the "cool" sensibility. And Stan responded strongly to their love affair with melody, their placement at the forefront of their art the making of moving and sophisticated songs. And he, the frequent prisoner of psychic pain and the creator of the aching cries of

"Early Autumn" and *Focus,* responded also to the strain of melancholy that ran through almost everything the Brazilians did. The American public latched onto the happy aspects of bossa nova, but, as Jobim said, sadness was deeply woven into the genre:

> It is in our music, this sadness of the Africans, the Portuguese, and the Indians, three races who understand the human condition. This is not a negative philosophy, but only people without soul cannot understand what there is to be sad about in life. Our music is beautiful because sadness is more beautiful than happiness. . . .
> What is so particular about Stan in comparison with the other players in the time, he had a soul . . . yes, a great soul.

And finally, Stan—who always swung so mightily—was immediately captivated by the sinuous beat, which always set feet and hips to movement.

Fortunately, Stan did not have long to wait to make music with his Brazilian brothers. They had no commitments to Audio Fidelity, and Creed Taylor quickly signed them to record with Stan for Verve. Taylor was anxious to bring everyone together in the studio because *Jazz Samba* had raced up the pop charts and began 1963 as number two, an unprecedented position for a jazz release. Taylor was also buoyed by two other developments: the *Big Band Bossa Nova* album had entered the pop charts on December 22, 1962, and Stan's bossa nova triumphs had rewon for him the *Down Beat* crown he had lost to John Coltrane the two previous years. He squeezed by his rival in the 1962 poll by a margin of less than one percent.

Taylor decided that he would team Stan up on separate albums with three major Brazilian musicians: Luiz Bonfa, João Gilberto, and Laurindo Almeida. Jobim, who helped Taylor greatly in organizing the sessions, played on all of them and contributed nine songs.

The Bonfa album, *Jazz Samba Encore,* was cut in February and put the spotlight on his compositions and guitar playing; it also features the singing of his blind girlfriend, Maria Toledo, an excellent performer whose voice projects a husky warmth and a supple swing. Jobim wrote the best songs on the album, the haunting "Insensatez (How Insensitive)" and the harshly poignant "O Morro Nao Tem Vez (The Slums Have No Chance)." The Brazilian musicians provided a firmer rhythmic foundation than did Charlie Byrd's accompanists, freeing Stan to dig more deeply into the material. His playing is superb, as he often reaches the combination of high intelligence and raw emotion that made *Focus* such an outstanding work.

On February 28 Stan was the subject of a *Down Beat* cover story, titled "The Resurgence of Stan Getz." The article began by recounting Stan's woes at the box office and in the record stores for more than a year following his return from Europe. It then leaped forward to the success of *Jazz Samba* in a happy present:

> Verve confirms that the single record of "Desafinado" out of the album has passed 500,000, and that the LP itself has sold "several hundred thousand," and should also wind up close to 500,000. At this writing, the album is in its 20th week on the best seller charts in the trade press. . . .
>
> All that matters to him (Getz) is that he is now able to produce whatever music he likes, and can be sure of an audience for it, and that when he announces "Desafinado" (or "Dis here finado" as he calls it), he introduces it as "the tune that's going to put my children through college—all five of them." . . .
>
> Getz now can command a nightly four-figure salary, the royalties from his albums are expected to run ultimately into six figures, and he can count on the kind of lifelong security that only a year ago seemed hopelessly out of reach. A year ago, nevertheless, Stan Getz was playing as brilliantly, as soulfully, as swingingly, and as sensitively as he does today. The difference is his successes—and that's show business.

Less than three weeks after the last Bonfa date, Taylor scheduled Stan for his collaboration with João Gilberto on an album that was to be called simply *Getz/Gilberto*. Jobim, who played piano on the record and wrote six of its eight tunes, imported his favorite drummer, Milton Banana, for the session.

One day, while they were rehearsing, Stan asked Gilberto's wife Astrud—the only one of the Brazilians who spoke English—to sing the words of the songs in English. Stan was immediately struck by the vulnerable sensuality of her voice, and asked that she sing on the album. Astrud had performed with her husband at parties, but had never sung professionally; her voice was a small instrument compared to that of Maria Toledo, and she had trouble staying in tune, but she seduced the listener with an intriguing combination of plaintive heat and cool reserve. As Stan remembered, he had to overcome substantial resistance to include Astrud on the date:

Gilberto and Jobim didn't want Astrud on it. Astrud wasn't a professional singer, she was a housewife. But when I wanted translations of what was going on, and she sang "Ipanema" and "Corcovado," I thought the words in English were very nice . . . and Astrud sounded good enough to put on the record.

While they were reworking the arrangements to make space for Astrud, the group was spurred on by the news that on March 9 *Jazz Samba* hit number one on the pop charts, the only jazz album that has ever done so.

Monica saved the group from disaster on the day of the recording, March 18, 1963. João Gilberto, a reclusive and almost pathologically shy man, refused to leave his hotel room for the session, and Monica, who spoke some Portuguese, was deputized to lure him out. She pleaded, argued, and cajoled for three and a half hours until, almost exhausted, João relented and the two of them emerged from his room and boarded a cab for the studio. João's dramatics forced the group to return the next day to complete the album.

João's performance at the sessions confirms the praise Miles Davis heaped on him when he said, "Gilberto, he could read a newspaper and sound good." He backs his deep voice with subtly chorded guitar rhythms to create moods of rare intimacy, and his dusky vocals create a sweet tension with Astrud's projections of erotic innocence as they collaborate on two Jobim songs, "Corcovado (Quiet Nights)" and "The Girl From Ipanema."

Stan's performance is elevated by the rapport he created with João, a deeper communication than that which he achieved with his other Brazilian collaborators. João's long experience listening to Stan may have had something to do with this. As he recalled:

> Some years ago, when I was young and searching in my country, I knew about Stan, though he didn't know about me. I was introduced to his music through Donato, a pianist friend of mine. Time and again we listened to Getz records with stirred emotions. . . . There isn't any American whom I'd rather hear playing the music of my country.

Stan created another kind of rapport with Astrud as he enveloped her vocals with sensuous, caressing lines. Jobim, Banana, and Brazilian bassist Sebastiao provide firm, subtle support throughout.

The mellow feelings projected by *Getz/Gilberto* belie the tensions besetting the marriage of João and Astrud; soon after the recording session, they separated.

Stan was back in the studio two days after the *Getz/Gilberto* date for his *Getz/Almeida* session. Guitarist Laurindo Almeida came to the United States in 1947 when one of his songs, "Johnny Peddler," became an American hit. This led to a three-year stint with Stan Kenton and subsequently a lucrative career in the Hollywood studios. Over the years he made a small number of records that, like Charlie Byrd's, combined jazz and classical elements; he was best known for *Brazilliance*, a 1952 album that bore some of the seeds of bossa nova.

In contrast to Jobim and Bonfa, Almeida was not an adept improviser, and since there was no singing on the album, almost all the interest lies with Stan's performances. He does not let the listener down despite a disturbing incident that would have thrown a less resilient artist off his form. He recalled:

> In the middle of this session we went out to get something to eat, and my horn was locked in my trunk. When we came back, it was stolen. I was heartbroken. Not only did I love that horn, but the mouthpiece had taken me years to work out. I had to finish the session on a borrowed horn and mouthpiece. Six years and one day later I had a phone call from a New York policeman. A fan of mine, he had been looking for my horn all the time and had finally come across it in an obscure pawnshop, but without the mouthpiece.

Among Stan's outstanding solos on the LP are a searing rendition of a tune called "Maracatu-Too" and a limpid reading of one called "Winter Moon."

The Grammy Awards Ceremony on May 15, 1963, was a roller coaster ride for Stan. He was deeply disappointed when *Focus* lost out to Vince Guaraldi's "Cast Your Fate to the Winds" as Best Original Jazz Composition, but his spirits bounced back when he won his first Grammy ever for Best Jazz Solo Performance on "Desafinado" from the *Jazz Samba* album. He gave his award to Creed Taylor, who still owns it. The top single of the year was Tony Bennett's "I Left My Heart in San Francisco," and Vaughn Meader's spoof of the Kennedys, *First Family*, won the voting for best album.

The day following the Grammys, Stan flew to Puerto Rico with Monica, Beverly, and Pamela for a three-day engagement at the Condado Beach Hotel. They brought with them a turntable and the first acetates, or test pressings, of Stan's recordings with the Brazilians.

Beverly awoke in the middle of their last night at the hotel to hear

Stan, in a drunken rage, pummeling Monica in the adjoining room as she screamed, "He's killing me. He's killing me. Help me, Beverly. Beverly, call the doctor."

Pamela remained asleep, as Beverly went toward the next room and found her father, blue eyes glaring, blocking her way.

"Go back to bed," he said. She retreated.

Beverly heard more screaming followed by Stan stomping out and slamming the door; she went in to Monica, who was bleeding from one ear.

"Mom, let's go," Beverly begged. "Let's get out of here before he comes back."

Monica rose sobbing and put a record on the turntable. It was the test pressing of "The Girl From Ipanema."

"It's okay, I'll be all right," she said through her sobs as the music filled the room. "Listen to this; it's going to make Daddy a huge star. Isn't it beautiful? Isn't he a genius?"

"Please, let's get out of here."

"No, listen. He's a genius; he's a good man. The alcohol makes him bad. It's the terrible alcohol."

Beverly returned to her bed and a confused sleep.

Stan was in a good humor the next morning as he and Monica acted as if they had never fought the night before. She took the girls home, and he flew to Chicago where he appeared in two benefit concerts for the Chicago Symphony. *Down Beat*'s reviewer responded to Stan's performance with a fourteen-piece orchestra assembled by Gary McFarland and with his quartet by writing, "Getz was in the best of forms, playing with an ease and a lyricism that leaves one in awe of the man's imagination."

Stan shared the bill in Chicago with a variety of performers including Muddy Waters, the Teddy Wilson Trio, the Count Basie Orchestra, Carmen McRae, and Jack Teagarden's sextet. He had a boozy reunion with his first mentor, who had returned to two-fisted drinking after several half-hearted attempts at abstinence. Stan would never see Big Tea again; he died at age fifty-eight in New Orleans on January 15, 1964, of pneumonia complicated by cirrhosis of the liver. His face was so ravaged by alcohol that his family opted for a closed casket at the funeral.

Charlie Byrd marred Stan's otherwise pleasant summer of touring when the two men appeared together for a week opposite Ella Fitzgerald in Washington in late July 1963. Byrd kept telling Stan that he was unhappy that Stan had not shared with him the Grammy for "Desafinado"; he also complained about his compensation for the *Jazz Samba* date. He and his wife Ginny went public with his grievances in a joint interview published in the August 29 issue of *Down Beat*. He said:

I made the big mistake of doing the date and not talking about any deal. The next thing I knew, I was out. I mean, no artist royalty—none at all. Just leader's scale, plus scale for the arrangements, all of which I wrote. All Stan had to do was come in and play. We had the rhythm section and the idea.

And Ginny added:

If the same situation had happened in reverse, I'm sure Charlie would have insisted that Stan get due credit, and he would have said when the record began to sell, "Look Stan, how did we know this was going to be a hit? Here's half of it."

In the same issue of *Down Beat*, Creed Taylor rebutted Byrd's claims about the Grammy:

"Desafinado" was nominated in two categories: Record of the Year and Best Jazz Solo Performance. It won an award only as Best Jazz Solo Performance. If it had won the award for Record of the Year, then the Grammy would have been presented jointly to Stan Getz and Charlie Byrd.

The edited version of "Desafinado" unfortunately precluded the use of any of Byrd's solo. Therefore, the award for Best Jazz Solo Performance went to Getz.

The Byrd brouhaha so unnerved Stan and Monica that they prevailed upon Verve executives to add a clause to Stan's contract indemnifying him against possible suits by Charlie.

Stan and Monica were frustrated with Verve management during the last months of 1963, because the company had not released the *Getz/Gilberto* and *Getz/Almeida* albums; the Bonfa album was the only one of the three that Stan had made with the Brazilians that was in the stores. The executives were sitting on the two recordings because they did not wish to compete with their own *Jazz Samba*; it was still comfortably ensconced on the pop charts in December 1963, nineteen months after its release.

Stan and Monica contended that what they would be competing with was schlock, records with names like *Boogie Woogie Bossa* and *New Beat Bossa Nova, Volume Two*, and that the Gilberto and Almeida albums with Jobim were authentic and superior products that the public would leap at immediately. They also pointed out that Stan was still first in the hearts of jazz fans; he had again nosed out Coltrane in the *Down Beat* poll for 1963.

The Verve executives were not moved; they stayed with their strategy and put *Getz/Gilberto* into release in March 1964 when, as Creed Taylor remembered, "We worked that record like it was the number one priority record at the company." They refused to do anything immediately with the Almeida album, which they kept on the shelf until October 1966.

In January 1964, Stan was having difficulty finding a pianist for a three-week Canadian quintet tour during which João Gilberto was to be added to Stan's regular group. Stan's old friend Lou Levy suggested that instead of a pianist he hire Gary Burton, a brilliant twenty-one-year-old vibraphone player who had recently left George Shearing's group.

Burton was a pioneer in the use of four mallets—rather than the conventional two—on the vibraphone and, as a consequence, could play resonant four-note chords on the instrument. Levy reasoned that, with such chords, Burton could approximate the richness of a pianist's accompaniment and urged Stan to take a chance with the young man.

Although Stan knew that Burton was an impressive musician, he hesitated. The sound of the piano is deep and full while that of the vibraphone is high and thin, and Stan was afraid that he could not achieve a proper balance with the vibraphone in a quartet. But at the last minute he was still without a pianist, and he hired Burton. As Stan remembered, they had a difficult beginning:

> At first it didn't happen, because vibes are not a swinging accompaniment instrument, but he knew what I wanted and taught himself how to do what I needed.

Burton also recalled the period of adjustment:

> We hated each other for about two weeks. Then I began to hear what he was playing in a different light. Stan plays the melody of a tune, and it sounds like he wrote it just then. . . . When he solos, sometimes the melodies he makes up sound richer than the written melody. That and his intensity towards music. He plays every night as if it's his last.

Burton, at the start of a very distinguished career, was bursting with new harmonic and rhythmic concepts and—like earlier bright young protégés such as Horace Silver and Scott LaFaro—he stretched Stan's imagination. Stan was pleased:

I believe in him as a person and musician. He's a person I find
stimulating to be around, a person too good to be true. He's a very
deep musician, which will become evident through the years. He's
made music his life's study. In other words, he's trying to be good.

By the time they had come back to New York, Burton was a member in
good standing of Stan's group. Gilberto was not; he was lonely and unhappy in frigid Canada, left his hotel room only to play the gigs, and
quit before the end of the tour.

Stan was so pleased with Burton's playing that he brought the quartet
into a recording studio on March 4, 1964, only three days after returning
from Canada; the resulting album was called *Nobody Else but Me*.

Stan welcomed his bossa nova success, but as Gary Burton has said,
"he was worried that bossa nova was burying his jazz identity." He had
grown bored with a steady diet of "Desafinado," "One Note Samba," and
"Insensatez (How Insensitive)" and felt a need to work out again on
straight-ahead jazz material. *Nobody Else but Me* fulfilled that need; it
was comprised of standards by Gershwin, Porter, Rodgers, Kern, and Van
Heusen and four fresh jazz tunes (including two written by Burton).

With Stan's bossa nova recordings continuing to sell well, Verve executives put the tapes of *Nobody Else but Me* aside for later release. Somehow, they became buried in a New Jersey warehouse and forgotten. They
were not rediscovered and released until thirty years later, in 1994.

For music lovers it was worth the wait. Stan is by turns romantic, lushly
evocative, fervent, and purely melodic. The lead track, "Summertime," is
a gem, an interpretation which rivals Miles Davis's and John Coltrane's
versions as the definitive jazz rendering of Gershwin's song. Stan makes
a ravishingly languorous statement of the melody and follows it with an
improvisation which builds subtly in intensity until his jabbing tones carry
the listener into the heat of an August noon in the deep South.

He uses wondrous shifts in dynamics to evoke romantic responses to
the melodies of "Little Girl Blue" and "Here's That Rainy Day," and he
shifts the mood abruptly as he slashes his way through a fast, fierce version
of "What Is This Thing Called Love." He is both mellow and fierce on
"Out of Focus," Burton's version of Sauter's "I'm Late, I'm Late" theme
from *Focus*. Burton shows that he had learned a lot in three weeks with
Stan, as he skillfully cushions his leader's flights with soft, billowy chords
and improvises with intelligence and intensity throughout.

Stan had returned from Canada in time to move with the family to
much grander living quarters in Westchester—a large, airy house more
in keeping with their new economic status.

Monica was so enthusiastic about the prospects for *Getz/Gilberto* that once she had put the travail of moving behind her, she talked the Verve executives into giving her a role in promoting the album. She took an office at Verve and helped convince the program directors at important radio stations to give significant air time to key singles from the album. She remembered:

> I just picked up the phone and I called the guy in San Francisco, and I said, "I know that you pick for popular programs, and that this is a jazz record, but I just want you to listen to it. Please just listen to it." So I sent it. . . . And sure enough, they picked that one. And then we attacked Los Angeles. Sure enough, it was a hit in Los Angeles and in some other areas.

The record built momentum quickly. Both the single, "The Girl From Ipanema," and the album, *Getz/Gilberto*, sold well in April and May, and they entered the charts simultaneously on June 6, 1964.

While Monica toiled in the Verve offices, Creed Taylor brought Stan into the studio to work in a quartet setting with a fellow master, the pianist Bill Evans. The bass chores were split between two powerful players, Ron Carter from Miles Davis's quintet and Richard Davis, and the quartet was completed by Coltrane's explosive drummer, Elvin Jones. The results were disappointing; Stan played comfortably throughout, but Evans was tentative and stiff. The volume and complexity of the playing of Jones, Carter, and Davis appeared to unnerve him, and he never found the inspiration to spin out his characteristically lyrical lines. The record—*Stan Getz & Bill Evans*—was not released for ten years, and as Evans told a reporter, he was unhappy that it ever reached the public:

> When the date was over, we both felt we had not got to the level we wanted. Stan had a clause in his contract that would prevent the release of anything he did not approve, and so the record was not issued. However, Verve released it later without approval.

Taylor made a deal with Columbia soon after the Evans date that allowed Stan and Burton to record for that label with Bob Brookmeyer on a sextet album called *Bob Brookmeyer and Friends*. Brookmeyer chose his friends well, and the results were spectacular all around. He borrowed an outstanding rhythm section for the session—Elvin Jones from Coltrane and Ron Carter and pianist Herbie Hancock from Davis—and they provide bristling, inventive support for their colleagues and solo with distinction as well. Stan burns on two up-tempo tracks and plays sensuously on three ballads: "Skylark," "I've Grown Accustomed to Her Face," and "Misty." Brookmeyer, as usual, plays with both fervor and intelligence, and Burton, the new kid on the block, more than holds his own in this august company.

Following the Brookmeyer recording and in response to the burgeoning sales of *Getz/Gilberto* and "The Girl From Ipanema," Stan expanded his touring group to include Astrud Gilberto. They drew enthusiastic, standing-room-only crowds as "The Girl From Ipanema" triggered waves of adulation that made the response to "Desafinado" seem pale in comparison.

Astrud became a pop icon and launched a career that is still prospering more than thirty years later. She personified for millions of people the youthful aura of sex and romance embodied by a teenager whom Jobim used to watch walking to the beach.

> Vinicius de Moraes, my partner who wrote the Portuguese words to the song, and I used to drink at a bar in Rio that, like a French bar, had chairs on the sidewalk. It was one block from the beach.
>
> She was a green-eyed girl, very beautiful. We didn't bug her. She would go to school and to the beach and we would see her. She was blonde and dark, a mixture that is so beautiful. She was a creature of God. . . .
>
> The girl is a symbol of something, of love and easiness. It's like a dream.

The actual girl from Ipanema was Heloisa Eneaida Pinheiro. Jobim and de Moraes became her friends and attended her wedding; today she is a TV talk show host, an actress, and the mother of four.

Astrud personified sex and romance for Stan as well as for the multitudes, and—despite constant squabbling about her salary and record royalties—the two of them began an affair while on tour in July 1964. Thus began the most notorious of Stan's infidelities while married to Monica. She claims that she never knew anything about them.

"The Girl From Ipanema" raced to number five on the pop singles charts that month and *Getz/Gilberto* peaked at the number two album spot in August. The album failed to emulate *Jazz Samba* in reaching the number one position only because it competed head-on with the Beatles' *A Hard Day's Night*. It outsold *Jazz Samba* by a wide margin, however.

Stan's success with *Getz/Gilberto* and "The Girl From Ipanema" proved that bossa nova was not merely a fad. After thousands of unsold bossa nova dancing dolls were thrown onto the scrap heap and scores of releases had found their way to the ninety-nine-cent remainder bins, he had shown that the music had a permanent position in the aesthetic firmament. Stan's success also demonstrated that he had contributed more than any other musician in taking bossa nova from obscurity as a Brazilian genre art form and in making it a force that stirred millions throughout the world. And he hadn't compromised; he made his landmark records in the true Brazilian idiom with the authentic creators of the music.

Stan was distracted only slightly during the giddy summer of 1964 when, on September 10, Charlie Byrd filed a suit against MGM, Verve's parent, for monies due on the *Jazz Samba* album. Byrd claimed that because he was billed as co-leader on the LP, he was entitled to a portion of the royalties; his case was weakened by the fact that he did not have a written contract to that effect. The suit meandered through the legal system until August 1967, when—in an out-of-court settlement—Byrd collected roughly $50,000 plus a piece of future royalties from MGM.

One of Stan's happiest memories of 1964 was a sold-out October 9 Carnegie Hall concert that he helped produce; it featured his quartet with Astrud plus João Gilberto and a backup group. Stan's band and Gilberto's ensemble played separate sets (which can be heard on the album *Getz/Gilberto #2*) and then closed the concert by joining forces for three songs (included in the CD compilation *Stan Getz: The Bossa Nova Years*). There were few incendiary moments; the event sounds like a bunch of old friends having a relaxed evening together making music in the kitchen over wine and beer. The high points are Burton's romping solo on "Stan's Blues," Stan's eloquent reading of "Here Comes That Rainy Day," and his sinuous backgrounds for Astrud and João on "Corcovado (Quiet Nights)."

The week before Christmas 1964 Astrud left Stan's band and bed when their dispute concerning her compensation reached a climax in a torrid shouting match.

John Coltrane beat Stan out in the *Down Beat* poll for 1964 by a margin of 7 percent. Although Stan's accomplishments were many that year, he was contending with Coltrane at the peak of his career—playing with Elvin Jones, McCoy Tyner, and Jimmy Garrison in his greatest quartet and making magisterial recordings such as *Crescent* and *A Love Supreme*.

A fine example of Burton's work with Stan occurs on a January 30, 1965, recording of a performance in Vancouver titled *Canadian Concert*. Burton builds wonderful structures under Stan but never gets in his way, and both men solo with verve and poignancy; Burton reaches a peak on

"My Funny Valentine," and Stan communicates eloquently on "My Romance."

While Stan was playing a concert at Duke University on April 13, 1965, Monica, Creed Taylor, and Astrud Gilberto joined a crowd of eight hundred crammed into the ballroom of New York's Astor Hotel for one of four simultaneous Grammy Award dinners; the others were held in Nashville, Chicago, and Los Angeles.

Getz/Gilberto won Album of the Year honors, and "The Girl From Ipanema" was voted the best single in an unprecedented victory for jazz. The competition included Barbra Streisand's "People," the Beatles' "A Hard Day's Night," Louis Armstrong's "Hello, Dolly!" and Henry Mancini's "Pink Panther." The *Getz/Gilberto* team won two more Grammys—Phil Ramone of A&R Recording, a Verve subcontractor, for Best Engineered Recording and Stan for Best Instrumental Jazz Performance. To show that he was still angry about the defeat of *Focus* two years before, Stan gave his statuette to Eddie Sauter.

Depression was a continuing and tormenting presence in Stan's life, independent of his successes and his failures. Psychic pain visited him all too frequently, and the only way he knew to banish it was to drink. One night soon after the Grammy Awards, during dinner with the family and guests, he hurt so badly that he wanted to jump out of his skin. He knocked back a half-dozen Scotches and his pain eased, but his rage burst loose.

It took over as he drank more and grabbed Monica and pulled her around by the hair, shouting obscenities. Then he let her go and started throwing things. He smashed lamps and broke windows while his wife led everyone to an upstairs room where they huddled fearfully.

Stan kept smashing things, railing furiously for half an hour until finally he sat down. He felt utterly desperate—unable to stop wounding his wife and children, unable to stop destroying his home. For a short time he was drained of emotion, but then the hurt came back like nausea spreading out from his solar plexus until every cell pulsed with anguish. No pain could be worse than this, he thought, and it will never end; he felt he could never escape. It was too much to endure.

He walked over to the stove, turned on the gas jets, opened the oven door, knelt, and put his head in the oven. The sour smell filled his nostrils as he inhaled and drifted and drifted into a deep, peaceful sleep.

After quiet had descended, Monica said to Steve, who was sixteen, "I want you to go back down and check on Dad. Please. You're the oldest."

Steve smelled the gas as he opened the kitchen door and saw his father lying limp, unconscious. For a moment he was torn in two directions.

One part of him was so angry that he wanted to leave Stan there to die. Another part drove him toward the oven. When he got there, he pulled Stan out and laid him on his back on the floor. He turned off the gas jets, found his father's pulse, opened a few windows, and ran back upstairs. Monica summoned the family physician, Dr. John Foster, who pronounced Stan out of danger and helped carry him to bed.

OUT OF CONTROL   FOURTEEN

AT THE TIME he attempted suicide, Stan was working on an intriguing project, collaborating with Eddie Sauter on the music for *Mickey One*, an Arthur Penn movie starring Warren Beatty as a small-time nightclub comedian on the run from the mob. Steve remembered:

> I could never understand how he could make such incredible music and at the same time create this incredible chaos. I remember him agonizing over *Mickey One*. . . .
>
> He'd bring home the work tapes. Dad plays all kinds of music in the movie—like Polish polkas and 1950s rock and roll. He's playing Warren Beatty's alter ego, performing all kinds of music from the joints that Beatty, as a comedian, is trying to make it

in. The music knocks you out. So much passion in that thing.
Dad agonized over it.

Mickey One was one of the few box office failures for Penn—who directed
such hits as *The Miracle Worker, Alice's Restaurant,* and *Bonnie and Clyde*—
but critics have valued the film as an absorbing and imaginative portrayal of
urban paranoia. Penn was enthusiastic about Stan's contribution:

> What is the sound of terror? The sound of loneliness, fear in the
> city? It is a contemporary sound. For *Mickey One,* it had to be a
> sound that would express the central character, and reflect his
> inner life.
>
> My solution to that phase of the film was a simple one. It
> would be the sound created by Stan Getz from an original score
> by Eddie Sauter. The sheer artistry of Stan Getz interweaving
> mood through improvisation, along with Eddie Sauter's written
> score, becomes a moving experience for the listener.... Stan's
> command of his instrument, his ability to express a desired sound,
> to reveal the feeling of each dramatic expression projected in the
> story, was simply a delight to me.

While Stan's creativity continued to blossom, his depressions, his drinking,
and his rages intensified. Steve referred to the late 1960s in his family as
"the war years":

> They were pretty rough years.... In those days he was drinking
> a quart a day. And he was in real bad shape. There was a lot of
> violence at home. He was off the wall. I don't know how we got
> through it.

For the Getz children the fearful symbol of "the war years" was a silver
mug, Stan's chosen instrument for drinking Scotch. It had come from
Rockelstad and had been made for Count Eric von Rosen, Monica's
grandfather. The Count had an aversion to milk in glasses, because he
hated seeing the filmy rings which the liquid left on the surfaces of the
vessels. So for drinking milk at Rockelstad he ordered a set of silver mugs
with his initials on one side and the von Rosen family crest on the other.
David remembered getting Scotch for his father:

> I hated this thing, this little mug.... It had two initials on it—
> E. R., Eric von Rosen.... Everything about it symbolizes fear,

this horrible fear coming from my stomach. He'd say, "Get me some Grant's." I'd be in so much fear I'd run like crazy and get him the Grant's. And then I would disappear.

And Steve recalled when he resigned as a bartender for his father:

I got real sick and tired of bringing him his silver chalice, his bottle of Dewar's, and his ice. I don't remember where I got the balls to do this, but I remember putting the tray down and I said, "This is the last time I'm going to be your personal bartender." And he got so mad, he chased me out of the house.

The writer of a September 3, 1965, *Time* magazine profile of Stan either did not know what was going on in Stan's home or chose not to reveal it. The journalist painted a picture of domestic tranquillity and reported that Stan would make "a cool $250,000" in 1965 from *Getz/Gilberto* royalties, the fee for *Mickey One*, sold-out engagements throughout the United States, and triumphant tours of Japan, South America, and Europe.

Both domestic tranquillity and a plate-glass door were shattered at Stan's home on December 18, 1965. He got drunk and, as he fought with Monica over a set of car keys, he put his right foot through the door and damaged several tendons and severed an artery as blood spurted everywhere. Surgeons at a nearby hospital repaired the damage as best they could and protected his foot and ankle with a cast, but Stan permanently lost movement in the last four toes of the foot. *Down Beat* reported discreetly that Stan had injured himself "while puttering around his home."

Stan went wild again when he returned from the hospital, smashing mirrors and furniture with his crutches and sending Monica with the five children scurrying for the safety of a motel.

The next night, numbed by painkillers and seated in a wheelchair, he played a concert at Carnegie Hall with Dionne Warwick and Joe Mooney, the blind singer who accompanied himself on the organ. Monica returned a day later with the children and cleaned up the broken glass and the other debris. Stan acted as if nothing had happened, and an uneasy calm settled over the family as he and Monica searched for a new home.

The Getzes were ready for a move in late 1965. They were unhappy that developers were building a series of small homes in the lush meadows surrounding their house, and they had plenty of money to move up in scale. Monica had inherited $52,000, and she was eager to add that to Stan's abundant cash flow to purchase something quite magnificent.

They were delighted when they came upon the Shadowbrook estate and stood in the twenty-three-room main residence and looked down at the majestic Hudson River through large trees that were set on a grassy lawn. The river—less than a half mile from them and two miles wide at this point—glinted in the sunlight as it rolled toward New York City, fifteen miles to the south. Shadowbrook wasn't Rockelstad, but it possessed a palatial air; it was comprised of four substantial buildings on nine acres.

The main structure was built early in the nineteenth century with exposed exterior beams in the Tudor style, and each of its rooms was expensively appointed. The walls of several were clad in burnished mahogany paneling, and all the fixtures and architectural details reflected an aristocratic taste. The mosaic-tiled entryway sported a ceiling of tooled leather, a domed music room was encircled with Tiffany glass windows, the nine fireplaces were carved from marble, the kitchen was enormous, and there were nine bedrooms and a working elevator.

The outbuildings consisted of a stable and a four-thousand-square-foot carriage house, each with dwelling space upstairs, and a five-room gardener's cottage.

The Getzes purchased Shadowbrook jointly for $125,000, using Monica's $52,000 as the down payment, and moved in during the spring of 1966.

As they were settling in, they were invited to an even grander residence, the White House, to attend a May 5 reception for the 113 chiefs of the Washington diplomatic corps. Stan, who never met a big band he didn't want to join, sat in for a few numbers with the scarlet-jacketed members of the Marine dance orchestra and, according to *Down Beat*, "rocked the joint." This was the second time he had done so; the previous October his quartet had played to an enthusiastic audience at a gathering hosted by President Lyndon Johnson for the nation's top college students.

Stan was back at the White House on June 7, 1966, playing with the quartet on the South Lawn at a reception for the 1966 Presidential Scholars, 140 outstanding high school students. The President's daughter, Luci, served as the hostess, and Steve, who had just graduated from high school himself, attended with Monica.

Stan was at the top of his game, a world class artist, but he remained possessed by the fears and anxieties of the twelve-year-old Bronx boy who peed in his pants at his first harmonica recital. Gary Burton, into his third year with the quartet in 1966, told *Down Beat*:

> He has more than the normal amount of worries over imagined inadequacies of his playing. That bothers him a lot. . . . He hates anyone making a big thing over him, the stardom thing. But he

likes playing Carnegie Hall, the TV shows, making the movies and records. He likes being important, as anyone would. But, the strain is great. He's getting more and more to feel that everything he does now must be his very best and better than he did before. . . .

He's never really worried about what kind of music he plays, just whether it's good or bad. But if he has a bad night, he gets very upset. He feels as if he's let everybody down.

Stan's performance anxieties did not prevent him from embarking on an ambitious concert project involving the talents of three major composers (Eddie Sauter, Alec Wilder, and David Raksin), a first-class arranger (Manny Albam), the members of his working quartet (Burton on vibes, Steve Swallow on bass, and Roy Haynes on drums) augmented by guitarist Jim Hall, and Arthur Fiedler and the Boston Pops Orchestra. The three writers created special works for Stan: Sauter labored for four months to compose "Tanglewood Concerto" for saxophone and orchestra, Wilder produced an arrangement of his haunting "Where Do You Go?" and wrote three new ballads, and Raksin crafted lush symphonic settings for two of his songs.

Stan invited Albam, whom he had known as a teenager in the Bronx, to write two arrangements for the concert. Albam was bowled over when he visited Stan at his new home to work on the project:

> I went over there to Shadowbrook and I was astonished, I mean it was a castle. This is not like where all our friends lived. This was an incredible place. It looked like it belonged to the Earl of Snowden or somebody.

Albam impressed Stan greatly with the richly harmonic setting he created for the Jewish lament, "Eli, Eli," and he wrote a fresh, fast, highly percussive version of "The Girl From Ipanema" that spotlighted Roy Haynes.

The concert—scheduled for performance on August 3, 1966, at the summer home of the Boston Pops, the outdoor Tanglewood amphitheater in Lenox, Massachusetts—almost met with disaster. Albam remembered:

> Between the time that we all wrote the music and had it copied and delivered, it got lost on the way to Tanglewood. It was all gone. It wound up that the kid in the mailroom decided he would save some money and sent it up as Parcel Post and it was sidetracked.

The rehearsal was supposed to be Monday and this was Saturday afternoon, and they had a copyist in New York working on that stuff. It was probably one of the most costly projects they ever did, and they didn't have time to get it all done. So "Eli, Eli" went down. That's one piece that Stan really wanted to do.

They finally found the scores on some railroad car in Connecticut.

The concert drew almost fifteen thousand people, a record for Tanglewood, and Stan played brilliantly; fortunately the performance was recorded. *Down Beat*'s reviewer awarded the album, A *Song After Sundown*, five stars and wrote:

> Getz' playing seems to become more lyrical as years go by. He soars through each of these selections with that distilled sweetness that only he can achieve—his tone is never saccharine, but full-bodied and joyous. This is a warm, wonderful session in which he and the Boston Pops under Maestro Fiedler are in perfect rapport. . . . This album is pure bliss.

And Richard Palmer, the British critic, was almost as enthusiastic:

> Stan's playing here . . . is the usual mixture of the exquisite and the muscular, the tender and the fiery. If "Tanglewood Concerto" is formally the most ambitious and thus the most enduring performance, the Wilder ballads are hardly less delightful. . . . The Orchestra acquit themselves well, as you'd expect from such a professional outfit. . . . That said, their role is very much a supporting one in this instance, and all the honors belong to Getz.

Stan's next major concert was a command performance—ordered by President Johnson for the other side of the world in Bangkok, Thailand. As part of their efforts to shore up support in Southeast Asia for the Vietnam War, the President and his wife scheduled a state visit in late October 1966 to Thailand's King Bhumibol and his queen, Sirikit. Aides told LBJ that Bhumibol was a jazzophile and an amateur saxophonist who had sat in with the bands of Benny Goodman and Jack Teagarden, and the President immediately summoned Stan and his quartet to play at his October 29 state dinner for the monarch and his queen.

At LBJ's urging, Stan and his group arrived a week before the state dinner to play nightly with the King at jam sessions at his palace. Bhumibol was delighted with the music and with the discussions he had with Stan about saxophone technique. Five days into the visit, Stan and Monica had a fearsome row, and Stan left her and boarded the next plane for New York. During the twenty-hour journey, he became remorseful about letting his President down and, on reaching New York, booked himself on a return flight. He never left JFK Airport or changed his clothes and reappeared in Bangkok just an hour before the state dinner.

The quartet's performance was a success, and after the Johnsons had retired for the night, Bhumibol brought the group back to the palace for a final jam session. Soon after the American ambassador cabled the State Department in Washington: "Embassy considers warm rapport established between Getz and royal family very advantageous."

Following performances for U.S. servicemen at five military installations in Thailand and Vietnam, Stan and the quartet flew to Europe on November 4, 1966, for a whirlwind fifteen-day tour of Germany, Denmark, Sweden, Finland, Holland, France, Spain, England, and Ireland.

Because European audiences still had a hearty appetite for bossa nova, the promoter had reunited Astrud Gilberto with Stan's group for the junket. Since her estrangement from Stan in December 1964, Astrud had divorced João and had married an American, who came with her to Europe. The first few concerts went smoothly, but about a week into the tour, the animosity between her and Stan erupted anew, and she demanded her own backup group. The promoter acquiesced, and subsequent audiences were disappointed when they heard the featured artists play separate sets.

The British critic Alun Morgan found that during Astrud's set at a London concert:

> ... the magic of Getz was notable by its absence. Her trio was efficient and Miss Gilberto sang in tune, but it seems that her best setting was with the Getz group some years ago.

Conversely, Morgan believed that Stan and his men — Burton, Swallow, and Haynes — were in top form:

> Getz has now reached such an incredibly high peak of musicianship, it is inconceivable that anyone could surpass him. Nothing seems beyond his capabilities. And the quartet he now leads is the finest of his career. . . . Stan made no concessions to anyone; he roared through the faster numbers, sweeping aside any

remnants of those slanderous rumors that he was just a player
of pretty tunes. His work now has a greater sense of urgency
than before.

Stan suffered two setbacks on returning to the United States in December
1966. John Coltrane edged him out in *Down Beat*'s poll for the third
straight time, and Gary Burton decided to leave the quartet after almost
three years.

Stan was disappointed that Burton was moving on, but he understood
that his young colleague had developed his talents to a point where he
needed to leave the nest. As Burton told a *Down Beat* reporter:

> I wanted to be my own person. It was getting frustrating to work
> for someone else when I had my own ideas and it wasn't in my
> place to express them.

He felt his time with Stan was fruitful, however, and he wrote years
later:

> I think I have only met or played with a handful of really great
> musicians in my life, and Stan was the first. I'm not even sure I
> was worthy of being part of his group. He influenced my own
> playing for years to come, and I'll never forget him.

Burton's agenda for 1967 was a full one; he had scheduled several
recording sessions as a leader, had contracted to write an instructional
book, and had lined up a number of lucrative freelance engagements.

Stan always sought challenging cohorts, and he replaced Burton with
the imaginative young pianist and composer Armando "Chick" Corea.
Chick was born in 1941 in Chelsea, Massachusetts, to Armando, Sr., who
played trumpet and bass in his own dance orchestra, a group that had a
wide following in the Boston area and on Cape Cod. Chick grew up
listening to his dad's records of Dizzy and Bird, and his first major influences on piano were Horace Silver and Bill Evans. After performing with
his father as a teenager, he opted for a conventional academic career at
Columbia University but quickly dropped out. He remembered:

> The second night I was in Manhattan, I went down to Birdland
> and heard Miles Davis's group with (John) Coltrane and (Wyn-
> ton) Kelly. . . . I couldn't get my head into the curriculum after
> that. So after two months at Columbia, I went back to Boston

and stayed for eight months preparing for a Juilliard audition. I got accepted, but after two months I got bored with that. It took me a year and a half after high school to realize that what I needed to do was just play.

Corea performed with four major bands in the five years between leaving Juilliard and joining Stan: the steaming Afro-Cuban combos of Mongo Santamaria and Willie Bobo; the Herbie Mann group, which combined straight-ahead jazz with both Afro-Cuban and Brazilian elements; and the bebop quintet of trumpeter Blue Mitchell. During these years Corea developed an impressionistic approach to improvising that emphasized Debussyesque washes of color; daring, bittersweet dissonances; and abrupt tempo changes.

Stan's integration of Corea's concepts into the style of the quartet can be heard on the album *Sweet Rain*, recorded on March, 30, 1967, with Ron Carter on bass and Grady Tate on drums. This LP was Stan's last collaboration with Creed Taylor and one of the finest; Taylor left Verve soon after to join A&M Records.

Stan responds to Corea's impressionism by improvising with a freedom and unpredictability reminiscent of his playing on *Focus*; everything sounds freshly minted as he explores the outer limits of harmony and meter. He chose two Corea compositions for the album; on "Litha," he takes the listener on a fierce harmonic adventure as he alternates thematically between the languidly pastoral and the urgently urban, and on the ballad, "Windows," he uses dissonance to lace the tune's lyricism with a deep poignancy.

The title tune, "Sweet Rain" by Mike Gibbs, is a dark-hued piece over which Stan effortlessly creates lines of ominous sadness. The other two numbers, Dizzy Gillespie's "Con Alma" and Jobim's "O Grande Amor," reflect a happier mood but, even here, Stan tinges his heated improvisations with a keening astringency. Corea imbues everything with a sophisticated lyricism, and Carter and Tate support the soloists intensely and resiliently.

Sweet Rain ranks highly in the Getz canon. *Down Beat's* reviewer gave it five stars and called it "a remarkable album," and the British critic Richard Palmer maintained that it was "utterly essential."

Several weeks before the *Sweet Rain* session, Stan undertook an unusual project for Verve. The company had prerecorded a large orchestra and a choir performing a dozen songs as a background setting for improvisations by guitarist Wes Montgomery, but before they could get him to a studio, he left the company for A&M Records.

To salvage Verve's investment, Stan agreed to put on a set of head-phones and take Montgomery's place. The resulting album, *Voices,* sold well but received mixed reviews. Dan Morgenstern gave it five stars in *Down Beat* and called it "a superb mood album," and Richard Palmer commented:

> This writer would cite *Voices* as one of Getz's finest albums. The crooning is quiet, subtle, and expertly arranged by Claus Ogerman.

His countryman Steve Voce disagreed:

> "Focus" had the enormous advantage of Eddie Sauter's scoring. "Voices" uses the arrangements of Claus Ogerman and they are uninspired and inappropriate. For once, Stan sounds off-form.

After touring extensively throughout the United States in the spring of 1967, Stan was reunited with the King and Queen of Thailand on June 27, when he and Monica attended a concert in honor of their Majesties at the White House; among the other guests were the John Waynes, the Allan Jay Lerners, and Duke Ellington.

President Johnson was proud that the entertainment came from his native state in the person of the North Texas State College big band. North Texas State, the alma mater of Jimmy Giuffre, Gene Roland, and Herb Ellis, was a pioneer in jazz education, and its powerful band boasted several good soloists. King Bhumibol was overjoyed when Stan and the Duke sat in with the group, swinging through the ensemble passages and playing sparkling solos. Although Stan had appeared in shows with the Duke's band on several occasions, this was the only time that they ever played together.

Stan was shaken and saddened when he heard that John Coltrane had died of liver cancer at age forty on July 17, 1967, in Huntington, Long Island, New York; he had been ill for a year. Stan could not attend the funeral at St. Peter's Church in New York City on July 21, but—along with Ellington, Max Roach, Horace Silver, and singer Nina Simone—he sent a large arrangement of flowers. One thousand mourners, who crowded into the church that sat only 650, heard original compositions played by Ornette Coleman and tenor saxophonist Albert Ayler. Instead of a eulogy, Coltrane's friend Calvin Massey read the religious poem, "A Love Supreme," which Coltrane had written for the jacket of his album of the same name. It ends:

Thank you God.
ELATION—ELEGANCE—EXALTATION—
All from God.
Thank you God. Amen.

Stan brooded angrily throughout his sets at the Rainbow Grill in Manhattan one night shortly after Coltrane's death. He was upset by what a friend of the family had told him during a casual telephone conversation earlier that day: His twenty-nine-year-old brother-in-law, the psychiatrist Dr. Nils Peter Silfverskiold, had lightly struck Beverly, now thirteen years old, during a quarrel while Stan had been away on tour. The hostility kept building in him, and by the time Monica and Beverly arrived in a car for the journey home, he was in a rage.

As Stan worked the car north toward Shadowbrook, he berated Beverly.

"Why didn't you tell me about Nils Peter punching you?"

"It was nothing, Dad. It wasn't a big deal."

"I'll kill that little bastard next time I see him. I'll break his balls. No one is going to do that to you."

"Dad, calm down. It was months ago. Really. Just an accident."

"Don't tell me to calm down, you little snot. Don't try to protect him."

Stan suddenly stopped the car in front of a bar and walked in. He ordered ten shots of Scotch, lined them up, and threw then back neat. He returned to the driver's seat reeking of alcohol and continued yelling about Nils Peter the rest of the way home.

Stan asked for a cup of bouillon when they arrived at Shadowbrook, and Monica told Beverly to crush up an Antabuse pill secretly and dissolve it in the soup. In her continued attempt to combat Stan's drinking, Monica had somehow obtained a supply of Antabuse, the prescription medicine that causes illness if taken in conjunction with alcohol. She had become familiar with the drug when a doctor prescribed it following Stan's destructive rampage at their home in Roomstead, Denmark, in late 1959.

Stan took a sip of the soup, spat it out violently, and screamed at Beverly, "Can't you make a cup of fucking bouillon? This is awful. What is wrong with you?"

"Dad, it's okay. Let me drink some."

Beverly swallowed a mouthful and found it to be the foulest, most bitter liquid she had ever tasted, but she said, "Yum. Tastes good to me." Stan gagged more of it down and headed for bed, leaving his daughter feeling very guilty. Monica was almost totally inexperienced with Antabuse and did not realize that it is tasteless when dissolved in cold liquids but unpalatable with hot ones.

About an hour later, Beverly was awakened by a commotion in her parents' bedroom and ran full-tilt toward it. She remembered:

> I just stormed into their room, and I stopped dead in my tracks. He was on top of her on the bed, her head hanging over the edge, and he was strangling her, and she was purple. And I yelled, "Dad," and he jumped. He flew off her. He went straight up in the air. He sat down on the bed and just stared at his hands. His hands were shaking badly and he was white as a ghost. He was so upset. He said, "I freaked out. I didn't know what I was doing. Why did I hurt her? Why did I hurt her?"

Monica called the family physician, Dr. Foster, who gave Stan a sedative, and he finally settled into a peaceful sleep. The next morning, he was crestfallen and apologized to everyone, and Monica asked the children to forgive him; she explained that he was drunk when he strangled her and wasn't in his right mind.

The incident so unnerved Monica, however, that soon after she booked herself for a week of pampering and reflection at the Hambletonian Spa in upstate New York. She became friendly there with a wealthy matron who was quite dignified and self-composed; Monica was therefore surprised one evening when the woman came into her room sobbing uncontrollably and seeking solace.

She told Monica that, after her husband had retired as the CEO of a very large corporation, he began drinking heavily and beating her, and she asked Monica to read letters that her husband had been sending her from a place called Hazelden, an alcohol rehab center he was attending in Minnesota. As Monica remembered, the letters were a revelation:

> There was that candidness and honesty. He said that he looked at his life totally differently now that he realized that he was an alcoholic. And he realized there were other people at this place who were brilliant and funny and good and acceptable and they were also alcoholics and they weren't ashamed to say it. These letters were just marvelous. And I thought I didn't admit that I was married to an alcoholic, but I did know it in my head. . . .
>
> I came home full of energy and said, "Stan, you have to go to Hazelden." . . . But he always changed the subject. So it took about a month to cajole him.

Monica traveled with Stan to Hazelden on September 7, 1967, for his admission to its nine-week rehab program. The institution, founded in 1949 and located forty-five miles northeast of the Minneapolis–St. Paul area in Center City, had pioneered the treatment of alcoholism as a disease and based its program firmly on the twelve-step philosophy of Alcoholics Anonymous.

Stan walked up to the receptionist when they arrived and asked to see the boss immediately. When Dr. Dan Anderson, the director, appeared, Stan told him, "There's only one condition that I check into this place: my wife comes, too."

"Does she drink?" Anderson answered.

"No, that's the problem."

"Okay, you go to the men's unit and she goes to the women's unit."

Thus Monica became the first person to participate in what has now become the "family" program at Hazelden. Anderson had improvised on the spot to secure Stan's participation, putting Monica in with a population made up exclusively of alcoholics.

Monica asked the director, "What should I do? Should I pretend that I'm an alcoholic, too—so they don't feel bad?"

"Tell the truth. This program is all about being honest. That's what it's all about."

Anderson gave Monica a sense of relief.

It was like a stone being lifted off my shoulders. I didn't have to worry about him. *He* had to worry about him.

She soon realized that the situation wasn't that simple.

Stan was bouncing off the walls. I came across one of their people, who said that Stan was the only person they ever took downtown to Center City, Minnesota, to give him a drink to get him to shut up, because he was so wild and agitated and everything. Of course, that didn't work either, and he took off.

Stan had lasted only four weeks. He returned to Shadowbrook while Monica worked her way through the full nine-week course.

Soon after she returned, Stan left for England for a short, successful tour with the quartet. Commenting on a November 25 concert in Manchester, Steve Voce was impressed by the new depths of expression that Stan was exploring with Chick Corea:

Although the melodic embellishment remains, the material used
is more important for the way it can be developed rather than
the way it can be made more beautiful. The exquisite melodic
improvisation remains, but only as an adjunct to invention. To
use an analogy, Getz's melodic improvisation is now like the
words used by a writer, for the purpose only to express ideas rather
than an end in itself. In the past it has been the beauty of the
words that came first. . . .

Corea would seem to be a linch-pin in the new order.

Stan returned from England to discover that he had won the *Down Beat*
poll again, defeating Sonny Rollins by a large margin. The news to him
was bittersweet, because he realized that his easy victory was due mainly
to the death of John Coltrane, his great contemporary who had beaten
him five of the previous seven years.

Stan's triumphs could not still his pain and rage, and he erupted again
after an uneventful dinner at Shadowbrook on December 19, 1967, with
Monica and two guests: her brother, Nils Peter, who was visiting for the
Christmas holidays, and Stan's accountant. Following the meal Stan became drunk, and an argument with the accountant erupted into a fistfight.
Steve, who was home on vacation from the University of Colorado, and
Nils Peter tried to help the man stop Stan's bull-like rushes but they
failed, and Monica called the police at 12:23 A.M. When they arrived, Stan
told them that it was he who had been attacked and asked them to arrest
the three other men.

The police left but were summoned four more times during the
night and the following day as Stan continued his destructive binge.
The last time—at 5:24 P.M.—they arrested him when Dr. Foster, who
had come to help Monica, told them he needed assistance to bring
Stan under control.

On Foster's recommendation they took him to the psychiatric ward of
a nearby hospital, where a resident psychiatrist examined him but could
find no reason to commit him. The police then transported him back to
Shadowbrook and Foster's care. By this time Stan was worn out and went
to sleep.

Monica and Nils Peter took the children away to a hotel in the nearby
Catskill Mountains for the remainder of the holiday season, and when
they returned, she obtained an order of protection against Stan from
Family Court Judge Albert Fiorillo. The order stated that—to protect his
family—coercive action would be taken against Stan whenever he became
drunk at Shadowbrook.

Stan was so shaken by his insanely destructive binges that he arranged to meet in New York on December 29, 1967, with Dr. Ruth Fox, a psychiatrist who specialized in the treatment of alcoholics. She suggested that Monica participate in their consultations, and Stan brought her to their next meeting a short time later.

Dr. Fox was an Antabuse zealot, and—despite the fact that the drug could only be obtained from pharmacies via prescription—she encouraged patients to fill their pockets with pills from candy jars that she had placed throughout her office. As Monica recollected, she recommended to Stan and Monica that he embrace a rehab regime which combined hospitalization to detoxify him, psychotherapy, Antabuse, and Alcoholics Anonymous, and that Monica also receive psychotherapy and join Al-Anon, a program for the families of alcoholics.

Dr. Fox's approach differed from Hazelden's in only one important respect: The institution had always been opposed to Antabuse. Its doctrine held that the only effective way for the alcoholic to fight the disease was to rely on internal spiritual resources to abstain from drink; it has maintained this position to the present day.

Dr. Fox said it was imperative that Stan take Antabuse every day, and she told them that if he neglected to do it, Monica should crush up and dissolve the pills in his orange juice. Stan said he understood his problems and would make every effort to take the Antabuse himself. Before the couple left, Dr. Fox reached into a jar on her desk and gave them handfuls of the pills.

Stan checked himself into Hazelden for a second time on January 16, 1968, and stayed until February 3, when he was allowed to leave to tour with his quartet; he returned on March 3 and remained until March 14. Both visits were counterproductive. Despite the bondage to his cycle of depression, booze, and destructive rage, he did not yet possess the will to get sober.

Security was lax at Hazelden in those days, and Stan managed to smuggle pills and airline vodka bottles into the place. He and Truman Capote became notorious for hiding their small bottles in the snow and their pills in bushes and retrieving them as they took what they averred were "brisk walks" for exercise.

When Stan returned to Shadowbrook drunk on March 15, Judge Fiorillo took coercive action by compelling him to "go to Hazelden Foundation, Center City, Minnesota forthwith." Stan was back at the institution for his fourth visit the next day and was discharged April 7.

Dr. Anderson believed that Stan's last sojourn was more productive than his three previous visits, and he wrote in an April 9 letter to Fiorillo:

Mr. Getz was required to attend 20 therapeutic lectures relating to alcoholism and addiction per week, plus five group therapy meetings per week. In addition, he was systematically given individual counseling by a number of staff persons. . . . Arrangements were also made near the end of his stay for him to visit with a rabbi for spiritual counseling. . . .

In comparing his response to treatment on this admission with his behavior on previous admissions, it is apparent that he has shown considerable progress.

Looking back years later, Stan viewed the experience differently than did Dr. Anderson:

I didn't want to get cured because I was sent there against my will. I just went through the motions. . . . You can't get the program unless you are ready. You can't be pushed. I didn't want it. I denied it. I was out there against my will. . . .

I had to keep working. I had to support this big house, this family, vacations, everything. . . . I was stupid enough not to see the message at that time, that I was an alcoholic. All I could do was my job. . . . I didn't want anyone to tell me what I could do after I had finished my job.

Stan resumed drinking the moment he left Hazelden on April 7 and told Dr. Fox about it when he saw her two days later. This prompted her to send Fiorillo a letter on April 12, 1968; she described the program she had recommended and suggested that the Judge commit Stan to a rehab institution in Pennsylvania.

Monica tolerated Stan's drinking until April 13, when she had him arrested again. Two days afterward he appeared before Fiorillo, who had received the letter from Dr. Fox. The Judge did not believe that another bout of rehab would benefit Stan this time; he merely ordered that he "be under the care and treatment of Dr. Ruth Fox."

Dr. Fox wrote the Judge again on June 6 confessing to the failure of her efforts with Stan. She said that he had been drunk a number of times since April, and she recommended that when he returned from a tour of Japan and the West Coast, he be committed to Falkirk Hospital, thirty miles from Shadowbrook.

Stan drank moderately until August 6, when he binged again and Monica had him arrested for a third time. He spent the night in jail and the next day consented to Fiorillo's order committing him to Falkirk.

Stan's breath smelled of alcohol when he arrived at the hospital, and he was sweating profusely. He was sent to the detox unit and subjected to a series of tests and interviews. An admitting physician wrote that Stan told him:

> When he drinks he loses a great deal of his self-control for the reason that he has had many difficulties with his wife . . . although he recognizes that he is a success in his profession and should be happy, this is not true, because he lacks a great deal of understanding at home. . . . He complains of her (his wife) showing a lack of affection when he required it most.

The next day Stan changed his tune; another physician reported that "he spoke very warmly of his wife, emphasizing her beauty and how much he loved her, how she in turn must love him, since she never left him or sued for divorce."

The doctors concluded that Stan had an "addictive personality" and showed "evidence of a deep-seated personality disorder." They wrote that he was a cooperative patient who "recovered both physically and in terms of his natural buoyancy and euphoria while at Falkirk, and was extremely optimistic about his future prospects when he left. . . . The prognosis, however, must be very guarded, indeed." The physicians recommended on discharge on August 16 that Dr. Fox supervise his care—which would include psychotherapy at the hospital—and that he be recommitted to Falkirk if he defaulted on his program. They also suggested that Monica undergo psychotherapy.

Chick Corea had had enough following the Falkirk episode and left Stan to join Gary Burton's quartet. All the members of this group were now Getz alumni; the other musicians were Steve Swallow and Roy Haynes. Corea and Stan parted on good terms and promised to work together in the future. On Thanksgiving weekend 1968, the Burton quartet shared billing at the Village Gate in New York with Stan's group, which now included Miroslav Vitous on bass, Jack DeJohnette on drums, and Jane Getz (no relation) on piano.

Stan again bested Sonny Rollins in the *Down Beat* poll in December, and Gary Burton was elected Jazzman of the Year. Stan's victory was surprising because the chaos of his life had curtailed his public appearances and had prevented him from making any albums in more than fifteen months. In fact, 1968 was the only year in which he had not been recorded since he embarked on the road with Jack Teagarden in 1943 at age fifteen. Stan's last recording, completed on August 31, 1967, with the backing of a large orchestra, was an album of Burt Bacharach tunes aimed at an "easy listening" audience and was called *What the World Needs Now*. Stan played beautifully throughout, but the album is short on jazz content.

Stan's personal demons continued to torment him as he made a short tour of England, France, and Scandinavia in January and February 1969. His playing was erratic and disturbing to audiences and critics alike; Benny Green of the London *Observer* was flabbergasted that Stan, previously always the sure one, veered perilously from one stylistic pole to the next, and Derek Jewell in the London Sunday *Times* wrote this about an evening at Ronnie Scott's nightclub:

> His performance was wildly uneven. Happily, it improved, and drew heavy applause from a baffled audience during a very good second set. But the first was something else. During this, Getz appeared disoriented, ill-at-ease with his listeners, unwilling to play for long, pausing at length, disappearing from the stand, muttering. The music was grave and unworldly, as if dragged from within him, the vibrato heavily pronounced, the structure blurred. It was moving and beautiful, and embarrassing and ugly at once. Genius in retreat.

Stan never adhered to his Falkirk rehab program; he broke all his psychotherapy appointments, he stopped taking Antabuse on his own, and he kept on drinking. He continued to be violent when drunk, and Monica continued to forgive his conduct. Her daughter Pamela remembered one of her parents' fights during that winter of 1968–1969:

> He was pulling her out of the pantry by the hair and she was trying to hold onto her hair so that he wouldn't pull it out of her head. And he was just yelling, "Cunt. Bitch. I'll show you."
>
> My mother was screaming, "Please call the police. Please. Somebody, Pam. Get help."
>
> And I went toward the phone and he just looked at me like he wanted to kill me, and I just ran away. . . .
>
> I was scared. I ran upstairs and my mother came up a little bit later and she said, "Don't be angry with him. He's only like this when he is drunk. He doesn't mean it."

Stan's behavior in late March 1969 was so outrageous that even Monica couldn't excuse it. He had been drinking for more than two days and became violent; Monica took the children to a motel, where she telephoned Judge Fiorillo and convinced him to arrest Stan for a fourth time. He was drunk when he was picked up on March 22 and hauled off to jail. After a court appearance two days later, he packed some clothes, picked up his horn, and headed for England, leaving the family behind.

EUROPE AGAIN   FIFTEEN

JUDY GARLAND, looking wasted and gaunt, came one night to hear Stan at Ronnie Scott's London club, where he had secured a four-week April engagement. Stan dedicated a couple of tunes to her, and when she reacted brightly, he coaxed her up onto the bandstand. As she approached him, he thought he had made a mistake; she was tottering uncertainly, and he had heard about a recent disastrous nightclub engagement when, fuddled by drink and drugs, she had forgotten the words to her songs and had been pelted with bread sticks and cigarette butts. But strength lit Judy's face as Stan's spotlight hit her, and she climbed onto a stool on the stage, rearranging her voluminous skirt so that it filled out her frighteningly frail figure. Stan gave Judy star treatment, standing in the background and playing quiet obbligatos as she sang two numbers in good voice.

247

When Ronnie and his wife took Judy's party and Stan and his musicians to a Chinese restaurant afterward, Judy's overriding concern was that Ronnie bring for her a liter bottle of a gin and lime drink. She ate almost nothing but emptied the bottle. Two months later, on June 22, 1969, she was found dead in her London flat of a barbiturate overdose; she was forty-seven.

Stan had settled into London's Dorchester Hotel that spring and managed his affairs from there. He came back to the United States for engagements but did not communicate with the family. While Steve, David, and Beverly continued their educations in the States, Monica took Pamela and Nicky to Sweden.

One night at the Dorchester, Stan and his friends, the comedians Peter Sellers and Spike Milligan, had drunk many liters of wine when Stan started boasting of his prowess as a swimmer.

"The Thames would be a sprint for me," he said. "It doesn't faze me at all."

"It's a treacherous river, Stan, and very cold," Milligan replied. "Two hundred quid says you won't make it across."

"You've got a bet."

"Here's another two hundred that says you won't," Sellers chimed in.

"You've got a bet, too."

Five minutes later, the three of them walked through the Dorchester lobby, with Stan clad only in swim trunks and a bathrobe, and hailed a cab to a nearby Thames bridge. Stan soon plunged into the river, and although he was stroking powerfully, Milligan panicked and called the police.

"This is Spike Milligan."

"Who?"

"Spike Milligan. You know, from the *Goon Show* on TV. I'm down here at the river with my good friend Stan Getz, who's trying to swim across. I don't think he's going to make it. I need your help."

"Even if you are Spike Milligan, you sound pretty drunk to me. I advise you and whoever is with you to go home and sleep it off."

The policeman hung up and Milligan and Sellers jumped back into their waiting cab and directed the driver to cross the bridge. When they got to the other side, they found Stan sitting nonchalantly on the riverbank.

"What took you guys so long?" he asked.

On May 1 in Los Angeles, Stan recorded *Didn't We*, his first album in twenty months. Like his previous LP of Burt Bacharach songs, it was aimed at an "easy listening" audience and utilized the same musical concept—romantic tunes played over lush orchestral settings.

Stan continued drinking at a prodigious pace. He stopped performing during the summer of 1969 and drifted down to Spain's Costa del Sol resort area, where he rented a small apartment by the Mediterranean in the town of Almuñécar, east of the city of Málaga. There he grew frightened as his depressions intensified and his health deteriorated. Despairing, he telephoned Monica in September and pleaded with her to rejoin him and help him get sober.

She agreed. Steve returned to the University of Colorado, David remained at Shadowbrook to complete his final year in high school, Beverly was enrolled at a boarding school in Pennsylvania, Nicky stayed in Sweden with relatives, and Monica traveled to Spain with Pamela, age eleven. Monica remembered how she found Stan:

> He was both mentally and physically in terrible shape ... He was ... emaciated. He was dirty. He was crying ... He said he needed help.

Monica took several steps to return her husband to health and sobriety. She plied him with nutritious foods, she arranged for him to enter a rehab facility in England, and she secretly sprinkled Antabuse into his food.

Dr. Fox, in her April 12, 1968, letter to Judge Fiorillo, had written:

> I have found it best for this (Antabuse) to be taken by the patient of his own free will and given by the wife. However, if we find as time goes on that Mr. Getz is remiss in taking it, then we would see that the wife gives it to him crushed up in orange juice.

Fox did not explicitly recommend here the secret administration of the drug, but Monica believed that with this paragraph the doctor had given her license to administer Antabuse to Stan without his knowledge.

The secret administering of Antabuse was an expedient but potentially dangerous course. The drug should be taken only under the careful supervision of a physician and with the patient's knowledge, because when it combines with alcohol inside the body, it creates a powerful toxin which can make the recipient seriously ill and can even cause death. The principal manufacturer of the drug, Wyeth-Ayerst Laboratories, prints this warning in its "Patient Guidelines for Antabuse":

> In the presence of alcohol, the most common effects produced by Antabuse are flushing, throbbing in head and neck, throbbing headache, respiratory difficulty, nausea, copious vomiting, sweat-

ing, thirst, chest pain, palpitation, dyspnea, hyperventilation, tachycardia, hypotension, syncope, marked uneasiness, weakness, vertigo, blurred vision, and confusion. In severe reactions there may be respiratory depression, cardiovascular collapse, arrhythmias, myocardial infarction, acute congestive heart failure, unconsciousness, convulsions, and death.

Stan experienced some of the devastating effects of the drug soon after Monica and Pamela had arrived in Almuñécar. Not knowing that there was any Antabuse in his system, he drank two glasses of red wine at a workingman's bar on the ground floor of his apartment building, walked across the street to a beach, and became immediately nauseated. He recalled:

> I will never forget it. I had the most ferocious reaction I have ever had to anything in my life. I thought I was going to die. I felt terrible. . . . I was vomiting uncontrollably into the Mediterranean. My heart was racing. I was just completely ill. I felt like I was going to die.

When he told Monica about it, she suggested that he might be starting to become allergic to alcohol.

Soon after, Stan, Monica, and Pam headed for England, where Stan cleaned himself up at the rehab facility, and he and Monica rented a small flat in London's posh Mayfair district. They soon returned to the Costa del Sol where they leased another residence, a house at Punta de los Monos just behind Gibraltar. On a clear day they could look out from their home and see Africa across the straits.

During the next two years London and the Costa del Sol became the twin poles of their existence; they bought land by the sea near Almuñécar but never built on it, and in 1970 they moved to another rented home in Fuengirola, near Málaga. Shadowbrook did not drain them financially during their European sojourn because the rents from apartments they had created in the three outbuildings covered much of their taxes, mortgage payments, and other expenses.

Stan had another severe Antabuse reaction when he flew alone to London to make a record called *Marrakesh Express*. It featured popular songs of the day like the title tune by Graham Nash, Paul Simon's "Cecilia," and Bacharach's "Raindrops Keep Fallin' on My Head," and it followed the commercial formula of his two previous albums by setting his solos over romantic orchestral arrangements. Stan remembered his difficulties that day:

Just before we went upstairs to the recording, I had a pint of strong English beer and I got upstairs, and I started to have a reaction. I just went to the bathroom and nobody saw me. Finally I did come out and somehow I got through the recording. . . . I was so sick. . . . It was the worst record I ever made. . . . I hear that record, and you can hear that I'm having an Antabuse reaction.

Beverly suffered from health problems of her own that autumn, and they were compounded by the indifference of the authorities at her Pennsylvania boarding school. She remembered:

I got appendicitis. Nobody in the school believed me. They left me lying in my room for three days and nobody bothered. I was throwing up. I was really sick and I was on the third floor of this house. I remember crawling down three flights of stairs and calling Dottie Foster because she was a nurse. And the next thing I knew, I woke up in the hospital having been operated on.

Dottie Foster, the wife of Dr. John Foster, the Getz family physician, had driven to the school, taken one look at Beverly's distended belly, and hustled her off to a hospital, where surgeons immediately operated to remove a ruptured appendix. Beverly was withdrawn from the school, and Mrs. Foster took her from the hospital to her own home.

While recuperating, Beverly received a letter from Stan addressed to her and David. It read:

Dear Good! Grown up Kids,

Have been Sober for 1 month. Don't lose hope. I haven't! I Love my family more than the Bottle; a million times more. As you you (sic) know, I'm a terrible letter writer, amongst other faults. The only thing i can do decently is play the Sax— Sometimes. Love me if you still can.

I Love you all,
Dad

Would you like my autograph? Okay, you twisted my arm. HERE GOES!!! big deal.

Beverly stayed with the Fosters until the Christmas holidays, when she and Nicky visited her parents and Pamela in Spain.

Stan and Monica had become friends with one of their neighbors, guitar master Andrés Segovia, and had talked him into giving Beverly lessons. She took a dim view of the enterprise, because she found Segovia gruff and forbidding; she was spared the ordeal of studying with him, however, when she became ill again, this time with the flu. When she recovered, Monica instructed her how to crush up the white Antabuse pills and sprinkle them into a variety of foods and warned her, "If you ever tell Daddy this, he'll kill us all." Beverly returned to the Fosters' after the holidays, as Monica and Stan began searching for a school in England for her.

Soon after Beverly left, Stan, while chasing Monica in a drunken rage, fell down a flight of stairs in their home and broke his heel bone and hurt his hand. After a delay of several weeks caused by a faulty diagnosis, the doctors put a cast on his foot, and he flew to London a couple of days later in great pain. He talked a doctor into prescribing morphine and proceeded to overdose on the drug in Monica's presence; she called the physician, who revived him.

During the first week of February 1970, Stan left London on crutches for Oslo and a short tour of Scandinavia and promptly came down with his second case of double pneumonia. He recovered much more rapidly than he had in Sweden in 1955, and he was playing at Ronnie Scott's club by the end of the month. Benny Green, in a London *Observer* review of the engagement entitled "Maimed But Masterly," found that Stan's artistry had triumphed over his travails:

> The last time Stan Getz came to London he brought with him an uncertainty about his own style which was so uncharacteristic of the man that nobody could believe it. . . . The crisis appears to be over. This time the handicaps he brings to Ronnie Scott's club are merely a broken foot, three semi-paralyzed fingers, and the after effects of pneumonia, and the musical result is infinitely finer. . . . The sensation most people associate with Getz is blinding speed of thought, to which the fingers respond with faultless precision, and in a theme called "Tour's End" there is all the proof we need that he retains this quality. Phrases move from chord to chord so sweetly that the time lapse between thoughts and execution seems to have been eliminated altogether. . . . He is one of the major figures in jazz history, perhaps the most felicitous of all saxophonists, and one of the very few whose mas-

tery of the process of improvisation transcends all considerations
of styles and school.

During the Ronnie Scott engagement, Monica flew from London to Sweden for a weekend and left Pamela with Stan. Pamela became apprehen-
sive one morning because Stan was angry and out of sorts, and these
moods often presaged a drinking bout. She took an Antabuse pill from a
hiding place in a kitchen cabinet, crushed it up, sprinkled it over pancakes
she had made, and topped it with butter and sugar. Stan ate the food
and later that day drank some alcohol and had a mild reaction. He
telephoned Monica and said, "Something wonderful has happened. I
might really be allergic to alcohol."

Monica was overjoyed because she reasoned that she could now control
Stan's drinking with carefully apportioned secret doses of Antabuse. Until
then she had administered the drug somewhat randomly; from now on,
she would do it systematically. At first, Beverly and Pamela were her only
associates in the Antabuse enterprise. Eventually, Monica would recruit
Steve and David as well as employees and friends; all were pledged to
secrecy. And the results pleased Monica, who looked back on the early
1970s as a golden era. She later said, "He showed for the first time he
was able to live without alcohol for longer and longer periods of time."

Lithium, the standard drug for treating manic-depressive illness in the
1970s, was prescribed for Stan by a physician in London and also contributed to his increased sobriety at this time. Depression was a root cause
of Stan's drinking, and alcohol released his manic rages; lithium worked
to reduce for him the severity of both destructive emotional states. The
drug was not totally effective in dealing with Stan's depressions, and in
the mid-1970s, another medicine, Elavil, was found helpful and was added
to the regimen. He took both of them until 1980.

Stan and Monica had found an all-girls boarding school for Beverly in
Oxfordshire, and she arrived in England in March to enroll.

In May 1970 Stan and Monica traveled to South Africa—at the time
in the grip of apartheid at its fiercest—for a three-week tour. Stan was
furious when they arrived because the promoters had promised he would
play for people of all races, and the local publicity stated the opposite.
Stan told a press conference that he would play for "all members of the
public," and he hounded the promoters to get him a permit to work in
the black townships.

The promoters obtained the permit but reneged on their promise to
organize the concerts, telling him they could never again book him in
the country if he played for blacks. On his own, Stan organized a date

at the Bantu Men's Social Center in Johannesburg; he performed with a black combo and then with his own all-white group and finally brought all the musicians on stage for a jam session. The audience mobbed him when the concert ended, and it took him an hour to wend his way through the crowd and out of the hall. "The Johannesburg audience was the best I ever played for," Stan later told Beverly. "I'm proud of what I did there."

Beverly felt lonely at her boarding school and had difficulty adjusting to a new curriculum in the middle of the school year, and one night, during Stan's South African tour, she ran away. She quickly lost her resolve and sneaked back in and her absence was never discovered. She returned to the United States at the end of the semester and spent the summer at the Fosters'.

David crossed the Atlantic in the opposite direction after graduating from high school in June 1970. He flew to Spain to spend the summer in the house at Fuengirola with Nicky (who came down from Sweden), his parents, and Pamela. On arrival David was told that Monica and Pamela were administering Antabuse secretly to his father.

Stan had just returned from Paris filled with enthusiasm about a French group that excited him so much that he felt he had to record with them. He remembered:

> We had come in June to watch the tennis championships and, as a criminal who always returns to the scene of his crime, I went to the old Blue Note where I had played thrice annually from 1959 to 1961. I had been told that jazz in France was dead, and sure enough, the club was almost empty.
>
> I walked in and my mouth fell open. I heard some hardcore swinging jazz, everybody was dipping in, really taking their piece. There was Eddy Louiss on organ, René Thomas on guitar, and Bernard Lubat on drums. . . . I found it sad that crowds will only turn out for an American name artist, regardless of the quality of the music. . . . These musicians deserve a better fate than a slow death before disinterested Parisians. I decided then and there to present these musicians to the rest of the world.

Stan promised that in the autumn he would return and begin rehearsing the musicians for a quartet album with him.

Stan threw himself into a new sport that summer when he began taking tennis lessons from jazz lover Lew Hoad at Hoad's facility in Marbella, just up the road from Fuengirola. Hoad, born in Australia, was one of the best tennis players of all time, but his career was cut short in his mid-twenties by a back injury. His powerful, attacking style excited the crowds and caused broadcaster Bud Collins to write:

> He blistered the ball and became impatient with rallying, preferring to hit for winners. It was a flamboyant style, and made for some bad errors when he wasn't in tune. But when his power was focused along with his concentration, Hoad came on like a tidal wave.

During the preopen era, when only amateurs could play in the major tournaments, Hoad won, within a span of five years, six Grand Slam titles in singles and seven in doubles. His best year was 1956 when, at age twenty-two, he took three of the four singles Grand Slams, losing only in the United States. After a Wimbledon triumph in 1957, he turned pro, but his back problems erupted the next year, and his career petered out in the early 1960s. In 1964 he and his wife, Jenny, who reached the Australian singles final in 1954, opened their tennis camp in Marbella, and it still flourishes. Hoad died from leukemia in 1994, but Jenny is carrying on.

As Nicky, age eight, watched Stan work his way through a sweaty lesson one morning, he criticized his dad's game from the sidelines. Stan said, "If you think you know so much about tennis, why don't you try it?" and handed his racket to his son. Believing that tennis was like Little League baseball, Nicky slugged several balls out of the court. Hoad then explained the rules to him, and he quickly began to hit powerful, accurate shots. Nicky did not realize it at the time, but he had found his life's work. He remembered:

> I just really enjoyed the feeling of hitting that tennis ball with the racquet, it was so easy compared to baseball, and from then on I was hooked on the game, and I used to practice on the backboard there for like five hours a day.
>
> My parents would just drop me off at the club, leave me there, and I would be hitting against the backboard and they would drive away and they would come back five hours later, and I'd still be hitting against the backboard. I got to be a pretty good player in a short amount of time.

Nicky showed so much promise that when the summer ended, his parents left him with the Hoads to develop his game more fully. He picked up Spanish quickly as he attended a local school in Marbella until the following June.

David returned to the United States for the 1970–1971 academic year to enroll at Loretta Heights College, a small liberal arts institution in Denver not far from his brother Steve at the University of Colorado in Boulder. Beverly rejoined her parents and Pamela in London and entered a finishing school outside the city where she boarded and studied such subjects as cordon bleu cooking, stenography, dressmaking, and flower arranging. Pamela was sent to a conventional girls' boarding school deep in the British countryside.

During the autumn Stan played with local musicians throughout Europe and rehearsed with the Eddy Louiss trio whenever he found the opportunity. He made his debut with the group in December in Paris at a club called Le Chat Qui Pêche. The engagement was a success, according to *Down Beat*:

> The saxophonist played with a fervor and enthusiasm and imagination which recalled the Getz of the Storyville LPs with Jimmy Raney. . . . Big and authoritative, the lyricism (of Stan) has no longer any need of prettiness to manifest itself. The sound is powerfully sonorous, the rhythmic aspect of the phrase is enhanced, the fast tempos are often provocative. He receives tailor-made support from the Eddy Louiss trio. . . . As for the organist, he has his unyielding originality, his never-ending invention, his fire, his thirst to play, and his unshakable love of the music.

Stan learned in Paris that he had beaten out Sonny Rollins in the 1970 *Down Beat* poll and that Miles Davis had been elected Jazzman of the Year.

Stan did not make any albums in 1970, but he broke his drought when he went into a London studio on January 3, 1971, for several days of recording with Louiss, Thomas, and Lubat. Beverly remembered the morning of January 6, when she wrote a letter to her grandfather Al:

> I went down to the mailbox, stuck it in the mail, walked up the stairs. As I walked in the room, the phone rang; Monica picked it up and I heard her say, "Benny," the name of Al's brother. And I knew it. The minute she said his name, I said, "Grandpa's dead, right?," and she nodded, "Yes." Heart failure. It was so freaky.

Monica told Stan when he came home, and he sat down and sobbed for a long time. The next day he flew alone to New York for the funeral. Al's health had been failing for several years, as he suffered several heart attacks and endured the amputation of part of a foot because of diabetes. He had married a third time, and his widow dictated the funeral arrangements, treating Stan and his brother Bob coldly. They were infuriated when she made no mention of them on Al's tombstone, which was inscribed "Beloved by his wife and stepsons." Stan did not remain for the full eight-day period of mourning and returned to London on January 9.

After one more day in the studio with the Louiss trio, he decided to record most of the tracks for their album before a live audience at Ronnie Scott's club in March.

Beverly came down to London from her boarding school to stay with her father one late January weekend when Monica was out of town. She remembered that when she tried to get into the family's small, second-floor Mayfair flat, she found that the doorbell was broken.

I called him up from a pay phone in the street, and he said, "I'll throw the keys down to you." Ten minutes went by, and nothing happened. I called back again, and he didn't answer. I finally got a policeman to chop down the door. I remember pushing my way in first, because I was afraid of what we were going to see, and I didn't want the police to see anything. He was slumped over this table with a needle hanging out of his arm.

I was trying to keep the police out, but they came in and they kind of picked him up. He came to, thank God, and they laid him down on the bed. It was these two young cops, two young Bobbies. When Stan saw me, he started crying, and then he saw them and he really got upset. Because he had been barred from England years before after a drug episode.

One of the cops asked, "What's your name?" He said, "Stanley." The cop replied, "Okay, Mr. Stanley. We're leaving now, and we haven't seen anything."

Stan keeps crying and saying, "I haven't done this for twenty years." And I'm putting my hand over his mouth, saying, "Okay, shut up, Dad, shut up."

They left. They came back the next day just to make sure he wouldn't say anything to anybody, because they would have lost their jobs.

I called his doctor, who came over and left two pills for me to give Stan when he woke up. Then Monica called. I was just waiting for him to wake up so I could give him those pills. Monica asked, "What are the names of the pills?" And they were sleeping pills. And she said, "Do not give him the sleeping pills." She was right. He was already down, and I could have killed him, because he was going in and out of ODing.

England always presented Stan with special temptations, because its laws allowed addicts to obtain drugs by prescription from cooperative doctors.

Following a highly successful two-week tour of Mexico, Stan and his group settled in at Ronnie Scott's for a three-week gig on March 1, 1971. As he told a French reporter, he was eager to atone for what he considered a seriously flawed engagement at Scott's thirteen months earlier.

> It was a disaster.... I hadn't played in eight months. I could hardly hold a saxophone in my mouth. I had no muscles, no lips. I shouldn't have played. I was feeling very uncomfortable because I had just stopped drinking five months before and I was not well. It takes a year to get really well from alcohol. I'm a hard drinking man when I drink. Two bottles a day for ten years. The Dylan Thomas of the saxophone.... Grant's Standfast or Grant's 12-Year-Old or Dewar's White Label....
>
> My wife was pushing me to forget my bad habits. Without her, I wouldn't have gotten well. And she stayed by me every minute.

Benny Green took a different view of the 1970 engagement, seeing it as part of a stunning Getz comeback. He wrote about this in a long *Down Beat* article:

> Getz has worked at Ronnie Scott's Club three times in the last three years, and during that time appears to have gone through what the Victorians used to call a spiritual crisis....
>
> When he arrived at Scott's for (his) 1969 engagement, Getz was 42 years old, and was, I think, experiencing the first, extremely disconcerting, intimations of the artistic menopause which afflicts so many creators moving into their middle 40s.... That Getz, one of the supreme masters of form in improvisation, should have felt himself impelled to fling himself into the deep and muddy waters of formlessness seemed to me one of the most depressing jazz events of the last ten years....
>
> In 1970 Getz returned harassed by the after-effects of pneumo-

nia, a broken foot, and two semi-paralyzed fingers. . . . His embouchure had quite clearly disappeared for the moment. . . . His
(engagement) was a tremendous relief. . . . There was no question
that apart from the physical struggles a much more important
one had recently been concluded with himself.

Quite apart from the fact that it was the most remarkable come-
back ever seen in London jazz circles, Getz' 1971 visit was a
crushing argument in favor of the theory that jazz is after all an
art form. . . . In my opinion he is now playing better than at any
previous stage in his career.

Fans everywhere were fortunate to hear Stan at his new peak on March
15, 16, and 17, when he and his group were recorded live at Ronnie Scott's
to complete the sessions begun in the studio in January. The resulting
album is called *Dynasty*.

Dynasty bristles with the energy and passion of Stan's previous major
jazz album, *Sweet Rain*, but it is more accessible to the listener. It swings
harder, and while its harmonies are totally contemporary, they avoid the
harsher dissonances of Stan's outing with Chick Corea.

Stan's new rhythm section displays a thrusting cohesiveness that propels him inexorably forward on his flights of improvisation. Guitarist
Thomas was a veteran of Sonny Rollins's group and a disciple of Stan's
old cohort Jimmy Raney; his solos intriguingly combined Raney's fleet
intelligence with a streak of gypsy sadness. Louiss on organ could easily
have drowned everyone out but showed admirable restraint as he reeled
off chorus after hot chorus at just the right volume; and Lubat at the
drums managed to drive his confreres along forcefully without ever
becoming obtrusive.

The nine selections on the album provide Stan with a variety of settings
in which to display his talents. There are two ballads, a crisp bossa nova,
two up-tempo swingers, an elegy for Al Getz, a low-down funk tune, and
two infectious Latin numbers; seven of the songs were written by Thomas
or Louiss.

Stan is expressively unerring as time and again he chooses the right
timbre, the right harmonic coloration, the right rhythmic nuance to give
surging life to a kaleidoscope of emotions; most of the time they are tinged
with pain. Twenty-two years before, with "Early Autumn," he limned the
aching melancholy of youth with a light, translucent tone. The tone of
Dynasty is full and muscular as he expresses the sadness of a mature man
who has suffered. Almost every note is conveyed intensely, as if he wished
to burn away life's pain with his searing cries.

Stan's friend Spike Milligan caught this aspect of Stan's psyche accurately when he wrote in the liner notes:

> If you are at all a sensitive person, you will detect in his playing
> a sadness; perhaps it was the sudden death of his father in the
> midst of the recording sessions coupled with an inherent sadness,
> a feeling of suffering, which is released or rather aborted from
> his being by unending flurries, suspensions, and cascades of notes
> which get into a trinity of feeling, intellect, and technique. One
> feels, that had he not had this superb musical gift, he might
> become suicidal. "Of suffering, beauty is born"; I feel this might
> be the essence of Stan Getz. Like Van Gogh—he suffers, but my
> God look what he gave us.

Milligan did not know when he wrote this that Stan had twice attempted suicide.

Lew Hoad told Stan and Monica that he believed Nicky had the makings of a tennis champion because the child combined great athletic ability with a steely competitive temperament. He was unhappy to see his young charge leave for a British boarding school in August 1971 after a year of spectacular progress. Nicky was crestfallen when he discovered that his new school had no tennis program, but his parents believed that at age nine his serious education should take precedence over his athletic ambitions.

Stan toured exclusively in Europe with the *Dynasty* group for the rest of 1971, playing to sold-out houses at both clubs and festivals. In November he recorded *Communications '72*, a collaboration with Michel Legrand for which Stan recruited Eddy Louiss. Legrand backed Stan and Eddy with a large string orchestra and a seventeen-piece vocal group, the Swingle Singers, featuring Michel's sister Christiane. Ten Legrand compositions are performed and, as *The New Yorker* reviewer noted, they reflect a broad stylistic palette:

> There is every sort of mood and music: a rolling fervent medium-
> tempo blues, in which Getz gets off close to a dozen brilliant
> choruses; a Bartok-like piece, in which he plays a difficult, almost
> acrid melodic line nearly straight; a couple of hymn-ballads; and
> a piece in which he exchanges Bach figures with the orchestra
> and chorus. The orchestrations are ingenious, if somewhat showy,
> but Getz is paramount throughout—in turn lyrical, declamatory,
> fleet, and wholly original.

While Beverly was in Paris in early December with Monica, she came upon a letter from Big Bev that Monica had inadvertently left lying about. Stan and Monica had told her that her mother had disappeared, and Beverly remembered that reading the letter had almost literally knocked the wind out of her:

> She (Big Bev) had read in some gossip magazine that Stan had gotten a divorce. She wrote that she was so sorry to hear about the divorce, and if there was anything she could do concerning the kids, please contact her. Because she missed her kids and loved her kids and wanted to have something to do with them.

Beverly ran to Monica with the letter and said, "I found this. My mother is alive. Why didn't you tell me?"

"The letter was a surprise to us, too, darling. We were convinced that she was dead."

Beverly was uncertain about what she would do.

> I remember sitting down and trying to write her a letter, and I couldn't get past "Dear." I didn't know what to call her. I just didn't know what to do. I didn't know what to say. I really regret not writing that letter, I really regret it. She died the next year.

By the end of 1971, Stan's drinking had stabilized at a moderate level. Monica had learned enough about Antabuse dosage to minimize the occurrence of serious reactions such as Stan suffered in the Spanish workingman's bar and at the London recording session; Stan endured a series of mild reactions, which he attributed to a newly developed allergy to alcohol. Because he had rebounded both physically and artistically from the crisis of late 1969, he and Monica decided that it was time to return to Shadowbrook. A lucrative contract to perform at New York's Rainbow Grill, starting on January 3, 1972, convinced them that they should move quickly.

They were frustrated when they failed to obtain union permission for Louiss, Thomas, and Lubat to perform in the United States, but fortune smiled on them when they ran into a temporarily unemployed Chick Corea in London. He talked enthusiastically about several new tunes he was working on and about a pair of excellent New York musicians with whom he wanted to work. His enthusiasm carried the day with Stan, who paid him to complete his compositions and told him to bring his new cohorts to Shadowbrook in late December to rehearse.

Before leaving Europe, Stan was happy to learn that he had bested Sonny Rollins for the fifth straight time in the *Down Beat* poll.

Beverly, Pamela, and Nicky remained in England to continue their schooling, and Stan and Monica returned home in the midst of a cold snap, a frigid reminder of the weather they encountered when they returned from their previous European sojourn eleven years earlier.

ANTABUSE YEARS SIXTEEN

CHICK COREA brought Stanley Clarke and Airto Moreira to the rehearsals at Shadowbrook. Clarke was a twenty-year-old prodigy on bass who had made a strong impact while playing for Horace Silver in 1970; Moreira was a thirty-year-old Brazilian percussionist whom Chick had met when they were both working for Miles Davis during the same year. Moreira's wife, the singer Flora Purim, came to the rehearsals and helped fortify the musicians against the frigid weather by cooking, along with Monica, the hearty dishes of her native Brazil.

Stan loved the tunes that Corea had written and he was impressed by Clarke's talents, but he was dissatisfied with Moreira; he enjoyed the percussionist's improvisations but found his accompaniments weak and scattered. Stan solved the problem by adding Tony Williams—for many the outstanding jazz drummer of the 1960s and 1970s—to the band and using Moreira to broaden the group's percussive spectrum. Williams had joined Miles Davis in 1963 at age seventeen and stayed with him until 1969, powering some of the greatest small groups in jazz history. The drummer had always admired Corea's talents and had talked Davis into hiring Chick in 1968. Williams had found only middling success as a leader during 1970 and 1971.

The quintet opened its three-week engagement at the Rainbow Grill on January 3, 1972, sharing the bill with João Gilberto. Gilberto played and sang with Stan's group and also created duets with his countryman, Moreira. John S. Wilson of *The New York Times* was very impressed:

> The rhythm section that is now playing at the Rainbow Grill is one of the most fascinating groups of its kind that can be heard anywhere. It is, for the most part, a Miles Davis alumni association. . . .
>
> Mr. Getz is currently blending the warm romanticism of his bossa nova period of the early 1960s with the explosively dynamic attack he developed later in the decade, producing a kind of slow-boil intensity on tunes by Mr. Corea, Billy Strayhorn's "Lush Life," and several bossa novas.
>
> The combination of Mr. Getz's highly experienced virtuosity with this remarkable rhythm section makes for jazz on an unusually sophisticated level.

The engagement broke all records for the venue as crowds stood in long lines in the lobby of the RCA Building to ride the elevator to the Grill on the sixty-fifth floor, where they could enjoy both the music and the breathtaking views of Manhattan. Stan's success came as a tonic to the world of jazz, which was enduring the full onslaught of the rock revolution and was in the middle of one of its periodic depressions.

The quintet went into a studio on March 3, 1972, to make an album that became known as *Captain Marvel*. The record contains five compositions by Corea, who plays electric piano exclusively, plus a short rendition of Billy Strayhorn's "Lush Life." Unlike the songs he wrote for *Sweet Rain*, Corea's new compositions all reflect the Spanish heritage of his mother (his father was Italian).

Except for the two-and-a-half minutes of "Lush Life," *Captain Marvel* never lets the listener relax. This is tough, take-no-prisoners music, and its main perpetrators are Stan and his drummer. Stan is in fierce fettle and Williams's intensity matches his leader's every step of the way.

Williams's most singular skill is maintaining a hypnotic pulse while embellishing it with an amazing variety of effects—cymbal crashes, piercing rimshots, deep bass bombs, thundering rolls. Moreira joins the fray by coaxing from an array of gourds, tambourines, bells, and bongos subtle counterrhythms that augment and color Williams's percussive barrages; Clarke and Corea add throbbing, serpentine figures to the musical stew.

Corea also contributes a couple of stunning solos, but Stan outguns him as he digs passionately into the material. On "La Fiesta" he catches fire as he takes the listener through four celebratory choruses, and he almost reaches this peak again with his improvisations on two other numbers—"Captain Marvel" and "Day Waves." The two Corea albums—*Sweet Rain* and *Captain Marvel*—and *Dynasty*, which came between them, capture a middle-aged man rising to meet the aesthetic challenges posed by younger colleagues; he does so with the energy of a youth and the skill of a mature artist.

At the time of *Captain Marvel*, Stan was negotiating to leave Verve after twenty years to sign a more lucrative deal with Columbia Records. As a consequence, the release of the album was delayed for three years, and its distribution was split; Columbia took the U.S. market and Verve the rest of the world.

By June 1972 Stan was free to record with whomever he liked, and on the second of that month he made a one-shot recording with Norman Granz, who had launched a new label, Pablo. It seemed like old times as Granz put him in a familiar JATP setting, and the resulting album, *Jazz at the Santa Monica Civic*, captures Stan jamming happily with Roy Eldridge, Ella Fitzgerald, Count Basie, trumpeter Harry "Sweets" Edison, trombonist Al Grey, and saxophonist Eddie "Lockjaw" Davis; they are backed by the sterling rhythm section of Ray Brown on bass, Freddie Green on guitar, and Ed Thigpen on drums. Stan is outstanding on a brooding "Blue and Sentimental" and on a wailing version of "C Jam Blues" with Ella and the Count.

Stan had not kept a close rein on his new quintet, and in late June Corea, Clarke, and Moreira told him that they wanted to start a band of their own. They added Flora Purim for vocals and Joe Farrell on saxophone and created "Return to Forever," one of the most successful jazz groups of the 1970s. Williams wanted to restart his career as a leader, and he left also.

Stan convinced Clarke and Moreira to remain with him for a July 1 concert at the Newport/New York Jazz Festival, and he recruited Hank Jones and Gary Burton to round out a quintet for the date. Two days later at the festival, Stan appeared with Zoot Sims, Al Cohn, Flip Philips, Red Norvo, and Chubby Jackson as guests of Woody Herman's orchestra. Stan, Al, and Zoot joined Woody's baritone player for a romp through "Four Brothers," Stan had "Early Autumn" to himself, and all the alumni joined in a fast, happy blues for a finale. Brothers Al and Zoot wore ties and rumpled business suits while Stan was resplendent in a white outfit with the insignia of the comic book hero "Captain Marvel" stitched across his chest.

During the balance of 1972, Stan toured extensively with a quartet consisting of Dave Holland, a brilliant Miles Davis alumnus on bass, Jeff Williams on drums, and Richie Beirach on piano.

In December Sonny Rollins ended Stan's five-year run at the top of the *Down Beat* poll. Stan's 1971 victory had been his seventeenth in twenty-two years and his last. During the following two decades, Stan finished second ten times and third seven times as Rollins won twelve times, Dexter Gordon five, and Randy Brecker three. Rollins was born two and a half years after Stan, and his art matured later; he is one of a very few jazzmen of Stan's generation whose life work has achieved the heights that Stan's did.

Big Bev died on December 10 of a cerebral hemorrhage at her home in Tehachapi, California; she was forty-five. Her husband of six years, David Bednar, a chiropractor, buried her in the cemetery of a Roman Catholic mission in San Bernardino under the inscription "Beverly Byrne Bednar, Forever in Our Hearts." After several difficult years that included jail time for theft, Big Bev had conquered her addictions by the early 1960s; she met Bednar while she was singing in a Santa Monica nightclub in 1965. When they moved to Tehachapi, a mountain town a hundred miles north of Los Angeles, she stopped performing professionally and managed her husband's office. Bednar remembered:

> Everybody liked her. All the patients liked her. My kids from a previous marriage liked her. She was a perky little thing who moved around very fast, always singing. She was very giving, but easily intimidated and vulnerable.
>
> She never stopped loving Stan and never talked bad about him. He did not treat her right, but he never hit her like I heard he did with the second wife.
>
> Losing those kids was the most devastating thing in her life. After she got over the drug problems, she didn't have the emotional and financial resources to fight for the children.

Big Bev had on her mantelpiece a framed picture of Stan, Monica, and the Getz children that had been cut from the front of an album cover; the Getzes did not learn of her death until Dr. Bednar wrote them more than a year later.

Stan returned to the Rainbow Grill for three weeks in January 1973 with Holland, Jeff Williams, Beirach, and the singer Yvonne Elliman, who was fresh from a Broadway triumph as Mary Magdalene in the hit musical *Jesus Christ Superstar*. Elliman, who was introduced to Stan by his daughter Beverly, had a dark, throaty voice that she projected with authority. Stan's backgrounds helped greatly to give shape to her performances, each of which ended emphatically with "I Don't Know How to Love Him," her hit from *Jesus Christ Superstar*. The engagement was a commercial success despite the fact that many audience members were thrown off by the contrast between Elliman's pop style and the uncompromising, sophisticated jazz played by the quartet.

During the last week of the Rainbow Grill engagement, Jack DeJohnette replaced Jeff Williams as Stan's drummer, and the quartet's personnel remained stable for eight months, until September 1973. DeJohnette, like Holland a Miles Davis alumnus, is an inventive percussionist who is also a fluent composer. Quickly, most of the group's repertoire consisted of tunes by DeJohnette, Holland, and Beirach, a Juilliard-trained musician with a quirky, densely harmonic style. Beirach was replaced in September by Albert Dailey, a more mainstream pianist with prodigious technique, a romantic sensibility, and roots in bebop.

Stan changed pianists frequently throughout his career. In the quartet format he preferred, the drummer and the bassist were there primarily to provide a rhythmic foundation; they soloed infrequently. The pianist played a more important role, supplying essential harmonies and colorations and soloing almost as much as Stan. He wanted his pianists to challenge and refresh him, and he kept replacing them because he sought from them a renewing inspiration. They knew the ground rules when they joined Stan and as a consequence felt little bitterness when they were replaced. Several—including Dailey, Corea, and Lou Levy—were employed by him more than once.

The year 1973 ended on a sour note for Stan when he suffered a herniated disc in his lower back while on Christmas vacation in the Bahamas. He could barely move, and he was forced to sleep on the floor. Monica took him in a wheelchair to a jet that flew them directly to Ohio, where he underwent an operation at the Cleveland Clinic. Aside from a few scary moments when Stan turned blue because the anesthetist pumped the wrong chemicals into his body, the operation was a success.

Following the surgery, Stan had to be carefully weaned from the morphine that had been administered to him for pain.

In June of 1974, after two years of negotiations, Stan signed with Columbia Records. He was pleased with his new affiliation because it was more lucrative than his deal with Verve had been, gave him considerably greater control over the packaging of his LPs, and called for fewer recording sessions. He liked the reduced work load because—except for *Getz/ Gilberto* and the other popular bossa nova albums—Stan had never earned big money from recordings; the great bulk of his income came from public performances.

He was eager to move forward with Columbia but was not prepared for the company's bureaucratic inertia or its penchant for recording him in gimmicky settings at tangents from the no-frills jazz which was his forte. Monica remembered:

> It was like molasses to deal with Columbia. The only person that was really nice was Bruce Lundvall. They had very little understanding of what Stan was all about. It took an enormous amount of time (to get anything done), but by then we were very invested in the relationship.

Stan's deal with Columbia allowed him to record albums for other labels, and he made several good freelance recordings while performing on tour. Monica frequently joined him on the road, and she gave him his Antabuse when she was with him. At Shadowbrook, she usually left the task to servants who were pledged to secrecy.

Following his return to the United States in 1972, Stan had become sick with some regularity when he drank while Antabuse was in his system. His average reaction was usually nasty and short; his face and chest would redden, his pulse rate would shoot upward, he would vomit, and he would feel clammy and weak. Following an hour's rest and several glasses of cold water, he would begin to feel better and, after another hour, he would be up and about. But sometimes something would go wrong; he would eat or sleep too little or drink too much, and the Antabuse-derived toxins would, as they did at the workingman's bar in Spain, almost tear his body apart.

His first reaction of this severity in the States occurred on July 3, 1974; scheduled that night to accompany Johnny Mathis and Mabel Mercer at a Newport/New York Jazz Festival concert celebrating the American song, he became nauseated after drinking and called in sick. Then he returned to Shadowbrook and fell violently ill.

He was retching and shaking, but he couldn't throw up. He was ministered to by Monica and by a Finnish servant who got him to induce vomiting by convincing him to stick his fingers down his throat. His symptoms then eased.

He slept through the night and had recovered sufficiently the next evening to enliven a dull festival concert, as John S. Wilson of *The New York Times* reported:

> An attack of food poisoning prevented his appearance (behind Johnny Mathis and Mabel Mercer) and left a big hole in the jazz and song program. However, by Thursday evening he had recovered and was on stage at Avery Fisher Hall with his quartet to join in a program that also included the Gerry Mulligan quintet and the Bill Evans trio. It was a good thing that he had recovered, because ... Mr. Getz's group was the only one that brought any life to the proceedings. ...
>
> The monotony of a steady diet of blandness was setting in when Mr. Getz came on and, with a few biting notes on his tenor saxophone, dug into a medium blues that, at the very least, shook off some of the accumulated lethargy. Mr. Getz has a good sense of theater—of dramatic structure and development in his programming as well as in his performances—and he used this sense to pick up what was left of the evening.
>
> He was helped immeasurably in this by his pianist, Albert Dailey, who followed an invitingly soft and furry solo by Mr. Getz on "Lover Man" with an unaccompanied solo built on a series of runs that were as effectively electrifying as Mr. Evans's had been quiescent.

Stan had two more severe Antabuse reactions during 1974—one in San Francisco, which he later suspected resulted from eating a box of pastries baked by Monica and brought to him by the singer Jon Hendricks, and one in Rome.

Beverly had, in June 1974, launched herself into a show business career with Hendricks's daughter Michelle and Buddy Rich's daughter Cathy in a singing group called "Hendricks Getz Rich," which toured with Buddy's big band. The three young women sang intermittently with the band for four years. Beverly remembered:

> I love music and I was drawn to it, but it was too much pressure being his daughter. It was fun; it was nothing serious. I mean,

we were pretty bad. But we toured all over Europe, sang with Dad at Carnegie Hall, and were on Johnny Carson.

Finally, our group fell apart, and I ended up being assistant road manager for the Buddy Rich band.

Steve Getz was also performing professionally as the drummer/leader of a jazz-rock group which gigged mainly in Colorado. He was married in 1969 to a high school sweetheart and in 1970 fathered a son, Christopher. By the summer of 1974, his marriage was breaking up, and he was heading for a divorce. That spring he had picked up his final credits at the University of Colorado to graduate with a degree in political science.

Steve's younger brother David was becalmed in 1974 after attending three colleges in four years and failing to graduate. He had always found Sweden congenial and moved there in May 1974 for a stay of five years, working in factories and as a hospital orderly.

The youngest Getz son, Nicky, returned permanently to the United States in June of 1974 after three years at the British boarding school where he could not indulge his love of tennis. Nicky was enrolled as a day student at the Hackley School near Shadowbrook, applied himself intensely to tennis, and quickly became a star on the school's team. Soon after, his parents built a court on the grounds at Shadowbrook where Nicky honed his game and the other family members enjoyed themselves.

Nicky's sister Pamela had returned from her British boarding school during the summer of 1972 and was sent as a day student to the Masters School, a few miles from Shadowbrook.

In Antwerp, Belgium, on August 16, 1974, Stan and the Bill Evans Trio played a concert that has a murky recording history; an album was released eighteen years later on an obscure label, Jazz Door, as *But Beautiful*. Both Stan and Bill perform much better than they did on their previous outing in May 1964, when they were so dissatisfied with their work that they tried to prohibit the release of the resulting album.

Evans was put off in 1964 by the accompaniment of musicians he was not familiar with—Richard Davis and Ron Carter on bass and Elvin Jones on drums—but in 1974 he had his own bassist, Eddie Gomez, and his own drummer, Marty Morell, and plays like someone totally at ease. Stan blended intuitively with Gomez and Morrell and found a deep affinity for Evans's classic lyricism. No one in the history of jazz could match Evans and Getz for expressing melancholy, and they didn't disappoint, spinning out lines of beautiful and chilling sadness on "The Peacocks," "Emily," and "Lover Man." Their up-tempo frolic on "Funkallero" showed that they could swing happily together as well.

In October 1974 DeJohnette and Holland left Stan to lead their own groups, and he replaced them with Billy Hart on drums and George Mraz on bass. Hart, a subtle, sensitive percussionist, had performed with Sarah Vaughan, Herbie Hancock, Stanley Turrentine, and Wes Montgomery and found an instant rapport with Stan; he remained with him for four years. Mraz was born in Czechoslovakia in 1944 and in the late 1960s came to the United States, where he worked with Dizzy Gillespie, Oscar Peterson, Ella Fitzgerald, and the Thad Jones–Mel Lewis Big Band. He had a subtle harmonic sense, and his solos were richly melodic. He remained with Stan through 1975 and rejoined him several times after that.

On May 21, 1975, Stan recorded his first album for Columbia almost a year after he had signed with the company. It was his first studio session in thirty-three months, the longest such hiatus of his career. The album was called *The Best of Two Worlds,* and it reunited Stan with João Gilberto. The arrangements are by Oscar Neves, who also plays guitar, and among the backup musicians are Airto Moreira, Albert Dailey, Billy Hart, and Steve Swallow.

After the heat and excitement of *Captain Marvel,* his previous studio recording, the new album is a letdown. Stan has little to do since most of the tracks are dominated by Gilberto and his countrywoman Heloisa Buarque de Hollanda, whose lusty voice contrasts sharply with Gilberto's quieter vocal instrument. Stan solos extensively on only one track, "Ligia," and contents himself most of the time with obbligatos and fills supporting the singers.

He has even less to do on his subsequent Columbia studio date in July 1975, when, with his distinguished colleagues Lee Konitz and Al Cohn, he joined Bobby Scott's orchestra to back a now-forgotten Japanese singer, Kimiko Kassei, in an album called *This Is My Love.*

His next visits to the studio, in October, were far more productive. They resulted in an album called *The Peacocks* featuring Stan's old colleague from Herman's Second Herd, Jimmy Rowles, in a number of settings; and a robust session called *The Master* with his working rhythm section—Albert Dailey on piano, Billy Hart on drums, and Clint Houston on bass.

One night in early July, after they had performed at the Newport/New York Jazz Festival, Stan and Zoot Sims dropped into Bradley's, a jazz saloon in Greenwich Village, and jammed into the wee hours with the resident duo there, Rowles and George Mraz. Rowles remembered:

> Stan and Zoot got into it down there and they just played up a
> storm. In fact Whitney Balliett even wrote in *The New Yorker* that

the best part of the whole festival was that night in Bradley's with
Zoot and Stan. They were really whooping it up.

Stan was so carried away that he told Rowles on the spot that he wanted
to do an album with him. They planned the session soon afterward during
an afternoon at Shadowbrook, deciding on a varied format.

The Peacocks spotlights Rowles as a songwriter; a singer; a piano soloist;
in duets with Stan; in a quartet with Stan, drummer Elvin Jones, and
bassist Buster Williams; and in the same quartet backed by four singers.
Rowles sparkles in all of these roles (no pun intended) as he and Stan
create a moving and totally delightful musical experience.

Some pianists—Corea, Beirach, Dailey—challenged Stan. Rowles
melded with him; they became a single spirit with two entwined voices.
Rowles spent a good part of his career as the chosen accompanist of the
greatest of jazz and pop vocalists—Billie Holiday, Ella Fitzgerald, Sarah
Vaughan, Carmen McRae, and Peggy Lee—and he enriches Stan's melodic lines as he would those of a singer; Stan returns the compliment
as he plays obbligatos behind Rowles's expressive, husky vocals. The two
men are by turns rueful, humorous, wistful, and sad. Their duets on
"Skylark," Rowles's "The Peacocks," and "The Hour of Parting" are exer-
cises in pure romantic feeling, and when they are joined by Jones and
Williams, they are propelled into an easy, joyous swing.

Jon Hendricks dropped into Shadowbrook one afternoon following the
Rowles session, and Stan played the tape for him. Hendricks was immediately inspired to compose lyrics for one of the quartet tunes, the up-tempo
"The Chess Players," and to write words to the notes of Stan's solo. Stan
was delighted and a few days later brought Hendricks, his wife, Judy, his
daughter Michelle, and Beverly Getz into the studio to overdub the vocals.
The quartet sang the tune, and Hendricks alone accompanied Stan's solo,
displaying great dexterity as he captured all the nuances of the sinuous
saxophone improvisation.

The Master, Stan's second October 1975 studio date, finds him both
relaxed and powerful, demonstrating what Richard Palmer calls a "breathtaking synthesis of tenderness, virility, melodic invention, penetrating instinct for structure, and rhythmic virtuosity." Dailey's inspiration almost
matches Stan's throughout, and the pianist reaches a high point on "Lover
Man," when he makes a richly ruminative miniconcerto from his unaccompanied solo at the end the piece.

Columbia did not wish to saturate what they believed was a fragile
market for Stan's straight-ahead jazz albums, and they delayed the release
of *The Master* for eight years, until 1983. They were following in the

footsteps of Verve, which in 1964 shelved Stan's mainstream jazz LP, *Nobody Else but Me*, in favor of more commercial bossa nova releases; as we have seen, *Nobody Else but Me* did not make it into the stores until thirty years later, in 1994.

Albert Dailey had already told Stan that he wanted to move on when they were making *The Master* album, and Stan knew whom he wanted as a replacement—Joanne Brackeen, a very powerful player who had spent three years with master saxophonist Joe Henderson. As she remembered, she was still with Henderson when Stan began calling:

> We were at Ratso's in Chicago when it started, and I told Stan then that I had an obligation to Joe. Ironically, the tour that Stan wanted me for was to start at the same club. Even more ironic is the fact that the prospective jobs Joe had lined up fell through, so I ended up with Stan.

Brackeen joined him at the Village Gate in New York on October 31, 1975. She felt very comfortable with Billy Hart and Clint Houston and in fact used both of them on a recording in 1977. Her professional relationship with Stan was marked by a healthy creative tension, as she told a reporter about the quartet:

> Now that I am playing with them, I know what it means to listen to everything at once. I don't hear Clint, or Stan, or the chords; it's all one. . . .
>
> Everything that I have done on records and all that I do with Stan has structure. It all has a certain amount of measures, and with Stan you have to stick with the harmonic structure as well. I prefer less and less structure. My next album will be freer. . . . I take the music as far out as I can but still try to make him sound good. His feeling and intonation are incredible.

Stan found inspiration in Brackeen's playing and was happy to let her roam freely. He told a reporter:

> I have always given my sidemen room to maneuver. I believe that if the talent is there, it should be heard. I want my sidemen to find themselves because when they do, it helps the group as well. I can never forget that I was a sideman once myself. . . . She (Joanne) is developing a following wherever we go. The fans really dig her and so do I.

Stan made no recordings for Columbia during 1976 and only went into a studio once; he played strongly at a session in May for the Inner City label in a small group backing the pleasant but undistinguished vocals of actress Cybill Shepherd. The album was called *Mad About the Boy*.

The quartet toured Europe during the summer, and before they left, Monica asked Joanne Brackeen to dispense Antabuse secretly to Stan during the trip. She adamantly refused, believing that she would be violating Stan's rights if she did so.

In the midst of a two-week engagement at Ronnie Scott's in July, Stan obtained, in accordance with British law, a legal prescription for heroin. He promptly overdosed and was in no condition to complete the second week of the gig. Scott wanted to hire a new group, but Stan convinced him to allow Brackeen to complete the engagement with Houston and Hart. Brackeen made the most of her opportunity, advancing her career considerably as she impressed critics and fans alike with her exciting playing.

A few weeks after returning from Europe, the quartet took off in September for a hectic tour of South America involving eighteen concerts in twenty-three days. Steve accompanied Stan on the trip and performed professionally with his father for the first time; he had spent most of the previous six years in California and Colorado away from his parents and was overjoyed at the opportunity to play with Stan and to spend more than three uninterrupted weeks with him. He was disquieted, however, when Monica talked him into giving Antabuse to Stan secretly. He remembered:

> At the time I had no knowledge of Antabuse. I was told, however, by Monica that since I was going on the tour, it was very important that I give this to him. I administered the Antabuse to him two—at the most—three times. And after searching my conscience, I decided to discontinue giving it, feeling it was not right. . . .
>
> He'd get sick. It (the Antabuse) worked. He used to turn beet red and break out in hives and his heart would pound very quickly.

The tour provided Steve with an intense musical learning experience as he alternated with Billy Hart between the drums and a set of congas. "I learned more music in three weeks sitting next to Billy Hart than I could in three years elsewhere," he later reflected.

Stan was pleased to have Steve at his side, but he did not want his oldest son to follow the itinerant life of a musician. These feelings are reflected in a letter Stan sent to Monica on September 19, 1976, from São Paulo, Brazil:

> My Dearest Lady:
> Nothing much to tell you. I am writing because I want to be close to you. . . .
> Steve has been sick twice. He's finding this life very difficult. I wish with all my heart that he realizes that this crazy gypsy life is not really living, and that a successful life is peace and regularity and that kind of life is an art in itself.
> I hear by the grapevine that you are buying me a present. Being a kept man, I feel that this is only proper in order that you won't lose me to a richer lover. . . .
> I love you. Will you be my Valentine?
>
> > > Stan

The quartet plunged into a full autumn schedule of U.S. dates following their return from South America; it was broken only on the night of November 20, when Stan performed with Woody Herman's band and several distinguished alumni in a Carnegie Hall concert celebrating Woody's fortieth anniversary as a leader.

Beverly Getz was working with the Buddy Rich band at the time, and she remembered that Buddy decided he could not miss the concert:

> He canceled a job paying several grand so that we could go. He and his wife and daughter and I got on a bus and came home so we could be there. That was really sweet. Buddy had a big heart that way.

The concert was a joyous and emotional event that was fortunately recorded by RCA. Stan was joined by Jimmy Giuffre, Al Cohn, and Zoot Sims on "Four Brothers," Ralph Burns on "Early Autumn," Jimmy Rowles on "Cousins," and Don Lamond and the 1976 Herman aggregation on "Blue Serge" and "Blue Getz Blue (Stan's Blues)." Stan sounded inspired throughout, but he reached a personal peak on "Stan's Blues." After two hot unaccompanied choruses, he showed that he still possessed an absolute command of the big band idiom as he drove the group in the ensemble passages and soared dexterously through its textures as he soloed.

Stan reverted to his old bad habits during the 1976 Christmas holidays, when he got drunk at a dinner at Shadowbrook attended by Monica,

Pamela, Beverly, Michelle Hendricks, and Oscar Neves, the Brazilian guitarist who had arranged Stan's 1975 album, *The Best of Two Worlds*. Pamela, who was a senior in high school at the time, later remembered that the incident started when Beverly's dog, Whippet, was making an unpleasant noise while chewing a television antenna in the hallway:

> My father got up, went out in the hallway, and he was kicking the dog and the dog was whimpering. . . . I went upstairs and I just sat down on my bed and I just was crying. It seemed like a minute later I heard footsteps down the hallway, just loud footsteps, and I knew he was coming after me.
>
> He came in the room and he started saying, "You bitch, don't you tell me what to do," and he started slapping me and hitting me. And I got on the bed and I put my feet up to protect myself because he was just hitting me . . .
>
> Then Oscar came in and just pulled him off me, and my mother came in and said, "Don't be mad at him; he's just like this when he's drinking. He doesn't know what he's doing." And I just said, "I'm never going to forgive him for this."

In late January 1977 Stan, accompanied by Monica and Brackeen, Hart, and Mike Richmond, a new bass player, traveled to Copenhagen for a series of performances at the Montmartre, some of which were to be recorded by Steeple Chase Records; the club was a new and much larger incarnation of the original Montmartre, which had been founded by Anders Dyrup and later sold by him. On January 27, 28, and 29 the outstanding Danish bassist Niels-Henning Ørsted Pedersen sat in for Richmond during the recording of the live quartet sessions. For the January 29 date Stan and Pedersen were also recorded with the Danish Radio Big Band.

The quartet sessions were released in the United States by Inner City records as a double LP set, *Stan Getz Gold*, and they received uniformly laudatory notices. The reviewer for *Cadence Magazine* called Stan "magnificent," Brackeen "remarkable," Ørsted Pedersen "amazing," and Hart "unforgettable," and decried the fact that Stan's recorded output in the 1970s was so small. *Stereo Review*'s writer said "the rhythm section, headed by Joanne Brackeen — a remarkable pianist with impressive past associations — cooks up a storm over which Getz rides with characteristic ease and agility; he is obviously very comfortable with this group, and he doesn't hold back," and *Down Beat* was unstinting in its praise:

Stan Getz Gold is a perfect distillation of the Getz approach . . .
a special joy, a celebration of the rite of improvised music. . . . a
landmark in the career of one of today's most brilliant masters.
Listen!

Dyrup now owned the Monastery, Copenhagen's most elegant restaurant,
and he was eager to celebrate Stan's fiftieth birthday on February 2, 1977.
He remembered:

> There was no plan for what was going to happen on his birthday,
> so I arranged that we all meet at my restaurant. We were a little
> party of, I think, twenty or twenty-five people, which I hosted.
>
> We didn't know how to celebrate Stan, how to make it festive
> for him. Then my wife, this is my second wife, got the idea to
> call around to all the saxophone players in Denmark and ask
> them to come to the Montmartre after the dinner at the
> Monastery.
>
> Every jazz saxophone player available in Copenhagen and sur-
> rounding cities, plus a lot of other musicians were there. Stan
> was scheduled to do his regular gig at the Montmartre, and when
> he went to the stage to play, all the lights went out and everybody
> lit their lighters, and up got about twenty saxophonists, and they
> played "Happy Birthday."

Stan and the quartet hardly had a chance to catch their breaths following
their Copenhagen engagement before they were hurried onto a bandstand
in Montreal. The reviewer for the newspaper Le Devoir reported that their
rushed arrival did not daunt them:

> Mr. Tenor Sax and the members of his quartet just stepped off
> the plane from Copenhagen and had time for a change, a shower,
> and maybe dinner before their first set. . . .
>
> Getz . . . is in better shape than ever. His technique has ma-
> tured to a smoothness which allows his every thought to flow with
> the superb colorings he has long been developing.
>
> His current pianist is Joanne Brackeen, and she floored me
> completely. She plays the entire keyboard with a very percussive
> approach, and weaves in the most intricate filigree of runs, full
> of novel ideas, with total assurance. . . . Mike Richmond on bass
> is also full of interesting ideas, and Billy Hart, one of the best
> contemporary drummers, is full of fire and humor.

Soon after, Stan waxed eloquent about Richmond to a *New York Times* reporter:

> Mr. Getz could not restrain his excitement at the presence of Mr. Richmond ... "I like musicians that float. Lately I don't like a bassist to play chuck, chuck—four, four. The bass is the instrument that has advanced the most in jazz. No one in particular is responsible for the advance. Nobody starts anything. From Jimmy Blanton to Oscar Pettiford to Charles Mingus, it's a natural evolution. That's what makes jazz the greatest thing in the world for me."

During April the quartet was in constant motion, visiting Europe again and embarking on a groundbreaking tour of Cuba. Soon after taking office in January 1977, President Jimmy Carter lifted a long-standing ban on American travel to Cuba, and a promoter quickly signed up Stan's group and those of Dizzy Gillespie and Earl Hines to play both on a cruise ship and in Castro's domain. The cruise was sold out, and the musicians played before large, enthusiastic crowds in Cuba. They jammed with outstanding local musicians, including Paquito D'Rivera and Arturo Sandoval, both of whom later defected to the United States. Stan managed to swim every day and acquired a healthy tan.

Brackeen left the quartet suddenly in July 1977—with three days remaining in an engagement at Blues Alley in Washington, D.C.—because she had to care for her father, who was extremely ill. While ministering to him, she decided to strike out on her own as a leader and never returned to Stan. At Mike Richmond's suggestion, he replaced her with Andy LaVerne, a twenty-nine-year-old whose credentials included two and a half years with Woody Herman.

On leaving Washington, the quartet embarked on a three and a half month tour that took them to Europe and Israel and to Europe again. Their principal stop on the first European leg of the trip was a jazz festival in Montreux, Switzerland, where Stan was recorded with an all-star big band that included Maynard Ferguson and Dexter Gordon; he performed on several free-blowing tracks which are included on a double Columbia album, *Montreux Summit, Volumes 1 and 2*.

The Israel sojourn is documented in a film, *Stan Getz in Israel: A Musical Odyssey*. Stan and Monica, both looking tanned and trim, are shown in a number of settings—eating a sabbath dinner, shopping in crowded Jerusalem markets, worshiping at a synagogue, attending a benefit for crippled children.

Most of the footage, however, is devoted to Stan performing with his own quartet and with native musicians—a Kurdistani pipe and drum group, an Arab quartet featuring a violinist, a Yemeni choral ensemble, a Klezmer band from the European diaspora, and a jazz-rock group that tried to incorporate several of the country's ethnic traditions into its music. He played with the last band, built around four members of the Piamenta family, in a major Jerusalem concert.

With lightning quickness Stan absorbed the rhythms and harmonies of the ethnic styles and performed with gusto with the local musicians. At one point he picked up a clarinet, an instrument he hadn't touched for twenty-five years, and coaxed a lovely, burnished sound from it as he played a lively duet with a Klezmer clarinetist.

One of the Piamentas, Yossi, became a guest of the Getzes at Shadowbrook for several months the following year; he eventually settled in Brooklyn and received considerable publicity in 1994 as the leader of "Hasidic New Wave," a band pioneering what he called "hasid rock."

In Israel Stan met Siga Weissfisch, a master masseur with whom he formed a deep friendship. Siga, a powerfully built, blunt-spoken Israeli who owned homes in both Tel Aviv and a New York City suburb, added Stan to a list of celebrity clients that included Leonard Bernstein and Zubin Mehta. He eased the strain on Stan's neck and shoulder muscles, which supported the ten-pound weight of his saxophone, kept his lower back supple, and became a confidant and father figure to him.

The visit to Israel brought Stan into contact with his Jewish roots and touched deep emotions in his secular psyche. He later told a reporter:

> I was in Jerusalem a few months ago and a friend suggested I visit the ancient wailing wall. I happen to be Jewish, and I am proud of that fact, but my first thought was, "Oh, that's just some sentimental monument." I went and stood there before the wall and, you know what, I cried—not carrying on hysterically—but the real tears came down.

Stan and his cohorts traveled from Israel to Europe in late August and became a quintet when they were joined by Efrian Toro, a young Puerto Rican percussionist who was a friend of Billy Hart. Toro was hired because he had impressed Stan greatly when he sat in with the band during a Boston engagement a few months earlier.

On September 15, 1977, the quintet entered a high-tech electronic studio in Montreux, Switzerland, for a Columbia recording session. Stan was in a mood to experiment, and he had in LaVerne a musician who knew a great deal about electronic instrumentation. Stan remembered the circumstances in Montreux:

> Andy came into the band playing both electric and acoustic pianos, just as Joanne had done. She had played acoustic to begin with, but in the last few months she was there, I decided to go with the electric instrument, because I liked the percussive effect it had on certain things. We stayed with those two instruments until we made this new record, when we had all those other instruments at our disposal in the studio. We started experimenting with overdubbing; that's how it came about. Then the experiment with the Echoplex occurred. I'd never touched one before; it happened to be right there in the studio.

The Echoplex, beloved of rock groups, allows the musician to make his phrases repeat themselves while he builds other phrases on top of them. Stan used the device to play layers of counterpoint with himself, and he turned LaVerne loose on an Arp string synthesizer, a Rhodes electric piano, and a Moog synthesizer, which could approximate the sounds of any instrument as well as those of many natural creatures.

The quintet created a double LP, *Another World,* in Montreux in two days, and roughly half the playing time is devoted to pieces with electronic instrumentation. Most of the electronic effects are done tastefully, but the Arp strings muddy the arrangements and have little sonority, and the synthesized bird calls sound gimmicky. Stan essays an unaccompanied Echoplex tour de force on the title tune, mixing blasts, echoes, stabs, and honks into a fevered climax.

The most effective of the high-tech efforts are "Pretty City," a sizzling Latin piece with an infectious melody, and "Club 7," where the electronic devices power surging riffs. The straight acoustical tracks are all excellent, and Stan is at his expressive best on "Willow Weep for Me," a modified blues called "Sabra," and "Blue Serge."

The quintet did not return from Europe until late October 1977, and they found themselves back at Washington's Blues Alley in early November.

Beverly had traveled to Washington to hear her father and was standing in the back of the club listening to the music when a strange man approached her.

"Are you the daughter of Beverly Byrne and Stan?" he asked.

"Yes."

"I guessed it. You look just like your mother," he said, "I'm your uncle. My name is Bob Mare, and I'm married to your mother's sister, Bobbie. She's sitting at that table over there."

"I can't believe this. This is incredible."

Bob led Beverly to his wife and said, "She's Bev's daughter." The two women embraced, stepped back, and smiled with joy.

Beverly sat down, and Bobbie explained that she and her husband had been in northern Virginia on business when they decided to come and hear Stan after seeing a Blues Alley advertisement in a Washington newspaper.

"Why didn't you kids ever answer the letters your mother mailed you?" Bobbie asked. "And what about the money she sent you? If she could scrape up a little money around Christmas, she would always send it to you."

"We never received any money. And we only got one letter—back in seventy-one."

When Beverly later asked Stan and Monica about this, they maintained that the single letter that Beverly had found in Paris in 1971 was the only communication from Big Bev that had gotten through to them.

Monica came into the club, and when Stan finished his set, the two of them joined Bev, Bobbie, and Bob at their table. They told the Mares how glad they were to see them, and Stan looked Bobbie in the eyes and said, "You know, with all the troubles your sister and I had, I always loved her." Monica's countenance did not change.

The Mares then invited Beverly to visit them across the river in Virginia, and Monica insisted that she come, too. Monica and Beverly drove over the next day, and the four people had a pleasant conversation over coffee and cakes.

Stan went into San Francisco's Keystone Korner in February 1978 with a load of electronic gear and an extra member of the band—his old friend Bob Brookmeyer, who had signed on for a four-month stint. The two men had not performed together since 1964 because Brookmeyer, during the intervening years, had battled alcoholism and pursued a career as a writer-arranger. Brookmeyer played with his usual wit and grace at the Keystone Korner but was at times thrown off stride by the noisy electronics. Stan was somewhat defensive about the equipment when talking to a reporter, explaining that it was still "an experiment and not a fully realized form of expression. I'm going to stick with it for a while, using it in spots. And I try to be subtle with it."

A *New York Post* reviewer the following month found nothing subtle about the electronics:

For the reunion of Getz and Brookmeyer, these master melodists, it was simply wrong. Too much, too loud—endless clatter and clutter, all obscuring rather than enhancing their gentle ways. More satisfying by far is a just-issued LP made in Copenhagen . . . *Stan Getz Gold*—all clarity and subtlety.

During 1977 Pamela's boyfriend Scot Raynor came to live with her at Shadowbrook while he attended a college nearby. They were rummaging around the attic one day in early 1978 when Scot discovered a loaded pistol, a box of bullets, and what they believed was a bag with marijuana and hashish in it.

When Pamela asked Stan about the gun, he replied that it had been lent to him by a California woman after he had been mugged in San Diego the previous year, and he added that he intended to return it to her quickly. A few months later, however, Pamela found out that he still possessed the weapon when, following a noisy ruckus between Stan and Monica, Monica came running into her room. Pamela remembered:

> She was white in the face and she was saying, "He's got a gun. He put a gun to my head."
> I said, "Let's leave now. Please come with me. You can't stay here. I can't leave you here with him."
> And she said, "Just leave us. Go. I'll call Dr. Foster to give him a sedative, and everything will be fine. Just go spend the night in a motel."

Pam and Scot spent the night in their car because they couldn't find a motel room, and when they returned, Pam insisted to her father that they get rid of the pistol. After a short argument, he gave her the weapon, and she took it down to the Hudson River and threw it into the water.

Jazz came in force to the White House on the sweltering Sunday afternoon of June 17, 1978, when President Jimmy Carter invited scores of his favorite musicians to celebrate the twenty-fifth anniversary of the Newport/New York Jazz Festival with a New Orleans food fest and a concert on the White House lawn. Carter loved music—and jazz in particular—and each evening he would order up six hours of recordings to be played the following day while he worked in a small study adjacent to the Oval Office. He took obvious pleasure in hosting the concert and listened to the music in total absorption.

Spectators ate steaming portions of jambalaya while they sat at small tables or spread out on the grass to hear the largest array of jazz masters ever assembled in one place. Stan, impeccably clad in a beige safari suit, was joined by Chick Corea, Zoot Sims, George Benson, Ray Brown, Louis Bellson, and Lionel Hampton for a spirited set. Among the others who performed that day were Dizzy Gillespie, Sonny Rollins, Ornette Coleman, Max Roach, Jo Jones, Eubie Blake, Dexter Gordon, Cecil Taylor, Gerry Mulligan, Herbie Hancock, Mary Lou Williams, Teddy Wilson, Benny Carter, Roy Eldridge, and Tony Williams. Highlights of the long afternoon included an impromptu rendition of "Salt Peanuts" by the President, Gillespie, and Roach and a tearful embrace by Carter and Charles Mingus, who was confined to a wheelchair by Lou Gehrig's disease, which killed him less than seven months later.

At the festival itself in New York later in June, Stan and Albert Dailey triumphed over a faulty sound system that had been plaguing several other artists; they simply had it turned off and performed unamplified. As a *New York Post* writer reported:

> They just let the music play itself, tender and noble. "The Winter of My Discontent" rose from a wistful little exposition to a great cry of anguish, resounding in the hall's upper reaches. Dailey, introduced by Getz as "one of the world's greatest piano players," bid fair to prove it with a pellucid reading of Wilder's "Ellen." Then to close, "A Child Is Born," leaving the audience rapt, stunned by the naked human vulnerability of what they'd just heard.

Stan returned to the Keystone Korner in August, but without his electronic gear. The reviewer for the *San Francisco Examiner* found this a blessing:

> There are mikes, but Getz has discarded the contact and electronic enhancement gadgets and wires and controls which, I thought, fouled his Keystone performance last winter. . . . Getz more than ever is blowing full, round, fully packed. He can wail and moan, cry and groan on the ballads, yet drive his band often like a whip-snapping cattle herd commandant spitting out a noisy string of hard note commands.

Stan gave the crowd at the Keystone Korner a chilling scare one evening when his eyes rolled up in his head and he passed out in mid-solo and slumped to the floor. The club owner, Todd Barkan, quickly pulled Stan offstage and summoned a team of paramedics, who gave him an injection which immediately revived him.

When Stan came to, he told Barkan that he had become confused about the prescription dosage of some sleeping pills he was using and had swallowed too many; he added that the medication was called Dilaudid. It is unlikely that a doctor would prescribe this drug—a morphine derivative which is usually given to dull pain—as a sleeping aid. Stan returned to the bandstand the next evening in good shape and played vigorously.

One night in October 1978, an attractive twenty-five-year-old woman walked up to Stan after a set at Blues Alley in Washington and reminded him that they had met three years before when he was performing in Rochester, New York. Her name was Jane Walsh, and she invited Stan to a cast party the next evening following the opening of a new play that had been choreographed by her cousin; Stan accepted. Jane had traveled to Washington from her home in Auburn, New York, to attend the opening.

At the party Stan was taken by Jane's vivacity, intelligence, and dark good looks. She had been a professional singer and talked knowledgeably about music, and she struck a chord in Stan when she told him that she had emerged sober from rehab a year before following a six-year derailment by alcohol. Stan decided he wanted to see her again.

After Jane's return to Auburn, he called her a couple of times every week from the road, and on each occasion insisted that she join him somewhere. In December she acquiesced and flew to be with him at a Colorado mountain resort where he had an engagement.

After Jane's father died early in 1979, she elected to move to Miami, where her brother and his family lived. As she remembered, Stan stayed in touch:

> He'd be on the road somewhere and he would want to come and visit, and he'd take these little reprieves down in Miami. He'd get right off that plane, and we would dash right over to the beach, and we'd be in the ocean. He always wanted to live by the ocean and be on the ocean.

In March 1979 Stan completed his last album for Columbia, a collaboration with arranger-composer Lalo Schifrin called *Children of the World*. The Echoplex is used sparingly, but the synthesizers are out in force. At least two appear in every number, and they are augmented by electronic pianos, basses, and guitars. The first track is the Andrew Lloyd Webber song "Don't Cry for Me, Argentina," and the remaining ten are by Schifrin. Stan provides almost all the improvised content of the album as he solos expressively over the kinds of backgrounds which would become popular in the 1980s behind pop-jazz artists such as Grover Washington.

The LP is pleasant but insubstantial, primarily because Schifrin's writing is weak. His ten tunes are bland and do not provide Stan with the kind of challenge he found in such songs as Corea's "La Fiesta," Louiss's "Dynasty," or Rowles's "The Peacocks." In fact, Stan's strongest outing on the record is his interpretation of Andrew Lloyd Webber's composition.

In September of 1979, Stan was on stage with Dizzy Gillespie at the Monterey Jazz Festival when the trumpeter coaxed Diane Schuur, an unheralded twenty-five-year-old blind singer from Arizona, to the bandstand for an unscheduled performance. She sang Harold Arlen's "Down with Love" and Joni Mitchell's tribute to Charles Mingus, "Chair in the Sky," and both Stan and the audience were bowled over by what they heard. He remembered:

> I just happened to be in the right place at the right time that night. . . . I had never heard of Diane. . . . She came up there all alone, played and sang one tune on acoustic piano and one on electric. She made seven thousand people stand up roaring. Now that's not my criterion, because show business is show business. . . . But her musicality and her passion and pathos, her soul, got to me immediately. . . .
>
> It was so beautiful. Musicians are critical of singers. But this was the girl I thought I had been waiting all my life for. Everything she listens to goes into her. Whatever comes out is her own conception, her own enhancement of the tradition.

Stan grabbed Diane backstage and told her that he believed in her talent and that he wanted to do something for her. Wherever he went during the months ahead, he looked for playing opportunities for her and talked her up with club owners, festival impresarios, and record executives.

Stan and Albert Dailey were making a duet album in the studio in the Shadowbrook carriage house on January 12, 1980, as Monica and a guest, Myrtle Ann Franklin, were looking on. When the musicians finished, they took a break to drink some beer, and the women went back to the kitchen in the main house to make sandwiches. Monica sprinkled some Antabuse on Stan's sandwich and explained to her guest what she was doing.

Myrtle Ann was so upset by what Monica told her that she ran to the studio screaming, "Get me out of this crazy house. This woman is crazy. . . . She's trying to put Antabuse into your food. Just get me to the train station."

Stan didn't play any more that day. He went back to his room to think about Myrtle Ann's outburst as Dailey finished out the session with two solo tracks.

When Monica came to Stan later, he blurted, "Are you trying to kill me? You know that you've been told by a doctor in my presence that to give a subject Antabuse without him knowing it, he might drink and have a reaction and it's possible he can die." He continued, "And if he doesn't die, he's going to be very, very sick and uncomfortable. I'm beginning to realize this marriage is pretty bad, and I think you'd rather have me either sober or dead."

Monica told Stan that the Antabuse dosings were an attempt to save him, and she promised never to give him the drug again.

Stan had descended to an unprecedented state of emotional and physical collapse when Monica rescued him in Spain in 1969 and began the systematic secret dosages of Antabuse. She believed that his becoming sick from Antabuse perhaps two hundred times in the years that followed was a reasonable price for Stan to pay because she was convinced that without the drug, alcohol would have killed him. And she reflected that the entire family benefited as his drunkenness and violence subsided markedly during the 1970s. But the deception associated with Antabuse now extracted its substantial cost; it undermined the trust that had held her marriage together through twenty-three difficult and turbulent years.

BREAKING AWAY

TEN DAYS AFTER the revelation by Myrtle Ann Franklin, Stan and his quintet interrupted an engagement in Fort Lauderdale, Florida, for seventy-two hours to perform at a record industry convention in Cannes, France. Monica joined them, and they played a concert on January 23, 1980, for which they received $10,500 plus all expenses.

An incident on the flight back to the United States increased Stan's unease about Monica. Soon after takeoff, he drank some champagne and got up to visit his guitarist. When he returned to his seat, the flight attendant told him that he had found the remaining champagne in Stan's glass cloudy and had replaced it. Stan rifled through Monica's handbag, found what he believed were Antabuse pills, and threw them down the toilet. Monica denied doctoring his champagne, they squabbled, and Stan was furious the rest of the trip home.

When he returned to Fort Lauderdale, he was surprised to hear that Beverly had—on January 25—gone off with her boyfriend, Mike McGovern, to a local justice of the peace and gotten married. They had met two years before while she was assistant road manager for the Buddy Rich band and Mike was its principal trumpet soloist, and they had been living together in the apartment above the garage at Shadowbrook for several months. They wanted a quiet wedding and became nervous when Monica began to talk about extravagant nuptials at Shadowbrook featuring the Count Basie band and Rosemary Clooney; their nervousness turned to unease when they heard about the altercation on the flight from France, and on the spur of the moment they decided that their least stressful alternative was to elope.

Their witnesses at the ceremony were David Getz and his Swedish wife, Lena; they had been married in Sweden on August 12, 1977, and had returned to the United States in August 1979, when David enrolled at a small college in New Hampshire. After the two couples returned to Shadowbrook, they celebrated quietly in the McGoverns' apartment with the estate's caretakers, Betty Ann and Harold Fried.

A few days later, Betty Ann and Harold, David and Lena, Pamela and her boyfriend, Scot Raynor, and Monica and her mother rendezvoused with Stan and his band at Club Med at Dakar, Senegal, in West Africa. The musicians were hired for a two-week engagement but were paid no money; they received instead free vacations for themselves and a goodly number of guests. The "payment-in-kind" arrangement was conceived by Bernie Pollack, the Club's manager, who was a saxophone player and an ardent jazz fan. Stan had made a similar deal with Pollack the previous year when he managed the Club Med at Guadeloupe in the Caribbean.

Stan was in a belligerent mood when he stepped off the plane in Dakar, still angry about what he believed were Monica's continuing attempts to dose him secretly with Antabuse. He was so hostile when they arrived that Monica decided not to share a room with him and moved in with her mother.

Stan became very drunk at Club Med, and when Monica feared that he would continue bingeing, she turned again to her old expedient, Antabuse. She sent David into Stan's room to sprinkle the drug into a container of yogurt that he was keeping there in a small refrigerator. David completed his secret mission successfully, the first and only occasion when he dispensed Antabuse to his father. Monica also gave Antabuse to Bernie Pollack and asked him to administer it to Stan, but she believes he did not do so.

Whatever the source, Stan suffered an Antabuse reaction that he described as "a thousand times worse than the flu," and as he vomited and his heart raced and his head throbbed with pain, his anger with Monica escalated. He was outraged that she would make him ill like this only three weeks after promising him never to give him Antabuse again. When his symptoms subsided, he invited a woman from New York to fly to Dakar; she arrived the next day and moved into his room with him.

This affront caused Monica, her mother, the Frieds, Scot Raynor, and Pamela to pack up and fly back to America; soon after their return, on February 6, 1980, Monica—for the first time in eleven years—obtained from a Family Court judge a protective order calling for Stan's arrest if he became violent or drunk at Shadowbrook. In less than four weeks, two botched surreptitious dosings of Antabuse—during Myrtle Ann Franklin's visit to Shadowbrook and in Dakar—plus a suspected one on the airplane from France had severely torn the fabric of the Getz marriage.

Monica decided that she would try to repair the damage by staging at Shadowbrook an "intervention," a classic procedure for dealing with the problems caused by addiction. Interventions are meetings where family members, friends, and coworkers forcefully confront the alcoholic/drug abuser with the need for immediate help.

Experts insist that interventions be carefully planned with the aid of a professional who coaches and rehearses the participants and, if appropriate, takes part in the intervention itself. And an authoritative guidebook cautions:

> It is not a time to beat up on the alcoholic/addict, to punish or get even. It's purpose is to help, out of love and concern. . . . Exclude those who always immediately trigger anger in the alcoholic/addict, which could blow up the intervention before it gets going.

Monica invited to the early February encounter her mother; Stan's agent, Jack Whittemore; his close friend Siga Weissfisch; his principal physician, Dr. Avram Cooperman; the caretakers, Betty Ann and Harold Fried; Steve Getz; David and Lena Getz; and Beverly and Mike McGovern. None of them had a moment's preparation, and Stan was not told that they were coming.

Dr. Cooperman led off the proceedings, but he did not get very far in his talk to Stan. As Beverly remembered, the meeting quickly turned into a debacle:

> Dad's in his own house. He's just come off the road. He's tired. He walks into the library in his robe and he sees all these people,

and everybody starts ragging on him. Steve got into it with him,
I think. And he got really angry at everybody, saying, "Who the
hell are you to come into my house and tell me what to do?"
He started drinking and getting angrier.

Everybody ran away from Dad, except for the caretakers and
Monica's mother. She stayed in the house with him for two or
three days. Dad couldn't cook for her, so he mostly fed her ice
cream.

Monica was so scared that she asked my husband, Mike, to
climb up the back window to rescue her mother from Stan. . . .
But someone called in and talked to Monica's mother and found
that she was having a good time.

The caretakers, the Frieds, remember him being alternately
angry and solicitous with Monica's mother. He would scream,
"What do you think you're doing interfering in my life? You're
always sticking your nose into my business. Keep out of it, you
old cow." Then his voice would change and he would say, "Is
there anything I can do for you? Anything I can get you? How
about some ice cream?"

As they listened to this conversation, the Frieds thought, "He's
going to hit her. He's going to kiss her. He's going to hit her.
He's going to kiss her." Etc., etc. Monica's mother ate lots of ice
cream that day and the days which followed.

Monica acknowledged that the intervention participants should have been
coached, but she laid much of the blame for the failure of the intervention
on Dr. Cooperman, who she believes spoke too tolerantly to Stan. Cooperman, for his part, felt he had been placed in an almost impossible
position. He knew he had to confront Stan about his alcoholism, but he
also knew the strength of Stan's feelings of hurt and distrust about the
years of secret Antabuse dosings, and he sympathized deeply with those
feelings. He is convinced that Stan's anger that day was triggered by a
deep sense of betrayal.

Monica believed that Steve was appropriately tough with his father,
and she was shocked to hear Steve reveal that he saw Stan using cocaine
in Florida in 1979. She remembered:

Steven was really very courageous. And that was the first time I
realized that coke was in the picture. And Stan swooped down
on Steven. "You little shit," he screamed at him. And Steven
became very upset and just walked out.

Monica later attributed much of her marital travail to the addition of cocaine to Stan's menu of narcotics.

Steve had just come to the New York area to become the manager of Fat Tuesday's, one of the city's premier jazz clubs, and he moved into a small flat in a town near Shadowbrook, where he lived alone. Fat Tuesday's owner had hired him on the basis of favorable reports about the job Steve had done during the previous couple of years working at management agencies where he handled such jazz headliners as Maynard Ferguson, McCoy Tyner, Elvin Jones, Ahmad Jamal, and Stephane Grappelli.

After the failed intervention, Stan took his group on a short tour of Australia and India, where, according to *Down Beat*, he was "the undisputed star" of the second Indian festival of jazz in Bombay. They then played a number of lucrative dates along the East Coast, receiving $10,000 for two weeks at Steve's club, Fat Tuesday's, and $7,000 for a week at Blues Alley in Washington, D.C. Stan was headed for an excellent year; he grossed more than $222,000 in 1980.

After a few drinks at a rehearsal at Shadowbrook on May 3, Stan got into a shouting match with his musicians—Andy LaVerne, Brian Bromberg, Victor Jones, and Chuck Loeb—and fired them all. They left quickly, and he drove off soon after. He returned drunk, roared into Monica's bedroom around 3:00 A.M., grabbed the telephone cord, and used it like a lariat to swing the telephone through the air. Monica squirmed to avoid the projectile, and banged her head on the night table as the telephone hit her knee. Badly bruised, she drove alone to a nearby hospital and got Dr. Foster to meet her at the emergency room; the admitting physician wrote the following report:

> The patient is admitted to my care from the emergency room, where Dr. Foster had kept her under observations since 4:00 A.M. following contusion to her skull with possible concussion. History given in the emergency room was that in an effort to avoid hitting another car, braked and banged her left knee on the steering column or dashboard. She also banged her head at the time. She was in the emergency room under observation until around 8:30 or 9:00, and she continued to be somewhat dizzy, her vision was blurred. I was called and advised that she should be admitted.

Monica later said that she had concocted the story about the auto accident because "I didn't want Stan to be hurt by the papers—by the newspaper reports or anything like that."

Monica's discharge summary from the hospital four days later on May

7, 1980, stated, "A neurological consultation . . . confirmed the diagnosis of possible cerebral concussion and cervical sprain. During her stay in the hospital, she improved remarkably and was able to return home with very little symptoms."

Stan got drunk again at Shadowbrook on May 11, and the following morning Monica had him arrested under the protective order issued in February and had him hauled off to Family Court. The judge ordered him to Hazelden for treatment but gave him a one-week grace period to fulfill performance commitments.

When the Hazelden authorities discovered Stan high from opiates and cocaine that he had smuggled into the facility, they called Monica and she flew out and participated in the family program; since Dr. Anderson's improvised inauguration of the program for her in 1967, family therapy had become a well-organized element of the Hazelden treatment regimen. Stan's sojourn was interrupted by a short leave to play, at President Carter's request, at the Tall Ships Festival in Boston on May 29. He returned to Hazelden but did not finish his course of treatment and left before Monica did.

Hazelden's program for the fifth time had little effect on Stan's addiction; soon after, while touring Europe with Monica, he drank heavily again. She left him after a fight in a Paris hotel room, but had trouble departing from France. He had thrown her passport away during their altercation, and she was forced to rely on the influence of members of her family to gain entrance into Denmark and Sweden without the document.

Stan and Monica had not communicated with each other for more than a month when he turned up unexpectedly at Shadowbrook and surprised her. He had returned to receive an honorary doctorate at Mercy College in nearby Dobbs Ferry, New York, and Monica accompanied him to the ceremony on August 18, 1980.

Stan had persisted in seeking opportunities for Diane Schuur to perform with him, and he found one in early September at the Keystone Korner in San Francisco. Diane flew down from Seattle, where she was living with her father after returning home broke after three difficult years in Arizona. She was hooked on cocaine and alcohol at the time, and Stan fed her addictions and his when she arrived in San Francisco. She remembered:

> I walked into Stan's hotel room, and because there was a limou-
> sine and everything for me, I felt like a big cheese, and Stan
> hugged me and kissed me on the cheek, and said, "Can we say
> a prayer?" I said, "Sure. No problem." So we prayed. And then

we tooted and then I did a sexual favor for him because I was so high.

If I was in the same spot today—clean and sober with the boundaries I have been able to establish in my life—I probably would have said no. My psychological thing at the time was, "Since he's given me these drugs, I'll do anything for him."

I performed with him that night. . . . He was very much addicted to alcohol and drugs, too. So he was a great enabler for me. . . . After I performed with him, I just felt I was the apple of his eye. I always looked up to authority figures, and I definitely considered Stan an authority figure, almost a daddy. . . .

I remember performing with him the next night and he says, "God, you're so high on this and that, you sound like you're half out of your mind." It didn't occur to me to retort, "What about you? Where are you at?" I went home a bit disillusioned when I came down from all of those drugs.

Following the San Francisco engagement, Stan left with Monica on a four-week tour of South America, but she returned early to the United States to undergo plastic surgery on her face and breasts. She recovered in time for the Christmas holidays.

Nicky Getz had entered San Diego State University in California on a tennis scholarship in September 1980, and he looked forward to returning to the East Coast in late December to play in the World Junior Tennis Championships in Miami, Florida. Coincidentally, Stan had a holiday engagement in nearby Fort Lauderdale, and he rented two condos in the same building there, one for Nicky and one for himself and Monica.

Nicky had prepared diligently for the tournament, "the Wimbledon of the juniors," and was playing well in an early round when he tore up a knee so badly that he was forced to submit to arthroscopic surgery. A couple of days later, he went on crutches to his parents' condo for dinner and found Stan smelling of alcohol and looking for a fight. Nicky remembered:

He starts yelling and screaming at me. He's just looking for anything—how disrespectful I was toward my mother, because we had been arguing in the car about the surgery. . . .

The next thing I know, he's taken my neck, and he's pushed me up against this door in the kitchen, you know, really hard. And he's about to hit me and stuff.

My mom's screaming and yelling at him. And now I'm just

scared to death because I cannot defend myself. I'm in so much
pain with my leg. . . . I manage to get out of there, get downstairs,
and lock the door.

Monica hurried down to visit Nicky after Stan had gone to work and
convinced her son that he should leave. He arranged to stay with a girlfriend in a town several hours north of Fort Lauderdale and rode a Grey-
hound bus to get there. He flew back to San Diego a few days later.

When Stan and Monica returned from Florida, their hostility had escalated to a point where she left Stan at Shadowbrook and went to stay in
a hotel. Monica knew that her marriage was in serious trouble, and she
concluded that the best way to revive it was to organize a second, scrupu-
lously prepared intervention that would get Stan into therapy again.

She started to work on the intervention when Stan flew to San Francisco for a January 20–25, 1981, engagement at the Keystone Korner. For
this gig Stan had hired Lou Levy on piano, Chip Jackson on bass, and
Shelly Manne on drums. The *Chronicle* reviewer found much to be
pleased with:

> Looking as fit as he sounded, Getz responded in Tuesday's open-
> ing set with some of his most inspired playing here in years. . . .
> Getz' burnished light amber tone, delicately feathered at its edges,
> gives everything he plays the feel of a song whose words just happen
> not to be audible. . . . [His music] is suffused with a gentle bitter-
> sweet melancholy that occasionally gives way to a shy affirmation
> or a fleeting surge of radiant emotion. . . . Lou Levy and Chip
> Jackson are perfect compliments to Getz' poetic shadings and sub-
> tly changing moods. . . . and [Shelly] Manne is marvelous.

Monica was well prepared for Stan's second intervention when he returned from California. To train and rehearse the participants, she chose
Dr. Keith Simpson, a California physician who had helped Stan on a
couple of occasions. Simpson, then president of the National Council on
Alcoholism, had treated more than three thousand patients for alcohol
and drug abuse during the previous decade.

Monica and Simpson decided whom to invite to the intervention:
Steve, Beverly, Jack Whittemore, Ellen Buentello (a new caretaker at
Shadowbrook), Stan's lawyer, Buddy Monash, his accountant, Marvin
Zolt, and an assistant of Simpson's who was an intervention specialist. He
and the assistant flew in early from California and worked the other
participants through a thorough intervention curriculum during several

sessions in New York City. The event was scheduled for a conference room in Monash's office, and Stan was not told about it in advance. He was to be lured there on the pretext that Monash wished to meet with him about some legal matters.

The group sat around Monash's conference table and fidgeted for forty-five minutes before they figured out that Stan was not going to show up. He had been tipped off by Whittemore's secretary and was on an airplane headed for the West Coast. A few days later, in early February, he appeared at Shadowbrook, packed his essential belongings, and moved out. Slightly more than a year had elapsed since the Myrtle Ann Franklin incident, which had fatally undermined his trust in his marriage and his wife.

As his marriage was disintegrating, Stan found solace in talking with and occasionally visiting Jane Walsh, the young woman who had so impressed him a couple of years before. He called to tell her that he had left Shadowbrook and that he would contact her on returning from a six-week European tour with five accompanying musicians scheduled to begin on February 9.

The trip was managed by Billy Hoogstraten, a twenty-four-year-old Dutch student who soon became a trusted associate of Stan's and one of his closet friends. Billy was working part-time for Wim Wigt (another Dutchman who was the tour promoter) while studying for an advanced degree in agriculture. Stan's European junket the previous summer was under Wigt's banner, and Billy had met Stan briefly then.

Hoogstraten in Dutch means "highstreet," and on March 3, 1981, Stan took the sextet into a Paris studio to produce an album that was called *Billy Highstreet Samba* when it was released in 1990. The release was delayed because of a dispute over publishing rights which Stan did not settle until 1989. The members of Stan's band—Mitchell Forman on keyboards, Chuck Loeb on guitar, Mark Egan on bass, Victor Lewis on drums, and Bobby Thomas on percussion—were all energetic and under thirty, and Stan gave them a broad opportunity to display their talents; five of the eight tunes are by Loeb and two are by Forman, and everyone gets a chance to solo at length.

The music, strongly influenced by Chick Corea, displays complex Latin rhythms, biting electric piano lines, and spicy harmonies. Stan burns passionately on three up-tempo numbers—the title tune, "Page Two," and "Tuesday Next"—and makes romantic tapestries of three ballads—the old standard "Body and Soul" and "Be There Then" and "The Dirge." He plays soprano saxophone on the two latter numbers, the only time in his recording career that he used this instrument. The soprano presents greater difficulties in maintaining pitch and tone than does the tenor, but Stan is undaunted and creates a buttery sound on the instrument quite similar to what he achieves in the upper register of the tenor.

When his European tour ended in late March, Stan took up residence in San Francisco, choosing an apartment on Pfeiffer Street in the funky North Beach section, where drugs and booze were freely available. Except for a couple of overnight visits, he never stayed at Shadowbrook again.

The Keystone Korner, one of Stan's favorite venues, was also located in North Beach, and he made a live recording there for Concord Records on May 12, 1981; the album was called *The Dolphin*. Stan had not been happy at Columbia Records, which had strongly emphasized commercial considerations with its electronic instrumentations, its Gilberto rehash, and its uninspiring Schifrin backgrounds, and he welcomed working with Concord, a small, independent label whose owner/producer, Carl Jefferson, was devoted to pure jazz. Stan told Leonard Feather, who wrote the liner notes for *The Dolphin:*

> My philosophy is very simple. There are four qualities essential to a great jazzman. They are taste, courage, individuality, and irreverence. Those are the qualities I want to retain in my music.
>
> You can try out something else just to get the feel of what's going on. I did that, but it didn't sit true with me. It wasn't the essence of the jazz art form. I don't want ever again to be subjected to pressures from record companies.

The Dolphin is jazz at its simplest and purest, a straight-ahead quartet session with no electronic instruments. Stan brought to the date one musician from his recently concluded European tour, the young drummer Victor Lewis, and teamed him with two veterans, bassist Monty Budwig and pianist Lou Levy. Levy spoke in awed tones that week about Stan to the *San Francisco Chronicle:*

> He is the complete player. He has perfect intonation and technique and an unsurpassed ear. When I throw substitution chords at him—upside down, inside or out, or even wrong—he'll grab them and match them. His horn is an extension of his head. He's the Jascha Heifitz of the tenor sax. If Stan has a flaw, it's that he's flawless.

In 1991 Steve Getz found audiotapes recorded during the Keystone Korner gig that Stan had not believed were worth releasing. The music on the tapes was excellent; Stan, his own most severe critic, had overreacted. When Billy Hoogstraten heard about this, he was not surprised:

> Stan could play the most beautiful concert and come offstage and say, "This was shit tonight. I was nothing. You guys played great. I didn't get one note right out of the horn."

The rejected tapes were issued in 1992 by Concord as *Spring Is Here*. Steve is listed as coproducer with Jefferson, and Steve's son Christopher, twenty years old in 1992, is credited as an assistant to the producers.

The material on *The Dolphin* and *Spring Is Here* consists of thirteen numbers—a gentle samba, five up-tempo tunes, and seven ballads. Stan was inspired both by the Keystone Korner ambience and by the opportunity to work with a quartet:

> The people react as though they're in church. Afterward you never heard such a small crowd express its admiration so voraciously.
>
> The band is like a classical string quartet. If I had another horn, it would get in my way, and I would almost be like playing arrangements. In a quartet, I'm able to phrase differently every night. I'm up there and I can freely do whatever I wish to do. And the quartet is small enough for everyone to solo, I like to hear everyone in the band solo. It's essentially a classical-jazz approach to music. . . .
>
> For my taste, there's really nothing in the whole world better than an acoustic rhythm section when it's popping. It seems to vibrate inside your body. You seldom get it, but when you get it, that can be felt. It's hard to achieve; you've got to have the right players and the right moods. A lot of times listening to electric music just feels like I'm taking shock treatments.

These circumstances produced his best recorded work since the memorable month of October 1975, when he made *The Peacocks* and *The Master*, the two outstanding albums of his five Columbia years.

Stan brings a fierce, hoarse, booting exuberance to the up-tempo stompers like "How About You," "That Old Devil Moon," "Joy Spring," and "The Night Has a Thousand Eyes," and the quartet as a whole is infected by his joyous feeling; Levy and Budwig dig in with several exhilarating choruses, and Lewis demonstrates the gutsy swing and delicate touch that insured his tenure as Stan's drummer for the next eight years.

In 1979 Stan told a writer:

> Ballads intrigue me. I let the mood do what it wants. I never intend to do anything, it just comes out as the piece dictates. You'll notice that I never even close my eyes, but my mind is on the music. Everything comes from within, no images are conjured up that are based on what I see. There are some ballads on which I just don't play anything but the melody . . . the melody is so beautiful it says everything for me.

Stan conveys the beauty of melody and more on the albums as he provides classic, intensely moving readings of ballads such as "My Old Flame," "Easy Living," "Spring Is Here," and Johnny Mandel's "Close Enough for Love."

The albums were acclaimed by fans and writers on both sides of the Atlantic, and the British critics chose *Spring Is Here* as the 1992 Record of the Year for the U.K. magazine *Jazz Journal.*

In late May 1981, two weeks after the Keystone Korner engagement, Stan was joined in the North Beach neighborhood by David Getz and his wife Lena. David had just graduated from college in New Hampshire at age twenty-nine, and had gone to San Francisco "because I never got a chance to spend some real good time with my father." He found a job at the San Francisco airport with Hertz Rent-a-Car.

As Stan enjoyed his independence in San Francisco, he began to think seriously about suing Monica for divorce. His resolve was strengthened when his lawyer told him that the twelve years of secret Antabuse dosings constituted "cruel and inhuman treatment," the basis for a solid case in New York State. Stan was slated to depart on June 25 for another European tour, and before he left, he told the lawyer to start drawing up divorce papers.

He took Jane Walsh on tour with him, and she happily remembered the whirligig traveling, "It was great. It was my first visit to Europe, and we covered just about every major country, like thirty one-nighters in forty-five days." Stan brought along Lou Levy and Victor Lewis but replaced Monty Budwig (who had studio commitments on the West Coast) with Marc Johnson, a brilliant twenty-seven-year-old who had made his reputation with Bill Evans.

The highlight of the tour was the large festival in Nice, France, which took place from July 17 to July 21. As Steve Voce reported, Stan outshone other stars such as Dizzy Gillespie, Terry Gibbs, Dexter Gordon, Art Pepper, John Lewis, Elvin Jones, and Lee Konitz:

Stanley was the prodigious figure of the festival and it needs to be said that he was at all times as enchanting as his music. Everyone found him friendly and cooperative and he was the musical catalyst at any jam session in which he took part. He played his ass off at 11 different sessions during the second part of the festival. . . .

Getz took everything as it came in his search for, and close approach to, perfection. If it sounded right to let a ballad finish in Lou's piano solo, then it did. Lou Levy was "mon vieux," Marc Johnson "mon nouveau ami," and drummer Victor Lewis, "mon tigre."

The band was mon favourite, and wherever it went there were consistently high tides of jazz inspiration. When Art Farmer and Konitz sat in, the improvisations were supernatural, with Art's "It Might As Well Be Spring," and Stan's "We'll Be Together Again," flanking Lee's opus. Marc Johnson's bass lincs stimulated everyone, and his solos were prodigious.

Stan and Jane were jolted by news from Florida when they returned from Europe. She remembered:

We flew back into New York, and I was going back to Florida, and we had talked about me moving to San Francisco.

I tried to call my family, and I couldn't find anybody, and then I called the secretary of my brother John, and she said, "Your nephew Adam is missing." I think that was the thirty-first of July, and Adam had been abducted on the twenty-seventh. . . .

I went down to Florida, and Stan stayed in New York another week and then he came down. He appeared on a local radio show and encouraged people to help search for Adam.

I stayed and helped the family. They found the remains of my nephew about two weeks later, and we had some fundraisers and my sister-in-law started the Adam Walsh Center for missing children in Florida. I worked with her and John my brother through Christmas of eighty-one and into January of eighty-two. . . . They never found Adam's murderer.

The Walshes made the center a clearinghouse for information about missing children, and it grew into a national institution which still flourishes. John Walsh, projecting strength and determination, became a hero. He now hosts the Fox network's hit TV show *America's Most Wanted.*

When Stan was in New York before rejoining Jane in Florida, he instructed his lawyer to file an action for divorce against Monica on the grounds of "cruel and inhuman treatment." The summons announcing the action, dated August 5, 1981, was served on Monica with some difficulty.

Marvin Potash, an assistant to Stan's lawyer, was stopped at the door when he tried to present the summons to Monica at her attorney's office on August 6. Locating her car in the parking lot behind the office, he positioned himself there, and sighted her and her attorney a couple of hours later leaving the building via a rear fire escape. He remembered:

> When they reached the ground floor, the attorney and Monica Getz saw me. I then ran over to serve the Summons on Monica Getz, and the attorney physically blocked me. I then bumped him with my shoulder and chased Monica Getz. I then tried to serve her with the Summons, and she refused to take it. I then threw it at her and walked away. This was at 4:40 P.M.

Four days later, on August 10, Stan and Monica reached an agreement in Family Court about such financial items as support payments for Monica and Nicky (which approximated $80,000 annually), the disposition of credit cards, lawyers' fees, and an appraisal of Shadowbrook. Stan's capacity to meet his obligations was strong, because he was on the way to grossing more than $335,000 for 1981.

Monica was convinced that she had an alcohol problem with Stan, not a matrimonial problem. She believed strongly that if he would undergo a treatment program that involved the family and was long enough and rigorous enough, he would come back to her and drop the divorce action. She pleaded her case to him at a meeting at her lawyer's office in New York on November 3, 1981, volunteering to enter treatment with him and the children. Stan did not agree to this, but he did invite Monica to join him in sessions with Dr. Richard Shore, a psychiatrist who had been treating him three times weekly when he was in San Francisco.

Monica flew out a few weeks later; she claims that she stayed with Stan at his apartment and had sex with him there. He denied both allegations, maintaining that they never had sex after 1980. Steve and his son Chris joined them in San Francisco at Christmas time and checked into the Hyatt, where Steve—on a leave of absence from Fat Tuesday's—was exploring the opportunity of booking acts into the Hyatt's new jazz room, Reflections. Coincidentally, Stan was opening Reflections with his quartet on January 18, 1982.

Steve feels sure that Monica hoped to bring Stan home for good from San Francisco, but he believes that Stan was uninterested in the idea. Steve's belief appears valid because at that time Stan was constantly telephoning Jane Walsh to insist that she leave Florida and come to live with him in North Beach. Steve recalled, "Monica hung around and generally made a nuisance of herself. Stan was annoyed and a little embarrassed."

Monica and Stan attended three or four therapy sessions with Dr. Shore, and at his suggestion they sought out two mediators. The mediators convinced them that the financial particulars of their separation, which had been further defined since their August 10 meeting, should be formalized in a document.

Lawyers prepared such a document, which was called an "Agreement Toward Reconciliation"; its name is misleading, however, because it is mute concerning steps toward reconciliation. It deals with Stan's support payments for Monica and Nicky, selling the land near Almuñécar in Spain, applying for a zoning change to build condominiums on the Shadowbrook property, paying legal fees, settling indebtedness with the IRS and the states of New York and California, and shipping Stan's 1977 Mercedes to San Francisco. The agreement also extends for six months the period in which Stan could serve a formal complaint in the pending divorce action.

As Stan prepared for the Reflections opening, he felt one of his periodic urges to change piano players. He told Marc Johnson that he wanted someone who played in a more advanced harmonic idiom than Lou Levy, and Johnson suggested an old cohort of his from the Thad Jones–Mel Lewis Big Band, Jim McNeely. Stan listened to McNeely once and knew that he had his man.

Reflections, perched thirty-six floors above Union Square, was transformed by Hyatt management from a garish discotheque into a posh supper club, and Stan accepted a reduced fee to help launch it successfully. The room had an unfortunate layout for a jazz venue as most of the listeners sat in narrow rows stretching sideways from the bandstand, but Stan and the quartet packed them in during the two-week engagement. The *Examiner* critic reported that:

> (Reflections') spectacular views were matched by the most beautiful jazz sounds imaginable. Getz uses no amplification, and the lush melodies of "I'll Remember April" or "Spring Is Here" rolled out from the small stage and more than matched the grandeur of the sparkling lights of San Francisco below.

And the reporter for the *Chronicle* wrote:

> Getz' band was superb. His new pianist, Jim McNeely, was thoughtful and swinging. Even more impressive was bassist Marc Johnson (formerly with the late Bill Evans), who contributed a gorgeous romantic piece, "Antigna." The drummer was Billy Hart (substituting for Victor Lewis), one of jazz's most underrated musicians.

Jane Walsh gave in to Stan's blandishments during the Reflections engagement and flew from Florida to San Francisco to live with him. She was upset when he turned up drunk to meet her at the airport, and she was appalled the next day when, during a postbinge depression, he put a gun to his head and threatened to kill himself. She was also appalled by the multitude of drug dealers, liquor stores, and saloons in North Beach, and in less than a week moved the two of them to the Marina, a quiet, middle-class neighborhood surrounded by yacht basins on San Francisco Bay.

Carl Jefferson brought the quartet into a studio for Concord during the last day of the Reflections engagement, January 30, and they began an LP which was called *Pure Getz*. The group did not complete the album, because Stan, McNeely, and Johnson were slated to leave for New York the next day for a gig at Fat Tuesday's, where Victor Lewis would reclaim the drum chair from Billy Hart.

This led Jefferson to ask Steve Getz to supervise the completion of the LP back east the following week using Lewis. Steve had not seen a secure future at Reflections and had returned to his duties at Fat Tuesday's in mid-January; his judgment proved to be wise, because Reflections folded in less than two years.

Stan shared the bill at Fat Tuesday's with an old friend of his, the zany comedian "Professor" Irwin Corey. Stan and Monica accepted separate invitations to stay at the Coreys' apartment in Manhattan for the first few nights of the run; Monica claimed that she had sex with Stan at the Coreys', but he denied it vehemently.

Opening night coincided with Stan's fifty-fifth birthday, and his uncle, Benny Getz, turned up to help celebrate the event with Steve, Monica, and the sixteen-year-old daughter of Stan's lawyer. A *New York Times* reporter attended the opening and wrote:

> If he keeps it up, it's just possible that someday Stan Getz will master the tenor saxophone. But after forty years, the most his

fans can apparently hope for, is that he continues his public quest for perfection. "I'm still learning," Mr. Getz said, after conducting yet another session seeking the elusive saxophone ideal. . . .

"I learn something new everyday—to edit," he said, "to take out all the extraneous matter and stress form, logic, and content. I try to play beautiful music."

Steve, who received credit as associate producer of *Pure Getz*, relished supervising the New York recording for his father:

We read each other—it was great—like telepathy in the studio. I listened for interpretations—whether it was a good take. We agreed right down the line. I know what he likes, and he knows what I like. It was a different dimension to our relationship.

McNeely's solos on *Pure Getz* are not as intriguing as Lou Levy's on Stan's two previous Concord albums, but his harmonies are more astringent, and this seems to inspire Stan to put more bite into his improvisations. With *Pure Getz*, he appears to have arrived at one of those higher artistic plateaus that he discussed at the time with an Associated Press writer:

To me, you go along for the longest time, so boring, not being able to improve. And then it'll go down a little. You get so bored and unhappy. Right after that, it will go up beyond where it was.

That is one of the few joyous moments I have in music. It is a certain physical feeling of being able all of a sudden to make more form, logic, and content with less effort, less wastage.

Stan's joy is palpable as he creates two of the greatest solos of his career on the album's outstanding tracks—Bud Powell's bebop classic, "Tempus Fugit," and Billy Strayhorn's deathbed composition, "Blood Count."

Stan's furious solo on "Tempus Fugit" almost maniacally affirms life while, at the same time, expressing deep pain at its brevity. The arching cries that blast from his horn show what he meant when he told a friend, "Every time I try to play black, it comes out sounding Jewish."

Billy Strayhorn, Duke Ellington's brotherly collaborator for twenty-eight years, was dying of cancer in a New York hospital in 1967 when he wrote "Blood Count" as a vehicle for Johnny Hodges, the Duke's wonderful alto saxophonist. Three months after Strayhorn's death, Ellington and Hodges recorded what was considered the definitive interpretation of "Blood Count"—until *Pure Getz*.

Stan was unaware of the Ellington-Hodges recording when he read the music for the first time on the day of the session:

> My pianist, Jim McNeely, brought it to me. . . . The take on the record is the first time I had played it. Sometimes, your first impression is the best.

Critic Gary Giddins has written, "With 'Blood Count,' Getz joins the relatively small group of jazz stylists who can lay personal claim to material by sole virtue of their interpretive integrity." Stan achieves this by mining instinctively the turmoil underlying the elegiac song with startling variations in volume and intonation; at the emotional peak of his improvisation, he alternates marrow-freezing cries with soft, bluesy moans to carry the listener to the poignant center of the piece.

On February 11, a few days after the second *Pure Getz* session, Stan and Monica got together in a lawyer's office and signed the "Agreement Toward Reconciliation."

Jane Walsh rejoined Stan in New York soon after and departed with him on February 25 for a lucrative six-week European tour with McNeely, Johnson, and Lewis; the junket earned the quartet $101,500.

They had no time to relax when they returned on April 6, because within forty-eight hours they were flying to Tahiti. Bernie Pollack had taken over the Club Med there, and Stan had made another "payment-in-kind" deal with him: In return for two weeks of performing, the quartet members and their families received a free four-week vacation at the resort. David and Lena Getz and Billy Hoogstraten and his wife and infant son joined them. Billy was excited:

> Can you imagine? I'm a student living in a little room and having very little money. Then all of a sudden I'm there on the plane with my wife and my little kid and going to Tahiti to Club Med—and Stan took care of everything. He insisted to buy the Pampers and to rent the car. We spent nothing at all. . . . And then he took us to San Francisco, and we stayed for a week at the house.

During an engagement at the Keystone Korner in May following his return from Tahiti, Stan collapsed in a room at the Hyatt Hotel while he was with the club's owner, Todd Barkan. As he had done four years previously when Stan keeled over in midsolo at his club, Barkan summoned paramedics, who gave Stan an injection that immediately revived him. Again the culprit was the painkiller Dilaudid, and again Stan attributed his collapse to a mix-up concerning the prescribed dosage. Stan recovered rapidly and missed only one night on the bandstand.

Barkan called Monica in New York to tell her about the incident, and she flew almost immediately to San Francisco. She managed to speak with Stan on the telephone there, but she could not convince him to meet with her and returned quickly to New York.

Jim Nadel, the director of the Summer Jazz Workshop at Stanford University, which is located roughly thirty miles south of San Francisco, learned from a newspaper column that Stan had moved to San Francisco. He remembered:

> The story said Stan was in the shower and he heard a dog fight going on outside his San Francisco apartment and he realized that his dog James, a yellow Labrador, had gotten out and was losing the fight. He ran outside naked, dripping wet, and kicked the other dog and pulled James back to safety, scandalizing the neighbors.
>
> So, I realized Stan really does live in San Francisco. Then I was thinking he'd be the perfect guy to come down to the work-shop. . . . I call and Stan answers the phone. I told him what was on my mind and he said, "Come on over."
>
> I went over to his pad in the Marina where he was living with Jane, and we had a big long discussion while he was getting a massage.
>
> He had a real interest in the program, because I think he had reached the point in his life where he was interested in doing something with jazz education, pursuing and exploring it.

By the end of their conversation, Stan had agreed to participate in the next workshop scheduled for early August.

That summer Jane began to understand what it was like living with an alcoholic.

> When we were at the Marina, Stan was still using. He was in pretty bad shape. It's one thing for him to come visit you in Florida, and you see him on the weekend on his best behavior, but to move in with somebody and understand what really is going on in their life, it was very scary.
>
> He had already tried several rehabs throughout the years. My

family is riddled with it. I was drinking from the time I was 18 and entered rehab at 24. I haven't had a drink since I was 24 years old. I went into rehab because my mother talked me into it.

I didn't join AA until I was with Stan, living with this practicing person in California who was drinking in the house. I thought, "I'm not going to be able to handle this alone."

He'd go in spurts. You never knew what was going to happen. Erratic behavior. He used coke sometimes, but he was not really a coke addict. It was very sporadic. The booze was really the killer for him.

To understand it, it's like trying to sit here with a bunch of diabetics. They're not going to tell you what it feels like when they need insulin. You don't get it. You never get it.

If you can—imagine when people know their sugar is low and they've got to go for the insulin. You're down or your body starts feeling weird and then you need to have something to bring you up to the level again.

Following a ten-day European tour, Stan threw himself into the Stanford Jazz Workshop during the first week of August 1982. Nadel, an alto saxophonist who graduated from Stanford in 1972, had started the workshop in 1973 and had built it gradually into a solid institution. Students could opt for either a one or a two-week program and paid $175 per week for tuition and $136 for room and board. The curriculum emphasized improvisation and included instrumental clinics, master classes, music theory, ear development, arranging, composition, and individual instruction. The faculty gave concerts every night and provided advanced players the opportunity to perform publicly. The faculty for 1982 included Stan and the members of his quartet (Johnson, Lewis, and McNeely), bassist Chuck Israels, alto saxophonist Lanny Morgan, and Nadel. Stan and the quartet were paid $2,200 for the week; they absented themselves one night to earn $7,000 performing at the Hollywood Bowl.

Stan was a sensation, as Nadel remembered:

It was outstanding. Everybody played for him, and he made comments and he played harmony with them. Everybody was inspired, but a few students really connected with him.

Some were into complicated modes, and Stan would tell then, "It's not the mode; it's the mood." He was nervous about teaching, but it went really well.

Stan was much more successful with music than he was with words. His only failure of the week came on August 5; he was asked to speak about "Forty Years in Jazz," experienced a severe case of stage fright, and became almost tongue-tied.

He was far from tongue-tied when he met Stanford art professor and painter Nate Oliveira and Nate's wife Mona backstage following his last evening performance at the workshop. His tongue was lubricated by half a bottle of Scotch, and Nate joined him for a nip as he told Stan how much he admired his work. Stan felt an instant rapport with the Oliveiras, and they soon established a close friendship.

A few days later at a barbecue hosted by Nadel, he and Jane met two more couples who soon became their friends—Dr. Bill and Pat Dement, and Andy and Eleanor Geiger. Dr. Dement, a former professional jazz bassist who was a world-renowned neurologist and director of Stanford's prestigious Sleep Disorders Clinic, and Geiger, another jazz buff who headed Stanford's Athletic Department, were both in awe of Stan's talent.

Soon Stan and Jane were being invited to visit their new friends in their large, comfortable, understated homes in the beautiful college town. Rubbing shoulders with such university dignitaries in their native habitat had a strong effect upon the high school dropout from the Bronx slums. The man who always felt embarrassed by his lack of education and who had made his living mostly in saloons—dealing for forty years with fast-buck promoters, sleazy drug pushers, and grubby nightclub owners—could not believe that such distinguished people were treating him as a social equal. As Stan told an Associated Press reporter in September, the academic life appealed to him:

> I would like to be their legend in residence. Even though I didn't go to school myself, forty years qualify me to tell them something. . . . I like to teach and live easily. It is nice to see how normal people live. . . .

Jane remembered what the Stanford workshop experience meant to Stan:

> That was the beginning of the idea that Stan could do something other than stay on the road for eternity. When Geiger suggested that Stan could be an artist-in-residence at Stanford, Stan said to me, "This is my chance to stay sober." The only problem with

that is, you don't stay sober on a contingency. You stay sober because of your faith.

Jane's admonitions about the basis of sobriety and her success in resisting temptation with the help of AA inspired Stan to yet another effort to overcome his addictions. When Steve recommended a rehab center friends of his had raved about—a small facility called The ARK in Colorado Springs, Colorado—Stan decided to give the place a try.

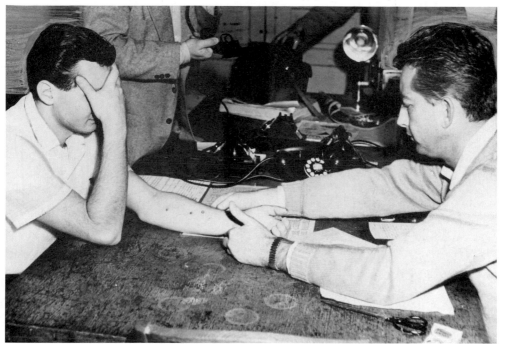

ABOVE: A Los Angeles detective examines the track marks on Stan's arm after his arrest on "vagrancy, drug addict" charges on December 19, 1953. *Photograph from the Security Pacific National Bank Collection/Los Angeles Public Library.*

BELOW: Stan being hauled off in a Seattle squad car after his arrest for an abortive holdup of the Olympic Drug Store on February 12, 1954. This photograph was sent nationwide on the UP wire service and elicited for Stan many supportive letters and telegrams. *Photograph from the Security Pacific National Bank Collection/Los Angeles Public Library.*

Rockelstad, Sparreholm.

Foto & ensamrätt: AERO-NORD, Ste
Godkänd av Försvarsstaben.

ABOVE: An aerial view of Rockelstad Castle in Sweden, the seat of the von Rosens, the family of Monica Getz's mother. *Photograph from the Collection of John and Dorothy Foster.* BELOW: Stan bids good-bye to Monica and Beverly as he commutes to work by bicycle in Denmark in 1959. *Photograph from the Collection of Beverly McGovern.*

ABOVE LEFT: Eddie Sauter, pictured here in the mid-1950s, collaborated with Stan in 1961 on what Stan believed was his greatest artistic achievement, the recording of *Focus*. Stan created dazzling improvisations over a beautiful seven-part suite composed by Sauter. *Photograph from the Collection of Frank Driggs.*
ABOVE RIGHT: Monica Getz smiles radiantly in this 1965 photograph. *Photograph from* New York Post.
RIGHT: Stan with five Getz children in 1963. David is to his right, Steve to his left. Nicky, Beverly, and Pamela stand in front of them. *Photograph from the Collection of Beverly McGovern.*

ABOVE LEFT: João Gilberto, Stan, and Chick Corea perform at New York's Rainbow Grill in January 1972. *Photograph by Katherine Bang; from Bettmann Archives.* ABOVE RIGHT: Stan performing with Astrud Gilberto in July 1964, the month when "The Girl From Ipanema" became a monster hit. *Photograph by Chuck Stewart.* BELOW LEFT: Antonio Carlos Jobim in the early 1960s when he was making wonderful music with Stan. *Photograph by Chuck Stewart.* BELOW RIGHT: Stan performing in 1965 with the brilliant Gary Burton; Burton was twenty-two at the time. He was a member of Stan's unit from February 1964 until December 1966. *Photograph by Lee Tanner.*

ABOVE: Nancy Reagan sent Stan this group portrait taken after the White House concert of December 4, 1982. From left to right: Marc Johnson, Roy Haynes, Dizzy Gillespie, Jon Faddis, Nancy Reagan, Miroslaw Vitous, Diane Schuur, Jim McNeely, Itzhak Perlman, Adam Nussbaum, Chick Corea, and Stan Getz. *Photograph from the collection of Jane Walsh.* RIGHT: The twenty-three-room main residence at Shadowbrook, the estate owned by Stan and Monica in Irvington, New York, a suburb north of New York City. *Photograph by David Godlis.*

LEFT: Stan working with students in a master class at Stanford University in 1986. *Photograph by Edward W. Souza, Stanford News Service.*

ABOVE: Stan and Diane Schuur share a happy moment in 1985. *Photograph from the Collection of Jane Walsh.*

RIGHT: Stan with Jane Walsh as they enter Stanford University Hospital on September 17, 1987. The next day, Stan underwent surgery to remove a cancerous lymphoma from behind his heart. *Photograph from the Collection of Jane Walsh.*

LEFT: Peter Torgner, whom Stan acknowledged as his illegitimate son, in a 1995 portrait. Torgner, born in 1958 in Sweden, has had a successful career on TV and the stage in his native country. *Photograph from the Collection of Peter Torgner.*

ABOVE: Stan with his close friend Herb Alpert in 1990. *Photograph by Michael Miller.*
RIGHT: Kenny Barron, whom Stan described as "the other half of my heart," was Stan's prime collaborator in his later years. *Photograph by Phoebe Ferguson.*

Samantha Ceseña and Stan in a 1990 photo soon after they became engaged.
Photograph from the Collection of Samantha Ceseña.

HEALING   EIGHTEEN

BEFORE HE CHECKED INTO The ARK, Stan indulged in one big drinking bout. It occurred at Pamela's wedding to Scot Raynor at Shadowbrook on Sunday, September 26, 1982. Stan had completed a gig in Chicago at 4:00 A.M. and had flown directly to New York without sleep, and he was angry with Monica. She had scheduled an afternoon wedding with the reception continuing into the evening, and this overlapped with Yom Kippur, which always begins at sundown and encompasses the holiest twenty-four hours in the Jewish calendar.

When the sun sets to begin Yom Kippur, observant Jews are enjoined to start a day of solemn fasting and prayer as they atone for the transgressions of the past year and prepare for the new one. None of Stan's Jewish friends or relatives attended the reception; the religious ones were at their synagogues, and the nonreligious ones stayed away because they were affronted, and Stan seethed about this as he knocked back Scotch after Scotch until he was totally inebriated.

He stayed on the East Coast during October to honor engagements at Fat Tuesday's and Blues Alley and flew to The ARK in early November. Because Stan only had a week to spare, the main purpose of his visit was to become acquainted with the place and with its director, Howard "Mac" McFadden.

Mac, six months younger than Stan, had—while a practicing alcoholic—carved out a successful career as a producer for NBC-TV during the 1950s and 1960s; his wife Shirley played the role of suburban matron, dividing her time between her country club and her work for community charities.

Mac had found sobriety at a small, rural treatment center in Connecticut called High Watch Farm, and in 1969 he felt a call to become a healer of the addicted. He wanted to create a facility using the intimate, low-tech approach practiced at High Watch, and he found that choosing a location was rather easy:

> I leave NBC at the end of 1969, and I sit there contemplating my navel, and I ask myself, "If you could go anywhere in the world, where would you go?" I had been to Colorado Springs just once on a drunken business trip, and it made an impression on me.
>
> I went home and asked my wife, "If you could go anywhere in the world—" and she said, "Colorado Springs"; she had been there once, before we had married. We looked at only one place and wanted it immediately. So we really felt we were led to it.

The McFaddens had chosen a pristine spot six thousand feet below the summit of fourteen-thousand-foot Pikes Peak in a meadow surrounded by tall trees; the site provided a panoramic vista across a spectacular valley. The patients lived in small cabins clustered around a treatment and administrative building, and Mac led them through a program rooted firmly in the principles of Alcoholics Anonymous:

> Our program was strictly based on AA's Twelve Steps, but it wasn't a high-powered facility like Hazelden, the granddaddy of them all. We ran the treatment center like a mom-and-pop place. My wife is cooking lunch and dinner seven days a week, doing housekeeping, and working with families. I'm cooking breakfast and running the program.

Mac was encouraged by Stan's attitude on arrival:

> Before he even came to us, he had made up his mind that he wasn't going to drink anymore. He came to The ARK trying to find a rcinforcement for that decision, a voluntary decision. Without a doubt, the fact that his wife was forcing him to go to Hazelden was instrumental in his refusal to accept what they were giving him.
>
> He wasn't that open and receptive to things. But he and I struck up a personal relationship, which I think he needed. It was very difficult for him to be close to people, because of a fear of being hurt.
>
> And he felt a tremendous amount of guilt in so many areas. I think one of the reasons he and I hit it off was that we shared that. He'd say, "Mac, you should have been born Jewish. You've got five thousand years of guilt and persecution built in." And we had both struggled hard with addiction; that was another tie.

Stan left The ARK with a solid commitment to return, primarily because the strong bond he had established with Mac.

He also left with a strengthened resolve to continue his battle for sobriety and began attending at least one AA meeting every day in the Bay area. He remained sober for days at a time, then weeks, then months.

Soon after he returned to the Marina from The ARK, Stan was invited to participate in a December 4, 1982, concert that was part of a series called "Young Artists in Performance at the White House." He and Dizzy Gillespie were asked to introduce protégés who deserved wider recognition; the performance was scheduled for a nationwide PBS-TV broadcast on December 21. This was the first time young jazz artists were featured in the series, which had previously spotlighted classical musicians. Jane Walsh remembered:

> Dizzy Gillespie was bringing Jon Faddis, and Stan goes, "Who shall I bring?" He says, "Listen to this tape and tell me what you think."
>
> Diane Schuur had sent a tape to our apartment and Stan said, "She's good. She's never done anything significant, and she's up in Seattle." I listened to her and I only had to hear thirty bars and I just said, "That's it. We're taking her." We got it together and she came down and stayed at our place, and then we went to Washington.

> With her blindness, she's so independent. I mean, "I can get my
> own cab and I can get my own room and I can dial my own
> phone." She has a lot of guts. And she can sing; she's phenomenal.
> Stan invited thirty people from San Francisco, including Andy
> Geiger. We had a wonderful time.

After Nancy Reagan made the introductions in the absence of her husband, who was traveling in South America, she sat down in the front row
next to George and Barbara Bush and turned the proceedings over to the
evening's master of ceremonies, the classical violin virtuoso Itzhak
Perlman.

Perlman began by making condescending statements about jazz as a
folk inspiration for classical composers and then presented Stan and
Dizzy; they led off with Dizzy's "Groovin' High" backed by the all-star
rhythm section of Chick Corea, Roy Haynes, and Miroslav Vitous. After
Stan told a surprised and delighted Corea that he was "the finest musician
who ever came out of any of the bands I put together," Corea, Haynes,
and Vitous performed a brilliant medley of an unnamed free-jazz piece,
the ballad "Autumn Leaves," and Thelonious Monk's "Rhythm-a-ning."

Then Stan introduced Diane, who wore a full-sleeved shimmering blue
dress and looked a decade younger than her twenty-nine years. As Stan
beamed at her from the crook of the piano, she accompanied herself on
the instrument and sang "Life Goes On" and "Love Conquers All" with
mesmerizing power.

Stan did a short set with his own quartet and Perlman brought on Dizzy
and his protégé, trumpeter Jon Faddis, who almost outdid his mentor with
his scintillating improvisations. Perlman joined everyone for the finale,
"Summertime," and Diane ended the number with some inspired scatting. As the applause filled the room, Nancy Reagan stepped forward and
embraced Diane, who has vivid memories of the incident:

> All of a sudden I feel these arms go around me and this really
> strong, fragrant perfume, and I'm thinking, "Who is this person?"
> Especially in the White House. And I said, "Who are you?" And
> she said, "Nancy Reagan."

The First Lady was genuinely moved by Diane's performance; she took
her on a personal tour of the White House and invited her back eighteen
months later to perform at a luncheon she gave for the "Ladies of the
Senate."

Jane had won an invitation for herself and Stan to meet with Mrs.

Reagan in the living quarters of the White House on the day following the concert; they looked forward to chatting with her about jazz, and Jane hoped that Nancy would give them the names and phone numbers of potential donors to the Stanford jazz program. As Jane recalled, it was not a fruitful meeting:

> She loved Stan. She was crazy about him, and she was crazy about his music. Stan and I sat down across from her and they chit-chatted a little, and Stan was very nervous. He'd be fine with a bunch of musicians, but he didn't have the presence to speak in these kinds of situations.
>
> What amazed me was, we talked about drugs, and she said, "I don't understand why anybody would take drugs." She didn't understand that they need it because they have a hole in their soul. . . . they're looking for something to make it all right. She doesn't understand that it's a compulsion. She thinks it is all a choice kind of thing. This woman heads the whole country's antidrug crusade.
>
> I went to Stan, "Let's go, let's get out of here. Because it's a wall; we're not going to communicate." And we left. . . .
>
> She gave us no phone numbers.

Larry Rosen, a producer and executive at GRP Records, was blown away by Diane's performance when he saw the PBS broadcast on December 21:

> I just happened to be watching the show that night and I flipped. Wow, this is incredible. This is simply amazing. The next day I called Stan Getz and said, "Who is this Diane Schuur? How do I get in touch with her?"

Stan sensed a good business opportunity and began negotiations to sign Diane simultaneously to a production company he had organized and to GRP.

One of Stan and Jane's primary 1983 New Year's resolutions was to move from the Marina to the Stanford area. Stan had been seduced by the academic lifestyle, and their new friends at the university strongly encouraged them to relocate. The two of them worked intensively with brokers, and after a few weeks they found a house to rent in Portola Valley, roughly six miles southwest of the campus. An apartment had been built above the garage there, and they invited David and Lena, who was eight months pregnant with her first child, to take it; occupancy was set for late February.

Jack Whittemore was working closely with Wim Wigt on a European/Saudi Arabian tour starring Stan and Chet Baker when the agent died suddenly of a cerebral hemorrhage at age sixty-nine on January 19, 1983. Stan performed at a New York memorial service for him on February 6 along with Hank Jones, McCoy Tyner, Phil Woods, George Wein, and Sonny Fortune. As he told a *New York Post* writer, his sense of loss was great:

> How do you say it? He was my agent, my manager, my friend, confidant, brother, father. So much. He stuck with me when I most needed him. . . . Jack proved himself a true friend. The best in the world.

Stan worked at Fat Tuesday's during the week before the memorial, and one night Monica came into the club and introduced him to an important new associate of hers, Dr. Sune Byren. Monica had met Byren the previous year when she started to mount a campaign against addiction in her native Sweden, where alcoholism was particularly widespread.

Following studies at Hazelden, Rutgers University, and elsewhere, she offered to work as a volunteer for the Swedish government but was stymied by its bureaucracy. She then offered her services to SAS, the Scandinavian airline, in a letter written to its CEO during the spring of 1982. He passed it on to Byren, who was the company's chief physician and who had been personally scarred by alcoholism because his daughter was afflicted with the disease.

Byren was intrigued by Monica's approach and that summer accepted her invitation to join her for a visit to Hazelden. He believed that the techniques that he saw there were more effective than anything being used in Sweden, and his convictions were reinforced when his daughter successfully completed a treatment program at Hazelden in November of 1982. At the time of the Whittemore service, he and Monica were proceeding with plans to form a nonprofit corporation, the Swedish Council on Alcoholism and Addiction (SCAA), to nurture the creation in Sweden of treatment centers modeled on Hazelden.

On February 7, 1983, the morning following the memorial service, Stan and Jane took off with Victor Lewis, George Mraz, and pianist Gil Goldstein for Holland and a rendezvous with Chet Baker. Goldstein was filling in for McNeely, who joined the six-week tour ten days later.

Jane remembered that she was deeply concerned about traveling with Baker, whose youthful gifts had been all but dissipated because of his voracious appetite for heroin, other hard drugs, and liquor:

> I said to Stan, "This is a precarious thing. You're just starting out on your sobriety. You've just begun at the university. You're going to be a professor. Your sobriety is shaky, and Chet is crazy and is going to be drinking and drugging."
>
> So we told Wim Wigt, "We'll do the tour, but we won't room with this guy. Don't put him on the same plane with us. We don't want to go through customs with him."

Wigt acquiesced, but the pressures on Stan's sobriety built quickly: Drugs and booze were everywhere backstage, and since Baker missed half of the gigs, Stan had to carry an extra performing load. By the second week of the tour, Stan had succumbed to temptation and was using both alcohol and cocaine.

Despite the chaos, the men managed to make decent music together—as evidenced by the recording of a February 18 Stockholm concert released as *Line for Lyons*. Stan's playing was the more forceful and expressive throughout, but Baker showed that he could still touch the heart by sculpting choruses out of pure melancholy on "My Funny Valentine" and "Stella by Starlight." Stan brought the audience to its feet with a touching rendition of the lullaby "Dear Old Stockholm," and he and Baker left their listeners calling for more when, without the aid of a rhythm section, they ended the performance by spinning out fascinating contrapuntal lines on the title tune.

Following a February 24 Paris concert that Baker missed, Stan was forced to fly to Saudi Arabia in the same plane with him because of the paucity of flights between there and France. They were traveling at the invitation of a cultural committee of Westerners—headed by the American, Swiss, and Norwegian ambassadors—who had organized two concerts in three days at a sports palace in the port city of Jiddah. They faced a difficult situation on arrival, as Jane remembered:

> Stan and Chet and I stay at the U.S. ambassador's home. Stan's scared to death to go to the country, changes his ID from Jewish to Protestant. The ambassador's home is a phenomenal place, Malaysian servants all over. We're going to have dinner at this long table, just he and Chet and Stan and me.
>
> Chet has taken heroin into Saudi Arabia. The boys on the

plane told me he was trying to give it to the bass player in the bathroom. I look over and Chet's face is on the dining room table; he's nodded out.

I immediately called Wigt and said, "You better meet us in Paris tomorrow. Either he goes home or we go home." And he dismissed Chet from the tour. Wigt did lose a lot of money, but enough's enough. Chet showed up (at the next concert), but the guards escorted him off.

Stan and Jane moved into the Portola Valley house immediately on returning to California after the tour ended on March 23. They were greeted there by David and Lena and their month-old son, Daniel, who had moved into the garage apartment in mid-March.

The Geigers, the Dements, and the Oliveiras saw Stan and Jane frequently after the move. Pat Dement remembered:

> It was at least weekly and usually more than weekly that we had dinner at somebody's house. If it was at their house, we would order in Chinese. . . . Everyone considered him a great cheapskate. Jane was embarrassed and did what she could to make sure he paid his share.

Their friends also remembered their noisy arguments when their tempers erupted unexpectedly. Jane recalled:

> I was blunt and outspoken, and often, when I criticized him, he would come back yelling. It didn't matter where we were. But it was just words. He could be verbally abusive but not physically abusive. He never tried to lay a finger on me.

As Stan renewed his battle with his addictions in the Stanford setting, he was subjected to additional emotional pressures as Monica began in earnest a long, bruising, expensive battle against the divorce. He had to deal with claims and counterclaims, depositions, discovery proceedings, petitions for support, and pretrial hearings as the case wended its Dickensian way through the American legal labyrinth.

He was sober again when he played a benefit for The ARK on April 27, 1983, in Colorado Springs; he was joined on stage by guitarist Johnny Smith, who had recorded the hit "Moonlight in Vermont" with him in 1952 and who had settled in Colorado Springs, where he owned a music store. Stan talked to a reporter about Smith and The ARK:

I saw Johnny here about four or five months ago. I love him. He's a real gentleman, righteous—he's a lovely man. We used to jam all the time when he lived in New York. That's how "Moonlight in Vermont" came about. . . .

The ARK is a marvelous place. That's why I'm doing the benefit. . . . It's very individualized, very homey, non-pressure—not like an institution at all. In a hospital, they can dry you out. But you have to learn about alcoholism—what it is—an incurable disease. . . . Once you know this, you treat it as such, a disease, and you know it's not for you. That's it.

Stan's recovery followed a bumpy road as he indulged again on July 24, when he played a concert at the Robert Mondavi Winery in California's Napa Valley. Bob Getz, who had moved to California, produced a videotape of the event, which was issued as *Vintage Getz, Volumes 1 and 2*. The brothers had been out of touch for several years when Jane invited Bob and his wife Pat to celebrate Thanksgiving with her and Stan the previous autumn, and their warm reunion led to the collaboration at Mondavi's. Bob remembered the concert:

I saw firsthand how difficult it was for him to stay sober, because in this beautiful setting, under this wonderful sky, up came these people from San Francisco. All these affluent friends of his bringing him these little gifts so that by intermission he was stoned on coke.

Stan may have been stoned, but on the videotape he appears steady and in control as his blue eyes burn in concentration when he plays. He opened the concert with three quirky Jim McNeely tunes. As Jim remembered, Stan preferred his knottier compositions:

I brought easier tunes in; those are the ones he'd reject. He'd eat up the more involved ones. We'd rehearse a tune a few times, and I'd see he was getting into it.

The two-hour concert took place on the sixty-ninth anniversary of the birth of Stan's father, and he dedicated the event to Al before launching into the fourth number, a soulful performance of Billy Strayhorn's "Lush Life."

Marc Johnson was inspired throughout the concert as he backed Stan with fat, soulful runs and soloed brilliantly on "Tempus Fugit," McNeely's samba "On the Up and Up," and a blues. The audience was with Stan all evening long, and they responded with particular enthusiasm to a gorgeous reading of "Spring Can Really Hang You Up The Most" and to the searing finale, Strayhorn's "Blood Count."

The following week Stan interrupted his second Stanford Summer Jazz Workshop to perform at another Napa Valley vineyard, Paul Masson's. This concert was videotaped and was released in Great Britain as *Harvest Jam*; Bob Getz was not involved.

For a second time Stan's only workshop failure was a lecture—a talk entitled "Jazz Then and Now." Even after hours of preparation with Ted Gioia, a management consultant, pianist, and writer who lectured on jazz at Stanford, he was woefully inarticulate.

Stan's friends at the university were sufficiently encouraged by his participation in the workshops to form a Committee for Jazz at Stanford to lobby the classically oriented Music Department for an expanded jazz curriculum involving him. The workshops were freestanding creations of Jim Nadel and had no official status within the department, whose involvement with jazz was limited to lectures by him, Gioia, and one or two others.

In addition to the Dements, the Geigers, and the Oliveiras, the committee's core group included Gioia and a real estate executive, Ryland Kelley, and his wife, Shirley; Bill Dement became its chairman. The committee made little headway because the department was strapped for cash and contained no leaders who were passionate about jazz.

Of all his Stanford friends, Stan achieved his deepest rapport with the painter Nate Oliveira. Nate remembered:

> When he came here, he looked at all of us as being stable, having homes, being successful, and he felt he didn't have it. It wasn't true. He did have it. He had a different kind of success. His thing was so much more vital and important.
>
> The association with him took me away from a lot of stuff that is academic. Being an academic professor is wonderful, but it's pretty much straightlaced. Meeting Stan was like meeting somebody that was vital and creative and from a different part of the world. It was very, very important to me.

Stan was willing to lower his defenses with the burly, down-to-earth artist:

> Stan was an internal kind of guy, and he put up a lot of fronts and protected himself. Every once in a while that would break down. It would break down in funny ways. He loved this house, he loved to come here, he loved to eat here with us.

We laughed a lot. He liked to come here and really laugh. We weren't straitlaced you know. I've got some great photographs of me and Stan in drag.

One time we had a Fourth of July party, and I was doing this stupid thing with a Roman candle, and he was just hysterical. I've never seen anybody laugh as much as he did.

You wouldn't see Stan that way all the time. He was always holding it in. He was an internal kind of guy, and that's what sages are, that's what artists are. He was protecting himself, protecting his identity. He was very fragile, very insecure. He was a terribly insecure guy.

Nate found a kinship with Stan in their art:

When you asked him about his feelings when he played, he would get pissed off and say, "What are you talking about. Getting sentimental. I don't think about those things." But he really did.

When he played, you could almost see him make marks like a drawing, a big painting—an abstract expressionist like Bill de Kooning. Wow. You could just really see it.

I said, "Stan, you know what we do, we color this goddamn world. If we weren't around, people like us, the world would be all gray."

And he said, "God." And he never forgot that; he kept bringing it up to me all the time. "You know that is really the most important thing, Nate. We really do color this world."

Stan came east with Jane in October to play a number of gigs and to sign up Diane Schuur with his production company and with Larry Rosen and Dave Grusin at GRP Records. Diane was eager to begin recording because her career remained in the doldrums during 1983 despite the success of the White House concert. She remembered:

I was still working in the Northwest doing club dates for a reasonable amount of money, although I was still living off the government. I had to get disability because my work just wasn't enough to pay the bills. That's all there was to it. The career just kind of pooped right along.

On October 30, 1983, before they returned to California, Stan and Jane attended the christening of his granddaughter Katie McGovern, who had been born on July 6 to Beverly and Mike.

During the Christmas holidays, Stan realized that he needed additional help in his struggle with addiction because he found he could only stay sober for weeks at a time. Jane remembered:

> When my mother came for Christmas is when he decided to go to The ARK. I remember that because we took him. He willingly got up one day and said, "I want to go there." It was successful. In the fourth week they have a family program, and I went with Steve and David.

Nicky and Pamela also flew to Colorado for the family sessions. Steve believed that the program was helpful to him because it forced him to deal for the first time with some of the painful aspects of his relationship with his father and with a drinking problem of his own, which had started to become serious. But his three siblings received little benefit. David and Nicky could not initiate meaningful dialogues with their father, and Pamela left quickly because she felt that Stan was abusing her verbally.

Stan, however, did profit from The ARK regiment—in large part because of Mac McFadden.

Mac saw guilt and anger at the heart of Stan's problems:

> I do something wrong that I feel guilty about. And I'm uncomfortable with the guilt, so I get angry. . . . And I put blame out there.
>
> In our recovery we understand that resentment is our number-one offender. It brings more people back to drink than any other offender. Resentment, of course, is reliving an old hurt—over and over again. And out of resentment can come anger and certainly self-pity and fear.
>
> An outward expression of anger isn't a bad thing. It saves you from going insane or committing suicide, or whatever. But when you take a drug that affects the central nervous system, judgment goes out the window, and boom, you're not yourself and out comes something destructive.

And Mac believed that Stan's mother Goldie played a central role in his psychic drama:

> We certainly talked about her quite a lot. He wanted to keep her on this revered, sainted plateau, but deep down there was this

understanding that she certainly was a destructive factor in him losing those precious years of adolescence and growth.

And in adding to his burden of guilt. Remember her making him feel guilty as a kid when he was the only one in the family who had meat for dinner?

And Mac recognized that Stan had in Jane a strong ally in his struggles:

Jane had a better Al-Anon program than Monica. In the end Monica was enabling and just feeding into Stan's addiction. Jane, being a recovering person herself, really knew what she could do and couldn't do. She certainly couldn't get him sober, and she didn't want to threaten her own sobriety. So she knew both ways. She handled herself a lot better than most people would.

Stan emerged from The ARK on January 24, 1984, with renewed strength to combat his addictions.

Monica was fighting addictions in her own way, as she and Sune Byren convened in Stockholm on May 12 the first SCAA conference on alcoholism. The Queen of Sweden opened the conclave, which was called "Focus on Recovery" and which generated sufficient support to start the first Hazelden-style centers in Sweden.

Stan had completed more than six consecutive months of sobriety when he began to prepare for his third Stanford Summer Jazz Workshop. Jim Nadel, emboldened by the success of Stan's two previous summer stints, planned an ambitious program for 1984. He had recruited Dizzy Gillespie to teach alongside Stan during both weeks of the workshop, and he scheduled a gala concert for Sunday, August 5, at which Dizzy would perform with Stan and the quartet. The president of Stanford was slated to make a welcoming speech and the entire event was to be recorded commercially. Jane and Stan, the Dements, and the Oliveiras planned a buffet supper for fifty guests following the concert.

Dizzy, who was both extremely articulate and amusing, gave a lecture on August 2, and Stan attended to get some pointers; he was scheduled to speak a week later, and he wished to improve on his failures of the previous two years. Dizzy handled himself so well that Stan became totally unnerved and left soon after the midpoint of the talk.

Fear flooded his psyche; he felt incapable not only of lecturing, but of holding his own in the concert with Dizzy. He brooded morosely during the next two days as pain and anger raged inside him. He began drinking again the night of Saturday, August 4, while visiting George Mraz and a graduate student at a rented home. His anger exploded and he began to trash the house, ripping paintings from the walls and slashing them and throwing a microwave oven through a window.

He had found a gun and threatened Mraz with it, and Mraz located a telephone in a remote part of the house and asked Joey Oliveira, Nate's son, to come and rescue him and the graduate student. Joey drove over and sat with the motor running as the two of them raced from the house and jumped into the car and safety. Stan made it to a local Holiday Inn, where he continued to binge. He never showed up for the concert the next night or for the party he was supposed to cohost.

A pall hung over the postconcert buffet as the Oliveiras, the Dements, and the Geigers consoled Jane while various Stanford dignitaries joined Dizzy, John Handy (a saxophonist who had been hurriedly recruited to take Stan's place), and Stan's musicians as they picked at the food.

Stan left Palo Alto and Jane lost track of him, but she suspected that he was holed up in San Francisco. She asked Steve to help her find him, and Stan's son flew out from New York; after a three-day search, he located his father at the Hyatt Hotel on August 14. Stan had been drinking nonstop for ten days and was in terrible physical shape. He ranted at Steve, blaming everyone but himself for his condition.

Steve understood that he could not reason with Stan. He told him that he was heading for the home of Stan's AA sponsor to spend the night and suggested that Stan meet him there the next day. To Steve's great surprise, Stan showed up; he was still drinking.

Steve and the sponsor reminded Stan that he had contracted to play with the quartet at a thirtieth-anniversary Newport Jazz Festival concert in Rhode Island in two days, and as the seriousness of this commitment penetrated his alcoholic fog, he decided to sober up. They somehow got Stan in shape to board the plane the next day, and he made it to Rhode Island.

He played creditably, although he looked ravaged. Jane remembered that he called her when he became fully sober:

> He said, "We need to get back together."
> And I answered, "If you ever want to see me again, you'll get off that plane from Rhode Island, and I'll be there with your sponsor from AA. We have to do therapy together and you have to go to AA, or I'm out of here."
> He said, "Okay."

When Jane and the sponsor met Stan at the airport on the afternoon of August 25, 1984, he was in a state of near collapse, but she rallied him to fulfill a long-held commitment—to perform at the wedding reception of the Dements' daughter Cathy in the backyard of their home. The band, which included Jim Nadel and Joey Oliveira on saxophones, was performing when Stan arrived. He was heard before he was seen as he walked in from the side of the house. Bill Dement remembered:

> This band was playing, and all of a sudden I heard him. He wasn't on the bandstand. My image is like golden leaves just sort of starting to drift down, because he was playing a ballad. Jesus, it was beautiful.

Stan dedicated the next number, "Lush Life," to the bride and groom. He raised his arm to give the downbeat, stopped, and returned to the microphone to say, "There's more than one meaning to the word *lush*, you know." He played that song and several others beautifully, and then Jane and the sponsor took him home. He slept there alone, because Jane had moved out.

The next day, Bill Dement had him admitted to the detox unit of the Stanford hospital. Stan was surprised when his Stanford friends rallied around and visited him there. He expected to be despised and rejected after he had let them down so badly. As Jane remembered, their support affected him deeply:

> It was a huge turning point, just huge. It was the biggest one of his life. All these Stanford and AA people came over. .
>
> These people were high profile. They were already tremendously accomplished in their own right. They didn't need anything from Stan. They admired his creativity and his sensitivity. They wanted to be friends, and they're smart. They loved him. But they made it clear that they weren't going to tolerate his crazy stuff again—where you insult the president of the university and don't show up for a concert. They were serious people.

Bill Dement, Andy Geiger, and Nate Oliveira frequently accompanied Stan to AA meetings, which he attended at least once every day. By early October he convinced Jane that his recommitment to sobriety was serious, and they moved in together again, renting a three-story town house in Menlo Park, just north of the Stanford campus.

They were disappointed a few weeks later when Lena Getz, pregnant with her second child and homesick, convinced her husband David that they should leave California for her native Sweden. Lena, David, and their young son Daniel departed on October 26 and settled in Malmö, where Stan's granddaughter, Jennifer, was born on February 8, 1985.

In November 1984 Elektra Musician Records issued the duet album that Stan and Albert Dailey had recorded the day in January 1980 when Myrtle Ann Franklin burst into the Shadowbrook studio to reveal that Monica had been secretly dosing Stan with Antabuse. Sadly, the LP, which was called *Poetry*, was released four months after Dailey's untimely death on June 26, 1984, at age forty-six; he was one of the early victims of the AIDS epidemic.

Stan and Dailey were mutually inspired that January afternoon as they slashed and burned their way through up-tempo numbers like Gillespie's "Night in Tunisia" and Parker's "Confirmation" and created almost unbearably poignant readings of ballads such as "A Child Is Born" and "Spring Can Really Hang You Up the Most." Pete Welding's review in *Down Beat* aptly describes the richness of their collaboration.

> The pair explore a program of five modern jazz classics and two standard ballads with taste, elegance, and a stunning interactivity of purposeful, focused invention that makes the duets bristle with plentiful life and keening beauty. Over Dailey's firm, prodding, ever helpful support, spare yet telling, Getz sings and jabs and tears into these pieces, revealing the beauty and easy power that always have been at the heart of his music. Dailey responds in kind, playing with a tensile, craggy strength and focused linearity that contrast well with Getz' more luxuriantly romantic approach. In tandem, the two produced performances that are absolutely gripping in their flowing, confident mastery. They should be heard and savored time and again.

Stan had become so strongly involved with his AA program that he tried to convert Diane Schuur to sobriety when she visited him and Jane in late 1984. She recalled:

> I noticed that he wasn't drinking. I thought, well, this is very different. And he gave me a book—AA doesn't want me to mention its name—that talked about alcoholism and the disease. And he suggested, "Diane, you might find this very interesting." Of course I was very much into denial of my own alcoholism at the time, but I read it from cover to cover. And thought, "Hmm, very interesting. Sure. It applied to him, but not to me."
>
> I'd spend some time with him and Jane at his house, you know.

And here I'd be drinking white wine and all of this kind of stuff, and he just had Perrier or whatever. And so I just thank God that he was able to be in my life.

Dave Grusin and Larry Rosen of GRP Records brought Stan and Diane together in a Seattle studio on December 6 for her debut album, scheduling her first recording session in her hometown to make her feel at ease. They provided Diane with a set of excellent arrangements and called the album *Deedles*, her childhood nickname; Grusin plays keyboards on every track.

The program is highly varied—ranging from show tunes to Jackson Browne to Duke Ellington to Billy Joel to gospel—but Diane's talent is strong enough to stamp her exuberant musical personality on all of it. She shows superb control throughout her four-octave range and, as the circumstances demand, moves easily from creamy smoothness to earthy funk to keening gospel shouts. She reaches an emotional peak on the album's final track, the hymn "Amazing Grace," where her pure, soaring tones limn a message of hope.

Stan accompanies her lovingly on two tunes, Joel's "New York State of Mind" and the ballad standard "I'm Just Foolin' Myself"; they swing hard on the former and glide happily through the latter. Diane was delighted to have Stan working with her and acknowledged her debt to him in the liner notes:

> I would like to dedicate this album to Stan Getz for being my mentor and my friend, and for all his encouragement. His appearance on this album makes the circle complete.

Deedles sold well, shooting to the top of *Billboard*'s jazz charts soon after its release in the summer of 1985 and staying there for five weeks; in addition, it became a freak hit in the Soviet Union, where it sold an unprecedented fifty thousand copies. It achieved critical success in the jazz press and in broad-circulation magazines such as *People* and launched Diane as a jazz-pop star.

As she remembered, her rendition of "Amazing Grace" from the album helped Stan through one of the crises of his addiction struggle:

> He called me on the phone and he was extremely depressed. Sounded almost suicidal. And he said, "Deeds, I don't know if I'm going to make it." And I said, "Well, just keep the faith." I tried to fortify his courage. And "Amazing Grace," my version,

was playing in the background. And the song ended and we were both listening, and he says, "I think I'm going to make it now."

"Amazing Grace" did not help him through his next crisis during Christmas week, as Jane recalled:

> Some guy Stan had met at an electronics store shows up to set up a stereo system. My mother had come again for Christmas. This electronics guy has a Swedish masseuse with him. She says, "I'm going to give Stan a massage," and they go upstairs into the bedroom for I don't know how long. A long time.
>
> He comes downstairs, and I was pretty upset. I was highly suspicious that something was going on. We had a couple of words in the dining room, and he goes right over to the bar and has a drink and proceeds to get plastered. That ended four months of sobriety.
>
> He leaves the house, and he comes back late and locks himself in the bedroom and perpetually drinks. My mother stayed in the house with Stan, and I moved over to the Geigers for about ten days.

Stan had lapsed for the third time since his first visit to The ARK two years before, but as Jane remembered, he convinced her that his resolve remained strong:

> He called me up and said, "I had a slip. I'm sorry. I need to try this again." I went back with him, and he went back to the program. After that short slip was when he really started to embrace the program.
>
> He really buckled down. He'd call his sponsor; he'd go out to dinner with the guys; he'd go to meetings. He started to get a lot of pride about it. In January we got another house about six blocks from where we were living before. Beautiful little house.

On March 24, 1985, Stan heard that Zoot Sims had become the second of the original Four Brothers to die when he succumbed to liver cancer on the previous day; Serge Chaloff had preceded him by almost twenty-eight years. Zoot's condition was diagnosed as inoperable during the summer of 1984, but he went down swinging and continued to play until six weeks before he died. During his final days he greeted his physician every morning by saying, "You're looking better today, Doc."

Zoot was forced to scuffle hard for a couple of decades following his departure from the Second Herd, but his career blossomed after 1970 as he led successful quartets on his own and quintets with fellow Brother Al Cohn. Stan loved Zoot's swinging lyricism, and he jammed with him many times over the years; he remembered most fondly their joyous reunion at Woody Herman's fortieth-anniversary celebration in 1976 and their final collaboration in June 1982, a concert tribute to Lester Young that included Al Cohn.

Stan flew down to Hollywood on April 12 to perform on a second Diane Schuur album, *Schuur Thing*. It was aimed at a broader market than *Deedles* and spotlighted, in addition to Stan, the pop stars José Feliciano and Lee Ritenour. Stan plays on two numbers; he enlivens an uninteresting ballad, "Love Dance," with a short, inspired solo, and he romps with Diane through a hot version of Ellington's "It Don't Mean a Thing (If It Ain't Got That Swing)," which features two choruses where they trade four-bar scat and sax improvisations.

Schuur Thing was released only four months after *Deedles*, and, with substantial sales, it built on the momentum established by the earlier album and solidified Diane's status as a star.

Steve Getz acknowledged his alcoholism after several years of denial and entered The ARK for four weeks of therapy early in July. Stan participated in the family program, where both men faced awkward truths about their relationship and became closer than ever before.

Stan attempted to build on the rapport they had achieved by inviting Steve to join his group during an August 1985 engagement at the Club Med in Gesher Haziv, Israel. During Steve's previous employment by his father in South America in 1976, he had shared percussion duties with Billy Hart; this time he would be the only drummer.

The Club Med engagement was the fourth one arranged by Bernie Pollack for Stan, and it followed their previously established formula; the performers would not be paid but would be given a free holiday for themselves and several guests. Stan and Jane brought with them the Geigers and Stan's lawyer, Elliott Hoffman, and Elliott's wife, Nancy.

Pollack arranged for Stan and his people to divide their time between the resort, which occupies a beautiful Mediterranean beach just two miles south of the Lebanon border, and a kibbutz, or communal farm, across the road. They sampled kibbutz life during the day, came over to the club to swim and to perform in the evenings, and returned to the kibbutz to sleep. Geiger, Hoffman, and Pollack were amateur sax players; they were overjoyed when Stan allowed them to sit in on a couple of occasions and tolerated their efforts with good humor. One Friday evening they celebrated the sabbath at the kibbutz and Stan played the Jewish lament, "Eli, Eli," with such feeling that he reduced himself, the Geigers, and several others to tears.

Steve remembers the Israel sojourn as one of the happiest times he ever spent with his father. They had buried several old hurts at The ARK and were at ease with each other, they were both sober, and they performed together with gusto. Steve learned a great deal because Stan did not compromise his music for him and forced him to master a number of difficult tempos.

Stan and his people left the kibbutz for Jerusalem, where the quartet gave a benefit concert for the crippled children's hospital that Stan had aided in a 1977 performance. They also met with mayor Teddy Kollek, heard the Israeli Philharmonic under the baton of Leonard Bernstein, and schmoozed with Bernstein backstage. They ended the trip at another Club Med resort in the Red Sea town of Elath; Stan amused everyone on their final night when he played David Ben-Gurion (a nonspeaking role) in a historical pageant.

When they returned, Jane flew back to the West Coast but Stan stayed at the Hoffmans' apartment in Manhattan because he was slated to record in a New York studio with a quartet on September 4, 1985. He felt depressed and devoid of inspiration at the session and called it off after two numbers. He walked out and headed for Bradley's jazz club in Greenwich Village and got drunk—breaking nine months of sobriety. He returned, forlorn and embarrassed, to the Hoffmans' the next day.

He never drank nor drugged again. Perhaps it was Jane; or Mac and The ARK; or his Stanford friends. Perhaps, as the AA saying goes, he "got sick and tired of being sick and tired." It could have been all of the above, or none of them. The fact is . . . he had achieved sobriety at last.

TRIALS NINETEEN

STAN FLEW HOME from New York on September 8 and three days later played an engagement set up for him by Bill Dement. The World Business Forum, an association of corporate leaders from the Bay area, had asked Dement to provide education and entertainment for an afternoon and evening of jazz at the Stanford Faculty Club, and he arranged for Andy Geiger to speak about jazz history and structure, for Jim Nadel's group to play during the cocktail hour, and for Stan's quartet to perform a concert following dinner.

Stan and the Dements met at the party Johann and Joann Blokker, jazz fans and major contributors to Stanford causes. Johann, a wealthy investment banker, had became entranced with the music while working as a teenager for the anti-Nazi underground in his native Holland during

World War II; he had stripped a radio from a downed British bomber and had listened clandestinely to BBC broadcasts of Armstrong, Herman, Goodman, Basie, and other 1940s luminaries. He owned a vast record collection, could hum every major jazz solo from Jelly Roll Morton to Ornette Coleman, and loved Stan's music. Joann, a Stanford alumna, shared her husband's musical enthusiasms.

A couple of days after the dinner party, Stan and Dement ran into Johann on a plane heading for southern California, and Stan struck up a conversation with him. Blokker remembered:

> I started talking to him, and we agreed that we needed to get together. Soon after, Jane, Stan, Joann, and I went out for dinner. And his dog was in the car. James, the dog.
>
> I talked about jazz music and found that Stan and I had the same favorites, Lester Young and those kind of guys. A lot of jazz fans really don't know what's good or what's not good, but Stan and I had the same prejudices and the same favorites. This is how we got to know each other.

When Stan told Dement about his dinner with the Blokkers, Dement sensed that the couple could become major allies of the Committee for Jazz in its efforts to make the music an important part of Stanford's curriculum. The Music Department had made it clear that the committee would have to generate on its own all the resources for a jazz program; the university would not put up a dime. Andy Geiger recalled:

> We felt that Stan was a giant, that there was terrific value to the university in having Stan as part of the faculty.
>
> But there was huge competition for the dollars that were available. A lot of programs exist at universities because somebody has gone out and gotten the money for them. That's what we needed to do. We weren't going to walk over to the provost and say, "You need to put $178,000 in a jazz program because we've got Stan Getz."
>
> Universities like Indiana and North Texas State with strong jazz programs are enrollment-driven. They're going to compete to enroll students who are talented performers.
>
> Stanford was not going to recruit gifted jazz players. It's not that kind of a place. They had a lot of kids who wanted to play jazz—to have the experience in college, then go off to be stock brokers or doctors or lawyers. The Music Department at Stanford was not performance driven; it was academically driven.

The Dements, Geigers, Oliveiras, and Kelleys got together and decided that Bill Dement should approach the Blokkers directly for the money to get the Stanford jazz program off the ground.

Dement called Johann and was sufficiently encouraged by his response to arrange immediately a breakfast meeting with him and Dr. Albert Cohen, chairman of the Music Department and a scholar of the baroque period. Dement made a strong pitch for a program with an emphasis on performance and with Stan as its centerpiece, and when Cohen offered his cooperation, Blokker requested that the Music Department send him a written proposal within a week.

Cohen, with the aid of Nadel and Gioia, met the deadline; their document stated that for roughly $100,000 a year the university could bring Stan on to teach performance and could also beef up the academic curriculum by expanding Nadel's and Gioia's roles as lecturers and by adding the jazz historian Grover Sales to the faculty.

While Blokker and Cohen were refining the concept, Stan came to Cohen and told him that he was terrible at lecturing and feared he would be a failure in a straight professorial role. Cohen countered with the idea that Stan be an "artist-in-residence" rather than a professor, and that he teach mainly by showing with his saxophone how to play jazz. Stan liked the idea, and Blokker bought into it, too.

Blokker did not want to be the only major contributor to the jazz program, and he obtained from Cohen a promise that the university would make a strong effort to bring in significant other monies. He then pledged $100,000 for a 1986 pilot program and sent his first check to the university in December. Soon after, he spoke to a reporter about his motivations:

> I have always regretted that so many jazz musicians have to live in kind of a sewer—in an environment that is not conducive to a healthy life. Society should award jazz a higher respect than it has. We want to make the Stanford jazz program the best in the United States and give the music the respect it deserves.

Stan was appointed artist-in-residence on January 1, 1986, and he committed himself to teach six hours per week, to perform four concerts a year with his quartet and selected guest artists, and to involve his musicians and the guests in student workshops.

He took an annual stipend of $40,000, which supplemented the $300,000 per year he was earning from personal appearances and record royalties. He needed every penny he could get because his seemingly endless, grinding divorce proceedings were absorbing more than half his

income and disrupting his schedule with time-consuming legal confer-
ences on both coasts.

Stan taught by critiquing the performances of the musicians in Stanford's two big bands and seven small groups, by playing with them, and
by giving master classes for the more advanced students. As he told a
reporter, he relied mainly on his horn:

> I don't consider myself a music teacher. I'm not integrated in the
> curriculum. I'm an artist-in-residence.
>
> In the last analysis, it doesn't mean anything more than playing
> with them. And that's the only thing I can do: to play and to talk
> a little, like I talk with my own rhythm section. And I think that's
> actually the same way I learned it. I went to school on the road.
> I played with musicians more developed than I was. . . .
>
> (The students) want to get right up there and play without
> knowing the language—the chord changes and the scales. They
> stand up there and move their shoulders and emote, but they
> don't know the grammar and syntax of the jazz language, so they
> can't converse spontaneously. When they can do that, they'll be
> improvising. . . . Jazz music is a marvelous thing. It allows you to
> express how you feel at the moment. It's like conversation on
> the stage. . . .
>
> What I try to teach them is that 25% of jazz consists of starting
> at the right time and finishing at the right time. Another 25% is
> just to have the guts to play. The most important thing is to give
> them self-confidence. . . .
>
> I'm a strong opponent of imitation. I always tell them that they
> have to be themselves. That's hard, because they don't believe in
> themselves, they believe in their heroes. And I will tell them:
> that's perfectly all right, but your hero is the only one who can
> play that way. If you want to try and do the same thing, it will
> only be an imitation, however perfectly you will do it. I keep on
> trying to convince them that they have to play what they feel
> themselves. But that's not easy.

And he hoped that he could convey to his students his love for jazz:

> When I got this saxophone, it became a religion. There wasn't
> TV, there wasn't much money, and there was just a real dedica-
> tion. . . . I never thought of it as an art. It was just work that I
> loved. Not just work, but work that I loved. I loved it so much,

I would play it if nobody listened to it. Any jazz musician, if there's nobody around to listen, would play just for the sheer joy of improvising music.

For all his dedication, Stan had a serious failing as a teacher: He concentrated almost all of his efforts on the students he felt comfortable with, the highly talented ones, and gave very little help to the others. Of the few who benefited from his largesse, Larry Grenadier has made the greatest strides as a professional; by the mid-1990s, he had found his way to the upper echelon of jazz bass players.

Grenadier was only sixteen when he first studied with Stan at the 1983 Summer Jazz Workshop. He was so good that the following summer, when Stan's bassist George Mraz could not play because of tendinitis in his arm, Stan felt comfortable having Grenadier substitute for him. When Grenadier matriculated at a college in nearby San Jose in 1985, Stan, Jim Nadel, and the Committee for Jazz lobbied with Stanford's admissions office and won him acceptance as a transfer student by mid-year.

Grenadier was helped significantly by Mraz and the other high-level professionals whom Stan attracted to Stanford, and he found Stan's oblique teaching methods of great benefit:

> He would make certain comments after he heard you play, just take you aside and say something—how to play with the drummer, what he looked for in a bass player, how to make it more comfortable for a horn player, stuff like that.
>
> Just listening to him helped a lot. His sound is so unique; it's so rare for people to have that individual sound and make that strong a statement just with their sound. It was so striking; it just hit you over the head. And his timing and rhythm were so strong; he was a master of space and silence.
>
> Playing with him taught me so much faster than being in a class. He would turn around and yell, "You're speeding up," or "You're slowing down." Not in a harsh way, in a fatherly way.
>
> Improvisation is such a hard thing to teach; you can't theorize about it or be abstract about it. You have to get in there and do it over and over again.

Stan's first concert under his Stanford contract took place on March 3, 1986, and he recruited George Mraz, Victor Lewis, and pianist Kenny Barron for it. Jim McNeely's four years as Stan's regular pianist came to an end in late 1984 as he took on other commitments as a performer and writer. In early 1985 Stan started alternating him with Larry Willis, and later in the year he added Barron to the mix.

The concert was a major success, and Barron made an important contribution. Under the headline "Getz Combo Thrills Crowd in Program's First Jazz Concert" the reporter for the local newspaper, *The Peninsula Times Tribune*, wrote:

> The tenor saxophonist and his quartet of superb musicians played to a sold-out house at Dinkelspiel Auditorium to the delight of the Committee for Jazz at Stanford.
>
> Key Committee members Andy Geiger, William Dement, and Ryland Kelley were bounding up and down the aisles at the interval, obviously pleased with both the attendance and the music. . . . The audience listened with an intensity and responsiveness one might expect at a chamber music recital. . . .
>
> Barron easily matched Getz' renowned lyricism and sweeping melodic lines, drawing his most appreciative response from the audience on Billy Strayhorn's "Blood Count" and "Lush Life." Barron never forced his inventiveness, planting effortless gardens of rich, lush chords throughout his thoughtful and melodic single-note solos.

Barron, age forty-two in 1986, already had been a major performer for twenty-five years and had appeared on more than two hundred recordings. As a seventeen-year-old prodigy straight out of high school, he performed, composed, and arranged for an album by the excellent saxophonist Yusef Lateef, and two years later he began a four-year stint as Dizzy Gillespie's pianist. He went on to play with such distinguished musicians as Freddie Hubbard, Ron Carter, Roy Haynes, Joe Henderson, Buddy Rich, and James Moody and to lead several excellent groups of his own. He started teaching theory, harmony, and piano at Rutgers University in 1973 and became a tenured professor there in 1980.

Barron joined Stan, Mraz, and Lewis for a recording session at a studio near the Stanford campus six days after the concert at the Dinkelspiel Auditorium. The resulting album was called *Voyage* and was produced by Berkeley educator and jazz broadcaster Dr. Herb Wong for Blackhawk, a small independent label that he managed.

Barron's presence carries *Voyage* to a higher level of excellence than the three fine quartet albums that Stan recorded for Concord in 1981 and 1982. Barron quickly convinces the listener that Stan had never before found a pianist whose sensibility so felicitously matched his own. The two men show an uncanny empathy based on a shared lyricism and an irresistible sense of swing, and they anticipate each other's moves almost telepathically.

These qualities are exhibited most strongly on two classic 1930s ballads, "I Thought About You" and "Yesterdays," where they move the listener with a joyous swing and a robustly expressed romanticism and on Barron's title tune, where they unfurl surging solos that grow almost organically out of the sophisticated harmonies.

Voyage put Stan's resolve severely to the test because it was the first album he ever made sober. Jane Walsh remembered:

> He got halfway through the session and he called me up and said, "I can't go through with it. I think I'm going to drink."
>
> And I said, "No you're not. You've got a lot of loving friends. You'll be fine." I swear, they really say your faith comes out.
>
> He said, "I'm going to try" and got off the phone and made it through without taking a drink.
>
> It was a strain, because he had this thing about being perfect— "I've got to be perfect; it's got to be perfect." It probably came from his mother.

Herb Wong recalled that the session drained Stan physically:

> He finishes and he's sweating like mad. He says, "Jesus, I'm worn out, worn out by concentrating on everything that's been going on."
>
> I said, "Don't you always do that on a record date?"
>
> Stan says, "This is the first date that my head was completely clear. That's what took so much energy out of me. My head was clear and I was concentrating on everything we were doing. I have never done that before, in over two hundred recordings. This was the first. Before I was either on something or I was drunk."

Stan followed up on the success of his first Stanford concert with excellent events featuring Bob Brookmeyer on April 6 and Diane Schuur on August 10; the Committee for Jazz hosted a festive dinner party after the Schuur concert at the home of the Oliveiras.

On July 16, Stan had played in a Hollywood Bowl concert celebrating Woody Herman's fiftieth anniversary as a bandleader. Stan was alarmed by Woody's physical condition; he was suffering from emphysema and other ailments and was very tired. Because of Woody's health and a paucity of alumni (Stan and Jimmy Rowles were the only old-timers who performed), the event wasn't nearly as festive as the fortieth anniversary concert at Carnegie Hall.

Stan had been preoccupied with legal matters during the spring of 1986, because—after many delays—his divorce trial was finally scheduled to begin on June 16 in White Plains, New York, the seat of the county in which Shadowbrook was located. Eight days before, however, Monica dismissed her lawyer and was granted a ten-week respite to find a new one. When the case came to trial on September 3, 1986, more than five years after Monica had been served with the original summons, she was represented by Abraham Reingold; Stan had retained Jeffrey Cohen.

Monica, as the defendant who was charged with cruel and inhuman treatment, had the right to choose either trial by jury or by judge, and she decided on a jury. Under New York State law, this trial—which would determine whether the couple would remain married—would be followed by another if the jury decided in favor of divorce. The second trial would deal with the disposition of assets and income between the two parties and would be decided by a judge. Shadowbrook was by far the largest asset at issue.

Steve, his son Christopher, and David refused to testify on Stan's behalf despite intense pressure from him; Beverly agreed to be Stan's witness if needed. Pamela Raynor, her husband Scot, and Nicky Getz volunteered to take the witness stand for Monica.

As Cohen was making Monica's secret dosing of Stan with Antabuse from 1969 to 1981 the overriding issue of the trial, Reingold clashed repeatedly with Judge Vincent Gurahian. From the start, Reingold made long speeches challenging the judge's rulings, and Gurahian, believing them to be disruptive and irrelevant, accused him of "trying for some reason to get a mistrial." When Reingold persisted after several warnings, Gurahian became exasperated and declared a mistrial on the sixth day of the proceedings, saying:

> Mr. Reingold, you have succeeded, and I wish you joy in your success. I think you made a great mistake, I really do, but that's your privilege. I'm happy to be rid of the case because for six months there have been attempts and maneuvers to avoid a trial of this case.

Monica takes a different view of Gurahian's actions, believing that he was reacting to strong evidence that her team had uncovered and that he was one of those judges who "just want to give people a divorce and get on with it."

The next development in the case shocked her:

> Now Stan goes—and he is really desperate—and they make up a new complaint. And I almost faint because the new complaint accuses me of adultery. The Mother Teresa of jazz who never ever had an affair with anybody except for Stan.

Stan's attorneys had added the charge of adultery when they found two people who were willing to testify that they had seen Monica and Dr. Sune Byren in compromising situations at Shadowbrook.

On September 19, a week after he returned to California from White Plains, Stan joined Woody Herman and his band to play at a benefit dinner for the Committee for Jazz. The Committee had not adequately promoted the event, which took place at San Francisco's elite Bohemian Club, and it netted a disappointing $1,700. For the second time in two months, Stan was alarmed by Woody's deteriorating physical condition.

Despite the meager return from the event and the university's failure to provide monies to supplement Blokker's, the benefactor was sufficiently pleased with the overall results of the first nine months of Stan's program to pledge $100,000 for a second year.

Three weeks later, on the evening of October 12, Stan performed in his fourth and final 1986 Stanford concert. Earlier in the day he recorded his third album with Diane Schuur in Los Angeles. For the LP, which was called *Timeless*, Stan provided sterling support on three romantic tunes as he blended his horn seamlessly with her voice and contributed two gemlike short solos. GRP had the good sense to team Diane with a group of outstanding big band arrangers for the album, and she showed a new maturity as she rode confidently atop the fresh and muscular backgrounds provided by Johnny Mandel, Sinatra's associate Billy May, Pat Williams, and Percy Lubbock. The collaboration with Stan and the four other veterans resulted in Diane's first Grammy as the Best Female Jazz Vocalist for 1986.

Diane's manager examined her GRP royalty statements soon after the *Timeless* session and concluded that she was being short-changed. Stan's lawyer, Elliot Hoffman, then made his own inquiry into the situation and countered with claims that both Diane and GRP had not met their contractual obligations to Stan. This led to a long legal wrangle whose main effects were to estrange Diane from Stan for three years and to prevent her from recording during that time.

As Stan was opening a five-night stand on November 5 at Yoshi's Club in Oakland, California, he learned that he had been elected to *Down Beat*'s Hall of Fame, an honor that rewards a lifetime of jazz achievement. The sellout crowd gave him a standing ovation when the award was announced, and Stan told them, "This is an unexpected honor. I am thrilled. Believe me." What he said to a Florida reporter two weeks earlier was an appropriate commentary on the source of his career achievement:

> I cannot play a lie. I have to believe in what I play or it won't come out. My expertise is in feeling. Bob Brookmeyer once said of me, I probably have the greatest instinct of any jazz musician he ever knew. Instinct is where it's at.

In January 1987 Stan told Jane that he did not want to live with her anymore. Paradoxically, the sobriety that she had helped him earn had changed his feelings about her. She recalled:

> A lot of people, after they get sober, really become who they're supposed to be. They've shed the million masks they've devised their whole life to survive, and they're really working on getting down to the core of who they truly are, should have always been.
>
> Then maybe you two shouldn't be together. You look up and go, "Oh, my God, who are you?" A lot of people who get sober don't stay together. When he started to get sober, he started pulling away from me.

Billy Hoogstraten saw the process from a different perspective.

> Jane was very instrumental for getting his stuff together. He could depend on Jane. She was like a mother for him. But once he got sober and got more self-confident and independent, there was still Jane playing that mother role and giving him advice on whatever he had to do. Then he couldn't stand it anymore.

Stan's announcement took Jane by surprise; she was hurt and confused, but she decided to go ahead with a gala sixtieth birthday party she was planning for February 2 at the house they were renting. The party lasted from 6:00 P.M. to midnight, and all their Stanford friends and a large contingent from San Francisco enjoyed themselves as they ate the lavish buffet dinner, listened to music, and drank champagne. Jane had told the guests that there would be no hard liquor, and she was forced to send a

San Francisco journalist home because he insisted on bringing a quart of booze into the house.

Jane had hired a rhythm section of Larry Grenadier on bass and San Francisco professionals on piano and drums, and Stan performed happily for two hours with them and with Bill Dement, Ted Gioia, and Joey Oliveira who sat in, respectively, on bass, piano, and tenor sax.

Soon after the party, Stan and Jane moved into separate apartments only ten minutes apart, and Jane took a job at Dement's sleep clinic.

During the spring of 1987, Stan concentrated most of his energies on preparing for his second divorce trial, where he charged Monica with both cruel and inhuman treatment and adultery. The proceedings were scheduled to begin in White Plains before Judge Nicholas Colabella on May 11.

Ten days before, Stan was hit with terrible news: His internist revealed to him on May 1 that it was highly likely that he had cancer. A routine physical checkup had shown the presence of a tumor the size of a grapefruit deep in his body just behind his heart, and the doctor had told him that the growth was probably a lymphoma, cancer of the lymph system. He also told Stan that he faced a serious operation, which could be delayed with little or no risk until September to accommodate a very full summer schedule.

Stan decided not to tell anyone about his condition because he did not wish to deflect his own energies or those of his associates from the task of winning the long-awaited trial. His resolve to keep his secret broke down only once.

It happened after the first week of testimony, when he performed at a memorial service for Buddy Rich on May 17 at St. Peter's Church in Manhattan; Buddy had died of a heart attack on April 2 while recuperating from a cancer operation. Shaken by thoughts of his friend's mortality, Stan spoke about his tumor with St. Peter's Pastor John Gensel. Gensel, whose unique ministry to New York's jazz community—which he called his "night flock"—stretched back thirty years, remembered:

> He'd gotten to know me because he and Steve frequently came to our church together for AA meetings. . . . He said to me after the concert, "I have a big tumor behind my heart, and I'm going to have an operation. I'm not scared, I'm going straight ahead. . . . I haven't even told any members of my family."

Stan's thoughts were far from his impending operation as he listened intently to his lawyer, Jeffrey Cohen, emphasize in his opening statement that Monica's secret dosing of Antabuse constituted cruel and inhuman treatment:

> We intend to prove that for more than a decade Monica Getz secretly, willfully, intentionally, knowingly administered a drug called Antabuse to Stan Getz. We intend to prove that Monica Getz knew, and experts will testify, and Mr. Getz will testify that no one should ever administer the drug Antabuse to someone without their full knowledge and consent. . . . We also intend to prove that each and every time Monica Getz gave Stan Getz Antabuse without his knowledge, without his consent, she committed an assault—the same kind of an assault as if she had struck him with a baseball bat . . . an assault to his system which caused him many times to become very sick.

New York law does not require direct proof of an act of adultery; rather, it allows a jury to determine that such an act occurred if both the inclination and the opportunity for it existed. Cohen told the jury that they would hear evidence proving that both conditions existed simultaneously many times.

Reingold, in his opening statement, described the two defenses he would use against the Antabuse accusations: First, that Monica did not on her own administer the Antabuse secretly but was directed to do so by Dr. Ruth Fox in a 1968 letter; and second, that Monica was saving Stan's life and defending her safety and that of her children when she gave Stan the drug without his knowledge.

Reingold dismissed the adultery charge as totally without merit and a desperate ploy by Stan.

A few minutes after Stan started testifying, Cohen asked him if he loved Monica, and he answered:

> I hate Mrs. Getz for what she has done to me. I have grown to hate her very much. She has made my life miserable.

Later, when Stan was asked whether he would ever have a sexual relationship with his wife again, he said:

> I couldn't live with her. I could never have a sexual relationship with her. I wouldn't even sleep in the same room with her again. I couldn't. This woman made me afraid to be around her. She is forceful and evil.

Stan spent three days on the stand; under direct examination he spoke mostly about getting sick from Antabuse, and under cross he was forced to discuss his long and violent history of drug and alcohol abuse. He invoked the Fifth Amendment when asked about ingesting heroin and cocaine, but he admitted that he had enjoyed drinking:

> I was a good drinker. And that's a problem . . . That's probably why I never thought I was an alcoholic, because you have a capacity to drink. You don't have to have one or two drinks. You can drink. You don't get sick. You love every minute of it.

And he spoke proudly of his sobriety after September 4, 1985.

> When I surrendered to the fact . . . that I had the primary symptoms of alcoholism, I surrendered to the fact that I was an alcoholic. And I embraced the program, the best program in the world.

Cohen presented testimony from Joanne Brackeen that she refused Monica's request to give Antabuse to Stan surreptitiously while on tour, from a servant who did so on Monica's orders, and from a Shadowbrook guest who was sworn to secrecy after she saw Monica sprinkle the drug into Stan's breakfast.

He also brought to the stand as expert witnesses two doctors who specialized in substance abuse. They stated that they would never countenance the secret dosing of Antabuse, and they averred that its effects could be life-threatening. One of them testified that during the previous three years, two of his patients had almost died after heavy drinking following a normal dosage of Antabuse; both were saved by life-support systems in emergency rooms.

The 1968 Ruth Fox letter that played such a large part in Monica's defense did not explicitly recommend the secret administration of Antabuse. As we have seen, Monica inferred such a directive from the following ambiguous passage:

> I have found it best for this to be taken by the patient of his own free will and given by the wife. However, if we find as time goes on that Mr. Getz is remiss in taking it, then we would see that the wife gives it to him crushed up in orange juice.

Fox could not testify because she was dead, and Cohen countered

Reingold by inserting into the record the following excerpt from an article by her:

> The patient should never be given disulfiram (Antabuse) against his will or without his full knowledge and consent and understanding.

To support the adultery charge, Cohen produced two former Shadowbrook employees who testified that they saw Monica and Sune Byren, dressed in bathrobes, in Monica's bedroom several times between 6:30 A.M. and 7:30 A.M. and between 10:00 P.M. and midnight. In addition, a boarder stated that he saw them in bed together early one morning.

Monica and Byren denied the adultery charge out of hand; he and his wife testified that a kidney disease had made it difficult for him to have sex after 1981, and that a stroke had rendered him totally impotent after 1985.

Monica's two medical experts downplayed the ill effects of Antabuse, and both stated they would recommend its secret dosing in desperate situations. The two of them, however, had never encountered a situation of such desperation during their entire careers—careers in which they had treated approximately five thousand alcoholics.

Reingold's rationale that Monica had administered Antabuse to protect both the family and Stan from himself demanded that he call upon his witnesses to describe at length the carnage that Stan had visited upon them when he was drunk. The media had a field day as Pamela, Nicky, and Monica recited horror stories of beatings, verbal abuse, hair pullings, gun threats, and arrests. Newspapers ran headlines such as "Drugs, Booze and All That Jazz," "Son Says 'Musician Was Out of Control,'" and "'He's Like a Psychopath.' Daughter Tells Court, 'Getz Went on Rampages.'"

During direct examination, Monica testified that she opposed the divorce because she wanted to save Stan and the family from his delusions about his sobriety:

> Reingold: Do you recall him testifying . . . that if he wanted a divorce you would give it to him if he did not drink for a year? . . .
>
> Monica: That is not true. I said that if he were to go into family treatment and be sober for a year and do all of the things that we had discussed, yes, that was true. . . . If all of the children and I would participate in a family treatment and if after a year, after the treatment, he came out, if he was willing to accept all of this, then I would be willing to accept that. . . .

Secondly, I think that a divorce would deprive this family of family treatment which I know in most cases works, and I feel very strongly that he should confront the symptoms of his disease and that we should all confront the symptoms of Stanley's disease in therapy. . . .

Cohen pursued the subject in cross examination:

Cohen: If he went through this family counseling, you would give him a divorce?

Monica: If he came out at the end of a year and had family therapy, and if that is what he wanted—a divorce—I would give it to him.

Cohen: So he has to do just what you want him to do. You won't give him a divorce will you?

Monica: No, because—

Cohen: Just answer the question. You will not give him one.

Monica: I know he is not in his right mind. . . .

Cohen: Do you think it is realistic and reliable for you to ask five people to come from all over the world to spend a year in therapy, to come from countries as far away as Sweden to spend a year in therapy with you and Stan? . . .

Monica: Absolutely, yes. It's done all the time. . . .

Cohen: Unless all of those things that you want happen, no divorce for Stan Getz. Isn't that a fact?

Monica: That's a fact.

Cohen: Now you know more about what Stan Getz wants than he does, isn't that a fact?

Monica: True, true.

The jury of four women and two men did not agree with Monica; they deliberated for only three hours before granting Stan his divorce on both counts—cruel and inhuman treatment and adultery—on May 29, 1987.

BATTLING TWENTY
TO
LIVE

WITH THE TRIAL behind him, Stan felt free to talk openly about his health. Billy Hoogstraten recalled that Stan's first reaction was to rail against the unfairness of his fate:

> I remember him calling me, telling me they discovered the tumor. And he felt like somebody was really mistreating him because he didn't deserve that.
>
> He said, "Why now? If it had been three years ago, I can understand, because I was misbehaving all the time, taking all that bad stuff, and I needed some punishment. But for the last two years I've been trying to make up with myself and the people close to me. I've been going the right way. Now I'm punished with this."

345

Stan put aside these bitter feelings quickly and began to plan with his friends and family an attack on his illness. Jane Walsh, still living apart from him, began a highly organized search for the best qualified surgeon to excise the tumor. Stan, who had long distrusted Western medicine, read everything he could about Asian practices and decided to adopt, even before the operation, a strict regimen involving acupuncture, Asian macrobiotic foods and medicinal herbs, and shiatsu massage. His daughter Beverly helped Jane with her investigations and resolved to be with him through the operation and his recovery.

As Stan prepared for a busy summer of performing, he had to reconfigure the quartet. George Mraz had decided to leave to join piano master Tommy Flanagan, and Stan recruited Rufus Reid to replace him. Fortunately, the new bassist was quickly able to meld his talents with those of Kenny Barron and Victor Lewis to maintain the cohesiveness and the high artistic standards of the rhythm section.

Reid, director of the jazz studies program at William Paterson College in New Jersey, had been a professional for sixteen years and had performed with his own bands and with groups led by Dizzy Gillespie, Dexter Gordon, Art Farmer, Benny Carter, Freddy Hubbard, and Joe Henderson. He played less melodically but with more power and rhythmic subtlety than Mraz, and projected a rich, plumy tone that enhanced the frequent romantic flights of Stan and Barron.

The quartet participated in an excellent concert on June 21, 1987, at the JVC Jazz Festival in New York, and two nights later Stan made a festival guest performance with the Mel Lewis Big Band and Diane Schuur. *The New York Times* reviewer was enthusiastic:

> Stan Getz joined the band and, standing away from the mikes altogether, sounded better than anyone the whole week. Diane Schuur joined Getz and wowed everyone, her voice powerful and passionate, in particular on "Come Rain or Come Shine" with Getz obbligati.

Stan and his group, accompanied by Jane Walsh, embarked on a European tour one week later. Their third engagement found them in Stockholm on July 5, where they were visited backstage by Peter Torgner. Torgner, an unmarried twenty-nine-year-old, bore a striking resemblance to Stan and long claimed to be his illegitimate son.

His unmarried mother, Inga Torgner, recalled that she was living and working in Manhattan during the summer of 1957 when Stan approached her in a Greenwich Village nightclub where he was performing:

After the jam session was finished, he came over to our table and asked me in particular if he could drive me home. I was lodging at the time at the Sherman Square Hotel, Sherman Square, New York City. I accepted his invitation, and he drove me back home in a large white convertible Cadillac. . . . After some while, Stan and I one night took in at—I *think* the name was Wellington Hotel. It was in New York anyway—and I suspect that this night Peter came to be.

In June 1958, when Stan, his three older children, and Monica—eight months pregnant with Pamela—had moved to Sweden, Inga invited him to her apartment in Stockholm:

He came one evening, and I showed him two-and-one-half-month old Peter. I then said to Stan that it was his baby, too. In short, after this Stan took a rather abrupt farewell of us and left the apartment.

Stan did not depart abruptly when Peter presented himself as his son to him and Monica in 1974 in Stockholm or when Peter dropped in after a concert there during the late 1970s. On the second occasion, Stan chatted at length with him, introduced him as his son to his musicians, and took away an autobiographical letter describing Peter's successful singing career on the Swedish musical comedy stage.

Peter remembered spending a pleasant evening with Stan and Jane after the 1987 concert:

He seemed glad to see me. He presented me again as his son for a number of people who stood nearby. After we went to a back-stage room (situated in a boat), and talked for a short while. . . .

He was polite toward me by inviting me to the cab that took us to a restaurant called Cafe Opera, where we had some food. In the cab there were two or three musicians and also at the time, his girlfriend Jane. . . .

We were together for two hours, and Stan gave me his address in U.S.A., handwritten on a card which I have saved.

The quartet appeared the next night at the Montmartre in Copenhagen in a performance that was recorded by Danish state radio and TV and later released on two CDs, *Anniversary* (1989) and *Serenity* (1991).

The music Stan made that night was—with the exception of *Focus*—

as fine as anything he had ever created. The listener is awed by the mastery of a mature artist galvanized by the fear that this might be one of his last opportunities to deploy his full powers. Stan was energized by his illness that night and every other night of the tour:

> I thought that those concerts could be my last ones, and that gave me the feeling of "Now I have to really try my best." I felt strong, although my life was in danger.
>
> I made quite a drama out of it. You know how people can overact in those situations. In my fantasy, I was singing my musical swan song. You know how things are going when everybody is ready to start playing the violins.

Billy Hoogstraten recognized a heightened energy also:

> That summer he was so up all the time. Totally sober. And every concert was the most beautiful concert you could imagine.

Stan felt physically fit, his mind was clear, and he was performing in what he regarded as his "classical" setting—the quartet—with three musicians who breathed with him as one. There was Barron, whom Stan described as "the other half of my heart," Lewis, whose rhythms drove the group with sinewy intensity, and Reid, whose accompaniments were so on target that he seemed to be inside the heads of Getz and Barron.

Stan and the quartet played twelve numbers of bracing variety during two sets on July 6, 1987. The group's repertory that night included four romantic ballads, four brisk swingers, a blues, two up-tempo scorchers, and one elegy, "Blood Count."

"I Can't Get Started" is a masterpiece, one of the most completely realized ballad performances in the entire jazz canon. Stan always tried to heed Lester Young's advice to absorb the meaning of a tune's lyric, and he listened carefully to this song's words of romantic frustration:

> You're so supreme, lyrics I write of you.
> I dream day and night of you
> And I scheme just for the sight of you.
> Baby, what good does it do? . . .
> I can't get started with you.

He moves from notes as dense and rich as heavy cream to breathy sighs to sharp plaintive cries as he transports the listener unerringly through moods of anguish, tenderness, querulous anger, and, finally, resignation. Barron does not attempt to duplicate this tour de force, but follows with pure cascades of melody, a crystal reverie in swing.

The other ballad renditions—"I Thought About You," "Falling in Love," and "I Remember You"—come close to the perfection of "I Can't Get Started"; "I Remember You" won Stan his fifth and last Grammy as the Best Jazz Solo Performance for 1991.

Two Cole Porter tunes, "What Is This Thing Called Love?" and "I Love You," are taken at blistering tempos, and Stan displays a liquid sense of time as he moves ahead of, behind, and on the beat and rips exuberantly through the harmonies with an assortment of cries, gritty assertions, and billowing torrents of sound.

The final number is "Blood Count," which is given a more contemplative and resigned treatment than the anguished rendition on *Pure Getz*. As Stan told a reporter, he was dealing at a deep level with the composer's mortality and his own when he made the Copenhagen recording:

> I have a special affinity with Billy Strayhorn. I think about Strayhorn when I play the song. You can hear him dying. When it's in a minor key, you can hear the man talking to God.

Watching a clip from the Danish videotape of the Montmartre performance, the viewer is drawn inexorably to Stan's blue eyes, the intense orbs which belied a calm within. Steve Getz asked him one day about his riveting gaze:

> "What are you thinking about when you are so deep in concentration?"
>
> He replied: "It's not forced concentration. Sure, I'm thinking about what I'm playing, but what I'm trying to do is to psyche myself into relaxing so the notes come out of the horn in a natural way."
>
> He was a master of relaxation. This was the secret which enabled him to play such fresh renditions time and time again.

The Montmartre session provided two hours and five minutes of music. The Danes, who did not intend to make records of the performance, gave Stan raw tapes of the event, which he took home with him. When he listened to them more than a year later, he knew he was on to something special and pressed the Danes to sell him the rights to the session. After a short negotiation, he bought the rights for $735 and held them for future sale.

Stan returned to Stanford in early August to find the jazz program thriving. He had worked especially hard to expose the full complement of his students to other important musicians because he realized that he was effective only in teaching the most talented pupils; he was pleased that he and Jim Nadel had succeeded in recruiting the outstanding saxophonist Joe Henderson for the Summer Jazz Workshop, the Modern Jazz Quartet for a weekend workshop and concert in October, and trumpet star Art Farmer for a four-day residency in November, during which he would join Stan's quartet to instruct the students.

He was also happy to know that his best pupils were winning unprecedented honors for the university. During the spring a Stanford group had won an award for the first time ever at the Pacific Coast Jazz Festival, the premier western college jazz event. "Stanford Combo #1" took first place, and three of its five members—Larry Grenadier on bass, Bob Adams on piano, and Dave Aguiar on saxophone—were deemed the best on their instruments in competition with individuals from 120 different bands.

The following day the group traveled to Indiana to compete in the Notre Dame Jazz Festival, the most prestigious and comprehensive college gathering in the U.S. They triumphed once more, tying for first place with a band from William Paterson College coached by Rufus Reid. Grenadier and Aguiar again received outstanding instrumentalist awards.

Johann Blokker had become tired of carrying the jazz program's financial load almost single-handedly, and he decreed that he would limit his annual contribution to whatever was raised at an August 9 concert by Stan and the jazz-pop vocal group Manhattan Transfer; Stan had secured their participation by promising to perform for nothing on one of their albums later that month. The benefit was wildly successful, netting $80,000, and when Blokker sent in his check, the program could count $160,000 in its coffers for the new year. Stan flew to Los Angeles on August 27 to fulfill his commitment to Manhattan Transfer, laying down a background track for them and Brazilian vocalist Djavan.

During the summer of 1987, Stan and Jane worked with Blokker, Ted Gioia, and Ken Oshman, a prominent electronics executive and a member of the Committee for Jazz, on the creation of a jazz record company called Quartet. Blokker and Oshman planned to fund the company with $300,000, make Gioia the CEO (with Jane as his full-time assistant), and give Stan a piece of the action for his roles as talent scout and producer. Stan never became part of the team because, confident that he could immediately draw money-making talent to the new label, he asked for a salary of $100,000 per year rather than equity in return for performance;

Blokker and Oshman turned him down. The futile negotiations about Stan's compensation strained his long-standing friendship with Gioia.

Jane had scoured the country for the best chest-cavity surgeon for Stan and was surprised when she found the right person for the job in their own backyard at Stanford University Hospital; his name was Dr. James Mark. The operation was scheduled for September 1, and Beverly and her daughter Katie, age four, arrived on August 28, 1987, to help Stan through his ordeal. Because Stan came down with bronchitis, the operation was postponed until September 18, and Beverly remembers that she and Katie spent a happy interlude with Stan marred only by the nearly tasteless macrobiotic food they were forced to eat every evening:

> He just really wanted to be relaxed. He was wonderful. He got up every day, and he made his bed. He made his McCann's Irish Oatmeal; it's consistent with macrobiotic principles, and he spent fifteen minutes stirring it on the stove. He cleaned all his dishes, put them away, and cleaned the coffee pot—which maybe to some people doesn't sound like a big deal. But to me—who had never been around him since his drinking days—it was, like, wow!
>
> It was the best quality time I ever spent with him. We got really close. I was so happy there.

Dr. Mark began the operation by making a sixteen-inch incision from Stan's left nipple around to his spine and exposing the chest muscles, which were so strong they could power a sound that filled Carnegie Hall without a microphone. Mark sliced the muscles open to get to the rib cage and with great force pulled two ribs apart to enter the chest cavity. He then collapsed a lung to make space and systematically cut his way to the grapefruit-sized object lodged between Stan's heart and his spine. He removed it, cleaned out all suspicious surrounding tissue, reinflated the lung, and sewed Stan up. The entire procedure consumed eight hours.

The growth, as the internist had predicted, was a malignant lymphoma. The physician's experience told him that cancerous lymphatic tissue would continue to live inside Stan's body but that there was only a slight chance that it would again grow dangerously. He did not believe that radiation or chemotherapy was needed, but he wished to monitor Stan carefully every few weeks to detect quickly any recurrence of the disease.

Jane Walsh had prepared everyone for the problems associated with the drugs Stan would need to combat his severe postoperative pain:

I knew they were going to give Stan a lot of painkillers, and that would trigger his addiction, and as soon as they gave them to him, he'd want more. So I went to Dr. Mark with Stan. Stan doesn't say anything; he's embarrassed.

I said, "He had an addiction problem. You're going to have to really monitor this. You can't be just giving him morphine, thinking he's a typical guy. He's going to be hoarding it, looking for it, wanting it."

And Mark was just one of these no-nonsense guys. "I know about addiction. No problem. We're not going to let him get on those drugs."

Stan was frightened, of course. He did the operation, and when he got on those drugs he was the old demon; he was throwing trays around.

The AA people came around and Stan understood that he would have to wean himself from the drugs in six weeks, and he had a lot of support and he got off them.

He went back over to his apartment and made his slow recovery, and Beverly stayed for a while. I was over there a lot. We talked about getting back together. Maybe. Maybe not. It was a very weird time.

Blokker, Oshman, Gioia, and Jane launched Quartet Records when Gioia went into a studio on October 19 to complete a trio album begun in 1986 with himself as leader on piano. During the next month they produced quartet sessions led by two little-known, young musicians, alto saxophonist Mark Lewis and trumpet and flugelhorn player Dan Bendigkeit; Larry Grenadier played on all three CDs. Sales were anemic, and Quartet made no more recordings. Its owners disbanded the company a year later and sold its assets to a Los Angeles organization.

Stan cried when he heard that Woody Herman had died on October 29, 1987, at age seventy-four. Woody had stayed on the road until March, when a combination of congestive heart failure and emphysema felled him; he deteriorated rapidly after that.

Stan relaxed during the Christmas holidays with Jane, David, Steve, Christopher, and the Blokkers at Cabo San Lucas, a resort town on the southern tip of the Baja California peninsula. Stan baked in the hot sun every day and even did a little swimming.

As he slowly built his strength back, he had come to rely heavily for care on Donna Seid, a Chinese-American masseuse and expert on Asian diet. One morning during January 1988, Donna sent him to a health-food store to buy adzuki beans, a Japanese vegetable known for increasing stamina.

Stan was attracted to the beautiful young saleswoman with long dark hair who found the beans for him, and he asked her, "Do you like music?"

"Of course. I love music."

"Who do you like?"

"Ella Fitzgerald, Sarah Vaughan, Duke Ellington, jazz music. I was a very strange kid. I listened to Duke and Ella while my friends listened to funk or Earth, Wind, and Fire."

"Do you know a musician called Stan Getz?"

"No."

"Well, that's me. I'm famous. I teach at a school near here. If you want to listen to some good music, give me a call and I'll get you good seats. Here's my card. I'm going to Palm Springs for a little rest. I'll write the number on the back. Call me there if you want. On the front I'm crossing out Artist in Residence and putting Music Department, so you don't think I'm a painter."

The woman, a part-time fashion model whose name was Samantha Ceseña, asked a music-store salesman the next day about Stan, and the man told her that Stan's music had changed his life—had brought him out of a deep depression—and that she should start getting to know it by listening to *Focus* and *Getz/Gilberto*.

Samantha bought the albums and was impressed by the emotional honesty and intensity of the music, and she called Stan in Palm Springs to tell him this. She remembered:

> He said, "It's so beautiful where I am. How would you like to come down for a visit? You can come down, have your own room, just hang out, and we'll get to know each other."
>
> I said, "I'll let you know." By that time I was listening to the albums more and more and I thought I really want to know this person. I decided to go down.
>
> We just started to get to know each other. I trusted him. And I really had feelings for him. One thing in my life that I'm an expert at is following my heart.
>
> When we left, we drove from Palm Springs all the way up the coast to San Francisco.
>
> I was staying with a friend who lived near him, and Stan and I started seeing a lot of each other. When I met him, I was about to leave for Paris for some modeling assignments. And I still wanted to do that.

Stan took up his sax again in January 1988, but he found that playing was both painful and fatiguing. Nonetheless, he undertook two projects to help Stanford. First, he made a recording for major pop star Huey Lewis under terms similar to the ones he had previously negotiated with Manhattan Transfer; he backed Lewis on the title track of his album *Small World* and also appeared on the video of the tune and took no compensation; in return Lewis committed himself to performing in a benefit with Stan for the university jazz program.

Second, on January 17 he played a sold-out concert at the university with an intriguing sextet. It featured Jack Sheldon, a veteran trumpeter-singer from Los Angeles; Kim Park, a gifted alumnus of the Stan Kenton saxophone corps; and a seasoned rhythm section composed of pianist George Cables, drummer Donald Bailey, and bassist Chuck Israels. The reviewer for the *Peninsula Times Tribune* wrote:

> The three horns presented an ensemble sensitivity normally found only in classical chamber groups. . . . Though Getz still is regaining the former strength he possessed before his surgery, the virtuosity and sensitivity remain uncompromised. . . .
>
> Two of Stanford's finest student musicians, saxophonists Stefan Cohen and Dave Aguiar, joined the Getz band for a blues set. The four saxophonists "traded fours" in nifty fashion.
>
> At a reception following the concert, Committee for Jazz members, musicians, and donors enjoyed a lavish buffet under a huge tent in the Blokkers' back yard. Neither the blustery winds nor chilly air dampened the enthusiasm of the gathering.

Stan kicked off a month-long European tour in Amsterdam on February 11 with Victor Lewis, Jim McNeely, and a new bassist, Anthony Cox; teaching commitments had forced both Kenny Barron and Rufus Reid to pass up the trip. Billy Hoogstraten remembers that Stan was filled with anxiety before the first concert:

> It was very painful for him. He was very, very nervous, and when he came on stage he was sweating all over and feeling miserable. He went up to the microphone and said, "Good evening, ladies and gentlemen, I'm scared. I'm really scared. I've had a bad operation, and this is my first major performance." And then he played a wonderful concert. The audience responded with its wildest applause when he turned off the mikes to perform a powerful, unamplified rendition of "Lush Life."

Afterward, Stan told a reporter:

> Because my ribs were painful, I postponed over and over again
> the moment to resume working. I hardly touched my saxophone.
> I've got fingers which will always do what I want them to do and
> to build up my embouchure only takes me about four days. But,
> I was worried about my lungs, because everything had to come
> from there. My ribs were hurting continuously, but I think one
> has to work through that pain like an athlete.
>
> After this performance, I'm sure it's there. It's still there. It's all
> right. It will be fun again.

It soon became evident that—at least for a while—it was not going to
be fun again. Stan was totally exhausted after each performance, and at
the end of the first week, he decided to stop the tour after a London
concert on February 22, 1988, and reschedule the rest of it for May.

When he heard in Trieste that Al Cohn had died at age sixty-two on
February 15 of liver cancer, Stan told a reporter:

> For a long time I had the idea in my head of making a record
> with Zoot Sims and Al Cohn. But unfortunately, it couldn't come
> to that. I really regret that very much, because those are my two
> heros—Zoot and Al.

Stan had heard that Joey Oliveira, the son of Nate and Mona, was
scuffling around London playing his sax in rock and roll bands and small
jazz combos, and he telephoned Joey from the Continent to ask him to
play with the quartet in London on February 22. Stan felt that by getting
Joey to perform he could kill two birds with one stone—he could boost
Joey's career, and he could rest a bit during the concert while Joey soloed.

Stan felt sure that his young friend would acquit himself professionally;
he believed that Joey was a raw talent who only needed a disciplined
study of harmony to become an excellent jazz musician. Joey joined the
quartet for two numbers and played well, and Stan received good notices.
The *Guardian Weekly* reported:

> Although he was clearly weakened by a massive operation for
> cancer, Getz played fast pieces with such a relish in mingling
> bubbling runs with hushed clamatory sounds, and ballads with
> such shimmering poise, that the audience would hardly let him
> off the stage after his encores.

Joey was elated and wrote to the Blokkers:

> The Stan Getz quartet played at the Royal Festival Hall. He
> called me up and asked me if I wanted to sit in!! WOW ☺ I
> did, and it was great. He is a very nice guy.

But Stan was so drained by the concert that he cried in his dressing room after it was over.

Stan's doctor examined him when he came back to California and assured him that his distress was not caused by a recurrence of the lymphoma; he had merely tried to do too much too soon. He rested more, exercised lightly, followed his diet, his acupuncture, and his massage, and regained his normal strength in time for his second 1988 European tour on May 17.

Samantha moved into Stan's apartment in April, but she was restless. She did not as yet want a long-term relationship and was still eager to try her hand at modeling in Paris. Stan agreed to take her on his tour and to leave her in the French capital when he completed his engagements on May 31.

He hurried back from Paris because the "equitable distribution" trial on the disposition of the Getzes' assets and income began before Judge Colabella in White Plains on June 6. It was closed down dramatically two days later when Monica complained that she suffered from depression and had suicidal urges. In response Colabella ordered that she be examined by psychiatrists to determine if she was fit to continue; Stan was compelled by New York law to foot $3,400 in charges incurred by the examiners.

He realized on returning home from New York that he was smitten with Samantha, and he called her in Paris almost every day to tell her how much he needed her and how she would find a wonderful surprise waiting for her when she came back to him. She was working successfully in Paris, but in the end Stan's arguments were persuasive, and she rejoined him in New York on July 1 as he was about to perform in a Buddy Rich memorial concert at Carnegie Hall.

When they arrived in California, he revealed his surprise: a new house. It was rented and came with a pool on a one-acre lot in Atherton, a couple of miles north of his old apartment; Stan had a white picket fence built around the property to fulfill one of Samantha's fantasies. Soon after they moved in, Stan bought a yellow Labrador puppy he called James II. The dog was a youthful replica of Stan's beloved James, who had expired at age fourteen the previous winter.

Claude and Tom Anyos, recent recruits to the Committee for Jazz, lived around the corner in Atherton and became close friends. Claude possessed a sophisticated knowledge of jazz and continually delighted Stan with her insightful comments about his music. She remembered a relaxed relationship suffused with the atmosphere of the romance between Stan and Samantha:

> He got the house and the new James, and he also had a new lady that he liked very, very much.
>
> Stan was one of those people that loved being in love. When he wasn't involved with a lady, he was in mourning. That's his term. He would say, "This is death. I'm in mourning. . . ."
>
> Samantha is one of the most poised people that I've ever met. And she is serenity. . . . She is such a serene person that you get very calm around her. Jane was the intellectual in Stan's life. He always said she was so much fun and so bright and so quick.
>
> But Jane is a pistol. There's nothing calming about Jane, not one thing. She is just pure energy. Stan did not need that. He was fighting cancer and all those stressful legal battles. He needed a lot of calm. And he got that in Samantha.
>
> We'd have dinner together, we'd bring our dogs together—Stan loved to swim, so he was always in the water. He'd always say, "Do you want to hang out?" It was always hanging out. And most of the time he just sat around.
>
> I even tried my hand at macrobiotic cuisine but soon gave it up because it's hours of cooking and minutes of eating. . . . He could gobble that stuff in no time, and it would take forever to do.

Just as he was settling in with Samantha and James II in late July 1988, Stan received the terrible news that he had liver cancer; it was detected by a CAT scan and confirmed by a biopsy. Liver cancer is far more virulent than the low-grade lymphoma that had been dogging him and that had remained stable and nonthreatening since his operation ten months earlier. His doctors added to his concerns when they told him that treating the cancer would be doubly difficult because a goodly portion of his liver had been rendered useless by his decades of heavy drinking— a condition known as cirrhosis.

They informed him that he could probably survive for four to six months untreated and for a year if he allowed them to cut away the diseased liver tissue and follow up with chemo and radiation therapy. The doctors' prognosis roused Stan's fighting spirit:

When you've been told you have a few months to live . . . you either lay down and die, or you get up and fight. Part of it is an attitude towards life, loving life. It's something a lot of people take for granted. But I got my ire up.

He decided to reject his doctors' counsel and to fight his cancer by relying on an intensified course of Asian therapy; he would follow his existing regimen more religiously than ever, and he would add a mix of five Chinese herbs called Sunrider, which his daughter Beverly pressed him to take after she had seen it help one of her cancer-stricken neighbors.

In addition, he would try to quit smoking. He had ceased using drugs and alcohol in September 1985, but his pack-a-day addiction to cigarettes continued unabated. And as Samantha recalled, there were moments for Stan when the temptations of tobacco proved irresistible:

He was in the kitchen and he was naked. I said, "What are you doing?" And he goes, "Nothing. Oh, nothing." Then he walked out without turning around. He shuffled sideways. And I said, "What have you got in your back?" Like I caught a six-year-old child is the look he gave me. I'll never forget this look. And he turned around. He had a pack of cigarettes in the crack of his butt. I just started laughing. I said, "That's pretty good."

While Stan was confronting the savage reality of liver cancer, Monica was given a clean bill of health by the psychiatrists appointed by Colabella in the equitable distribution trial. Before appearing in court for the resumption of the proceedings on August 8, however, she pushed forward on another front: She mounted the first of several appeals from the jury verdict in the 1987 trial, appeals that dragged through the courts for six more years. The equitable distribution trial was concluded on August 15, 1988, when Colabella told the litigants that he would render his decision early in 1989.

The media mogul and megastar trumpeter and singer Herb Alpert stood in awe of Stan's talent, and when he heard that Stan had no record company contract, he became intrigued with the possibilities of working with him. He had told a reporter:

I'm a great fan of Stan Getz. I just think he plays wonderful, free, honest jazz. He has a magic touch. It's very melodic, very touching. . . . He says he never played a note he didn't mean. That's a hell of a commitment. I think that's the key word right

there, commitment—to commit to something you believe in. Stan
Getz . . . he's standing there with a handful of giants.

Alpert telephoned Stan in October of 1988, introduced himself, and suggested that they meet soon to discuss a collaboration. Stan was scheduled
to play at a cancer foundation benefit in Los Angeles on the evening of
November 10, and they arranged to get together earlier that day at Alpert's
house on the Pacific Ocean in Malibu, just outside of Los Angeles.

Alpert, who has a prodigious gift for creating songs and arrangements
that pop audiences love, stood on a pinnacle of music business success
when he met with Stan. He and his partner, businessman Jerry Moss,
had started their company, A&M Records, in a garage in 1962 with $200
and had built it into a corporate giant by making Alpert a megastar and
by helping create other megastars like Sting, Carole King, Cat Stevens,
the Carpenters, Styx, Supertramp, and Janet Jackson.

Alpert and his band, the Tijuana Brass, created fourteen million-selling
("platinum") records, exceeded 72 million in collective sales, and made
it to number one on the pop charts five times; he won seven Grammys
and garnered Record of the Year honors in 1965 with "A Taste of Honey."

Alpert, a lanky southern Californian who prefers casual clothes and
wears a ponytail, impressed Stan with his warmth and enthusiasm during
their two-hour meeting on November 10, and Stan responded in kind.
Alpert told him that he wanted to explore fresh musical formats with him
and would commit considerable resources to any joint projects. He even
suggested that Stan move down to Malibu so that they could work together
more easily. Stan's encounter with Alpert came at a time when the Stanford jazz program, so vibrant only a year earlier, was beginning to lose
momentum. Bill Dement, the main force in the Committee for Jazz, had
been forced to reduce his involvement severely to focus on the rehabilitation of his daughter Elizabeth, who had been severely injured in an auto
accident. And Stan's input was limited because he needed almost all
his energy to fight his illness and to earn money for his court battles
with Monica.

In addition, he was bitterly disappointed when bureaucratic inertia and
opposition to rock and roll from jazz purists on the committee scuttled
the Huey Lewis benefit that he had set up by appearing for nothing on
a Lewis recording. Lewis was at the height of his popularity as a pop
icon, and the benefit with him had been expected to produce more than
the $80,000 raised at the Manhattan Transfer concert the previous year.
When two "pure" jazz events netted only $10,000 and the university again
failed to provide any monies for the program, Johann Blokker announced

that—after three years as a mainstay—he would make no contribution for 1989.

Alpert, encouraged by his meeting with Stan, followed up with a persuasive barrage of telephone calls, and Stan began to see an association with him as an attractive alternative to the umpromising prospects he faced at Stanford. He called Elliot Hoffman and told him to begin talks with Alpert about a contract.

Stan had gained strength during the autumn months, and he looked forward to the results of MRI scans that he was scheduled to undergo in mid-November. On November 21, 1988, he was talking to Judith Share, a friend in New York, and said, "Hold on. The MRI report is coming in on the other line." There was excitement in his voice when he returned to her. "The tumor shrank at least ten percent. The doctor never heard of a liver cancer hepatoma shrinking, and he won't acknowledge the effect of the herbs. That Sunrider stuff of Bev's is terrific."

Stan's elation was short-lived, because the next day he experienced chest pains so severe that Samantha had to rush him to Stanford University Hospital. He had suffered a mild heart attack caused by a blocked artery, and the doctors immediately performed an angioplasty. For this procedure they inserted into the artery a tube capped with a deflated small balloon, moved it to the obstructed site, and broke up the blockage by filling the balloon with air. Samantha recalled that Stan was conscious throughout the operation and talked to her.

> I got to see the balloon. There was a TV screen with pictures from a small camera going through his veins. It was out of his view, so I told him, "This is really cool, Stanley, you should see what I'm seeing." And we were making jokes to each other.

The doctors put Stan on morphine to relieve the postoperative pain and sent him home in three days. No one had told them that Stan was addicted to the drug and had been weaned carefully from it following his lymphoma operation at their hospital fourteen months previously.

Five days later Samantha found him passed out in bed and breathing shallowly; he had taken too much morphine. She called for paramedics, who revived him and took him back to Stanford University Hospital. She then reached out to Jane Walsh, who met with Stan's heart specialists and told them about his detoxification procedures the previous year. They followed her advice and had Stan drug-free and out of the hospital four days later, on December 2.

Discussions with Alpert were going so well that when Steve and Beverly came to visit Stan and Samantha during the 1988 Christmas holidays, the four of them took a one-day expedition to Malibu to look at rental homes there.

Despite the near-miraculous remission of his liver cancer and his quick recovery from the angioplasty, Stan was continually grumpy in early 1989 because he could not play his saxophone. His lawyers, fearing that reports of successful performances would hurt his chances in the equitable distribution case, forbade him from performing until Judge Colabella made his decision.

Stan's disposition improved radically on February 9, 1989, when the judge gave Monica what Stan had been offering throughout their arduous legal battles: a half interest in Shadowbrook and the land in Spain and half of future royalties on all recordings made from the date of their marriage, November 3, 1956, through January 31, 1981, the day Stan left Shadowbrook for good.

After Colabella's decision, the negotiations with Alpert quickly came to closure. Elliot Hoffman remembered:

> There's no doubt that Herb Alpert was the first show business guy who was truly, truly kind to Stan. He gave him the first long-term generous record contract that I ever saw Stan get. . . . I was able to ask for just about anything that I always wanted Stan to have. And Herb was only too happy to give it to him.

The contract was signed in early March. When Alpert called a couple of weeks later with the good news that the house just north of his on Malibu Beach could be rented reasonably, Stan told him he would take it. He and Samantha moved down in early April; on arrival Stan changed into his bathing suit and plunged into the Pacific for a long swim. A few days later, he told Judith Share:

> We're grooving in this place. We have a pool and a hot tub and it's quiet and relaxed. I walk a mile on the beach every day. And a gardener is planting a vegetable garden for me on the property. Just nice. James is grooving here, too. . . . Sam's fine. She's a wonderful girl, the love of my life—Miss Sam here. . . . I've got to beat this thing. Life is too beautiful.

FULLY ENGAGED

STAN TOOK OFF in early June of 1989 with Samantha, Donna Seid, his grandson Christopher, Kenny Barron, bassist Ray Drummond, and drummer Ben Riley for a seven-week European sojourn. They began by spending five busy days in Paris—a city that they found caught up in a whirlwind of cultural and ceremonial events that culminated in the bicentennial of the French Revolution on July 14.

Stan's first order of business was to make the record *Just Friends* on June 11 and 12 with an old friend, singer Helen Merrill. Merrill's producer, Jean-Philippe Allard, had asked her whom she would most like to perform with on the date, and she chose Stan. When Allard contacted him, Stan proposed a three-record deal; he would play on *Just Friends*, but he also wanted to sell to Allard the 1987 Montmartre recordings, which he had purchased from Danish radio and TV and which contained enough material for two CDs.

Allard was very impressed with the Danish tapes, but he countered by asking Stan to throw in, for the same price, a third recording that Stan had produced in 1981 and that had been tied up in a publishing dispute— *Billy Highstreet Samba*. Stan settled the dispute, a deal was struck, and Allard's company, Polygram, paid Stan $240,000 for his three-CD package and roughly $20,000 for performing on *Just Friends. Billy Highstreet Samba* had cost Stan roughly $5,000, and he had paid $735 for the Danish session, which resulted in the CDs *Anniversary* and *Serenity*. Billy Hoogstraten recalled, "Stan was thrilled having that deal with Polygram because he never had that money for records."

Merrill's husky voice is frayed around the edges, but she knows how to use it to express both a mature romanticism and a bright joy. Stan's obbligatos are masterful as he is by turns challenging, caressing, and conversational, and on three numbers—"It Don't Mean a Thing (If It Ain't Got That Swing)," "Yesterdays," and "It Never Entered My Mind"— he unleashes solos of stunning vitality and passion.

Two days later—in a bicentennial ceremony—Danielle Mitterand, the wife of France's President, and Jack Lang, the Minister of Culture, inducted Stan, Dizzy Gillespie, Max Roach, Hank Jones, Phil Woods, Milt Jackson, Percy Heath, and Jackie McLean into France's prestigious Order of Arts and Letters. That evening and the following one, in what was billed as "one of the most glittering celebrations of the two hundredth anniversary of the French Revolution," Mme. Mitterand presented the newly minted Members of the Order in concert; the program of this dream band was a tribute to a prime inspiration of all its members— Charlie Parker.

An album of the second performance on June 15, billed as *The Paris All-Stars—Homage to Charlie Parker* with a cover featuring a photograph of the medal of the order, is marked by scintillating solos, precise ensemble work, and roars from the enthusiastic audience. Stan shines throughout; he plays a solo feature on Ellington's "Warm Valley" and performs spirited improvisations on "Birks Works," "A Night in Tunisia," and "Oo Pa Pa Da."

After the concert Stan headed for Cap Ferrat on the Riviera, where he had rented a villa which was to be his base during a six-week tour that took him and his musicians to eight countries. Hoogstraten remembered:

> It was a very complicated tour. Lots of cities all over the place.
> Samantha and Donna and Chris would stay behind in the house,

and Stan and I would go and meet the musicians where the gigs were.

It was a beautiful, beautiful big house right on the seaside. Every morning at 7:00, we walked through the garden, down steps to some rocks, and dove off into the sea. There were only rocks there, no beach. . . .

Jean-Philippe Allard came down there with the photographer Jean-Pierre Larcher to make photos for the jackets and liner notes of *Anniversary, Serenity,* and *Billy Highstreet Samba.* Samantha is featured with Stan on the first two, and I'm on the third one.

Larcher was fascinated with Stan and right away began talking about doing a documentary on him. Stan trusted him and was impressed by the work he showed him. And that's how the *People Time* film got started.

People Time is not a conventional documentary but a moving, impressionistic portrait of Stan filterd through Larcher's sensibility. It was completed in 1993, when it was shown on the French-German cultural TV channel, La Sept/Arte.

The bassist Ray Drummond, who had been on the road for months before teaming up with Stan, quit in mid-tour because of fatigue, and Stan quickly found a quality replacement from Sweden, the Japanese musician Yasuhito Mori.

Stan was upbeat when he returned to Malibu in early August and telephoned Judith Share:

> The tour was excellent. We ended stronger than we started. Our next-to-last gig, Aarhus in Denmark, was a crowning success.
>
> We got reviews there that you cannot believe. One said, "The heavens opened up." I believe it, but I don't feel it. I just do the gig, man. It's work. You just work to make it the best you can.
>
> I'll tell you one thing: I don't feel like I'm dying.

Stan was able to test his hypothesis on his mortality when he flew to the Bay area on August 28, 1989, to submit to one of his periodic MRI scans. He cried with joy when his doctor, who had given him less than six months to live thirteen months before, told him the remarkable news that the MRI showed that the liver cancer had shrunk by 70 percent. Stan celebrated again the next day at the Palo Alto Alcoholics Anonymous, where the members welcomed him warmly and gave him a small party and a medallion marking four years of sobriety.

Stan called Shorty Rogers with his good news, and Shorty remembered:

> I'm a born-again Jew. I'm Jewish, but I go to a Christian church.
> It's standard procedure there to form groups to pray for people.
> When Stan became ill, I got members of a band there to pray
> for him daily, and he was very touched.
>
> One day he calls me up, and he was sobbing; he could hardly
> talk. I said, "Cool it. What's going on here?"
>
> He says, "They just got the results, and the tumor decreased
> in size seventy percent. Tell everyone to keep praying for me."
>
> I answered, "I don't have to. It goes on and on and on."
>
> He was so moved, he said, "Shorty, I want to come to the
> church when the band's rehearsing. I just want to thank everyone.
> And maybe I'll bring my horn and sit in with them." Here's this
> great international star, genius of jazz, and it's a band made up
> of guys that work in the shoe store during the day.
>
> He comes with Samantha, his lady. The band leader says, "This
> is Stan Getz. He loves you guys, just wants to say a few words."
> And Stan very emotionally thanks everyone for praying for him,
> and then he asks, "Can I sit in with the band?" They had some
> little blues arrangement, and Stan just started roaring away, took
> around fifteen choruses, and sounded beautiful, and everyone just
> adored it. For the band guys that's the big experience of their life.
>
> Then he says, "Can I sit in the saxophone section? I just want
> to read some parts." The guy sitting next to him is around eighty
> years old, and they're playing real simple things, but he's just
> reading the parts and having fun. Playing in a sax section was
> something he just loved.

During late August and early September, Stan worked intensively with Herb Alpert and musician/composer/arranger Eddie del Barrio on his first recording project for Alpert. Alpert was almost euphoric at the time because he and his partner Jerry Moss were completing a deal to sell their company, A&M, for roughly $500 million to Polygram, the media conglomerate that employed Allard. The transaction, which was consummated a month later, stipulated a continuing role in management for both Alpert and Moss.

The Alpert-del Barrio album was very different from the acoustic quartet sessions preferred by Stan; it involved sixteen musicians, a heavy dose of synthesizers and electric pianos, and meticulously crafted arrangements. Del Barrio and Alpert created the arrangements, which are showcases for

Stan's improvisations and, to a much lesser extent, Kenny Barron's; they all have a Latin flavor. Stan remembered how the album evolved:

> We couldn't figure out what material to play. I got together with Herb and Eddie del Barrio. . . . I went up to Herb's house every day for three weeks and sort of put the skeleton together. That was the preparation we had. The melodies for Eddie, "Waltz for Stan" and "Lovely Lady," were written out. The rest were all à la *Focus,* made up over the background.

Stan went to Colorado to play a benefit for The ARK the week before he was scheduled to record; he wished to divorce himself from the project for a few days because he wanted his solos to be as fresh as possible when he went into the studio on September 13, 14, and 15.

Alpert tried to create a soothing environment for Stan at the first session. He set the lights low, placed a cup of Stan's favorite tea near his stand, and had all the technicians and musicians ready and in place. Then his worst nightmare happened. Stan became upset with a couple of wrong notations on his lead sheet and started cursing del Barrio, who had supervised the preparation of the scores. Del Barrio took umbrage and stalked off, and Stan stormed out as well.

Alpert set to work massaging their egos and in ten minutes had them back in the studio. Stan was still muttering obscenities when del Barrio walked up to him and said, "Fuck you."

Stan answered, "Are you apologizing? I think you're apologizing." When del Barrio said nothing, Stan went on, "Apologies make me so horny."

Then he rushed toward the arranger and embraced him. "Kiss me, you savage," he said, and smacked him on the lips. Del Barrio laughed, the tension dissolved, and everyone got down to work.

Apasionado has structural similarities to Eddie Sauter's *Focus,* but it is not nearly as ambitious. Alpert and del Barrio created rich, beautiful backgrounds for Stan's improvisations, but they are backgrounds and nothing more; Sauter created a complex symphonic composition that could stand on its own without Stan's contributions.

Stan solos at a consistently high level on the CD, alternating between a tough, piercing sound that contrasts dramatically with the lush arrangements and a plaintive timbre which melts into them. His most expressive improvisations occur on the funky "Amorous Cat" and the romantic "Waltz for Stan."

Samantha faced her twenty-fifth birthday on October 8, 1989, and she had come to realize that she had defined her life in terms of men for the previous eight years—Stan and, before him, a high school sweetheart to whom she had been engaged. She began to feel stifled during the European tour, and her frustrations intensified after they returned. She felt an insistent need to explore on her own who she was. She remembered:

> I was just too depressed within my own self, because I wasn't able to express who I was—or feel comfortable expressing or finding out who I was.

By the end of September, she was emotionally spent; on October 3 she told Stan that she had to leave, and two days later she was gone. After an initial burst of anger, he rapidly became depressed but found some solace in attending Yom Kippur services with Alpert on October 7.

Stan's mood was improved by the prospect of performing on October 17, 1989, for the largest audience of his career. He was slated to play the "Star Spangled Banner" for 26 million TV viewers and 63,000 fans as a prelude to a World Series game at Candlestick Park in San Francisco. He had strapped on his saxophone and was about to step onto the field when, for fifteen terrifying seconds, the ground shook and the stadium groaned and trembled; a powerful earthquake had struck.

Stan was rushed to an office in the bowels of the structure and chain-smoked for an hour until Candlestick executives secured a car and driver for him. He directed the driver to take him to Donna Seid's home, where he spent the night. Stan's schedule was too full to allow him to perform at the Series when it was resumed ten days later.

Stan wished to own a home rather than rent one, and in late 1989, Alpert devised a deal which would accommodate his desires; Stan would move a mile up the beach to a house Alpert owned, and he would credit Stan's monthly rental toward an eventual purchase. The house required extensive renovations, and they proceeded after Stan moved in.

Soon after he settled into his new digs, Stan flew to New York with Steve's son Chris to attend Steve's marriage to his second wife, Sharon. The two had met three years earlier, when Steve managed the Fat Tuesday's club and Sharon was a musicians' agent. Pastor John Gensel presided over the nuptials at his church in Manhattan, St. Peter's, on March 10, 1990. Eleven days later, Steve's brother David called Stan to tell him that he had taken a second wife, Marcela, in a ceremony performed at the City Hall of Nibro in Sweden by the city's mayor. David and his first wife, Lena, had divorced the previous year.

Steve and Sharon moved to southern California soon after their wedding, and when they visited Stan, they were deeply disturbed by the depth of his depression at losing Samantha. When she left him, she moved in with a girlfriend whom she had met at an acting class and found a job as a waitress at a posh Beverly Hills restaurant, Maple Drive. Stan came to eat often, leaving large tips for Samantha and notes telling her how much he missed her.

Initially she was wary, but he persisted with his attentions and she became more friendly, occasionally staying in a guest room at his new home. Her ardor stopped, however, at accepting his invitation to join him on his six-week summer tour that would take him to New York and Europe.

Before departing, Stan flew to the Bay area to play a June 8, 1990, benefit for the Stanford Summer Jazz Workshop on a three-decker cruise ship, the *City of San Francisco*. The Stanford Jazz Program, deprived of Stan's presence and the Blokkers' largesse, had survived in 1989 and 1990 through severe belt-tightening and a $10,000 grant from the university. Stan was delighted to help again, particularly since part of the proceeds were destined for a fund in his honor that would benefit disadvantaged students. Jane Walsh accompanied him, and they were happy to be re-united with Jim Nadel, the Oliveiras, the Kelleys, the Anyoses, and other old friends. Stan's eyes misted when he told Jane that he could never repay her and his Stanford friends for helping him attain his sobriety and his dignity.

The 150 guests on the ship, each of whom had paid $125 to attend, enjoyed a cruise along the bay under a full moon as they ate a gourmet dinner and listened to a concert by Stan's quartet. He employed Lou Levy on piano and two musicians who later accompanied him on his summer tour, Alex Blake on bass and Terri Lyne Carrington on drums.

The tour featured several *Apasionado* arrangements that used the electric bass, and Blake had been chosen because he was equally adept at both the acoustic and electric variety; most jazz bassists concentrate on the acoustic instrument and develop only rudimentary skills on the electric one. Blake had been recommended to Stan by Manhattan Transfer, with whom he had played for thirteen years; he passed muster after auditioning only three numbers.

Carrington, twenty-four years of age and a former prodigy, had gradually taken over from Victor Lewis, who wished to explore other career options after eight years with Stan. Carrington had learned to play on the drum set of her grandfather, who had performed with Fats Waller and Duke Ellington, and had become at age twelve the youngest winner of a scholar-ship to the Berklee College of Music. She came to Stan from the band of the Arsenio Hall TV show and had previously performed with Rufus Reid, Wayne Shorter, James Moody, and Clark Terry.

Following the full-moon benefit cruise, Stan visited his doctors in Palo Alto for another of his MRI checks. The result was the best ever: His liver tumor was now so small that it was barely visible. Stan had won himself a nearly complete remission of his cancer and at least two years of life, an almost unheard of outcome.

On June 17 he called Judith Share to tell her the good news about his remission and to muse, "Maybe I can get well without Samantha." He also told Judith that Jane had agreed to accompany him during part of his tour, which kicked off with a concert at Carnegie Hall on June 29, and that he was taking Donna Seid along to provide massages and oversee his diet.

For Jane the trip was a final vacation before the start of an important new job. She was slated on August 1 to begin working for Bill Walsh (no relation), one of America's most famous football personalities. Walsh had quit as Stanford's coach in 1979 to join the San Francisco 49ers professional team, and he won national renown as he led them to three Super Bowl victories. After ten years, the intense pressures of the professional game became intolerable for him, and he left the 49ers at the height of his fame after winning his third Super Bowl in 1989. Walsh had become a mini-industry as a national figure, and Jane was hired to manage his affairs as he broadcast football games for the NBC-TV network, wrote books, made TV commercials for a variety of products, and gave high-priced lectures.

Jane remembered the European tour:

> We were buddies. We weren't sleeping together. My major blow was when he left in 1987. By 1990 there was healing done.
>
> It was good to see that Stan was still growing in his sobriety. My theory of AA is that it takes a very long time to take the onionskins off, to peel the onion. Lightbulbs go off year after year. You say, "My God, this is why I did this, and this is why I felt that way." It's like therapy.

Jane left the tour during the last week of July to begin her work with Bill Walsh.

Stan used two formats during the tour: an acoustic quartet with Barron, Carrington, and Blake and, for selections from *Apasionado*, an electronic sextet created by switching Blake to electric bass and adding Eddie del Barrio and Frank Zottoli on synthesizers. The quartet selections were much longer and constituted roughly 70 percent of each concert.

A videotape of a July 18 concert before a large Munich audience shows Stan performing with great bite and vigor. He looks robust and tan and totally in command of the varied material he plays during the long program. He appears to have completely subdued his cancer.

Beverly flew out to meet Stan at the Los Angeles airport when he returned from Europe on August 12. He was pleased with the tour but tired, and he refreshed himself as they spent ten lazy days at the beach. While they soaked up the sun, Stan harped on the fact that he was lonely and was tired of living alone.

He did something about it in early September. After a mutual friend told him that Samantha had come to realize that she still loved him, he telephoned and told her that he could not live without her. He asked her to join him to talk about a reconciliation, and he suggested that they get together in Colorado Springs, where he would have a couple of free days after playing a benefit for The ARK on September 8, 1990.

Samantha remembered:

> We went to this lake, which was right near Colorado Springs, and we sat down and made a verbal contract. I led off, "I love you, you love me. This is what I need." I set out what I wanted, and then Stanley said, "This is what I need," and we came to an agreement and decided to marry. We set a date, June 23, 1991. . . .
>
> Stanley had to fly into San Francisco from there, and I joined him. That's when we had dinner and Stanley asked my father for my hand in marriage. . . .
>
> I remember my dad asking my mom and me to go powder our noses. He wanted to talk to Stanley alone. When I came back, Stanley had this face. It was like he was an eighteen-year-old who had gotten a talking to—that was the expression on his face. Later I asked, "Dad, what did you say to him?" Basically, he had said, "Look—you better take care of her, you better not be fooling around, blah-blah-blah. . . ."
>
> They loved Stanley. The bottom line is my dad had said, "You know, Stanley, I see how Samantha has that glow back. And I know she's really happy. And that's all I want for her. And if you can make her happy, I don't care what you look like or how old you are."

After receiving the green light from Mr. Ceseña, Stan headed down the coast to perform at the Monterey Jazz Festival on September 23 with an acoustic quartet that included Alex Blake, Kenny Barron, and Victor Lewis filling in for Terri Lyne Carrington.

Dizzy Gillespie, who was scheduled to open the evening program at 7:30, schmoozed with Stan backstage before Stan went on to finish the afternoon concert at 5:15. Dizzy took a seat in the audience to listen and was so taken with the music that he headed onstage to join in, and the audience went wild.

Stan was taking a drag on a newly lit cigarette when Dizzy bounded up, pulled it from his lips and a pack from his breast pocket and tossed them into the audience. Stan took it in good humor, and then he and Dizzy blazed through a high-energy set.

On September 30, 1990, Monica—having been rebuffed on appeals on at least six different divorce issues by New York's primary appeals court, the Appellate Division—took her case to the United States Supreme Court. The Supreme Court is inundated with potential litigants and is extremely selective in choosing cases to consider; less than 2 percent are accepted. The Court's principal selection criterion is that a case raise an important legal or constitutional issue.

Monica believed that her case raised such an issue because her brief called into question the entire rationale and structure of divorce law in New York State. She argued that New York unfairly favored husbands because it thrust divorce cases into the commercial court system, where money mattered most and where breadwinning husbands could place a "crippling economic burden" upon their relatively impoverished wives. She demanded that divorce cases be shifted to the family court system, where expenses were lower and judges were more experienced with child and spouse support and other matrimonial problems.

Monica pictured herself as a standard-bearer for families everywhere, telling a reporter:

> For many families across the United States, the ordinary system that is used to deal with family problems is dinosaurian. I'm not interested in my own case. I'm just interested because it's such a blatant illustration of the malfunctioning of the system.

In a reply Stan scoffed at her rhetoric, saying:

> She would like to picture herself as Florence Nightingale and me as a combination of Attila the Hun and Jack the Ripper, and she couldn't get it past a jury.

The Supreme Court rejected Monica's arguments without comment on November 26, 1990, and she reacted with defiance:

> You haven't heard nothing yet. We've just begun to expose what is going on in matrimonial and divorce cases in New York. This will not be the end of it. I can't talk about it now, but this is just the beginning of something.

In a closing salvo, she quoted poet James Russell Lowell, "Right temporarily defeated is stronger than evil triumphant."

The Supreme Court decision thrust Monica back into New York's courts, and she continued her battles in the Appellate Division. She also took her case into another forum, prime-time television. At 9:00 P.M. on March 12, 1992, 14 million CBS viewers watched her inveigh against the economic burden placed upon wives by the legal profession; she was appearing in a segment concerning the high price of divorce on *Street Stories*, a news magazine show hosted by Ed Bradley, the veteran *60 Minutes* commentator.

Monica describes her marriage on-screen as "a modern love story, a Romeo and Juliet story, and it was also a modern tragedy . . . a lawyer-manufactured tragedy." An interviewer comments, "Stan Getz was struggling with alcohol and later cocaine, was in and out of treatment centers, in and out of affairs with other women, increasingly out of control."

Then Monica says:

> He attacked our son on crutches during a crazy spell. I got a protective order. . . . He started all kinds of counter actions. And even though we loved each other at the time, the lawyers eventually—especially his lawyer—saw this as an opportunity to enrich himself at our family's expense. . . .
>
> We had an eleven-year nightmare which systematically drew all our resources and energies. and for what? No one gained by it—only the lawyer.

Monica may not have liked it, but she was forced to continue her reliance on lawyers as she persevered with her campaigns in the courts after the CBS show. On May 10, 1993, the Appellate Division affirmed both the 1987 jury verdict and the 1989 equitable distribution decision, but Monica was not undone. She came back fighting sixteen days later, carrying her case to New York's highest court, the Court of Appeals. They rejected her arguments on September 9, 1993, and the case finally ended twelve years after Stan initiated it and after the litigants had spent more than $1 million on lawyers.

Judges in three separate courts over a six-year period had found no merit in any of Monica's appeals from the jury verdict and the equitable distribution decision. She attributes her string of defeats to rapacious lawyers, perjured witnesses, and biased judges.

FAREWELL

TWENTY-TWO

TWO WEEKS AFTER he rejoiced at Monica's rejection by the Supreme Court on November 26, 1990, Stan received bad news from his doctor. A key blood test showed that his liver cancer was no longer in remission but was growing again. Soon after, when the tumor began to cause him sharp stomach pain, he told only Samantha and the Alperts.

Diane Schuur was proud that she had achieved her first year of sobriety on October 9, 1990, and she wanted to thank Stan in person for his help in fighting her addictions. She also wanted to close the wounds caused by their contract dispute, which had been settled in 1990 after three years of wrangling. Diane remembered seeing Stan in late December:

Herb Alpert was having a big party for Stan, and we made amends there about stuff that had happened in the past. He said he was really sorry. We hugged. He was pretty healthy. He asked me to sing at his funeral and at his wedding.

He was very sober. He must have had a spiritual awakening; he must have really gotten into contact with God and was able to be at peace.

I'm grateful to him, really. And I'm glad we were able to see each other in sobriety. He was quite a different man after he sobered up. He was completely different. It was quite a relationship that Stan and I had. God bless him, you know. It led me to where I'm at today, which is sober. I love Stan.

Herb Alpert was also impressed by Stan's transformation in sobriety:

He tried to find everyone that he was an asshole to, as he put it, (and make amends). He didn't like his old behavior. It was out of his control. It wasn't the real him. It was an aberration. It was drug-induced. It was craziness. . . . Booze, drugs, pills, whatever it was, that combination.

I met the real guy. I knew the person inside there. I knew the person that we loved to hear. That romantic, sensuous, sensitive, sound musician. I met that person.

Stan had been pressing Billy Hoogstraten for years to leave Wim Wigt and to start his own artists management business with Stan as the cornerstone, and he finally convinced him to do so in December 1990. Hoogstraten flew out to Malibu for ten days in late January to plan with Stan a short trip to Europe in March and an extensive tour there in July and August.

Hoogstraten remembered that his stay in Malibu was both congenial and relaxed:

He was pretty healthy, yeah. We had a good time. And he took me everywhere—taking our swim early in the morning together—having breakfast together.

I met Herb at the studio. Then both Herb and his wife would come down to the house once in a while and hang out over there. We had a birthday party together. Stan's birthday is February 2. But I was leaving, so we did it one day early. At his house in Malibu.

> Mostly people I never met before. I think Shorty Rogers was there. Herb was there, and Lani, his wife. There weren't many people, maybe ten people all together. It was just a small, intimate birthday party.

Stan did not tell Hoogstraten that on the day of the party, doctors told him they had found a second cancer growing in his liver. During the next few weeks he experienced difficulty in eating and suffered recurring bouts of stomach pain as the cancers put increasing pressure on his internal organs. He lost weight and became tired very easily, but he convinced himself that he was in the midst of a temporary setback and must push forward with his plans.

The March trip that Stan and Hoogstraten had committed themselves to involved only Stan and Kenny Barron as performers. When Stan played with Barron in a quartet setting, he usually included in the program a duet with the pianist. These performances were so brilliant that Hoogstraten, Jane Walsh, Jean-Philippe Allard, and other people close to the two men suggested that they make a duet album; during the autumn of 1990, Allard checked with fellow Polygram executive Herb Alpert and found that Alpert had no plans for such a project. Then Allard talked Stan and Barron into making a recording, which he scheduled for March 3 through 6, 1991, before a live audience at the Montmartre in Copenhagen.

Stan and Barron rehearsed their repertoire on February 24 during an engagement at the Charles Hotel in Boston with David and Marcela Getz and Samantha in the audience. This repertoire was a fresh one: It was comprised of tunes which Stan had never recorded before or had neglected for over a decade.

The next day Stan and Samantha flew down to New York for a two-day recording session with singer Abbey Lincoln, who had asked Allard, her producer, to secure Stan for the date. Allard again cleared the project with Herb Alpert and then assembled a stellar group of musicians to back Lincoln on the album, which was called *You Gotta Pay the Band*. In addition to Stan, he hired Hank Jones—who had performed on Stan's first record as a leader forty-five years before—on piano, Charlie Haden on bass, and Mark Johnson on drums. Maxine Roach, daughter of Lincoln's former husband Max Roach, played viola on two tracks.

Lincoln's voice was still strong, in tune, and pliant at age sixty-one, and she projected, like all the fine jazz singers, a distinctive sound. She is an excellent actress, having starred in such films as *Nothing but a Man*, *For Love of Ivy*, and *Mo' Better Blues*, and throughout her career had infused her songs with an astute sense of drama. She knew that Stan would enhance the dramatic and emotive content of her art because of a special rapport she felt with him.

> He's been everywhere I've ever been, and vice-versa, and he knows everything about life. So, for the songs I picked, I picked songs that I thought he would like to perform.
>
> It was easy, because we lived a similar life, Stan and me. . . . He understood everything that was in my heart. My heart was his heart. We never had a chance to work together before, but I knew him when my name was Anna Marie, when I was about twenty-five and he was about twenty-seven.

As they mesh their voices and hearts, Stan and Lincoln create a document of great warmth and intelligence, evoking intense layers of emotion in the listener.

The highlight of the album is "I'm in Love," as Abbey and Stan engage in a witty and warm dialogue at a bright tempo; his solo is extroverted and incisive, a declamatory exercise. He limns a mood of stoic resignation on Abbey's song about death, "When I'm Called Home," and he backs her with particular passion on two Johnny Mandel tunes, "Summer Wishes, Winter Dreams" and "A Time for Love," and Freddie Hubbard's waltz, "Up Jumped Spring."

The recording pleased Lincoln for more than aesthetic reasons:

> I'm really thankful for that album . . . because it started something special for me. It's my first hit album. And I know it's because of Stan. I'm not stupid. He has a lot of people who love him, a wide audience.

Billy Hoogstraten met Stan, Samantha, and Barron when they arrived in Copenhagen, and he was stunned by the change he observed in Stan's appearance. He remembered how different he looked from the man whom he had last seen in the United States on February 1. "In California, it's a man who still has ten years ahead of him. One month later, it's a man who's really dying."

Stan fought both pain and exhaustion during the nights at the Montmartre. Barron remembered:

> Stan's stomach was on fire. . . . I noticed that after each solo he was literally out of breath. It was taxing for him, as he had to

play more and harder without a bass and drums. He couldn't coast, and it really took its toll.

The music they made in Copenhagen, which was issued as a two-CD set called *People Time*, bears no trace of Stan's illness. It is vigorous and feisty and full of humor and expresses an entire rainbow of emotion. It showcases their new repertoire of five ballads and nine exuberant swingers, and it is on an aesthetic par with their previous Montmartre session, which produced the superb quartet CDs, *Anniversary* and *Serenity*.

Barron's mind seems uncannily bonded to Stan's as he creates with him, on every track, passages of daring and felicitous counterpoint. The pianist uses his solo opportunities to indulge brilliantly in a variety of styles—playing 1920s Harlem stride on "(There Is) No Greater Love," high-speed bebop on "The Surrey with the Fringe on Top" and "Softly, As in a Morning Sunrise," and Brahmsian romanticism on "I Remember Clifford" and Eddie del Barrio's "I'm Okay."

The ballad highlight of the CD is Charlie Haden's "First Song (For Ruth)," where Stan and Barron bring forth the tune's deep sadness and longing without indulging in a moment's sentimentality. Stan stomps through the fast numbers, knocking out wickedly wailing, thrusting solos on "(There Is) No Greater Love," "Night and Day," and "East of the Sun" and strutting jauntily through "Gone with the Wind," "The Surrey with the Fringe on Top," and "Like Someone in Love." The principal emotion the musicians convey to the listener throughout the two hours of this recording is joy: joy in mastery, joy in connecting with an audience, joy in invention, joy in swinging.

The Montmartre engagement was scheduled for four nights, March 3 through 6, and when they had created enough material for the CDs during the first three, Stan wanted to cancel the last one because he was feeling so bad. But Hoogstraten convinced him that the Copenhagen audience had a particularly deep affection for him, and he consented to an abbreviated performance on March 6. When Hoogstraten saw how thoroughly the effort had drained Stan, he regretted that he had encouraged him to play.

They journeyed to Paris to appear on March 8 at a large festival called Banlieues Bleues, and Stan's performance was subpar. He tried hard, but pain and fatigue prevented him from creating his powerful sound and from spinning out long phrases.

Stan was very ill and totally exhausted when he and Samantha returned from Paris on March 10, 1991. They rested at Malibu and took a short vacation in Hawaii, where his pain became more intense. His illness

motivated Stan to revise his will, and soon after their return, he invited John
Cohan, Herb Alpert's estate lawyer, to his home to discuss it with him. The
meeting took place on March 29, and Stan interrupted it for short intervals
several times, because he was suffering bouts of intense pain.

Stan had signed a will on February 16, 1989, which divided his estate
equally between Samantha, Steve, David, and Beverly. When Samantha
left him, he signed a codicil on October 10, 1989, removing her from
consideration, but he restored her in another codicil when he met with
Cohan. Because he believed that Samantha was extremely naive about
financial management, he instructed Cohan to put her one-quarter share
in a trust to be managed by Herb Alpert. Cohan argued strongly that
Stan should leave nominal amounts to Nicky and Pamela because under
California law such a course would make it much more difficult for them
to challenge the will. Stan adamantly rejected this suggestion.

Cohan returned to Malibu on April 12 with the new will, and Stan
executed it. It was challenged successfully by Nicky and Pamela, and on
July 8, 1993, an agreement was signed giving each of them 8.4 percent
shares. The shares of Steve, David, and Beverly were reduced to 19.4
percent, and Samantha's was left at 25 percent.

On May 22, 1991, Samantha signed Stan's name to a $100,000 check
on his Dreyfus Money Market account, and on June 4, 1991, she deposited
it to a bank account that she and Stan held jointly. She claimed that
Stan had instructed her to do this. She spent $23,500 on household,
medical, and business expenses and the remaining $76,500 on herself.
Steve, Beverly, and David sued her for the $76,500 and on July 1, 1993,
she agreed to give to them the first $75,000 in income earned by her trust.

On April 3, 1991, Stan suffered a severe internal hemorrhage. The
marauding cancer had eroded major blood vessels in his stomach, requir-
ing surgical repairs and a transfusion at nearby St. John's Hospital.

He was back at St. John's frequently during the remainder of April to
have fluids drained from his stomach. The liver and other internal organs
filter such fluids prior to expulsion from the body, and as the filtering
process begins to fail, the fluids accumulate painfully; drainage affords
immediate relief. Stan's doctors provided additional relief by putting him
on a regimen of painkillers.

Jean-Philippe Allard stayed with Stan and Samantha in Malibu for two
weeks in April as the two men worked with the tapes of *People Time* to
choose the best tracks for release on the CD. Allard remembered:

> He went to see a doctor every day, and he spent most of his time
> in bed. He was hanging out in his beautiful house resting and

listening to the music. He was enjoying the sun. We had dinner and lunch every day together.

During late April the cancer rampaged on and attacked Stan's stomach and intestines, making adequate nutrition impossible. He had entered a condition called cachexia. It is "characterized by weakness, poor appetite, alterations in metabolism, and wasting of muscles and other tissues," according to Dr. Sherwin Nuland, author of *How We Die*. Stan was back at St. John's for the first two weeks in May, but his optimism was undiminished. He felt sure that he would fight through this crisis and emerge strong and healthy by summer. Samantha participated in his denial. She remembered:

> I was very young. I was in the middle of it. I was heartbroken. I was planning a wedding even through all this. That was my dream. I thought how could all this be—I was in denial. . . .
>
> In fact, it would take me stepping out of the situation to make a mature decision. And first of all, I was obeying Stanley. Second of all, I couldn't see past my nose.

Randi Quat, Stan's principal nurse at St. John's, had just emerged from the operating room there in blood-splattered scrubs and rubber gloves when she was approached by two men with pony tails: a tall one—Herb Alpert—and a short one—Eddie del Barrio; Stan's two friends hated seeing Stan in the impersonal surroundings of the hospital and had decided to seek a nurse who could provide and supervise high quality care at Stan's home.

They were directed to Randi because she had extensive experience with the seriously ill, and they asked her whether she could handle difficult patients. When they revealed that they were talking about Stan, she said, "Sure, it's worth a try"; she had already dealt with Miles Davis and Elizabeth Taylor, and she didn't expect Stan to be any more fractious than they had been.

Stan and Samantha were still in denial about the seriousness of his condition after he was brought home badly weakened in mid-May; they clung to the hope that he would recover in time to make his summer tour of Europe following their wedding on June 23. Billy Hoogstraten sensed Stan's true condition and called several times suggesting that they cancel the tour; he finally prevailed on May 23.

Randi tried to make Stan as comfortable as possible after she got him home. She ignored Samantha's strictures and sneaked him cigarettes, and

they ate pizza and talked for hours as they looked out over the Pacific.
He impressed her:

> There was just something about him. You knew you were around
> greatness. I mean, it was like he owned the ground he stood on.
> Even being sick, even in a bathrobe, even knowing I had the
> final say over whatever he wants to do—you knew it. There was
> something about the way he walked, the way he talked.

By Friday, May 31, it was obvious that Stan did not have long to live,
and Samantha telephoned his children and urged them to come quickly
to be with him. Everyone made arrangements to travel to Malibu except
Pamela; her brother Nicky believes that she carried too much bitterness
within her:

> She's really, really angry. She's really mixed up. . . . She didn't fly
> out here when she knew he was sick. She has a tremendous
> amount of anger and resentment in her. I felt that way, too, but
> I feel like ten years down the line, I think you might mess yourself
> up more if you don't go and make your peace.

Nicky found his mother in Sweden when he called her about Stan's
condition, and Monica passed the news on to Peter Torgner and his
mother Inga there. Monica had gone to Sweden to gather evidence in
her ongoing struggle to reverse the divorce verdicts. She had Peter's
and Inga's blood tested for DNA evidence of Stan's paternity, and she
had gotten them to sign affidavits concerning their relationships with
him.
 Peter remembered:

> First, I got the positive DNA results. And then they said he was
> going down very fast. Then I said, "I'm going there." So, I bor-
> rowed some money at the bank to fly to LA. I couldn't afford it,
> but I really wanted to be there.

Nicky, Beverly, David and Marcela, Steve and Sharon, and Billy Hoogstraten arrived during the weekend. Hoogstraten flew in on Sunday, June 2,
responding to a call from Stan on Saturday:

> Later on I learned that everybody was surprised that he got out
> of his bed and got his voice together to call me. Because he

couldn't speak normally anymore. I could hear on the phone that he had a problem speaking.

He said, "Well, Billy, could you come out?"

I said, "Sure, I'll come out—as soon as possible. It's time to say goodbye, isn't it?"

He said, "No, no. I'm not dying, Billy. But I would love to have you over here for just a couple of days."

Hoogstraten brought from Holland two dozen of Stan's favorite flowers, long-stemmed red roses, and placed them in a vase by his bed. He and Beverly stayed in the house with Stan and Samantha, and David and Marcela bunked in with Bob Getz and Stan's secretary, Maggie Crim, who shared an apartment just minutes away. Nicky, Steve, Sharon, and Steve's son Chris visited from their homes nearby.

David was dismayed when he encountered his father:

I went into his house saying, "Well, where's Dad?" And I went to a room and there was a man sitting there, and I was still saying, "Where's Dad?" I didn't even recognize him; he was so emaciated.

The two managed to share a beautiful moment soon after:

It was very difficult because he had great difficulty talking, but one of the everlasting, most beautiful fantastic memories of my life—I'll never forget till the last breath of my body.

I was sitting on the couch in the living room, and we were watching the Lakers play the Bulls for the championship. And Dad came in and they helped him sit on the couch next to me. And he put his head on my shoulder. That was such a beautiful feeling. And he put his arm around me. . . . He couldn't talk, he could hardly talk. But it sort of didn't need any words.

Randi found it difficult to achieve her principal goal, which was to maximize Stan's comfort, as Samantha, the family, the Alperts, Hoogstraten, a holistic chiropractor, and assorted visitors swirled around him.

Samantha wanted so much to believe that Stan could recover that she followed the holistic chiropractor's advice and took Stan off his painkillers:

I remember now the sedative thing. I had some hope of maybe he would get better. I wanted him to live. And this is still the fact of—in denial. I was losing someone who I really much loved.

After several agonizingly painful hours, Beverly countermanded the sedative order, Stan found peace again, and tensions built between the two women. Other tensions grew when Nicky suggested several times that Monica fly out to Malibu. Samantha, backed strongly by the Alperts, told him that she was not wanted there, and he replied, "I'll tell her that, but I can't stop her."

Stan's comfort level was not enhanced by daily psychiatric sessions in which Samantha participated, therapy from the holistic chiropractor, a tearful visit on Tuesday afternoon by Shorty Rogers, Charlie Haden, Lou Levy, and Johnny Mandel, and the appearance the same day of a man named Steve Pettijohn who claimed he was Stan's illegitimate son. Pettijohn never pressed his claim, and the family doubts its legitimacy.

In the midst of this hubbub, Samantha managed a few reflective moments with Stan:

> We were in the room, and he said, "Why is this happening to me?"
>
> And I said, "Well, I guess because it needs to happen to you."
>
> He said, "It's not fair, I have everything I ever wanted, and now I have to go away."
>
> Then we held on to each other and cried.

And Herb Alpert achieved a silent communion with him:

> I saw him every day. It was at times unbearably sad to see him because he was such a handsome, robust guy and he just withered away. Two days before he died I spent some alone time with him. . . .
>
> He was sitting in the chair. I walked in the room and we were alone together and he looked at me with that great penetrating look and he put both his thumbs up as if to say, "Thanks; and everything is okay." I think he had come to terms with what was happening and he was at peace with it. . . .
>
> He touched me deeply. . . . I will remember him as the best friend a person could ever hope for.

Stan spent most of Wednesday, June 5, with Beverly, alternately talking and napping as his condition deteriorated. Sores in his mouth prevented him from eating, his stomach was painfully distended, and he was developing pneumonia. Randi gave him morphine to ease his pain and cigarettes for pleasure. She decided to stay till morning, working through a twenty-six-hour shift.

Stan moved in and out of sleep until 3:00 A.M., when he decided he wanted to look at the Pacific. Randi remembered:

> He got up into the wheelchair. It was kind of hard to manipulate him with the big belly. And you couldn't see a damn thing; it was too misty. And he said, "What's the fucking point?" He had spent all this energy.
>
> So he gets back into bed. He's in a lot of pain at that point, and I gave him some morphine. After that, he turned on his side. I'm listening to his lungs and they sounded terrible.
>
> That was when he called for Bev. I said, "Do you want me to go wake up Beverly?" He said, "No, not her." He was hallucinating about his first wife—regressing.

Stan then fell into a deep sleep. Randi left at 10:00 A.M., after cleaning him up and turning him over to a relief nurse. He never woke again. When Randi returned at 3:00 P.M., his breathing had become very labored, and she, the other nurses, Samantha, his children, his brother, and Billy Hoogstraten sat a vigil at his bedside. As Hoogstraten remembered, they were interrupted by a phone call:

> At four o'clock somebody called the house, and nobody knew who it was. I heard, "Some guy from Sweden is calling from the airport." And I said, "Wait a minute. Give me the phone." It was the guy Peter nobody knew about. I was the only one who knew about him.
>
> He said, "I'm here at the airport and I want to see my Dad." I said, "Peter, listen, man, nobody knows about you. Stan is dying. He's going to die within half an hour, forty-five minutes. Whatever. Please call me back in fifteen minutes."
>
> I got everybody together and said, "Listen, it's a weird surprise at this moment, but I have to tell you guys. There's this guy at the airport who is a son of Stan, and in a way, brother to you. He's there and he wants to come." And they said, "Let him come."

Randi remembered that Stan died at 5:00 P.M. "He just stopped breathing. We took a blood pressure, and there was no blood pressure. It was actually kind of peaceful. They were all at peace with it at that point."

Hoogstraten was giving directions to Peter Torgner at the moment Stan died, but he returned to the room seconds later.

> We were all gathered around the bed. Samantha closed his eyes and took one of the roses I had brought and put it in his hands. We were standing there, and nobody was saying anything. Nicky broke the silence by saying, "Well, we may feel sad about him now, but let's not forget that he hasn't been that nice to us all the time." Like giving himself some comfort that way. We were still standing all around the bed. And everybody was in tears.

Hoogstraten introduced Torgner to everyone when he arrived at 5:30 P.M. Peter remembered:

> When I got there, he had been gone for twenty minutes or something. I said, "Wow, is it too late? Don't tell me it's too late. I've come all the way from Sweden." I was shocked to see his wasted form.
>
> I got out of the room and cried a bit. Then I asked to be alone with him. They said, "Okay." I was just sitting and talking to him. When you see a dead person, you get into another stage. It's like something relieved from your chest.

That evening after Stan's body was taken to a funeral home, Samantha created a shrine in Stan's living room with his horn, his photograph, and candles, and Herb and Lani Alpert came over to help plan the funeral service. Stan had requested that he be cremated, and everyone felt that it would be appropriate for his grandson Chris to scatter his ashes into his beloved Pacific. Shorty Rogers, Stan's Bronx friend of fifty-one years, agreed to make his boat available for a service; it was a forty-six-foot, wide-beam trawler that could accommodate more than twenty people. Then Alpert said that he would take responsibility for the arrangements and that he would bring a CD player to the boat and play Stan's recordings chosen by those dear to him.

Later that evening, Beverly telephoned Monica at Nicky's request, and between sobs, Monica asked if she should fly out for the service on the boat. She agreed to stay home after Beverly insisted that her presence would be inappropriate.

The family, Samantha, Herb Alpert, and Billy Hoogstraten were joined by Jean-Philippe Allard (who flew in from Paris), Donna Seid, Eddie del

Barrio, Lou Levy, Samantha's parents, Steve Pettijohn, and Peter Torgner for the service. Pamela sent a wreath with the legend, "I Forgive You."

They boarded the trawler late Sunday morning from Shorty's yacht club down the coast at Marina Del Rey. He remembered:

> It was a . . . gorgeous day out on the water. We went out over six miles, and the water's flat like a pane of glass, no other boats, no other activity around us. Herb's wife Lani didn't come; she looks at a boat and gets seasick.
>
> It must have taken us forty minutes to get there. [People were] just chatting, just kind of mingling around listening to Stan's beautiful music.
>
> I put the boat in neutral and let it slow down until it stopped, and everyone goes up on the front deck to gather together. Herb proceeds to play "Blood Count," ringing out over the water. It was too heavy, everyone with heads bowed, looking the other way, just tears flowing, very quietly, very, very dignified.
>
> Stan's grandson came with the tenor saxophone case. In it was the box with the ashes, and he put the ashes in the water.
>
> I thought before it happened that someone would say a prayer or something, but the music said it all. Stan spoke to us through the music, and it was very heavy, the dignity and beauty of it. I'm sure it was pleasing to Stan. And then we went back.

Lani Alpert greeted everyone when the boat docked, and they ate a quiet lunch at Shorty's yacht club. Then they left and went their separate ways.

NOTES

Quotations without notes are from interviews by the author and his staff.

FOREWORD

Page

v–vi   **It's like a . . . is all about.** Stan Getz on Phil Schaap's radio show *Traditions in Swing,* WKCR-FM, New York, 3/4/89.

vi   **My life is . . . in my life.** Stan Getz, liner notes for *Another World,* Columbia Records, 1978.

TWO
FROM MINEVICH TO BIG TEA: A MUSICAL JOURNEY

16   **The physical training . . . one of you."** Don DeMichael, "A Long Look at Stan Getz, Part 1," *Down Beat,* 5/19/66.

17   **My life is . . . reaching and reshaping.** Stan Getz, liner notes for *Another World*, Columbia Records, 1978.

21   **It's like a . . . is all about.** Stan Getz on Phil Schaap's radio show *Traditions in Swing*, WKCR-FM, New York, 3/4/89.

25   **The time of . . . way it was.** Gary Giddins, *Riding on a Blue Note* (New York, Oxford University Press, 1981), p. 76.

26   **We were sitting . . . He was tremendous.** Stan Getz on Phil Schaap's radio show *Traditions in Swing*, WKCR-FM, New York, 3/4/89.

26   **Listen closely to . . . horn to lips.** Ibid., pp. 75, 76, 78.

26–27   **Teagarden was the . . . seamless lyrical shapes.** Gunther Schuller, *The Swing Era* (New York, Oxford University Press, 1989), pp. 590–591.

27   **"In my early . . . and it's logical."** Les Tompkins, "Giving It Back to God," *Crescendo*, reprinted 3/89.

27   **"Can you imagine . . . was some training."** Max Jones, *Talking Jazz* (New York, W. W. Norton & Company, 1988), p. 53.

THREE
THE PRESIDENT AND THE NEEDLE

31   **"They still had . . . Jewish building owner."** Don DeMichael, "A Long Look at Stan Getz, Part 1," *Down Beat*, 5/19/66.

33   **"a lifetime product . . . the Puritan ethic,"** Carol Easton, *Straight Ahead: The Story of Stan Kenton* (New York, Da Capo Press, 1973), p. 90.

33   **He got in . . . to the people.** Buddy Childers on the videotape *Back to Balboa Highlights: The Kenton Discussions*, Goal Productions, 1991.

34   **"We were the . . . in that band."** Al Harding on the videotape, Ibid.

34   **When it comes . . . built to thrill . . .** Carol Easton, *Straight Ahead: The Story of Stan Kenton* (New York, Da Capo Press, 1973), p. 120.

34   **Some of the . . . all their own. . . .** John S. Wilson, "Stan Kenton, Band Leader, Dies; Was Center of Jazz Controversies," *The New York Times*, 8/27/79.

34–35   **Whenever you play . . . listening, you're free.** "In Tribute to Stan Kenton," *Crescendo*, 10/79.

35   **"What's the idea?" . . . at your shoes."** Carol Easton, *Straight Ahead: The Story of Stan Kenton* (New York, Da Capo Press, 1973), p. 83.

35–36   **This fellow came . . . Stan Getz, folks.** Anita O'Day on the videotape *Back to Balboa Highlights: The Kenton Discussions*, Goal Productions, 1991.

36   **In 1944 it . . . dancing to it.** Anita O'Day, *High Times Hard Times* (New York, Limelight Editions, 1981), p. 134.

36   **We can't cut . . . was really blowing.** Ibid., p. 135.

38   **Technically speaking, I . . . did to me.** Ibid.

38–39   **The key aspect . . . teenaged Louis Armstrong.** From Phil Schaap article included in Lewis Porter (editor), *A Lester Young Reader* (Washington, Smithsonian Institution Press, 1991), p. 10.

39   **I always felt . . . shortened to Pres.** Bill Crow, *Jazz Anecdotes* (New York, Oxford University Press, 1990), p. 203.

40   **He would say . . . And he did.** From Lee Young interview with Patricia Williard included in Lewis Porter (editor), *A Lester Young Reader* (Washington, Smithsonian Institution Press, 1991), p. 36.

41   **Lester Young was . . . his third chorus].** From Louis Gottlieb article included in Ibid., p. 215.

41   **If you have . . . the usual progression.** From Nat Hentoff book excerpt included in Ibid., p. 71.

42   **He was the . . . it comes out. . . .** Don DeMichael, "A Long Look at Stan Getz, Part 1," *Down Beat*, 5/19/66.

42–43   **White people were . . . your left hand."** Whitney Balliett, "Pres," *The New Yorker*, 2/23/81.

FOUR
BENNY, BEBOP, AND BEVERLY

47   **Benny hired and . . . all over again.** Ross Firestone, *Swing, Swing, Swing* (New York, W. W. Norton & Company, 1993), p. 327.

47   **Once in London, . . . rid of him."** Nat Shapiro and Nat Hentoff, *Hear Me Talkin' To Ya* (New York, Dover Publications, Inc., 1966), p. 372.

48   **My father was . . . real best friend.** Rachel Goodman Edelson in the PBS-TV documentary *Benny Goodman: Adventures in the Kingdom of Swing*.

48   **He never could . . . everything was "Pops."** Terry Gibbs in Ibid.

49   **. . . Through no fault . . . identity he needed.** Ross Firestone, *Swing, Swing, Swing* (New York, W. W. Norton & Company, 1993), p. 115.

50   **The band was . . . bigger and bigger. . . ."** Ibid., p. 78.

51   **When we got . . . were the audience.** Ibid., p. 200.

51   **The Goodman Orchestra's . . . of its manifestations."** Ibid., p. 199.

52   **The whole point . . . jazz was art.** James Lincoln Collier, *Benny Goodman and the Swing Era* (New York, Oxford University Press, 1989), p. 219.

52   **"Teddy and I . . . a real kick."** Ross Firestone, *Swing, Swing, Swing* (New York, W. W. Norton & Company, 1993), p. 135.

53   **I was in . . . bands. So wonderful . . .** Max Jones, *Talking Jazz* (New York, W. W. Norton & Company, 1988), p. 52.

54   **Great musician, Benny . . . music, Benny Goodman.** Stan Getz on Phil Schaap's radio show *Traditions in Swing*, WKCR-FM, New York, 3/4/89.

54   **How do I . . . first major influences.** Max Jones, *Talking Jazz* (New York, W. W. Norton & Company, 1988), pp. 52–53.

54–55   **Benny Goodman was . . . over by it. . . .** Stan Getz on Phil Schaap's radio show *Traditions in Swing*, WKCR-FM, New York, 3/4/89.

55   **Once every 20 . . . still being explored. . . .** Max Jones, *Talking Jazz* (New York, W. W. Norton & Company, 1988), p. 51.

55   **When I first . . . was just great.** Howard Lucraft, "Looks at the Past and the Present of Stan Getz," *Crescendo International*, 2/90.

55   **"Koko" was the . . . a gleeful audacity.** Gary Giddins, *Celebrating Bird: The Triumph of Charlie Parker* (New York, Beech Tree Books, 1987), p. 88.

58   **It was beautiful . . . times in jazz.** Ira Gitler, *Swing to Bop: An Oral History of the Transition in Jazz in the 1940s* (New York, Oxford University Press, 1985), p. 141.

58–59   **In the old . . . never forget that.** Max Jones, *Talking Jazz* (New York, W. W. Norton & Company, 1988), p. 52.

59–60   **As marvelous as . . . an unfamiliar voicing.** James Lincoln Collier, *Benny Goodman and the Swing Era* (New York, Oxford University Press, 1989), p. 329.

60   **The band had . . . of your life.** Ross Firestone, *Swing, Swing, Swing* (New York, W. W. Norton & Company, 1993), p. 329.

61   **I thought Stan . . . him another chance.** Nat Shapiro and Nat Hentoff, *Hear Me Talkin' To Ya* (New York, Dover Publications, Inc., 1966), p. 372.

61   **Most obvious change . . . even better things.** "Gene Krupa," *Metronome,*
3/46.

FIVE
WOODY'N YOU

68   **"I played alto . . . Herbie Steward's horn."** Dan Morgenstern, "Blindfold
Test; Stan Getz," *Down Beat,* 5/10/73.
69   **We had a . . . for jam sessions.** Joseph Woodard, "Stan Getz; Back on the
Beach," *Down Beat,* 7/90.
70   **Stone is living . . . trained seal acts.** "Butch Stone's New Coast Crew Tops,"
Down Beat, 8/13/47.
71   **Gene wrote and . . . just like syrup.** As recorded by author at "Early Autumn—An All-Star Celebration of the Woody Herman Orchestra, the Second Herd
Panel," Newport, California, 9/24/93.
71   **We were all . . . still the daddy.** B.H., "Zoot," *Metronome,* 12/1/50.
71–72   **That was a . . . then a transfer.** Ira Gitler, *Swing to Bop: An Oral History of
the Transition in Jazz in the 1940s* (New York, Oxford University Press, 1985), p. 161.
72   **I was listening . . . factory in Milwaukee.** Woody Herman and Stuart Troup,
The Woodchopper's Ball: The Autobiography of Woody Herman (New York, E. P.
Dutton, 1990), p. 5.
74   **"There will always . . . the whole thing."** Herb Wong interview of Woody
Herman, Jazz Oral History Project, The Smithsonian Institution, Cassette 1, December
28, 1978, p. 36.
74   **"With the personnel . . . pieces for us."** Woody Herman and Stuart Troup,
The Woodchopper's Ball: The Autobiography of Woody Herman (New York, E. P.
Dutton, 1990), p. 39.
74   **"he liked my writing so much."** Dizzy Gillespie with Al Fraser. *To Be or
Not to Bop: Memoirs—Dizzy Gillespie* (Garden City, New York, Doubleday & Company, Inc., 1979), p. 186.
74   **His arranging ability . . . gone the farthest.** Herb Wong interview of Woody
Herman, Jazz Oral History Project, The Smithsonian Institution, Cassette 1, December
28, 1978, p. 43.
75   **Ralph Burns was . . . the next state.** Woody Herman and Stuart Troup, *The
Woodchopper's Ball: The Autobiography of Woody Herman* (New York, E. P. Dutton,
1990), p. 52.
75   **"Yes, this is . . . Woody Herman Herd."** Ibid., pp. 49–50.
75   **"I called it . . . that really stuck."** Ibid.
75   **"he could blow . . . into the horn,"** Steve Voce, *Woody Herman* (London,
Apollo Press Limited, 1986), p. 36.
75   **"wild and yet . . . and to see."** Gene Lees, *Meet Me at Jim & Andy's: Jazz
Musicians and Their World,* (New York, Oxford University Press, 1988), p. 95.
76   **On one-nighters, Woody . . . the boss wished.** Woody Herman and Stuart
Troup, *The Woodchopper's Ball: The Autobiography of Woody Herman* (New York, E.
P. Dutton, 1990), p. 52.
77   **He was completely . . . and not jazz.** Steve Voce, *Woody Herman* (London,
Apollo Press Limited, 1986) p. 47.
77   **"I can listen . . . in about five."** Ibid., pp. 47–48.
79   **I was disturbed . . . up the band. . . .** Woody Herman and Stuart Troup, *The*

Woodchopper's Ball: The Autobiography of Woody Herman (New York, E. P. Dutton, 1990), p. 69.

79 **It had nothing . . . was destroying Charlotte.** Gene Lees, *Meet Me at Jim & Andy's: Jazz Musicians and Their World* (New York, Oxford University Press, 1988) p. 87.

79 **Being off the . . . into the bathtub.** Woody Herman and Stuart Troup, *The Woodchopper's Ball: The Autobiography of Woody Herman* (New York, E. P. Dutton, 1990), p. 70.

79 **Abe decided to . . . got bumped off.** William D. Clancy with Audree Coke Kenton, *Woody Herman: Chronicles of the Herds* (New York, Schirmer Books, 1995), p. 109.

80 **One night, some . . . something productive again. . . .** Woody Herman and Stuart Troup, *The Woodchopper's Ball: The Autobiography of Woody Herman* (New York, E. P. Dutton, 1990), p. 72.

80 **When I heard . . . put it together.** Herb Wong interview of Woody Herman, Jazz Oral History Project, The Smithsonian Institution, Cassette 1, December 28, 1978, pp. 61–62.

81 **The Second Herd . . . terrific bebop charts.** Woody Herman and Stuart Troup, *The Woodchopper's Ball: The Autobiography of Woody Herman* (New York, E. P. Dutton, 1990), pp. 74–75.

81–82 **From the very . . . a moment's hesitation. . . .** Larry Kart, "Leading Survivors; Reunited Woody Herman & Stan Getz Reflect," *Chicago Tribune*, 3/29/87.

82 **It sure makes . . . out of you.** George Hoefer, "Stan Getz: Always a Melodist," *Down Beat*, 5/22/65.

SIX
FOUR BROTHERS

84 **"Within one year . . . in American music."** Ted Hallock, "New Herd Frenetic, Frantic, Flashy, Faffy, Factual, Fine, Period," *Down Beat*, 12/31/47.

86 **"Pres, what do . . . me a song?"** Stan Getz on Phil Schaap's radio show *Traditions in Swing*, WKCR-FM, New York, 3/4/89.

86 **Al Cohn loved . . . recognize Al's greatness.** Woody Herman and Stuart Troup, *The Woodchopper's Ball: The Autobiography of Woody Herman* (New York, E. P. Dutton, 1990), p. 77.

86 **Cohn was renowned . . . in Jersey City."** Bill Crow, *Jazz Anecdotes* (New York, Oxford University Press, 1990), pp. 320–321.

87 **I remember playing . . . was near us.** Joe Smith, *Off the Record: An Oral History of Popular Music* (New York, Warner Books, 1989), pp. 48, 49.

87 **It was no . . . show his ability.** Woody Herman and Stuart Troup, *The Woodchopper's Ball: The Autobiography of Woody Herman* (New York, E. P. Dutton, 1990), pp. 80, 84.

88 **They were seven . . . down Serge's leg.** Ibid., p. 81.

88 **"What do you . . . them by heart."** Steve Voce, *Woody Herman* (London, Apollo Press Limited, 1986), p. 57.

90 **"When Fate deals . . . tab on you."** Ross Russell, *Bird Lives!* (New York, Charterhouse, 1973), p. 277.

90–91 **The most startling . . . wonderful rhythmic smack.** "With Dramatically No Weak Spots, Herman Herd Gives Magnificent Performance," Michael Levin, *Down Beat*, 11/17/48.

91   It was a . . . compare with us? Ira Gitler, *Swing to Bop: An Oral History of the Transition in Jazz in the 1940s* (New York, Oxford University Press, 1985), pp. 235–236, 239.

93   That was like . . . Woody Herman band. As recorded by author at "Early Autumn—An All-Star Celebration of the Woody Herman Orchestra, the Second Herd Panel," Newport Beach, California, 9/24/93.

93   Ava Gardner was . . . and leave Ava. William D. Clancy with Audree Coke Kenton, *Woody Herman: Chronicles of the Herds* (New York, Schirmer Books, 1995), p. 135.

93–94   The audience that . . . until the mid-1950s. Woody Herman and Stuart Troup, *The Woodchopper's Ball: The Autobiography of Woody Herman* (New York, E. P. Dutton, 1990), p. 75.

95   The fourth movement . . . and forgotten about. Stan Getz on Phil Schaap's radio show *Traditions in Swing*, WKCR-FM, New York, 3/4/89.

95   Woody's a smart . . . pointed to Stan. Ira Gitler, *Swing to Bop: An Oral History of the Transition in Jazz in the 1940s* (New York, Oxford University Press, 1985), p. 237.

96   My wife had . . . going to leave. Don DeMichael, "A Long Look at Stan Getz, Part 1," *Down Beat*, 5/19/66; Larry Kart, "Leading Survivors: Reunited Woody Herman & Stan Getz Reflect," *Chicago Tribune*, 3/29/87.

97   Schoenberg: You have . . . melody, and singing. Loren Schoenberg and Dan Morgenstern, "Jazz from the Archives" radio show WBGO-FM, 7/19/92.

97   I needed the . . . the ten dollars." Don DeMichael, "A Long Look at Stan Getz, Part 1," *Down Beat*, 5/19/66.

98   Woody was a . . . guy's musical personality. . . . Larry Kart, "Leading Survivors: Reunited Woody Herman & Stan Getz Reflect," *Chicago Tribune*, 3/29/87.

98   He adored standing . . . good musicians play. . . . Ibid.

98   That was the . . . on the horses. Jean-Louis Ginibre, "Stan Getz—Toute Nouveau, Tout Beau," *Jazz Magazine*, 4/71.

99   Pee Wee had . . . the other end. Bill Crow, *Jazz Anecdotes* (New York, Oxford University Press, 1990), p. 177.

100   "half a mother-fucker." Ibid., p. 202.

101   What did people . . . like that forever? Gary Giddins, "Forty Years Later: Charlie Parker and His Brood," *Village Voice*, 8/22/89.

101   The acclaim for . . . "Early Autumn" side. *Metronome Yearbook*, 1950.

SEVEN
A NICE BUNCH OF GUYS

104   "Unlike most all-star . . . turned them out." "Diggin' the Discs with Mix," *Down Beat*, 5/5/50.

104   Herewith, . . . some comment . . . first-rate add Stan. Barry Ulanov, "The Editors Speak," *Metronome*, 2/50.

105   Buddy Stewart was . . . North Hollywood, Calif. "Buddy Stewart Killed in Wreck," *Down Beat*, 3/10/50.

106   The prospect of . . . together in 1950. Jack Chambers, *Milestones I; The Music and Times of Miles Davis to 1960* (Toronto, University of Toronto Press, 1983), p. 125.

107   *Birth of the . . . hum it also.* Miles Davis with Quincy Troupe, *Miles—The Autobiography* (New York, Simon & Schuster, 1989), p. 119.

107   ...there is little ... of cool jazz. Barry Ulanov, "The Sound: Stan Getz, that is, and that's cool jazz," *Metronome*, 6/50.

107   **I can play ... stompin' tenor man.** Leonard Feather, "Stan," *Metronome*, 12/50.

108   **I had been ... about the music.** Herb Wong, "Stan Getz: A Memorial," *Jazz Educators Journal*, Fall 1991.

111–112   **Stan Getz's quintet ... in many months.** Jack Tracy, "Chicago Band Briefs: Fresh Ideas, Crack Men Make New Getz 5 Great," *Down Beat*, 10/19/51.

112   **"Parker 51," written ... friend Ray Parker.** Letter from Lee Raney to Dan Morgenstern and Loren Schoenberg, 7/28/92.

112   **...how much jazz ... of human potential.** Stanley Crouch, "Jordan/Harris in the High-Speed Present," *Village Voice*, 12/9–15/82.

113   **I can imagine ... absence from NBC.** "Getz Gets Going at NBC, Spurns Road for Studios," *Down Beat*, 5/21/52.

114   **It was just ... the studio work.** Don DeMichael, "A Long Look at Stan Getz, Part 1," *Down Beat*, 5/19/66.

115   **Heroin had a ... bunch of guys!"** Bill Crow, *From Birdland to Broadway*, (New York, Oxford University Press, 1992), p. 95.

116–117   **He was leaning ... any of you."** Ibid., pp. 95–96.

118   **My aims should ... to sell jazz.** "Critics Still Irritate Granz as Another Season Ends," *Down Beat*, 12/28/51.

119   **My concerts are ... was segregated seating.** Nat Hentoff, "Uncompromising Impresario," *Quest*, February/March, 1980. Leonard Feather, "Jazz Millionaire," *Esquire*, 1/57.

122   **I'm going out ... for the band.** "Stan Getz Excited Over Idea of Joining Gerry Mulligan 4," *Down Beat*, 2/25/53.

122   **I don't know ... it with anyone.** "Combine with Getz? Not For Me: Mulligan," *Down Beat*, 3/11/53.

122–123   **The important part ... on young talent.** "Chords and Discords: Mulligan Stew Getz Boiled Down By Stan," *Down Beat*, 4/8/53.

123–124   **I'd assumed that ... of driving time.** Steve Voce, "John Williams; Time Remembered," *Jazz Journal*, 6/94.

125   **He's one of ... just the best.** Burt Korall, "Remembering Tiny Kahn," *Modern Drummer*, 4/91.

125   **"a high-energy face-off ... to the limit";** Berg, *Down Beat*, 7/12/78.

125   **... "the fastest tempo in captivity."** Stan Getz, liner notes for *Stan Getz*, Book-of-the-Month Records, 1980.

EIGHT
BUSTED

128   **One time they ... and get it.** Charlton Price interview of Jimmy Rowles and Gary Foster, 11/2/92.

132   **"Give me a ... drugs, I'll kill."** "Jazz Man Collapses in Jail Cell," *Seattle Daily Times*, 2/13/54; "Crazed By Dope: Noted Musician Collapses in Jail After Holdup Fails," *Seattle Post-Intelligencer*, 2/13/54.

133   **I'm a good ... clean for life.** "Crazed By Dope: Noted Musician Collapses in Jail After Holdup Fails," *Seattle Post-Intelligencer*, 2/13/54; "Jazz Man Collapses in Jail Cell," *Seattle Daily Times*, 2/13/54.

134   **I started fooling . . . any day now.** "Stan's Blue Note: 'Heroin Got Me,' "
Seattle Daily Times, 2/15/54.
135   **You have talent . . . waste of time."** "Jazz Musician Gets 6 Months as Dope
Addict," *L.A. Times,* 2/18/54.

NINE
THE ABYSS

139   **Someday I hope . . . about this problem?** Jack Tracy, "In This Corner: Narcotics and Music," *Down Beat,* 3/24/54.
139–140 **God didn't want . . . you, Stan Getz.** Ibid., 4/21/54.
142   **"The polytonal aviary . . . in since 1949."** "Birdland Marks 5 Swinging Years
With Big Blowout," *Down Beat,* 1/26/55.
143   **"playing with Basie . . . how I feel."** nat, " 'I Have the Right Band, Attitude
Now,' Says Getz," *Down Beat,* 3/9/55.
143   **"To all the . . . fifth straight time."** *Down Beat,* 1/26/55.

TEN
AN ANGEL OF DELIVERANCE

152–153 **After a bumpy, . . . in the grounds.** David Irving, *Göring: A Biography* (New
York, Avon Books, 1989), p. 30.
153   **It was so . . . torrent of life.** Ibid., pp. 39–40.
153   **After it was . . . ever be swollen."** Ibid., p. 47.
154   **Göring flew up . . . on her tomb."** Ibid., p. 135.
154   **"with its crossguard . . . Eric to Hermann."** Ibid., pp. 172–173.
155   **Few pharaohs' wives . . . the steps alone.** Ibid., pp. 143–144.
160   **We were filming . . . as a joke.** Stan Getz, liner notes for *Stan Getz,* Book-
of-the-Month Records, 1980.
160   **"as easy as . . . off a log."** Richard Palmer, *Stan Getz* (London, Apollo Press
Limited, 1988), p. 27.

ELEVEN
A NEW DIRECTION

170   **With Stitt you've . . . the starting gate.** John Tynan, "Meet Dr. Getz," *Down
Beat,* 2/20/57.
171   **"The usual background . . . and empty bottles."** Robert Reisner, "Elegy for
Tony Fruscella," *Down Beat,* 2/19/70.
173   **"the shapely Beverly . . . and a halter."** "Pep Pills Trip Trumpeter," *New
York Post,* 4/10/57.
176   **A terrific feeling . . . needed, nor missed.** Stan Getz, liner notes for *Stan
Getz,* Book-of-the-Month Records, 1980.
177   **Getz produces one . . . the great masters.** Richard Palmer, *Stan Getz* (London, Apollo Press Limited, 1988), p. 31.

TWELVE
CHALLENGE AND RESPONSE

182   **"You're my singer."** Don DeMichael, "A Long Look at Stan Getz, Part 1," *Down Beat*, 5/19/66.

184   **I'm tired of . . . in the States.** Jack Lind, "The Expatriate Life of Stan Getz," *Down Beat*, 4/14/60.

184   **In my opinion . . . the racial thing.** Max Jones, " 'No race bias here,' Stan Getz," *Melody Maker*, 8/22/59.

188—189 **Coleman invents, as . . . another new idea.** Ekkehard Jost, *Free Jazz* (New York, Da Capo Press, 1981), p. 50.

190   **When Gil Evans . . . do with them.** Nat Hentoff, "An Afternoon with Miles Davis," *The Jazz Review*, 12/58.

191   **During the year . . . PRAISE TO GOD.** John Coltrane, liner notes for *A Love Supreme*, Impulse/ABC Paramount Records, Inc., 1964.

192   **He'd play one . . . tune a day.** C. O. Simpkins, *Coltrane: A Biography* (Baltimore, Black Classic Press, 1975), p. 64.

192   **Monk gave me . . . a magnifying glass.** J. C. Thomas, *Chasin' the Trane* (New York, Da Capo Paperback, 1976), pp. 84, 90.

192   **Working with Monk . . . it to him.** C. O. Simpkins, *Coltrane: A Biography* (Baltimore, Black Classic Press, 1975), p. 67.

193   **I called his . . . a space ship.** J. C. Thomas, *Chasin' the Trane* (New York, Da Capo Paperback, 1976), p. 106.

193   **What he does . . . five different ways.** Nat Hentoff, liner notes for *Giant Steps*, Atlantic Recording Company, 1959.

197   **More than just . . . must surely fail.** Bill Coss, "Caught in the Act: Stan Getz, Village Vanguard, New York City," *Down Beat*, 6/8/61.

197   **Getz is playing . . . in this country.** John S. Wilson, "Stan Getz Back in U.S.," *The New York Times*, 3/23/61.

198   **"We would all . . . if we could."** Liner notes for *Stan Getz*, Book-of-the-Month Records, 1980.

198—199 **The *Focus* album . . . really believe in."** Les Tompkins, "Giving It Back to God," *Crescendo*, reprinted 3/89.

201   **I conceived the . . . a musical poet.** Coss, "Footnote to *Focus*," *Down Beat*, 3/29/62.

201—202 **You rehearse as . . . let it go.** Michael Aldred, "Stan Getz: herb and the alpha state," *Jazziz*, 8–9/90.

202   **I saw what . . . to be me.** Arnold Jay Smith, "Influentially Yours, Stan Getz," *Down Beat*, 8/12/76.

202—203 **What impresses me . . . and absolutely successful.** Richard Palmer, "Stan Getz at Sixty: A Further Appraisal," *Jazz Journal*, 7/87.

203   **The record I'm . . . and feel proud.** Joseph Woodard, "Stan Getz; Back on the Beach," *Down Beat*, 7/90.

THIRTEEN
STAN'S BOSSA

206   **What you are . . . that humans have.** Bill Coss, "Bob Brookmeyer: Strength and Simplicity," *Down Beat*, 1/19/61.

206   "You can't expect . . . its own locals," "Strong Action Against Jim Crow," *Down Beat*, 12/7/61.

207   "a big fish . . . a little pond." Tom Scanlan, "Chukatuck's Gift to Guitar," *Down Beat*, 7/21/60.

208   In Portuguese, a . . . a "new flair." Neil Tesser, liner notes for *Stan Getz: The Girl From Ipanema; The Bossa Nova Years*, Verve, 1989.

209   The guy who . . . of the samba. "Jazz News," PolyGram Classics biographical press release on Antonio Carlos Jobim.

209   Naturally the purists . . . They repelled everything. Ibid.

213   It is in . . . beautiful than happiness. . . . George W. Goodman, "Jobim and His Songs At Carnegie Hall," *The New York Times*, 3/29/85.

213   What is *so* . . . a great soul. *Stan Getz People Time*, un film de Jean-Pierre Larcher, produced by Le Sabre, 1993.

214   Verve confirms that . . . that's show business. Leonard Feather, "The Resurgence of Stan Getz," *Down Beat*, 2/28/63.

215   Gilberto and Jobim . . . on the record. Neil Tesser, liner notes for *Stan Getz: The Girl From Ipanema; The Bossa Nova Years*, Verve, 1989.

215   "Gilberto, he could . . . and sound good." Leonard Feather, "Blindfold Test: Miles Davis," *Down Beat*, 6/18/64.

215   Some years ago, . . . of my country. Joao Gilberto, liner notes for *Getz/Gilberto*, Verve, 1963.

217   "Getz was in . . . the man's imagination." Don DeMichael, "Caught in the Act: Jazz Supports the Symphony," *Down Beat*, 6/16/63.

218   I made the . . . and the idea. Leonard Feather, "Jazz Samba: The Other Side of the Record," *Down Beat*, 8/29/63.

218   If the same . . . half of it." Ibid.

218   "Desafinado" was nominated . . . went to Getz. Creed Taylor, "Jazz Samba: Still Another Side of the Record," *Down Beat*, 8/29/63.

219   At first it . . . what I needed. Don DeMichael, "Gary Burton: Portrait of the Artist as a Young Vibraharpist, *Down Beat*, 7/29/65.

219   We hated each . . . it's his last. Ibid.

220   I believe in . . . to be good. Ibid.

220   "he was worried . . . his jazz identity." Liner notes for *Stan Getz: Nobody Else but Me*, Polygram Records, Inc., 1994.

221   `When the date . . . later without approval. Richard Palmer, *Stan Getz* (London, Apollo Press Limited, 1988), p. 47.

222   Vinicius de Moraes . . . like a dream. BMI 1965 Press Release for "The Girl From Ipanema."

FOURTEEN
OUT OF CONTROL

228   What is the . . . delight to me. Liner notes for *Stan Getz Plays Music from the Soundtrack of the Motion Picture* Mickey One, MGM, 1965.

229   "a cool $250,000" "Jazz, Back from the Wild Side," *Time*, 9/3/65.

229   "while puttering around his home." "Potpourri," *Down Beat*, 2/10/66.

230   "rocked the joint." "Stan Getz Rocks White House Party," *Down Beat*, 6/16/66.

230–231 He has more . . . let everybody down. Don DeMichael, "A Long Look at Stan Getz, Part 2," *Down Beat*, 6/2/66.

232   Getz' playing seems . . . is pure bliss. McPartland, "Stan Getz—Boston Pops; *Stan Getz at Tanglewood*," *Down Beat*, 3/21/68.

232   Stan's playing here . . . belong to Getz. Richard Palmer, "Stan Getz: A *Song After Sundown*," *Jazz Journal*, 9/88.

233   "Embassy considers warm . . . family very advantageous." BMI Press Release, 1/67.

233   . . . the magic of . . . some years ago. Alun Morgan, "Stan Getz in London," *Jazz Monthly*, 12/66.

233—234 Getz has now . . . urgency than before. Ibid.

234   I wanted to . . . to express them. Dan Morgenstern, "Gary Burton: Upward Bound," *Down Beat*, 8/8/68.

234   I think I . . . never forget him. Gary Burton, liner notes for *Nobody Else but Me*, Verve, 1994.

234—235 The second night . . . was just play. Simon Adams, "Chick's Career," *Jazz Journal*, 1/86.

235   "a remarkable album," Don DeMichael, "Record Reviews—Stan Getz: *Sweet Rain*," *Down Beat*, 9/21/67.

235   "utterly essential." Richard Palmer, *Stan Getz* (London, Apollo Press Limited, 1988), pp. 50–51.

236   "a superb mood album," Dan Morgenstern, "Record Reviews—Stan Getz, *Voices*," *Down Beat*, 1/11/68.

236   This writer would . . . by Claus Ogerman. Richard Palmer, "Stan Getz in the Sixties," *Jazz Journal*, 2/70.

236   "Focus" had the . . . Stan sounds off-form. Steve Voce, "Record Reviews: Stan Getz—*Voices*," *Jazz Journal*, 1/68.

237   Thank you God . . . you God. Amen. John Coltrane, liner notes for *A Love Supreme*, Impulse!, 1964.

240   Although the melodic . . . the new order. Steve Voce, "It Don't Mean a Thing," *Jazz Journal*, 1/68.

241   "go to Hazelden . . . City, Minnesota forthwith." Certificate of Order of Protection issued by the Family Court of the State of New York County of Westchester, Monica Getz, Petitioner, against Stanley Getz, Respondent, signed by Judge Albert L. Fiorillo, 3/15/68.

242   Mr. Getz was . . . shown considerable progress. Letter dated 4/9/68 addressed to Judge Albert L. Fiorillo, Family Court, Westchester County, 216 Central Avenue, White Plains, New York, signed by D. J. Anderson, Ph.D., Director, Hazelden, Center City, Minnesota, 55012.

242   I didn't want . . . finished my job. Cross-examination of Stanley Getz in Stanley Getz, Plaintiff, against Monica Getz, Defendant, 5/13/87, pp. 126, 166.

242   "be under the . . . Dr. Ruth Fox." Temporary Order of Protection (Extended) in the matter of Monica Getz, Petitioner, against Stanley Getz, Respondent, 4/15/68.

243   When he drinks . . . required it most. "History of Patient (Doctor's notes); Chief Complaint," regarding Stan Getz and recorded at Falkirk Hospital on 8/7/68.

243   "he spoke very . . . sued for divorce." Report of the psychological examination of Stan Getz by William Wolfson, Ph.D., Certified Psychologist, 8/8/67.

243   "addictive personality" and . . . very guarded, indeed." "History of Patient (Doctor's notes); Mental State," regarding Stan Getz and recorded at Falkirk Hospital on 8/9/68.

244   **His performance was . . . Genius in retreat.** Derek Jewell, "Moods of Getz," London Sunday *Times*, 1/12/69.

244   **He was pulling . . . doesn't mean it."** Direct testimony of Pamela Raynor in Stanley Getz, Plaintiff, against Monica Getz, Defendant, 5/21/87, pp. 4163–4164.

FIFTEEN
EUROPE AGAIN

249   **He was both . . . he needed help.** Direct testimony of Monica Getz in Stanley Getz, Plaintiff, against Monica Getz, Defendant, 5/27/87, p. 115.

249   **I have found . . . in orange juice.** Letter of April 12, 1968, addressed to Honorable Albert L. Fiorillo, Family Court, Westchester County, 216 Central Avenue, White Plains, New York, signed by Ruth Fox, M.D., 150 East 52nd Street, New York, New York, 10022.

249–250 **In the presence . . . convulsions, and death.** "Partial Guidelines for Antabuse (disulfiram) 140 and 500 mg Tablets," Wyeth-Ayerst Laboratories, Philadelphia, PA 19101, 1993.

250   **I will never . . . I felt terrible. . . .** Cross-examination of Stanley Getz in Stanley Getz, plaintiff, against Monica Getz, defendant, 5/13/87, p. 195.

250   **I was vomiting . . . going to die.** Ibid., 5/18/87, p. 271.

251   **Just before we . . . through the recording. . . .** Direct testimony of Stanley Getz in Stanley Getz, Plaintiff, against Monica Getz, Defendant, 5/12/87, p. 35.

251   **I was so . . . I ever made. . . .** Redirect testimony of Stanley Getz in Stanley Getz, Plaintiff, against Monica Getz, Defendant, 9/9/86, p. D98.

251   **I hear that . . . an Antabuse reaction.** Direct testimony of Stanley Getz in Stanley Getz, Plaintiff, against Monica Getz, Defendant, 9/4/86, p. 24.

251   **Dear Good! Grown . . . deal. Stan Getz.** Defendant's exhibit in Stanley Getz, Plaintiff, against Monica Getz, Defendant, 5/11–29/87.

252–253 **The last time . . . styles and school.** Benny Green, "Maimed but Masterly," London *Observer*, 2/22/70.

253   **"Something wonderful has . . . allergic to alcohol."** Direct testimony of Monica Getz in Stanley Getz, Plaintiff, against Monica Getz, Defendant, 5/27/87, pp. 120–121.

253   **"He showed for . . . periods of time."** Ibid., p. 124.

253   **"all members of the public,"** "Apartheid Defied by Getz in South Africa," *Down Beat*, 8/6/70.

254   **We had come . . . of the world.** Stan Getz, liner notes for *Dynasty*, Verve Records, 1971.

255   **He blistered the . . . a tidal wave.** "Lew Hoad, 59, Tennis Champion of the 1950's," *The New York Times*, 5/7/94.

256   **The saxophonist played . . . of the music.** Alain Gerber, "Caught in the Act: Stan Getz, Chat Qui Pêche, Paris, France," *Down Beat*, 4/1/71.

258   **It was a . . . me every minute.** Jean-Louis Ginibre, "Stan Getz—Toute Nouveau, Tout Beau," *Jazz Magazine*, 4/71.

258–259 **Getz has worked . . . in his career.** Benny Green, "Stan Getz in London: 'Very Like a Miracle,' " *Down Beat*, 5/13/71.

260   **If you are . . . he gave us.** Liner notes for *Dynasty*, Verve Records, 1971.

260   **There is every . . . and wholly original.** *The New Yorker*, 2/17/73.

SIXTEEN
ANTABUSE YEARS

264   The rhythm section . . . unusually sophisticated level. John S. Wilson, "Rhythm Succeeds at Rainbow Grill," *The New York Times*, 1/8/72.

269   An attack of . . . had been quiescent. John S. Wilson, "Stan Getz, Recovered, Enlivens Fisher Program, *The New York Times*, 7/6/74.

273   We were at . . . up with Stan. Arnold Jay Smith, "Profile: Joanne Brackeen," *Down Beat*, 3/10/77.

273   Now that I . . . will be freer. . . . Ibid.

273   I take the . . . intonation are incredible. Leslie Gourse, "Joanne Brackeen: Swinging Dissonance," *Down Beat*, 11/88.

273   I have always . . . so do I. Arnold Jay Smith, "Influentially Yours," *Down Beat*, 8/12/76.

275   My Dearest Lady: . . . my Valentine? Stan. Defendant's exhibit in Stanley Getz, Plaintiff, against Monica Getz, Defendant, 5/11–29/87.

276   My father got . . . him for this." Direct testimony of Pamela Raynor in Stanley Getz, Plaintiff, against Monica Getz, Defendant, 9/10/86, pp. 415–417.

277   *Stan Getz Gold . . . brilliant masters. Listen!* Berg, "Record Reviews: *Stan Getz Gold*," *Down Beat*, 4/20/78.

277   Mr. Tenor Sax . . . fire and humor. Nighthawk, "Jazzman Getz just gets better," *Le Devoir*, 2/4/77.

278   Mr. Getz could . . . world for me." John S. Wilson, "Stan Getz, at 50, Is Still Studying the Saxophone," *The New York Times*, 5/6/77.

279   I was in . . . tears came down. Conrad Silvert, "A Look at the New Stan Getz," *San Francisco Chronicle*, 2/17/78.

280   Andy came into . . . in the studio. Richard Williams, "Stan Getz: Presenting . . . the Stanley Steamer of the 80s," *Down Beat*, 1/12/78.

281   "an experiment and . . . subtle with it." Conrad Silvert, "A Look at the New Stan Getz," *San Francisco Chronicle*, 2/17/78.

282   For the reunion . . . clarity and subtlety. Richard M. Sudhalter, "Comparing Getz in Two Settings," *New York Post*, 3/23/78.

282   She was white . . . in a motel." Direct testimony of Pamela Raynor in Stanley Getz, Plaintiff, against Monica Getz, Defendant, 5/20/87, p. 171.

283   They just let . . . they'd just heard. Richard M. Sudhalter, "Stan Getz Plays It Cool & Quiet," *New York Post*, 6/29/78.

283   There are mikes, . . . hard note commands. Philip Elwood, "Ageless Jazz from Getz," *San Francisco Examiner*, 8/30/78.

285   I just happened . . . of the tradition. ABC-TV, 20/20, 3/87.

285   "Get me out . . . the train station." Direct testimony of Stanley Getz in Stanley Getz, Plaintiff, against Monica Getz, Defendant, 9/4/86, pp. 9, 10.

286   "Are you trying . . . sober or dead." Ibid., p. 10.

SEVENTEEN
BREAKING AWAY

289   It is not . . . it gets going. A.I.J. Mooney, M.D., Arlene Eisenberg, Howard Eisenberg, *The Recovery Book* (New York, Workman Publishing Co., Inc., 1992), pp. 508–509.

291   The patient is . . . should be admitted. Defendant's exhibit in Stanley Getz, Plaintiff, against Monica Getz, Defendant, 5/11–29/87.

291   "I didn't want . . . anything like that." Redirect testimony of Monica Getz in Stanley Getz, Plaintiff, against Monica Getz, Defendant, 5/28/87, p. 159.

292   "A neurological consultation . . . very little symptoms." Defendant's exhibit in Stanley Getz, Plaintiff, against Monica Getz, Defendant, 5/11–29/87.

294   Looking as fit . . . Manne is marvelous. Thomas Albright, "Inspiration from Stan Getz," San Francisco Chronicle, 1/23/81.

296   My philosophy is . . . from record companies. Leonard Feather, liner notes for The Dolphin, Concord Jazz, 1981.

296   He is the . . . that he's flawless. Don Asher, "Bebop Rabbi Joins the Silver Fox," San Francisco Chronicle, 5/10/81.

297   The people react . . . admiration so voraciously. Leonard Feather, liner notes for The Dolphin, Concord Records, 1981.

298   "cruel and inhuman treatment," New York State Domestic Relations Law, Section 170 (1).

299   Stanley was the . . . solos were prodigious. Steve Voce, "Nice Festival Roundup," Jazz Journal, 9/81.

300   "cruel and inhuman treatment." New York State Domestic Relations Law, Section 170 (1).

300   When they reached . . . at 4:40 P.M. Deposition of Marvin Potash taken 8/6/81 in Stanley Getz, Plaintiff, against Monica Getz, Defendant.

301   (Reflections') spectacular views . . . San Francisco below. Philip Elwood, "Stan Getz High on Jazz," San Francisco Examiner, 1/19/82.

302   Getz' band was . . . most underrated musicians. Conrad Silvert, "Getz Jazzes Up Reflections," San Francisco Chronicle, 1/29/82.

302–303 If he keeps . . . play beautiful music." "Stan Getz's 55th," The New York Times, 2/4/82.

303   To me, you . . . effort, less wastage. Mary Campbell, "Getz: Always Improving; Bringing Beauty to People," Apolis News, 9/15/82.

304   My pianist, Jim . . . is the best. Ibid.

307   I would like . . . normal people live. Ibid.

EIGHTEEN
HEALING

312   "the finest musician . . . I put together," Stan Getz on PBS TV show Young Artists in Performance at the White House, 12/21/82.

313   I just happened . . . touch with her?" Harry Rosen as quoted on ABC-TV, 20/20, 3/87.

314   How do you . . . in the world. Richard M. Sudhalter, "Riff for More Than an Agent," The New York Times, 2/5/83.

317   I saw Johnny . . . you. That's it. Judy L. Stewart, "Getz, Smith Ready to Jam Wednesday," Colorado Springs Sun, 4/22/83.

324   The pair explore . . . time and again. Pete Welding, "Record Reviews," Down Beat, 12/84.

325   I would like . . . the circle complete. Diane Schuur, liner notes for Deedles, GRP Records, 1984.

326   "You're looking better today, Doc." Bill Crow, From Birdland to Broadway: Scenes from a Jazz Life (New York, Oxford University Press, 1992), p. 261.

NINETEEN
TRIALS

331   **I have always . . . respect it deserves.** William Johnson, "State-of-the-Art Jazz at Stanford; Artist-in-Residence Stan Getz Heading Strong New Program," *Peninsula Times Tribune*, 1/26/86.

332   **I don't consider . . . than I was.** Simon Korteweg and Bert Vuysjo, "I Don't Want Pity: The Miraculous Come-back of Tenorist Stan Getz," *De Volkslerant*, 2/19/88.

332   **(The students) want . . . on the stage. . . .** Bob Protzman, "Saxophonist Loves Career as 'Professor' Getz," *St. Paul Pioneer Press Dispatch*, 3/26/87.

332   **What I try . . . that's not easy.** Simon Korteweg and Bert Vuysjo, "I Don't Want Pity: The Miraculous Come-back of Tenorist Stan Getz," *De Volkslerant*, 2/19/88.

332–333   **When I got . . . of improvising music.** KRON-TV, San Francisco, news feature on Stan Getz at Stanford, 8/82.

334   **The tenor saxophonist . . . melodic single-note solos.** William Johnson, "Stanford Stan: Getz Combo Thrills Crowd in Program's First Jazz Concert," *Peninsula Times Tribune*, 3/4/86.

336   **Mr. Reingold, you . . . of this case.** "Brief of Respondent, Stanley Getz, in opposition" to Monica Getz, Petitioner, vs. Stanley Getz, Respondent, in the Supreme Court of the United States, October Term 1990.

338   **"This is an . . . thrilled. Believe me."** Black Hawk news release, 11/7/86.

338   **I cannot play . . . where it's at.** Eric Snider, "Stan Getz: Playing the Sax by Instinct," *St. Petersburg Times*, 10/17/86.

340   **We intend to . . . become very sick.** Opening statement of Jeffrey Cohen before the Supreme Court of the State of New York County of Westchester in Stanley Getz, Plaintiff, against Monica Getz, Defendant, 5/12/87, pp. 27, 29.

340   **I hate Mrs. . . . my life miserable.** Direct testimony of Stan Getz before the Supreme Court of the State of New York County of Westchester in Stanley Getz, Plaintiff, against Monica Getz, Defendant, 5/12/87, p. 4.

340   **I couldn't live . . . forceful and evil.** Ibid., 5/13/87, p. 48.

341   **I was a . . . minute of it.** Cross-examination of Stan Getz before the Supreme Court of the State of New York County of Westchester in Stanley Getz, Plaintiff, against Monica Getz, Defendant, 5/13/87, p. 201.

341   **When I surrendered . . . in the world.** Ibid., p. 156.

341   **I have found . . . in orange juice.** Letter of April 12, 1968, addressed to Honorable Albert L. Fiorillo, Family Court, Westchester County, 216 Central Avenue, White Plains, New York, signed by Ruth Fox, M.D., 150 East 52nd Street, New York, New York, 10022.

342   **The patient should . . . consent and understanding.** Cross-examination of Dr. Nicholas A. Pace in Stanley Getz, Plaintiff, against Monica Getz, Defendant, 5/18/87, p. 61.

342   **"Drugs, Booze and All That Jazz,"** "Drugs, Booze and All That Jazz," *New York Post*, 5/14/87.

342   **"Son Says 'Musician . . . Out of Control.' "** Richard Liebson, "Son Says Musician Was 'Out of Control' When He Was Drunk," *Gannett Westchester Newspapers*, 5/22/87.

342   **" 'He's Like a . . . Went on Rampages.' "** Richard Liebson, " 'He's Like a Psychopath.' Daughter Tells Court, 'Getz Went on Rampages,' " *Gannett Westchester Newspapers*, 5/21/87.

342–343 **Reingold: Do you . . . disease in therapy.** Direct testimony of Monica Getz before the Supreme Court of the State of New York County of Westchester in Stanley Getz, Plaintiff, against Monica Getz, Defendant, 5/28/87, pp. 199–201.

343   **Cohen: If he . . . Monica: True, true.** Cross-examination of Monica Getz before the Supreme Court of the State of New York County of Westchester in Stanley Getz, Plaintiff, against Monica Getz, Defendant, 5/28/87, pp. 14–15, 28–29.

TWENTY
BATTLING TO LIVE

347   **After the jam . . . came to be.** Acknowledgement and Statement of Inga Torgner dated 5/30/91 and submitted as part of the Appellant's Reply Brief to the New York State Supreme Court, Appellate Division—Second Department in Beverly P. McGovern, Administrator, on Behalf of the Estate of Stan Getz, Plaintiff-Respondent, against Monica Getz, Defendant-Appellant, 10/15/92.

347   **He came one . . . left the apartment.** Ibid.

347   **He seemed glad . . . I have saved.** Acknowledgement and Statement of Peter Torgner dated 5/30/91 and submitted as part of the Appellant's Reply Brief to the New York State Supreme Court, Appellate Division—Second Department in Beverly P. McGovern, Administrator, on Behalf of the Estate of Stan Getz, Plaintiff-Respondent, against Monica Getz, Defendant-Appellant, 10/15/92.

348   **I thought that . . . playing the violins.** Simon Korteweg and Bert Vuysjo, "I Don't Want Pity: The Miraculous Come-back of Tenorist Stan Getz," *De Volkslerant*, 2/19/88.

348   **"the other half of my heart,"** Joseph Hooper, "Stan Getz: Through the Years," *The New York Times*, 6/9/91.

349   **I have a . . . talking to God.** Steve Voce, "And There's *More* Where That Came From . . . ," *Jazz Journal*, 1/92.

349   **"What are you . . . and time again.** Steve Getz on liner notes for *Spring Is Here*, Concord Records, 1992.

354   **The three horns . . . of the gathering.** William Johnson, "Mr. Sax Is Back," *Peninsula Times Tribune*, 1/19/88.

355   **Because my ribs . . . be fun again.** Simon Korteweg and Bert Vuysjo, "I Don't Want Pity: The Miraculous Come-back of Tenorist Stan Getz," *De Volkslerant*, 2/19/88.

355   **For a long . . . Zoot and Al.** Ibid.

355   **Although he was . . . after his encores.** John Fordham, "Ballad of the Cool Tenorist," *Manchester Guardian Weekly*, 6/7/91.

356   **The Stan Getz . . . very nice guy.** Postcard from Joey Oliveira to the Blokkers, 2/25/88.

358   **When you've been . . . my ire up.** Gene Santoro, "The Man," *Pulse!*, 5/90.

358–359 **I'm a great . . . handful of giants.** Michael Aldred, "Stan Getz: herb and the alpha state," *Jazziz*, 8–9/90.

TWENTY-ONE
FULLY ENGAGED

367   **We couldn't figure . . . over the background.** Joseph Woodard, "Back on the Beach," *Down Beat*, 7/90.

367   **"Fuck you." Stan . . . me, you savage,"** Letter of 9/5/91 written by Bruce Kelley to his parents.

372   **For many families . . . of the system.** David McKay Wilson, "Stan Getz's Former Wife Takes Battle over Divorce to U.S. Supreme Court," *Gannett Westchester Newspapers,* 7/2/90.

372   **She would like . . . past a jury.** David Margolick, "Ex-wife of Stan Getz Testing a Divorce Law," *The New York Times,* 11/21/90.

373   **You haven't heard . . . beginning of something.** David McKay Wilson, "Monica Getz Vows to Expose NYS Divorce-Law Problems," *Gannett Westchester Newspapers,* 11/27/90.

373   **"Right temporarily defeated . . . than evil triumphant."** Ibid.

373   **"a modern love . . . only the lawyer.** CBS-TV, *Street Stories,* 3/12/92.

TWENTY-TWO
FAREWELL

378   **He's been everywhere . . . was about twenty-seven.** *Stan Getz People Time,* un film de Jean-Pierre Larcher, produced by Le Sabre, 1993.

378   **I'm really thankful . . . a wide audience.** Ibid.

381   **"characterized by weakness, . . . and other tissues,"** Sherwin B. Nuland, *How We Die* (New York, Alfred A. Knopf, 1994), p. 217.

384   **He touched me . . . ever hope for.** Herb Alpert, "Stan Getz: 1927–1991," *Rolling Stone,* 8/8/91.

Index

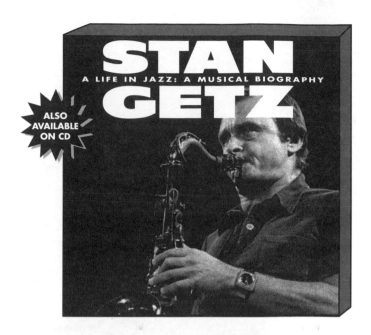

A Life in Jazz: A Musical Biography

Available on compact disc from Verve Records

The 11 songs selected by Donald Maggin for this introduction to Getz highlight his many talents and ability to create fresh and beautiful melodies in improvisation.

- **Night Rider** from *Focus*
- **Billie's Bounce** from *Stan Getz and J. J. Johnson at the Opera House*
- **Corcovado (Quiet Nights of Quiet Stars)** with Chick Corea from *Getz/Gilberto*
- **Litha** with Chick Corea from *Sweet Rain*
- **You're Blasé** playing behind the legendary Ella Fitzgerald
- **What Is This Thing Called Love** with Kenny Barron from *Anniversary*
- **Hymn of the Orient** from *Stan Getz Plays*
- **Summertime** with Gary Burton from *Nobody Else But Me*
- **I'm in Love** with Abbey Lincoln from *You Gotta Pay the Band*
- **Who Could Care** a great collaboration with valve trombonist Bob Brookmeyer
- **Night and Day** duet with Kenny Barron from *People Time*

Catalog #314535119-2

To be on the Verve mailing list (US only) please write to:
Verve Records, Dept. WM
825 Eighth Avenue
New York, NY 10019

Verve interactive: http://www.jazzonln.com/verve.htm